THE COLOR OF ANGELS

BY RUSTY KONTOS

Copyright 2023

All rights reserved.

Table of Contents

CHAPTER ONE 5

CHAPTER TWO 12

CHAPTER THREE 20

CHAPTER FOUR 34

CHAPTER FIVE 55

CHAPTER SIX 70

CHAPTER SEVEN 77

CHAPTER EIGHT 91

CHAPTER NINE 95

CHAPTER TEN 98

CHAPTER ELEVEN 104

CHAPTER TWELVE 114

CHAPTER THIRTEEN 122

CHAPTER FOURTEEN 128

CHAPTER FIFTEEN 136

CHAPTER SIXTEEN 151

CHAPTER SEVENTEEN 159

CHAPTER EIGHTEEN 165

CHAPTER NINETEEN 169

CHAPTER TWENTY 173

CHAPTER TWENTY-ONE 182

CHAPTER TWENTY-TWO	195
CHAPTER TWENTY-THREE	207
CHAPTER TWENTY-FOUR	216
CHAPTER TWENTY-FIVE	230
CHAPTER TWENTY-SIX	235
CHAPTER TWENTY SEVEN	259
CHAPTER TWENTY EIGHT	264
CHAPTER TWENTY NINE	272
CHAPTER THIRTY	275
CHAPTER THIRTY ONE	285
CHAPTER THIRTY TWO	299
CHAPTER THIRTY THREE	319
CHAPTER THIRTY FOUR	324
CHAPTER THIRTY FIVE	331
CHAPTER THIRTY SIX	341
CHAPTER THIRTY SEVEN	345
CHAPTER THIRTY EIGHT	366
CHAPTER THIRTY NINE	374
CHAPTER FOURTY	386

CHAPTER ONE

April 17th 1958

The old blue pickup pulled into the dirt driveway of the old white rental house. Standing on the side porch was a little chubby balding landlord. His name was Clark Hanson. He owned several of the old houses on, the tree-lined street. Hanson wiped his baldhead and brow with his hanky. "Howdy!" he called out to the young couple as they got out of the truck. "You must be the folks I talked to on the phone!!" Hanson held out his hand to shake with the tall young want-a-be Elvis.

"Yeah! I'm Billy Joe Martin. This is my wife, Sue Ellen! Glad to make your acquaintance!" Clark said, as he shook Billy Joe's hand. "And who might this pretty little thing be?"

"This is our little girl, Sissy," Sue Ellen quickly spoke up. The little blond three year old clung to Sue Ellen's leg as she tried to shyly hide.

Billy Joe broke in, "can we look inside the house now?"

"Oh, sure, sure you can. Follow me," said Hanson as they headed for the porch; Billy Joe stopped and took hold of the little girl's shoulder. "Not you Sissy. You wait here," he sternly said. Sissy's big blue eyes widened with a fearful look, as she quietly sat down on the edge of the porch

Hanson and Sissy's parents went on into the house. "As you can see, it is a nice size house, it's just right for a growing family," Hansen said smiling, as he went on to say, "There is a small garage lout back and almost an acre of yard for the little one to play. Colored town is just past that field behind you though. But they are all pretty good folks. They don't bother anyone, if you need a little something from a store, they have one that is just across the field. They don't mind selling to white folks. The nearest white store is about two miles down the street, next to the Mill.

"We won't be doing no business with NIGGERS. If we want something we will go ten miles if that is how far we have to go to a white man's store. AND as far as NIGGER TOWN goes, they stay on their side of the fence and we wills stay on our side," Billy Joe snarled.

"AUH, yes, I understand. I didn't mean anything other than, it would be convenient, that's all," Mr. Hanson said nervously.

"How much is the rent?" Billy Joe asked.

"AUGH it's twenty five dollars a month. First month in advance."

"We'll take it, here. I need a receipt. We won't move in till the weeks end," Billy Joe said as he handed Mr. Hanson the money.

"I will just go out to my car and get you a receipt. I won't start the rent date till you move in. A short time later Mr. Hanson returned back into the house. "Here you are Mr. Martin. The house is all yours. I' hope you enjoy living here. He handed Billy Joe the rent receipt. "OH yes you'll also be needing these," Hanson handed Billy Joe the keys to the house. "Well folks I hate to just rush off like this, but it is getting late and my MRS. is waiting dinner for me, she just hates it when I'm late. Well, then I'll see you folk's next month."

"Yeah, sure, thank you Mr. Hansen." Billy Joe, said as he shook hand's once more, as they said good by. After Hanson left, Billy Joe and Sue Ellen, came out to the porch where Sissy was still sitting. Billy Joe looked down at her. "Sissy, mommy and I are going down the street, you stay here till we get back. This is where we are going to live. You can play around, But don't leave the yard. You Hear Me?" Sissy looked up at him, "Yes daddy."

"Good girl. Now remember don't leave the yard. lf you do I will Whoop your ass. HEAR ME?"

"Yes Daddy."

"Billy Joe, it's going to be dark soon, why can't we just take Sissy with us?"

"No we can't take her. The Brass Rail don't want no kids in there. And besides that; I don't want to take no kid with us. I want to play some pool, and dance a little bit with my woman. Remember she's your screw up not mine. You said nothin would change for us, if you had her. Remember?" Billy Joe snarled through clenched teeth.

"I know, I know. But she hasn't had anything to eat yet." Sue Ellen said.

"So, it's only four blocks from here you can get her a hamburger and coke, and bring it back. If she gets tired she can get in the truck and lie down. Ain't that right Sissy? You get tired you get in the truck, or you can lay in that big old chair over there." Billy Joe pointed at the big overstuffed chair sitting on the porch.

"Yes Daddy, I will." Sissy said shaking her head yes.

"Good girl. Now you see, Sissy ain't afraid. Now come on let's go before it get's dark." He took Sue Ellen's arm, leading her down the porch steps. Billy Joe, called back over his shoulder. "Remember what I said Sissy, we won't be gone too long."

"OK Daddy." Sissy sat hand's folded on her lap, as she watched her father and mother disappear down the street. Sissy stood up and decided to explore her new home. She went out back to the old garage. She saw some boxes in one corner. She approached the boxes. Sissy's big blue eye's sparkled with delight as she stared at what was lying in one of the boxes. "A baby," she squealed with delight. Sissy reached down to pick it up. She hugged it close to her tiny body, swaying from side to side, murmuring "You are my baby now, you are so pretty." She held the doll out in front of her by the arms, "My name is Sissy. Now I must give you a name." The doll she held was actually a large Christmas tree angel topper. It had no legs under its white flowing satin dress; only a wire spring that was used to mount it on a tree. It had long well groomed golden locks of hair, and very soft fury type wings. "Your hair is just like mine, and so are your eyes, so that makes me your mommy now. And I'm gonna call you, Angel baby, cause you are an angel. She hugged the doll one more time and left the garage, heading back to the porch. She climbed in to the old chair, hugging the doll close to her. She lay there talking to her new doll as she watched the sun go down.

Sue Ellen sat at a table drinking a beer as she watched Billy Joe playing a game of pool, with another guy. Billy Joe's muscles flexed as he bent over the table to take his shot. His skin tight Tee shirt and jeans showed off his well muscled body. The only bulge that wasn't a part of his body was his pack of Lucky Strike cigarettes, tucked neatly in his shirtsleeve. An Elvis song started playing on the jukebox. "Love me tender, Love me true, may all my dreams be fulfilled." Sue Ellen got up from the table, and walked over to Billy Joe. "Honey, it's getting late, I need to go check on Sissy. We told her we would bring her something to eat." Billy Joe looked at her annoyed. "OK. OK, take her some food, then you get your ass back here. The band will start soon and I want to dance with you baby. Now go on now. I'll just play a few more games and take these suckers' money." He grinned as he slapped Sue Ellen's behind.

Sue Ellen went to the bar and ordered Sissy's food. "Hi, can I get a cheeseburger, fries, and a bottle of coke to go please?"

"Yes Mam, it will be just a few minutes." The bartender replied. Sue Ellen sat at the table, watching Billy Joe play pool as she waited for her food order. She sat there remembering back to when she first met Billy Joe. It was 1951 in Tupelo, Mississippi. Sue Ellen was working as a carhop, at THE DOG AND SUDS drive up. The first time she saw him, she fell head over heels in love with him. His coal black hair combed back in a ducktail, long side burns, and his piercing blue eyes. Billy Joe was with two of his buddies as they drove up in one of the boy's hot rod convertible. Billy Joe was in the back seat. "Hi, beautiful. What's your name?" He said with a Boyish grin on his face. "Sue Ellen. What can I get for you?" She smiled back. "How about your phone number Miss Sue Ellen?"

"How about you just give me your food order?"

"AUH, come on baby give me a chance. PRETTY PLEASE." Billy Joe begged.

"Stop it. You're embarrassing me. Just give me your order." Sue Ellen said, her face flushed.

"OK. OK. Give us three, cheeseburgers, and three large root beer floats, and three orders of onion rings. And what time do you get off? So I can pick you up, and we can go out somewhere?"

"Thank you, I'll get your order, right away. And no, you can't pick me up. And no we can't go out somewhere." She turned and walked away, smiling.

"HA. HA. Busted." The boy in the driver's seat howled. "Shut the hell up. Can't you see, she's crazy about me, and we are going out on a date?"

"Yeah, sure you are. And Marilyn Monroe is going to give me a blowjob."

"Fuck you, Berry Collins. I'm going to make it with her. You just wait and see."

"Yeah, sure you are. I'll bet you five bucks you can't get a date with her, let alone, fuck her." Berry challenged Billy Joe. Billy Joe slapped the palm of Berry's hand. "You got a bet, and let's make it a ten spot."

"Deal. But you got to prove you made it with her."

"How? You want to watch?"

"No man, just get her panties or bra. We will follow to our spot by the lake, and after you make it with her, we'll wait for you at the end of the stone road. Then you can wave her underwear out the window of your truck. Then we will know if you did or didn't."

"You got it." Billy Joe grinned smugly in agreement. Sue Ellen returned with the boys' order. They all had a sheepish grin on their faces, as they gave her the money for the order. They each gave her a dime tip. She thanked them and walked away, "ASSHOLES," she thought to herself as she walked away. The Dog and Suds closed at midnight. Sue Ellen walked out the back door. She walked across the parking lot, as she looked up she saw Billy Joe, setting, in a green parked pickup truck. Across the street, she saw the other two boys parked in their car that Billy Joe had been in earlier.

"HEY, Beautiful, how about a ride?" Billy Joe called out to her. "No thanks, I'm waiting for my father to pick me up."

"Augh, come, tell your daddy, you got a date with me." Billy Joe gestured.

"No thanks. I don't date customers. Goodnight. My dad is here now." The black forty-nine Buick pulled up in front of her. "Hi daddy." She said as she got into her father's car. She gave Billy Joe a little wave as they drove off out of the Dog And Suds parking lot. The two boys, Berry Collins and Marty Blake drove into the parking lot from were they were parked across the street earlier. "HEY. HEY. OLD BUDDY, you struck out. Now PAY UP." Berry said as he stopped his car next to Billy Joe's pickup. "OK. OK. I'm not done for yet." Billy Joe said as he slapped a ten into Berry's palm. "THANK YOU MY MAN." Berry said as he put the money in his pocket.

"Tell you what, let's say you give me a week, and if I don't score with her I will double the bet. But If I do, you pay me twenty. HOW'S THAT FOR A BET?"

"YOU'RE ON, MY MAN. I could use another twenty bucks." Berry said with a confident grin on his face, as the two boys shook on the bet.

"Hey MAN, let's go cruisin for a while." Berry said to Billy Joe and Marty.

"YEAH, man, let's go!" Marty said excitedly

"No man, I got to help my old man cut some wood in the morning. I need to go home and get some sleep, you know he like's to get an early start.

"OK, MAN. SEE YOU TOMORROW NIGHT?" Berry asked.

"Yeah, I'll meet you guys here. Besides I got to work on Sue Ellen, don't I? I got to get my ten bucks back." Billy Joe said smiling, as he climbed into his truck to start it.

"Tomorrow night." Berry replied. The boys waved goodbye to each other as they drove out of the lot.

Sue Ellen sat in her bathtub, slowly soaping her arms as she closed her eyes. Images of Billy Joe flashed in her mind. She was remembering his shiny black hair, his flashing sweet smile and those piercing deep blue eyes. She leaned her head back against the tub, "OH, You DUMMY," she murmured to herself. "Why are you playing so hard to get? You know you want to go out with him." "Well," she thought, "if he is really interested, he will come back. Maybe I should wait and see if he is really interested in me, or just trying to impress his friends. If he is he will keep coming back until I say yes, and till I get to know him, and he knows me. OH he is so gorgeous though, I hope I'm doing the right thing by playing hard to get." She giggled to herself silently. After her bath she went to bed that night her dreams were filled with her and Billy Joe.

CHAPTER TWO

"Mam, your order is ready." The Burly bartender called out to Sue Ellen from behind the bar. Sue Ellen's thoughts returned back to where her surroundings were. "Oh yes thank you. How much do I owe you?"

"That will be two, seventy five." Sue Ellen took out a five, handed it to the bartender, waited for her change and left to take the food to Sissy, who was fast asleep in the old chair on the porch. "Sissy, Honey, wake up. Mommy's here. Look baby I got you a cheeseburger, French fries and a coke, come on baby, sit up here and eat for Mommy." Sissy sat upright, rubbing her sleepy eyes. The Doll still clutched in her tiny little arms. "Thank you Mommy," Sissy said in her sleepy little voice. "WHAT you got here Honey?" Sue Ellen asked as she took hold of the doll to look at it. "She's My Dolly. I found her out there in the old building."

"Why she is very pretty, Sissy, but Honey she isn't a dolly, she's a tree topper for a Christmas tree. She's an angel. See Honey, she's got wings." Sue Ellen said as she held up the angel to show her little daughter how the angel was meant to go atop a tree.

"Don't want her on a tree, I want her for my baby doll. I can keep her, can't I Mommy? Please say I can." Sissy said pleadingly. "Of course you can baby. Now here, you eat, and Mommy has to go back to where Daddy is, "Are you cold Honey?"

"A little." Sissy replied as she took a bite from her cheeseburger. "Thank, you Mommy."

"For what, Honey?"

"For the burger, and most of all for letting me keep my baby."

"Augh, Honey, of course you can keep your baby. After all, you found her, so that makes her yours to keep. As for the burger, Honey you don't have to thank me and I told you I would bring it to you. But you are welcome. I'm going to get you my sweater out of the truck; you can cover up with it if you get cold. OK?"

"OK, mommy, I will." Sissy replied as she nodded her head. Sue Ellen went to the truck to get her sweater for Sissy. As she came back, "Now baby, if you get cold, as I said before, you just rap yourself, and your new baby doll up. And Mommy and Daddy will be back very soon. OK?"

"OK, Mommy."

"You'll be OK Honey, you just stay here on the porch or get in the truck if you want. And I will be back before you know it." She gave Sissy a quick hug, and a kiss on her cheek, smiled at her, walked away, turning to wave as she left, her brave little girl, all alone sitting in the dark of night, eating her food. Afterward to curl up in the old chair, and drift off to sleep.

Sue Ellen walked into the bar just as the band started to play. "A whole lot of shaken going on, yeah, I said there's a whole lot of shaken goin on," the band played, as the loud music filled the bar. The dance floor crowded with people, dancing to the loud music. Sue Ellen looked around for Billy Joe. The Bar had filled with people since she left. Billy Joe came up behind her, locking both hands around her waist, he whispered in her ear. "What took you so long baby?"

"I wasn't to long. You were still playing pool with the guys and I took Sissy some food. I needed to make sure she was OK.

"OK. OK. You're here now, and I'm not playing pool. So let's have some fun." Billy Joe said as he pulled her toward the dance floor. They danced almost every dance, Billy Joe stopping only long enough to jug down a bottle of beer. The band took a break, Billy Joe and Sue Ellen were sitting at a table, Billy Joe ordered another round of drinks. "Billy Joe, it's getting late, I don't want another drink. Sissy's all alone and, besides..." Sue Ellen didn't get to finish her sentence, Billy Joe angrily cut in. "SISSY. SISSY. That's all you think about. You said things wouldn't change for us if you had her. I told you I didn't want any kids. But no, you had to go and let yourself get knocked up." Billy Joe scowled.

"Well now you're saying it's all my fault? You had fun making her. It's up to the woman to make sure she doesn't get knocked up. NOT THE MAN," he yelled back at her.

"Look Billy Joe" I don't want to fight, all I'm saying is it's getting late, and that Sissy is just a little baby, and she might get scared all alone. And thing's haven't changed for us, we still go out together, we still have time alone together, I have always done everything you have asked of me haven't I? HAVEN'T I?" She asked soothingly, "Billy Joe my love has not changed for you, I still love you deeply, and I love our baby. I know you love her too. YOU just need time to adjust to being a father."

"OK. OK. I just want to have some fun while I'm still young. Besides we have to move into the house this weekend, and I have to start work on Monday morning at the mill. It might be a long time before we can go out like this again. I'm sure Sissy is OK, she is probably fast asleep anyway. So come on Honey What do say, just give us tonight together. Please, PRETTY PLEASE" He begged Sue Ellen.

Finally she smiled at him and gave in. The Band started to play again. Billy Joe took Sue Ellen's hand and they went to the dance floor. He held her close as they slow danced to the song, Love Me Tender. They stayed till closing. "Last CALL" the Bartender called out. "It's a quarter of two, we got to close in fifteen minutes. Billy Joe gave Sue Ellen a deep kiss, and they headed out the door. "Thank you sweetie, for giving me this night." Billy Joe said soothingly.

Billy Joe and Sue Ellen arrived back to the house at two thirty A.M. Billy Joe went directly to the truck, Sue Ellen stepped onto the porch. Sissy was all curled up in a little ball, sound asleep, in the old chair. The angel doll rapped tightly in her arms. Sue Ellen slipped her arms underneath, picking the sleeping little girl up, Sissy murmured softly, in her sleep, as Sue Ellen carried her to the truck After climbing into the truck, Sue Ellen cradled her in her arms on her lap. Billy Joe Backed the truck out of the driveway, onto the street, were they started on their thirty-mile ride for home.

Billy Joe pulled to a stop, the curb in front of the apartment building were they were still living. Sue Ellen carried Sissy up the two flights of steps to get to their apartment inside. She held Sissy over her shoulder, holding her tightly with one hand, and opening the door with the outer hand. Once inside, she took the sleeping, Sissy over to the sofa, she laid her down, took off the sandals from her tiny feet. She left Sissy's faded blue, tattered dress on, as she then covered her over with a blanket. Sue Ellen stood over Sissy, smiling down, as she brushed aside one of her golden curls gently with her hand. "You are so beautiful my little angel," she whispered softly. "Mommy loves you." Sissy lay peacefully sleeping with her angel doll still clutched tightly in her arms. Sue Ellen turned out the light, and went into her bedroom. Billy Joe was stretched out on the bed naked. He perched himself up on one elbow, and patted the bed with his other hand. "Come on woman. Come to Papa. I need you."

"Awe, Billy Joe. I've got to start packing, so we can move, next week." She said with exhaustion in her voice.

"YOU'RE TELLING ME NO?" Billy Joe scowled at her with a hateful glare.

"No Billy Joe. I'm just saying I'm a little tired, that's all."

"Get your clothes off AND GET YOUR ASS OVER HERE. I'm in the mood, and I want some of that pussy, IT'S MINE AND I WANT IT NOW"

"ALL RIGHT, ALL RIGHT." Sue Ellen snapped. "Just give me a minute to get undressed."

"WELL, HURRY IT UP OR I'LL COME OVER THERE, AND RIP THEM OFF."

Sue Ellen undressed, and climbed into bed next to Billy Joe. She just lay there as he savagely took her. He wasn't concerned with, whether she was enjoying having sex or not. Sue Ellen just closed her eye's waiting for it to be over. He wasn't making love to her, he was cruelly raping her. He clawed her as he thrust himself inside her, he was biting her shoulder, "Billy Joe, YOU'RE HURTING ME. PLEASE NOT SO ROUGH."

"SHUT THE FUCK UP BITCH, I'M ABOUT TO COME...OH YES OH." He said as he thrust harder and faster. "AWE," he panted, and then his body went limp, on top of her. He lay there for what seemed like an eternity to her. Then suddenly, he rolled off her. He was flat on his back when he said. "WELL. Get off your ASS and go clean me up!"

Sue Ellen got out of bed, went into the bathroom. A moment later she returned with a washcloth wet with soap and water and a towel. She cleaned Billy Joe, then returned to the bathroom to take care of herself. She looked at herself in the mirror. Her neck and shoulder was all bruised with bite marks. She ran a cool cloth over them trying to sooth the pain. She stared at herself in the mirror for a moment. She turned off the light and went back to the bedroom. Billy Joe was fast asleep. She climbed in next to him, closed her eyes and drifted off to sleep.

April 18th

Sissy woke around seven thirty; she rubbed her eyes as she yawned. She held up her new baby as she lie on her back, she pulled the doll's face to meet her face giving it a big kiss. "Good morning Angel, how are you today?" She said in a child like whisper. She gave the doll a large grin as she sat up, trying hard to be quiet. "I'm so glad I found you, I know you are to! We are goin to have so much fun together, I won't be alone anymore, and you won't either. We will always have each other. I'm hungry, aren't you? Come I will fix us breakfast. SHOOSH," she whispered. "We can't make no noise." She said as she climbed off the sofa. "We don't want to get Daddy mad," Sissy whispered as she tiptoed into the kitchen. Sissy scooted a chair up to the cupboard, were she took, out two slices of bread from a loaf. She slid down from the chair, pushed it back to the table, went over to the frig, and took out a slice of bologna, and a bottle of coke. She climbed back on to the chair, placed the bologna between the two slices of bread, opened the coke with a pop opener, took a drink, then offered the doll a bite of her sandwich, and a drink of coke.

After Sissy finished, tiptoed back to the living room, put on her sandals She then very quietly went to the front door, holding the doll in one hand, she opened the door with her free hand. She went out into the hall and down the steps to the outside. Once outside, she went around the building to her favorite place in the back yard. It was an old tall oak tree; Sissy sat down on the grass, under the tree. She played pretend games with her new doll.

Sue Ellen drug herself out of bed, still feeling tired. She looked at the clock on the nightstand next to her bed. "Ten after one," she groaned. The. whole day is almost gone she thought. Billy Joe was still sound asleep. She sat on the edge of the bed, glanced over at Billy Joe for a moment. She then got up and went to the bathroom for a shower and dressed for the packing chore so they could move into their new house.

As she was getting dressed, she thought of Sissy. She knew Sissy must have gotten up hours before her. She hurried to throw on a tee shirt, and pair of old jeans. She called out to Sissy as she entered the living room, "SISSY, where are you baby?" she called once more, as she headed for the kitchen. She saw the empty coke bottle, and breadcrumbs on the table. She cleaned up before going to where she knew she would find Sissy.

Sue Ellen came down stairs, and out to where Sissy sat playing with her doll. It was well after two in the afternoon. "There you are," she smiled down at Sissy. "Hi, Mommy."

"You want some lunch?" Sue Ellen said as she knelt down by Sissy.

"What we havin?" Sissy asked.

"OH, I was thinking maybe you and I would go down to the Dog and Suds and get us the big special"

"WOWWE, can Angel come to?"

"YOU bet she can, then after we have to come back home and pack our things, OK?" Sue Ellen said as she brushed Sissy's hair back from her face. She took Sissy by the hand pulling her up, they headed out of the yard for the street. The Dog and Suds was just three blocks down the street from their apartment house. Sue Ellen figured that Billy Joe would sleep till after they returned.

Sue Ellen returned back to her apartment, with Sissy, a little after four. She unlocked the door and went in. Billy Joe was sitting at the table drinking a beer. "Where you been?" He asked.

"I took Sissy to The Dog and Suds," she replied. "Here I brought you a sandwich and fries." She handed him the bag.

"You couldn't cook supper here at home for me?"

"Billy Joe, I want to pack things up for the move." She replied, her voice slightly aquiver.

"You can pack every thing up except the kitchen stuff, and what we might need. We have four days before we move. And I expect to have my meals cooked by my wife right here at home. I DON'T want fast food, from that shit 'Hole' where you work. DO you understand?"

"Yes Billy Joe, I understand."

"Fine. Now throw this shit in the trash, and make me a real chicken dinner. I got to go meet the guys. I want my dinner on the table when I get back."

"What time do you want to eat?" She asked.

"I'll be back by seven." He said, then jugged down, the rest of his beer. He got up from the table, and headed for the door.

"Sissy, GET YOUR LITTLE ASS IN THE KITCHEN AND HELP YOUR MAMMA."

Sissy flinched at his gruff words. "Yes Daddy," she said timidly as she scurried off to the kitchen.

Sue Ellen couldn't see throwing away a perfectly good sandwich, so she wrapped it in foil, after Billy Joe left, and put it in the frig. She thought she could give it to Sissy for lunch the next day.

Sue Ellen stared at the clock on the wall, as she put the plate of chicken in the stove warmer. "Billy Joe," she said aloud, "where are you?" It was now after ten, she had dinner done and on the table, since seven. She fed Sissy at eight, and put her to bed.

Sue Ellen kept herself busy, packing things she knew she wouldn't be needing any time soon. It was well after midnight now. Sue Ellen had just finished with her tenth box. She taped it up and stood up from her kneeling position. She stretched out her arms yawning; she walked into the kitchen, she glanced at the clock on the wall. "TWELVE THIRTY," she groaned. She took the chicken from the warmer, wrapped it up and put it in the frig. "The hell with you Billy Joe Martin. If you want supper, you will get it your damn self." She said to herself out loud. She slammed the door on the fridge, turned off the light and went to her bedroom to go to bed.

After climbing into bed, she propped herself up with her pillow behind her back, she took a book from the nightstand and began to read, trying to get over her anger with Billy Joe.

CHAPTER THREE

Chicago General Hospital. Monday, April Tenth.1957.The tall young black doctor was standing at the nurses' station. "Here you are my last chart. Make sure, Doctor Davis gets all of my patient's charts. He said to the nurse as he handed her his chart.

"Yes Doctor Green. Now you better scoot, your wife has called three times. You don't want to be late for the start of your vacation," the nurse said with a smile.

"No I sure don't, get my wife on the phone. I'll take it in my office."

"Right away Doctor Green." the nurse replied. He went into his office, taking off his white smock as he went to his desk to answer the phone that was now buzzing.

"Hi Honey, sorry I'm running a little late," he said into the phone.

"Darling you are always a little late." His wife's voice said over the phone.

"How is our baby doing?" He said lovingly.

"OH he's sleeping right now." She said as she rubbed her hand over her large stomach.

"So now how are you feeling?" He asked.

"I feel fine." She replied.

"Honey are you sure you are up to this trip?" He asked.

"Mark, you are not talking me out of this vacation. We haven't been anywhere since we got married."

"OK. OK. Point taken." He replied. "I just wish Mom and Dad could come here, and we could go to Canada or somewhere with them."

"Oh Honey you worry to much. You know your parents are getting too old to travel such a long distance. Besides, no one will never even know we are there. WE will just keep a low profile while we are there."

"Yes I guess you are right, as usual." He sighed. "I guess I worry to much, but I did grow up in Tupelo, and things haven't changed much. The white people stay on their side of town, and the coloreds stay on their side. But if they see a colored man with a white woman, well they could really make trouble for us." He said with deep concern in his voice.

"I tell you what I will put on a black wig and die my skin and pass for a colored. Will that make you feel better?" She joked.

"No Dear. If we time it just right we will get there at dusk, and leave at night, when we come home."

"Well if you don't get home here and help me finish packing, we won't get there at all." She said.

"Ok I will be home in an hour, see you then. I Love you."

"I Love you too. Now hurry home."

"ON my way, bye." He hung up the phone, checked on some last minute things in his office, locked the door and left for his home.

Mark Green met his wife Jane while he was doing his residency at the hospital. Jane was a nurse there. They were married a year later. After nine years of marriage they are having their first child. Mark was worried about making a trip with her, because she is almost eight months pregnant, and the fact that he is black and she is white. Making a trip to Mississippi, wasn't the greatest idea, with the way things were in the south. But Jane wanted to meet his parents, as they did her. His parents were almost eighty, his mother has a bad heart. His father is almost blind. He hasn't seen his parents in almost twenty years. His father worked for the railroad, scraped and saved so Mark could go to medical school. So he really needed to see his family, at least once before they passed away.

Dr. Green took the Dan Ryan expressway to his exit taking him to Skokie, where he and his wife Jane lived together in a very modest house on a tree lined street. The suburbs of Skokie had only well maintained homes and well groomed yards. It was a great place to raise a family. Dr. Green pulled in to his driveway. He stopped in front of his attached two-car garage. He got out and went into his two story white cape cod with black shutters. He opened the front door. Their little white poodle Toby, came running up to him barking excitedly, happy to see him. "Toby my boy," he said as he picked the little dog up into his arms. "Where is your Mommy?" Toby licked his face and made little growl sounds as if trying to answer him. After hugging Toby he gently put him down as he went to the foot of the staircase, calling out to his wife. "Jane, are you up there? Jane Darling where are you? I'm home." He started up the stairs Toby on his heels. "Jane."

"You don't have to shout. I'm down here." She said smiling.

He looked back over his shoulder as he turned to come back down. He put his arms around her embracing her as he kissed her ever so lovingly. "EMMM, I missed you." He whispered."

"Missed you to darling." She murmured. He ran his fingers thru her long chestnut hair. He looked deep in to her hazel brown eyes. "Have I told you I love you?"

"Not for at least two hours.

"Well I do." He kissed her once more and mussed her hair. "Hey why isn't Toby at the boarding kennel?" He said as he bent down playfully patting his curly foretop.

"The kennel called, said they were running a little late, they should be here in an hour."

"Well I will load the car, and close everything up while we wait for them." He said as he started back up the stairs. "Are the bags all packed?" he asked.

"Hours ago." Jane answered. "I was covering the furniture, when you came in."

"Can you handle that ok?" He asked.

"Of course I can, I'm pregnant not crippled." She laughed as she headed back to the living room.

"Ok wise guy. I will get the bags, after I load them I will take a quick shower, and then shut off the gas and water."

The Kennel picked Toby up, they said their goodbyes to him, and then they closed up the house, got into the blue Cadillac, drove out of Skokie heading off for Tupelo Mississippi. It was well after seven, P.M. when they finally got started. They stopped and had a late supper in Springfield. They spent the night in Saint Louis. It was nearly five A.M when they stopped. They got back on the road again about five P.M that evening. They arrived in Tupelo at four A.M. Jane was asleep, her head tilted back on the back of the front seat. Mark turned onto highway six, Jane, Honey wake up. Jane drowsily opened her eyes; she smiled as she looked over at her husband. "Are we there?" She asked.

"Almost, just a few more miles up this road." He replied.

"It's so dark and deserted," Jane said as she noticed they were the only car on the road.

"It is best that there aren't any other cars on the road." Mark said as he lit a cigarette.

"Now why on earth would you say that?" She asked.

"Because when you see more than two cars on this road after midnight, that only means one thing."

"What do you mean Mark?!"

"The Klan." He said, his voice being very seriously concerned. "The only time they are out on this road late at night, is when they are hurting or harassing colored people

"Oh Mark, that doesn't still go on, does it?" She said in a worried tone of voice.

"Honey that stuff still goes on and on. As long as the ignorance of the Klan exists it will never stop. And if we are seen together by the Klan, they would probably kill us both."

"Oh Mark you can't mean that."

"Oh yes Honey I do. That is why I am afraid for you. When we get there you must not let any white people see you. You must stay in the house during the day; we can go out into the yard after sundown. When I was ten years old I saw the Klan hang my uncle Jack.

23

They killed him just because he accidentally brushed by a white woman touching her shoulder. And for that he lost his life."

"Oh my." She gasped.

"That's why we can only stay a few days, and we must leave at night. Once we get out of Mississippi and back into Illinois, then we can have a real vacation at the lake. I wish your parents were able to come with us to the lake."

"So do I, but they are just getting to old to travel."

"Well we are here." He said as he turned on to the dirt road that led up to a very well kept two-story farmhouse. "You wait here until I get someone to open the door. Love you." He said as he leaned over giving her a quick kiss on the cheek. Mark went to the front door, and knocked on it with his knuckles. A few moment's later the porch light came on, then went off, as his mother came out on the porch throwing her arms around him, giving him a big long hug. They talked a moment, and then Mark left her standing on the porch as he came down the steps to the car. He went to Jane's side and opened the car door for her. "Come on Honey. Lets go meet my mother." He smiled. Mark led her by the arm to the porch were his mother waited.

"Hurry child come inside." The old woman hugged her then hurried her inside. Jane followed the thin frail silver haired black woman inside. She was still holding onto the old black woman's bony frail hand as she looked into gentle smiling face. She had very kind eyes, Jane thought to herself.

The old woman took hold of Jane's other hand held them outstretched, as her eyes looked her up and down. "EMMM, Markus has good taste, but of course he always has. Welcome to the family child." She said as she embraced Jane again, giving her a hug and a peck on the cheek. Mark came in the door carrying the luggage. "Were do we sleep Mother?"

"Take the suitcases up to your old room."

"But Mother my room only has a single bed."

"Not anymore." She giggled. I bought one of them new king beds when you told me you were bringing your wife. Now take those upstairs and come back down to the kitchen, and I will fix you whatever you want. Come Jane, let's get to know each other." Jane followed her to the kitchen, as the old woman tightened the belt on her deep purple quilted robe.

Jane looked around the very clean and well-kept kitchen. She sat down at the round solid oak table. The oak hardwood floors shined. Not a speck of dirt any were Jane thought to herself. "How bout some herb tea Dear?" The old woman asked as she put a copper kettle on the stove burner.

"That will be fine." Jane replied.

"Good. I was hoping you didn't want coffee, because I hope you know caffeine isn't good for my grandson."

"Grandson? Oh Mother Green, it could be a girl you know."

It's a boy. You're carrying high and to a point. That's how boy babies sit. Trust me I know." She smiled at Jane, sounding very confident, she knew what she was talking about.

You know Dear you can call me, Cora, if you like, Mother Green sounds too old. She laughed."

"Ok Cora it is." Jane replied.

"I wish I could show you off to my friends. But that would be to dangerous for all of us." She sighed.

"Maybe someday you can Cora, times are changing."

"Maybe where you come from Honey, but they won't ever change here."

Mark came into the kitchen; he joined them at the table. They talked till nearly sunup, and then they went to bed. Jane slept only a few hours. She did that a lot lately. Her baby was due in about six weeks so she was having difficulty in finding a comfortable way to sleep. She looked over to Mark who was having no problem at all. He was sleeping like a baby. "Lucky you." she thought to herself. She got up and dressed to go downstairs. She tiptoed trying to be as quiet as possible. She didn't want to disturb anyone in the house. As she was coming down the stairs, she stopped midway down. She was staring at the old photos on the stair case wall. Jane reached out and touched one of the oval shaped photos on the wall, as if she knew the person in the photo.

"That's Thomas Green. Mark's great grandfather," Cora's voice broke into Jane's thoughts from the bottom of the stairs. Jane looked down to her as she said, "He looks like Mark." Cora broke in.

"Was he white?" Jane asked.

"Half. His mother was a slave, and Edward Green's mistress. Come on down and I will tell you all about our family. Want some breakfast?" Cora asked as they went into the kitchen. "Maybe some tea and toast, I can fix it. You are probably tired too."

"Tired, Lord no child, when you get my age you will find that you don't need much sleep. How about bacon and eggs, along with that toast?"

"Yeah, that's sound's great." Jane answered with a big grin on her face.

Cora laid strips of bacon in the large cast iron skillet. The bacon sizzled as it hit the skillet. Jane scrambled the eggs. Mark's father entered the kitchen, he was tapping his way to the table with a cane. "I could smell the bacon frying all the way down the hall."

"Sit yourself down at the table, and meet your daughter-in-law, Jane...Jane, Henry, Mark's father. Mark and Jane arrived while you was asleep."

"Come closer child so I can see you better." Henry said, as he reached out a hand to Jane. Jane leaned in close to him and gave him a hug and quick kiss on the forehead. "You are a pretty one I must say. They all sat at the table enjoying the food and talking. "That was a great breakfast girls. But I got to go out back and check on my flowers, see you all later, so to speak," He said a little humor in his voice. Henry got up from the table, and tapped his way out of the kitchen.

Cora and Jane cleared the table of dishes and sat down to have some tea. Cora poured tea into Jane's cup, and then her cup, as she sat the kettle down on the metal tray, "As I was saying, Thomas Green was the love child of Edward Green, the woman he was married to did not want children. They had separate bedrooms on separate floors in that big old mansion. So Thomas's mother, who was a slave on the plantation, became his mistress. It has been said they were really in love. They must have been something; Thomas was the oldest of ten children. Thomas was his favorite. He sent Thomas to Europe, were he got the best education money could buy. Well when Edward died, he left this house and five hundred acres to Thomas, along with a hundred thousand dollars. By the time Thomas had returned home, he found out that his Mother and his brothers and sisters had been sold at auction. Mrs. Green could not sell him because Thomas carried the Green name and had been declared Edward's son. Edward had made sure the lawyers had all the documents on paper in his will. So Thomas had the one piece of paper that was worth its weight in gold. That paper declared that Thomas was a free man. Thomas became a lawyer in Philadelphia. He didn't return here until a few years after the war was over, and the slaves freed. He tried for years to locate his mother and siblings. He found out that his Mother died two years after she was sold. She was beaten to death by a cruel slave foreman. She was killed for taking a few extra potatoes to feed her youngest child."

"What happened to the children?" Jane asked.

"Well it's said that because they were too young to work, and that they were girls, they were shot and thrown into the same grave with their mother." Cora said clearing her throat, as her voice began to break up. "Thomas located two of his brothers and one sister. He never did find the other four. It's been told that they died in the war. They were all young boys, they ran away from there owners, and joined up with the union army."

"So that is how Mark and Henry and Henry's father got their lite skin from."

"And of course their good hair. They all have the white man's hair."

"Yes I know, when I first met Mark I thought he was Spanish, or Greek. I almost could not believe he was colored. Jane said with a smile."

Do you think it would have made a difference if you had known?" Cora asked, searching Jane's face for the right answer.

"Of course not, I fell in love with Mark, not his color. If Mark had been coal black, I would have still loved him."

"I'm glad to hear that, but you know you are in for a lot of criticism and snide remarks from people who don't understand;" Cora added. "I only hope your love for each other is strong enough to undergo, all the strain you will incur." Cora said as she took a sip of her tea from her china teacup.

"Don't worry Cora, the love we have for each other is very strong." Jane said assuringly. "Cora, do you think it would be ok if we went out back into the garden? I really would like to see it."

"Well I guess so, I don't guess anyone can see into the backyard. I need some fresh air too." Cora said as she stood up taking the teacups to the sink. The two of them went out the back door onto the large back porch. It overlooked to a very large picturesque backyard. It looked like something from the Homes and Garden magazine.

"OH Cora it's just breath taking. Why it's just so beautiful. I never thought it could be this gorgeous, I have never seen anything like it in my life." Jane said as she soaked in all the beauty of the roses, and numerous other flowers that surrounded the well-manicured yard. Jane stepped off the porch steps onto the cobblestone walkway. She bent down touching and smelling the roses, and other fragrant flowers. Jane felt free and exhilarated as a child running barefoot in the soft summer grass. Cora stood on the porch admiring how happy and resilient her daughter-in-law looked. Mark was standing in the kitchen doorway, looking through the screen door.

"Do you think it wise that Jane and yourself be out here in the open?" Mark asked concern in his voice.

"I thought of that Mark, but we are surrounded by the woods and the fields, and the entire yard has tall lilacs surrounding it. The only way someone could see back here, is if they come in the backyard." Cora said her voice very reassuring.

"I guess you are right Mother." Mark said.

"I see you are up and among the living." Cora kidded.

"OK, I hear you. Now can a man get a cup of coffee, around here?"

"Yes you can. There's a fresh pot on the stove, help yourself. Are you hungry?" Cora asked.

"Well how bout some of your peach pie? You got any?"

"You know good and well I always got peach pie. It's your father's favorite." Cora laughed.

"Jane." Cora called out. "Your husband is up, he wants some peach pie. You want some?" Cora asked.

"Yes, sounds good. I will be in in a moment." Jane answered across the yard, where she was watching Mark's father trim some roses.

"Ok." Cora answered, as she turned and went back into the house where Mark was now pouring himself a cup of coffee.

"Mother, I think I will take father into town with me." Mark said as he sat down at the table. "Is there anything you need?"

"No, I can't think of anything right now." Cora replied as she cut him a piece of pie.

"I need something." Jane said as she came into the kitchen.

"Now what on earth could you possibly need? You packed everything except the house." Mark chided.

"That's not true. Cora don't listen to him. I need some chocolates."

"Chocolates?" Mark said.

"Yes chocolates, you know I have a craving every now and then."

"OK. I will get you some chocolates." Mark laughed. "You gonna be ok while I'm gone?" Mark asked."

"Of course she will be fine, Jane and I will have a good time together while you men are gone. Won't we Jane?"

"You bet, Cora." Jane said in agreement with Cora.

"Now eat your pie and get your father, and you two have fun in town. Jane and I will be just fine."

Mark finished his pie, and took his father to town. Cora cleaned up the kitchen, and retired into the living room. Cora brought out the family photo album, and the two of them spent the rest of the day reminiscing.

April 12th

Melvin Gumm and his brother Elvin were in the woods behind the Green's farm. They were poaching for rabbit and squirrel. Melvin and his brother were both a little on the retarded side, mostly from being just dumb and uneducated. They were twins. Not identical, but they did favor each other. Elvin was looking through a pair of binoculars, when something caught his eye.

"Melvin, LOOK AT THIS. Come on take a look" He jumped up and down all excited, making hand motions to his brother to come see what he was seeing.

"What the Hell you want Elvin? You makin all this noise gonna scare away all the game." He said angrily at Elvin. Melvin snatched the binoculars from his brother's hand. He looked through them.

"Now what in the hell am I supposed to be looking at?"

"Look over to old Nigger Greens place. Tell me now what do you see?"

"What the hell's the big deal? Just some white woman, and that old white nigger Green standin in the yard. She's probably a social worker or a nurse."

"Look again, how many social workers or nurses you know with belly's stickin out like that? Hua. Hua. How many Melvin, Hua. How many? I heard that Nigger Green's son married himself one of them Yankee white women." Elvin said with authority in his voice.

"Well, how you know she just ain't one of them lite skin niggers like the Greens?" Melvin said trying to sound like he knew what he was talking about. "Well anyway, they just visiting, so what do we care? It be different if they was movin in." Melvin said. "Besides, I don't care. Now lets do what we came out here for." Melvin demanded.

"All right. You're no fun at all" I still think she's white. I'm still gonna tell the wizard." Elvin groaned.

"Shut up Elvin. Tell whoever you want to, after we get done here." Melvin growled.

April 19th

The week passed quickly, and it was time for Mark and Jane to leave. Jane was glad she got to know Mark's parents, she felt sad to leave. But on the other hand a little relieved. It was Sunday late afternoon, Jane was packing her suitcase, Cora sat on the foot of the bed.

"Cora, I hope that you and Henry can come to Chicago when the baby comes."

"Don't worry. Got it all worked out with my sister. She is going to take us to the train station, and we will riding a big passenger car to come stay with you. I wouldn't miss seeing my grandson for nothing in this old world."

"I'm going to miss you Cora." Jane said as she gave her a hug.

"I will miss you to, but look on the bright side, we will see each other in just four weeks, and that will go very fast. You'll see." She hugged Jane back.

That Sunday night, around seven o'clock, Mark loaded the car, they said their goodbye's, and Mark and Jane left his parents house heading back to Illinois where they planned a week to end up their vacation at Lake Placid. They were driving down highway six, they were just a few miles from Mark's parent's home. They saw red lights flashing just ahead of them. Mark slowed down; he reached over and took Jane's hand in his. He saw the Police officer flag him to a stop. Mark rolled down his window. "What's the problem officer?" Mark asked. The officer smiled at him. "Evening Sir, Mam." He nodded. "There has been an accident just ahead. "You'll have to take a little detour, just go up this dirt road, and it will bring you back here on the main road. Its a little bumpy, but it's pretty good in all. Mark looked at him as he asked, "I'm a doctor can I be of help?"

"That's nice of you to ask Doc, but there were no survivors."

"I'm sorry to hear that." Mark replied.

"Well doctor you just go down that road like I said and you will be back on the highway in no time at all." The policeman reassured Mark.

"Thank you officer, sorry I could not been of more help." Mark replied.

"Well that's what happens when you mix speed with alcohol." The policeman nodded, and Mark turned down the dirt road. They were driving about fifteen minutes.

"Good Lord Mark, when are we going to get back onto the black top? This road is so rough." Jane complained.

"I know Honey it shouldn't be to much longer. The cop said it was rough, but only a few miles." Mark answered Jane.

"Mark look at the road. It looks like its getting muddy." Jane said.

"I think you are right Honey, in fact it seems to be getting real slick. Damn," he said as the Cady began to slide, then suddenly the tires spun out and the Cad slid sideways, suddenly they came to a jolting stop. Mark looked over at Jane. "You OK?"

"Yes." She shakenly replied.

"Well you sit tight, and I will see how bad we are stuck." Mark opened the car door to get out.

"Look, Mark headlights." Jane pointed in the rear of the car.

"Give me the flashlight, I need to warn them before they become stuck like us. Mark got out waving the light at the approaching headlights.

CHAPTER FOUR

April 19th

Sue Ellen Sat with her back propped on pillows against the headboard. She had just turned the page in her book, when the sound of the key turning in the lock of the front door got her attention. She heard Billy Joe's footsteps coming down the hall to the bedroom. Billy Joe walked into the room; Sue Ellen glanced up from her book.

"Where and the hell have you been?" she asked angrily.

"I had something to do with the guys, it took longer than we thought."

"Well you know you made such a fuss about dinner. You said you be home by seven, and it is now two thirty, A.M., in the morning. I kept it warm as long as I could, when you didn't get home by eleven. I put it all away, in the fridge. So if you still want dinner, you can just warm it up yourself. I am not going to take much more of your macho bullshit. If you think you are going to treat me like shit, while you go out and harass some poor coloreds, for looking at one of them dumb ass Klan Kluckers wrong, then you can do it with out me."

"Fuck you bitch. I'm tired I'm going to take a shower now. I'll settle this with you later. But you hear this bitch, if you got any idea about leaving me, you better think again, because if you do I will hunt you down and kill your ass. THAT'S A PROMISE." He said glaring at her as he pointed a finger at her. "And one other thing, I am a Klan member, and if some Nigger needs to be taught a lesson on how to keep his place. Well so be it. That's what we do. And no wife of mine will be a Nigger sympathizer. So just shut the hell up and put the book away, and go to sleep. That's your whole problem, you read to damn much." He dropped his hand at his side and started for the bathroom. Sue Ellen raised up on her haunches in bed.

"Fuck YOU, BILLY JOE MARTIN. YOU HEAR ME?" she screamed at him.

Billy Joe lunged at her from the doorway, he was on top of her, hitting her and slamming her head against the wall.

"You don't talk back to me like that. YOU HEAR ME?" He shouted as he kept hitting her again and again. Then suddenly he stopped.

"Don't you even, try leaving; or don't even open your mouth to me." He moved off her and left her crying on the bed. He went into the shower. Sue Ellen heard the water running in the shower. She got up, taking her pillow and a blanket from the bed. She went into the living room and layed down on the opposite side of the couch from the still sleeping Sissy.

Billy Joe came out of the shower, found her gone. He started for the living room, to make her come to bed with him, but he decided against it. He knew he had to get up for work in a few hours so he went to bed.

The alarm went off at six A.M. Billy Joe reached over and turned the alarm off. He put his hands over his face, rubbing it as he yawned. Then the memory of his fight with Sue Ellen ran through his mind. After getting up and dressing, he went into the living room where Sue Ellen lie sleeping with Sissy on the couch. He started to wake her but changed his mind. He went into the kitchen, and made himself some coffee instead. He went to the fridge, took out two pieces of chicken, wrapped them in foil, took some chips down from the cupboard, took out a handful, put them in a baggie, filled his thermos with coffee, put it all in his lunch bucket and left the apartment for his work.

Sue Ellen awoke when she heard the front door close. She went into the kitchen to look at the time on the kitchen clock. It was six thirty five. She put the coffee pot back on the stove to warm it up. Then she went into the bathroom, she looked at herself in the mirror. She gently touched her cheek and eye. Her cheek was swollen and bruised. Her left eye was nearly swollen shut. She had a swollen split lip.

Sue Ellen put a cold cloth on her face. She then returned back to the kitchen were she fixed herself a cup of coffee and sat down at the table. Thoughts began to flood her mind. "Why has Billy Joe been so violent lately?" She was remembering back to when they first met, and how loving he was. He has always had a little mean streak in him, she thought to herself, but he never used to hit her. But he has always ordered her around. She always knew he never wanted Sissy, but she thought he would come to accept and love her in time. Time she thought, I got to do the laundry and finish the packing. So I guess I better get started, she said aloud to herself. She got up from the table and went into the bedroom; she began by picking up clothes from a hamper and sorting them. She went into the bathroom, picking up Billy Joe's clothes from the floor he had taken off when he took his shower. As she picked up his shirt, she noticed some dark red spots on the sleeve. Then she held it up to examine it closer.

"What on earth." She said aloud. "This looks like blood." Then she turned to check herself out in the mirror, then back to the shirt. The whole sleeve was blood soaked, and had blood splatters all over the front. Then when she picked up his jeans, examining them very closely. She saw more blood splatters. His socks were covered with blood spots. "Billy Joe what have you done?" She said to herself out loud. She threw his blood stained clothes in with the rest of the laundry.

Sissy woke around eight. Sue Ellen got her ready after she fed her, and took her with her to the laundromat. They arrived back at the apartment around noon, Sue Ellen sent Sissy out to play while she finished the packing. Sissy was still outside when Billy Joe came home at five.

Billy Joe came through the front door, he saw Sue Ellen taping her last box. He saw her face. It made him feel very bad, and feelings of guilt welled up in him, as he felt a lump in his throat. He walked over to her. "Sue Ellen" I'm so sorry." Tears welled in his eyes. "I did not mean to ever hurt you like this. Honey please forgive me. I swear I will never hit you again. I swear to God Almighty. May he strike me dead." He said begging for her forgiveness, as he reached down to her. Sue Ellen stared up to him, searching his face for his sincerity.

"What about the blood Billy Joe?

"Blood, what are you talking about?" He stammered, looking puzzled.

"The blood stains I found on the clothes you were wearing last night."

"Blood on my clothes? I don't know what you are talking about." He said trying to think of an explanation.

"Yes the blood, Billy Joe." She said coldly.

"What did you do, and where did it come from, or should I say, who did it come from?"

"Sue Ellen you got it all wrong, baby, I must have got some blood on me when Red shot a big old raccoon. He scared the hell out of me when he shot it. I was probably only two feet away from it.

"Two feet away huh, then how did the front of your pants and the whole shirt sleeve get soaked? Tell me that Billy Joe."

"That's easy. I probably got it when I picked it up and took it to him."

"Auh come on, Sue Ellen. What do you think I did, kill somebody?"

Sue Ellen thought for a moment, then she answered in a low voice.

"No I guess not." She said.

"So you forgive me?" He said as he pulled her into his arms. "Come on you know you want to say yes." He crooned. "Come on give me that pretty smile of yours. COME ON NOW." He teased.

Sue Ellen gave in. "Oh all right, I forgive you. But you promise you won't ever hit me again like last night, right?" Sue Ellen said, in a child like voice.

"I promise." He said holding up his right hand as if swearing in court.

April 23rd

Friday morning, moving day for Billy Joe and Sue Ellen. Billy Joe had picked up his check from the textile mill. Thursday was his last day for that mill. He was to start on Monday, at their other plant in Cottonwood.

"Sue Ellen." Billy Joe called out to her as he came in the front door.

"I'm right here, dear." She replied. "We got room for six more boxes. How about those boxes in the corner?" Sue Ellen said pointing to a stack of boxes in the corner of the room.

"Yeah, I think those will fit. Oh, I'm going to take you and Sissy on this load, and you -can stay at the house. By the time we unload, and I get back here Red, and Berry will be here to help me with the heavy stuff." Billy Joe said as he bent down to pick up two of the boxes.

"Let me get the door, and I will get a box and bring it down to you."

"OK, but just take one. This shit is heavy. What the hell you got in here anyway?" Billy Joe asked as he strained to carry the boxes.

"That shit, is yours." She giggled.

"My stuff? Like what?"

"Like all your books." She chided.

"Oh yeah, I forgot I had a lot of books and records."

"Let's see, there's Elvis, and Elvis, and Elvis." Sue Ellen teased.

"OK. Just get the door, you made your point." He laughed.

They were loaded and on their way a little after one that after noon. They pulled into the driveway at ten after two. Sue Ellen got out of the truck with Sissy to unlock the side door.

"The lights are on." Sue Ellen called out, as she tried the kitchen light.

"Well they said they would have them on by today." Billy Joe called back to her. Billy Joe untied the ropes that were tied to the truck holding the boxes on, when a. tall young man approached Billy Joe.

"Hi. My name is Carl Holt, I live across the street," he pointed at the old two story white house.

"Welcome to the neighborhood."

"Thanks." Billy Joe said as he shook Carl's extended hand.

"Can I give you a hand unloading?" He asked with a smile.

"Sure, here, take this one." Billy Joe said as he handed Carl a box off the truck. They had the truck unloaded in less than an hour with Carl helping.

"Wow, I almost forgot what it's like to move," Carl said wiping the sweat from his brow with his hanky he took from the back pocket of his jeans.

"Is this everything?" He asked.

"No this is just the packed stuff. I still have to go back to Tupelo for the furniture." Billy Joe said.

"Could you use another strong back?" He grinned.

"Yeah, sure, if it's not too much trouble?" Billy Joe said happy to have the offer.

"No trouble at all. Just let me go close up my house and leave my wife a note and I will be right with you.

"You bet." Billy Joe answered. "Hey, and thanks again."

"You're welcome. Glad I can be of some help." Carl said as he headed across the street to his house. Billy Joe watched the tall blond man named Carl cross the street.

"Seems to be a nice guy." He commented. "I think I'm going to like it here. What about you?" Billy Joe turned to Sue Ellen asking what she thought.

"You bet I'm going to like it here. We have our own house, a big yard, and our neighbors are not the next wall over." Sue Ellen smiled.

Billy Joe and Carl jumped in the truck and left to get another load.

"Mommy, can Angel and me go out and play?" Sissy asked Sue Ellen as she started unpacking boxes.

"Sure Honey, just don't wander off too far from the house. Ok?"

"I won't Mommy, I promise."

"OK. Now scoot, Mommy's got a lot to do before Daddy gets back."

"Wee," Sissy said to her doll as she ran down the porch steps. Sissy went out back by the garage, then to' the fence line. There was a block wire fence separating the field from Sissy's back yard. There was a large hole in the fence, it was large enough for Sissy to walk through.

"OOOH look Angel, flowers. Let's go pick some for Mommy to put in the new house. We can make it smell all pretty." Sissy wandered into the middle of the field were she smelled and began picking flowers.

"Who are you?" A voice came from behind Sissy, as she looked up a little startled.

"I'm Sissy, who are you?" She asked her blue eyes opened wide as she asked the little colored girl that was standing just a few feet away.

"My name is Marcy, and I'm four years old. And this is my brother William, he's only two and a half. How old are you?" She asked as she sat down next to Sissy and began picking flowers.

"I'm three years old and this is my dolly. Her name is Angel." Sissy said as she held up her doll for Marcy to see.

"She don't got no legs." Marcy observed. What kind of Doll is she?

"She's an angel, silly. That's why I named her Angel." Sissy said firmly.

"Oh, I guess that would be right, she does have wings." Marcy said standing corrected. Sissy looked at her then with a big smile.

"Hey, you want to be my friend?"

Marcy thought for a moment. Then very seriously said, "William too?"

"Why of course. William too. I like him too." Sissy said as she hugged him.

"Where do you live?" Marcy asked.

"Over there." Sissy stood up pointing to her new house. "We just moved in today."

"I'm glad. I only have William to play with, and he don't talk too much, and sometimes he don't want to play. I have my older brother Ben. He is ten years old. But he won't play with me and William either. He says we are too young to play with him. He is always helping Daddy in the garden."

"Gee I wish I had a brother or sister," Sissy said. "But my Daddy says he don't like kids. He don't like me. He tells me that all the time and he is so mean to me." Sissy said as tears started to fill her eyes.

"What about your Mommy?" Marcy asked.

"Oh my Mommy likes me, I guess. She just has to do what my Daddy says."

"Gee, I guess me and my brothers are lucky. My Mommy and Daddy tell us they love us every day, and every night, before we go to sleep."

"I wish mine did." Sissy said.

"Well William and I will always like you." Marcy said as she put her arm around Sissy's shoulder.

"I'm glad I have always wanted a real friend. Now I have two friends." Sissy beamed.

The children played together until Marcy heard her mother calling.

"I got to go home now." Marcy said. "Will you be here tomorrow?" Marcy asked.

"Yes, this will be our secret place, Ok?" Sissy asked.

"Ok, I got to go now. Bye Bye now. See you tomorrow." Marcy said as she started for home. "Come on William, Mommy's calling us," Marcy said as she took William by the hand leading him in the direction of her house. Sissy waved till they were out of sight.

"Well Angel, I guess we better go too. We got a lot of flowers for Mommy, she is going to be so surprised." Sissy stood up as she gathered-up the flowers and scurried home, to give the flowers to her mother.

"Mommy look, flowers." Sissy proudly held them out for Sue Ellen to see.

"Oh, they are lovely. Let me smell." She bent down to take a sniff.

"Oh, they smell just wonderful. Where did you ever find them?" she asked.

"Over there." Sissy pointed to the field behind the house. "There are lots of them everywhere." Sissy boasted.

"Well let's take them in the house, put them in a. jar of water."

"OK Mommy." Sissy said as she followed her mother inside. Sue Ellen got a mason jar filled it with water, and put the flowers in the jar. "There now," she said as she finished arranging the flowers.

"Let's put them on the kitchen table. There now, my don't they look pretty there?" Sue Ellen said smiling at Sissy.

"Oh, yes, Mommy. They are so beautiful." Sissy beamed. Just then Sue Ellen turned her head at the knocking sound on the screen door.

"Hello, is anybody home?" A woman's voice called through the door.

"Yes, can I help you?" Sue Ellen said as she went to the door. She opened the screen just a little to see the nicely dressed dark haired woman standing on the other side.

"Hi. My name is Margie Holt. I live across the street, and I found a note from my husband Carl, saying he was helping you folks move in."

"Oh yes. He went with my husband to get another load of stuff. Come on in." Sue Ellen said as she held open the door for her. "Everything is a mess." Sue Ellen said. "Would you like some coffee?"

"Sure if it's not to much trouble?" Margie said as she sat down at the kitchen table. "Oh what lovely wild flowers," she said as she bent to smell them.

"I picked them for Mommy" Sissy beamed.

"Oh, how nice of you, and what might your name be?" She asked.

"Sissy. But my real name is Sarah. But everyone calls me Sissy."

"Sarah is a pretty name. But so is Sissy. What would you like me to call you?" She asked.

Sissy thought for a moment, then a big grin came over her face. "Sissy. You can call me Sissy."

"You got it. Sissy it is." She took Sissy by the hand to shake on it. Sissy giggled, then took her doll and got down from the table.

"Mommy, can I go out on the porch and watch for Daddy?"

"Yes Honey. You stay out on the porch now." Sue Ellen said firmly.

"I will." Sissy replied as she went out the door.

"I would show you around. But as you can see, I don't have furniture yet."

"Oh, I understand that. We were the same way last year when we moved in."

"Even with what I've got, I'm going to have to get more now. We had just a tiny little apartment. Now we have this big old house to fill.

"Well what do you still need?" Margie asked.

"Well, I'm going to need a bed and a dresser for Sissy now that she is finally going to have a room of her own." Sue Ellen said.

"You got some time, come over to my garage, I got just what you need."

"Oh, I couldn't afford to buy it now." Sue Ellen said.

"Buy it? My no. I will give it to you. I been trying to get Carl to get rid of that stuff for months." Margie said. "Come on. Lets go get it. I think the two of us can carry it over here, and set it up for your little girl so she can sleep on it tonight.

The two of them had managed to carry a single bed, mattress and box springs, dresser, and even a bookcase and a box of children's books. Margie even had all the bed linens to go with the bed.

"Oh, Margie. Thank you so much. I don't know what to say." Sue Ellen said thrilled.

"You already said it." Margie smiled. "I'm glad I could finally get rid of it."

"But it all looks so new." Sue Ellen said as she ran her hand across the dresser top.

"Well it was two years ago." Margie replied a slight sigh in her voice.

"I don't understand. If they were new, why haven't you used them?"

"Well two years ago Carl went out and bought all this stuff. It was for our son's room."

"Your son? You have a son?" Sue Ellen asked.

"Yes. You see when he was born; I had to have an emergency Caesarian. I hemorrhaged and they did a total hysterectomy on me. So I can't have any more babies. Anyway Carl was so proud just to know we had at least one baby, he went out and bought all this to furnish a boy's room. That is for when he outgrew the baby crib and stuff. I had all that to until last year, I gave it to my sister, for her baby, with all the baby clothes. My baby lived for a month. He died before he ever left the hospital." Tears filled Margie's eyes as she told Sue Ellen her story.

"Oh, Margie, I'm so sorry." Sue Ellen said putting her arm around Margie's shoulder.

"Oh, I'm alright. It's just that I haven't thought about him for so long. I could never bring myself to look at this stuff until today. It was such a long time ago. You think I would be over it. But I guess I know deep down in my heart, you never get over losing your child.

"No I don't think anyone can really get over losing a child; I know I would just go crazy if anything happened to Sissy." Sue Ellen said.

"Sissy," Margie said, "She hasn't seen the room yet."

"You're right, she will be thrilled." Sue Ellen said as she turned to call Sissy in from the porch.

"Sissy, come into the kitchen, dear." Sue Ellen called through the screen door.

Sissy came into the kitchen, "Ok, Sissy, remember the room I told you that was yours?"

"Yes Mommy, that one over there." Sissy pointed to the doorway off from the kitchen.

"Well close your eyes. We got a surprise for you." Sue Ellen told her as she took her by the hand and lead her to the bedroom. "Now keep your eyes closed."

"I will, Mommy."

As they entered the room, "Ok Honey now open them." Sue Ellen told Sissy.

"Oh Mommy!" She squealed, "Is this all mine?"

"Yes Honey it's all yours."

"Oh, thank you Mommy, Oh, thank you."

"Don't thank me, thank Margie. She's the one who was so kind to give it to you. I only helped carry it from her house to here and set it up.

"Oh, thank you, Margie." Sissy wailed as she ran to Margie giving her a big hug and a kiss on the cheek.

"Oh, Honey, you are more than welcome. It has made me very happy inside just seeing how happy I have made one lovely little girl." Margie said, as she hugged and kissed Sissy back.

The bed was made_ of solid maple, the bright red bedspread and sheets set it off. The bookcase and dresser along with the nightstand were also solid maple. On the nightstand was a, brown rearing horse lamp. The shade was white with a western cowboy scene. Suddenly the happy scene was interrupted by the sound of Billy Joe's truck pulling into the driveway.

"Your Daddy's home. Let's not show him the room till later. We will surprise him too." Sue Ellen said.

She went to the screen door and propped it open, so they could bring in the furniture. Then Sue Ellen saw the other truck pull in with the fridge and kitchen stove on it. It was Red Avery, and Berry Collins. Berry was Billy Joe's old friend from high school. But Red Avery was the one Sue Ellen did not like because he was the one who got Billy Joe into the Klan. She always thought Billy Joe wouldn't be such a racist if it weren't for Red. She always thought he was the one who filled his head full with all the hate he had for colored folks. She knew he was some kind of big shot in the Klan, but she wasn't sure how big.

"Well Hello there miss Sue Ellen." Red said as he wet his lips with his tongue. He brushed back his thick red curly hair with his fingers. He always made Sue Ellen think of him as a cartoon evil wolf, ready to pounce on his prey and eat them up. She didn't like him at all.

"I'm just fine, Mr. Avery." Sue Ellen said coldly.

"Well now, you can call me Red, you know. After all it's not like we are strangers."

"If you insist. I'm only being respect full."

"Oh, I insist, and thank you for being honest." Red replied.

After everyone left, Sue Ellen finished, putting things away. Billy Joe was sitting at the kitchen table when Sissy climbed on the chair across from him.

"Daddy look at the pretty flowers I picked. She said as she reached for the Jar to hold up for him to smell. "Here Daddy smell." She said, as she then accidentally dropped the jar tipping it over spilling the water on Billy Joe. He jumped up as the water spilled onto the front of his jeans.

"GOD DAMN YOU Sissy. Look what you did YOU STUPID LITTLE BITCH." Sissy eyes widened with fear, as she backed off the chair, stammering as she headed for her room.

"I'm sorry, Daddy."

Billy Joe grabbed up the jar, he threw the glass jar at Sissy, it missed her, but shattered against the wall. It sent pieces flying everywhere. A large piece struck Sissy on the arm, causing a gash to open on her arm. Sissy screamed out in pain. Another piece hit her little leg. Blood spattered on the floor and the doorway woodwork to her room. Sue Ellen came running into the kitchen when she heard Sissy scream.

"What happened?" She yelled.

By this time Billy Joe was beating Sissy across the face with what was left of the flowers causing red stinging marks across her face.

"Billy Joe, stop!" She screamed at him as she grabbed his arm as he raised it to hit Sissy again. He stopped, then he backhanded Sue Ellen across her face knocking her to the floor.

"Billy Joe, DAMN YOU, STOP IT!" Sue Ellen cried out as she scrambled to her feet, trying to protect Sissy.

"She has to learn it's her fault." He yelled.

"Can't you see she is bleeding bad? You hurt her. PLEASE BILLY JOE. PLEASE STOP." She pleaded to him. Then he came to his senses. He stopped hitting the little frail child who was now just whimpering cowered down against the doorway.

"Fine." He said as he put his hand down. "I'm going down to the club. I want this mess cleaned up when I get back. And I want that little bitch to do it. And I want her out of my site, when I do get back. Is that understood, Sissy?" He glared down at Sissy.

Sissy answered with sobbing gulps, as she said "Yes Daddy."

Billy Joe went out the door and to his truck and drove off.

Sue Ellen ran over to Sissy. "OH, baby, let mommy see. Come on sweetie. Let's go over to the sink so I can clean it and put a bandage on it." She took a clean cloth and put it on Sissy's arm. She could see that there was a large piece of glass sticking out from her wound. Sue Ellen very carefully tried to pull it out without causing too much pain for Sissy.

"Got it." Sue Ellen said as she pulled out the glass. Then she drew her attention to the cut on Sissy's leg. "You hold this cloth, Sissy, on your arm real tight while Mommy looks for the medicine and bandages. OK Sweetie?" She said to Sissy, with a painful look on her face.

"Hurry Mommy, it hurts; it hurts so bad." Sissy said with a whimpering cry.

"I will Honey." Sue Ellen said as she ran to the boxes in her bedroom. She began frantically searching for the box marked medicine cabinet. She found it, she took out some gauze tape and cotton, and mercurochrome bottle. She hurried back into the kitchen. As she was tending to Sissy's arm. She knew in her heart the gaping wound needed stitches. She poured the mercurochrome on the wound and then squeezed it together, then wrapped snugly, being careful it wasn't to tight. She did the same to Sissy's leg.

After she took care of Sissy and held her in her arms, as she sat on a chair in the kitchen, she got her to stop crying, and rocked her till she fell asleep. She put Sissy in her new bed, and covered her with a bright red blanket. She had just finished cleaning up when Billy Joe walked in the kitchen door.

"I see you cleaned the mess up and not Sissy." He said hatefully.

"Yes I did." Sue Ellen snapped back.

"It's one thing for you to hit me. But it's quite another for you to hit Sissy. She is only three years old, and you could go to jail for what you did to her tonight, do you know that? Or do you even care?"

"I Know, I know, it's just that she made me so damn mad. Is she ok?"

"Do you even care how she is?" Sue Ellen snapped.

"Of course I care. I wouldn't be askin if I didn't. Now would I?" He said trying to sound concerned and remorseful. "Look. I'm sorry. I will take you both down to the Dairy Queen tomorrow and buy us a. Sunday or whatever you want. OK?"

"Ok. But Billy Joe this just can't happen again. No more understood?"

"I understand." He said as he nodded his head yes.

"I'm going to take a shower and go to bed. You coming?" He asked as he headed for the bedroom.

"I will be there in a few minutes, I got a few more things I need to do in here. Then I will be in." She said as she put some dishes in the cabinet.

"Ok, try not to be too long, ok?" He gave her that I want you smile.

"Ok," she replied. But inside she was still very angry with him. She went on with her putting things away, it was well after midnight. She checked on Sissy, she was still sound asleep in her new bed. She went into the bedroom to get another box, and found Billy Joe in bed also sound asleep. "Good." She thought to herself with a sigh of relief. She wasn't in the mood to make love to him. She carried the box into the kitchen, sat it on the table. Then decided to have herself a cup of coffee before getting started on the box.

Sue Ellen sipped on her coffee, as she thought back to when she started dating Billy Joe. He was very persistent back then. Still is, she thought. They dated five months. Then she broke up with him, because she had found out he made a bet with his friends he would get in her pants in seven days. He lost the bet. But he didn't care because he fell in love with her. He had got down on his knees to her and begged for her forgiveness. She loved him too, so she took him back, and a year later they were married. Billy Joe always had a bad temper, but nothing like he has now, she thought. Seems like it got worse after he met Red Avery, she murmured to herself. It was at a Fourth of July picnic,1954 that was put on by the textile mill where Billy Joe worked. Her and Billy Joe were lying on a blanket next to the edge of the lake. They were just lying there soaking up the sun, watching the water games some people were playing, in the swimming area. When all of a sudden, the stocky built red haired man stood over them.

"Hi. Aren't you Billy Joe Martin? You work at the Tupelo Mill, am I right?"

Billy Joe perched himself up leaning on his elbow. "Yeah, that's right. How did you know?" He asked surprised the man knew his name.

"I work in ordering at the Cottonwood plant, I've seen you a couple of times when I had to come to Tupelo. And besides the boss told me who you were when I asked about your name on some shipping orders. He pointed you out. And this lovely lady, she your girlfriend?" He asked as he undressed Sue Ellen with his eyes. He made Sue Ellen feel very uncomfortable, the way he looked at her. Much later she would know why she never liked him from the start.

"She is my wife." Billy Joe replied as he gave her a little pat on the leg. "Sue Ellen, that's her name, Billy Joe grinned proudly.

"Well Sue Ellen, glad to make you acquaintance." Red said in a wolf like tone as he held out his hand to her. Sue Ellen sat up on her haunches, and shook Red's sweaty Hand.

"Hey, the reason I came by is I want to invite you to my rally tonight."

"Rally? What kind of rally?" Billy Joe asked, a little interest in his voice.

"I'm the leader of the white Christian Knights." Red said proudly.

"You mean the Klu, Klux, Klan, don't you?" Sue Ellen said snidely.

"Some folks call it that." Red said as his smile left his face.

"Sue Ellen, don't be rude." Billy Joe said agitated at her remark.

"Oh no. That's Ok, lots of people don't understand what we stand for. That is all the more reason you should come, Sue Ellen. I think if you come see for yourself you might find that we are making a better place in America to raise are kids. We just want to keep our race pure. Now I ask you, is that so bad?" Red asked.

"Yeah, I think we should go, Sue Ellen, lets just see for ourselves. It might be fun. Come on Sue Ellen don't be a stick in the mud. Come on he pleaded."

"All right I'll go." Sue Ellen gave in.

"Great. Where and what time?" Billy Joe asked all enthused.

"Eleven o'clock, right after the fireworks. We will hold the rally just across the lake. There is an open field just off old gave road. You can't miss it. You will see the large bonfire we always have. So till tonight. I will see you there. Please come Sue Ellen I know you won't be disappointed." He smiled at her, shook Billy Joe's hand and walked off in the direction of some picnic tables.

"Billy Joe, I can't believe you could possibly be interested in the Klan."

"Oh, Sue Ellen what's it gonna hurt to go see what they do at those things. All we have to do is just watch and listen to what's going on. It don't mean we have to agree with them. Now does it?" He hugged her.

"Oh, all right, but we aren't going to get involved with them." Sue Ellen said firmly.

"Ok, that's settled, now give me another beer," he said pointing to the cooler.

"Billy Joe you just finished one." Sue Ellen said as she handed the beer to him.

"So? Hell I work hard all week. I'm entitled to a few beers, aren't I?"

"I'm sorry, Billy Joe. But it seems like you are drinking a lot lately."

"I have a few beers after work, to unwind and a few on the weekend. So how you figure that I'm drinking too much? Do I get drunk and disgusting? Well do I? Have you ever saw me that way?" Billy Joe demanded.

"No you don't get disgusting. But you seem to be more, I don't know. You just get different."

"Like how?" Billy Joe asked.

"I guess I'm trying to say you get mean, and you seem to get angry over little things and you get rough with me when we make love, if you have a lot to drink. That's all I'm trying to say."

"If I do that to you, I'm sorry. I never knew you felt like this. Honey, I will try to not drink so much if it's making you feel this way. If I get to rough with you, Honey, just tell me, and I will stop. Ok?"

"OK, I will tell you. Believe me I will." Sue Ellen said.

"Let's go get some food before it's all gone." Billy Joe said as he stood up taking Sue Ellen by the hand helping her to her feet. Then they went to were the food was being served.

That night they sat on their blanket and watched the fireworks. They were spectacular. They thought as they held hands, with arms around each other, as they leaned their heads on one another's shoulders. "I wish this night would never end." Sue Ellen said as she kissed Billy Joe on the ear.

"I wish it too." Billy Joe said, as he laid her back onto the blanket, kissing her as he whispered, I love you Sue Ellen. He slipped his hand in her shorts, caressing her between her legs. Then he pulled her shorts down, "Billy Joe. Not here someone might see us." She protested.

"Shhush." He whispered as he covered his mouth on hers. He managed to get the shorts off, and then he reached over next to them pulling another blanket over them as he pushed his way between her legs.

Then he was inside her. Their bodies becoming as one as they thrust hard against each other in perfect rhythm. Sue Ellen moaned with pleasure as the fireworks exploded overhead, lighting up the night sky.

Billy Joe's movement became faster, as he panted and groaned with pleasure. "I love you, Oh, baby, I'm going to come..."

"Oh Billy Joe, I'mmmm coming with you."

They reached their biggest wave of ecstasy they had ever experienced in a climax together. It was the first time it had been so exciting for them.

Billy Joe laid their exhausted, on top of her. Then he moaned as he rolled off next to her. They both layed on their backs just staring up at the beautiful colors lighting up the sky trying to understand what they had just experienced together. Billy Joe took her hand then he leaned over and kissed her ever so gently. "Honey was it as good for you as it was for me?"

"Oh, Billy Joe it was the greatest feeling I have ever had. It was great." She groaned to him.

"Does that mean we will have to wait till next Fourth of July to do it again?" Billy Joe teased

"What are you telling me? You need fireworks to make perfect love to me?" She teased back.

"I don't know, maybe." He teased back, with a grin.

"Well I guess we better get going. The fireworks are over." Billy Joe said as he pointed at the people starting to leave the park.

"We have time to run home and take a shower before the rally." Billy Joe said as he looked at his watch, with its illuminated dial.

"Oh Billy Joe, you still want to go to that thing?" Sue Ellen said trying to not sound discouraging.

"You promised." Billy Joe remind her.

"Yes. I said I would. So if it will make you happy, I will go." Sue Ellen said.

"Enough said. Let's get going so we won't be late." Billy Joe said as he picked up the small cooler and blankets. They headed off for Billy Joe's truck.

CHAPTER FIVE

They saw a glow of burning light, as they road down the old road across the lake. Billy Joe turned into the field on the left of them, and parked next to another truck, loaded with hay. As they looked around them they couldn't believe their eyes.

"Man. Look at all these cars and pickups, there must be five hundred of them. He awed.

"Yeah. And look over there by the burning cross. Five hundred white bed sheets, there must be a lot of naked mattresses." Sue Ellen said sounding sarcastic.

"Sue Ellen," Billy Joe said, giving her an impatient look.

"Well it's true. Look at them." Sue Ellen giggled.

"Come on." Billy Joe said, opening the truck door to get out.

They walked toward the crowd of white sheets, and stopped just a ways from the circle of people wearing the sheets were standing in. There was a platform at the head of the gathering.

"Do you see Red anywhere?" Billy Joe whispered to Sue Ellen, as she clutched his hand tightly.

"No I don't, and I don't see how you can identify anyone. Let's just go." Sue Ellen said trying to pull Billy Joe by the hand back toward their truck.

"Come on, Sue Ellen, give it a chance. We just got here." Billy Joe said pulling her back to him. Just then they heard a voice come over a loud speaker.

"Welcome, all my CHRISTIAN soldiers."

The crowd roared at the man's speech. He held up his hands to the crowd, as if he was the pope. He began to speak once more as the crowd stopped cheering to listen to his every word.

"My fellow Klansmen, we are here tonight to talk about what those men in Washington who call themselves true Americans."

"Those so-called true Americans want us to believe it's all right to let the Jew bankers run our banks and take our farms when we can't make the high cost of loan payments when our crops fail from drought or from storms that wipe out our fields, from floods, or hail. They want our children to go to school with niggers, and Jew's. They tell us we have to integrate. I say they can burn in HELL WITH ALL THEM NIGGERS AND JEWS, THEY ARE SO FOUND OF."

The crowd roared with clapping and cheers. He raised his hands once more, as he went on to say, "If they integrate our children with theirs, that means that it's ok for niggers and Jews to marry our white women and produce mongrel children with brown skin and nappy hair with monkey features. I say are we going to stand for it? HELL, NO, WE ARE GOING TO STAND UP FOR A PURE WHITE RACE, AND TO KILL ANY NIGGER OR JEW BASTARD WHO DARES TRY TO HAVE INTERCOURSE WITH OUR WHITE RACE AND ANY WHITE WOMAN WHO LOWERS HERSELF TO ALLOW A NIGGER TO HAVE INTERCOURSE WITH HER AND MAKE HER PREGNANT. THEN DEATH TO HER FOR EVEN WANTING TO HAVE A MONGREL CHILD BY A NIGGER OR JEW. I SAY TAKE THEM OUT AND DISEMBOWEL THEM BOTH. SLAUGHTER THEM LIKE THE PIGS THEY ARE ALONG WITH THEIR HALF BREED OFFSPRING."

The crowd went crazy with cheering and singing. A Shiver went up Sue Ellen's spine as she listened to the man's chilling words .As for Billy Joe, he was cheering and applauding with the rest of the crowd. Sue Ellen looked at Billy Joe's face. He was lit up with excitement like a child on Christmas day. She didn't like what she was seeing on his face.

"Billy Joe, let's go home. I've heard quite enough."

"We haven't seen Red yet. I want him to know that we did come."

"Who do you think that was giving the speech?" Sue Ellen asked.

"That was Red? Na, couldn't be. How do you know?" He asked surprised.

"Trust me. I remember his voice. And I'm telling you that was him." She said firmly. "Billy Joe, let's go home. We came, we saw, now it's time to go."

"Ok Honey. But let me just go up to the stage and let Red know that we did come. OK?" Billy Joe pleaded.

"Fine. But I'm going back to the truck. Go find him, but please, Billy Joe, don't take to long." She said with a little pouting in her voice.

"Great. Thanks Honey," he gave her a peck on the cheek. "Wait in the truck I promise I won't take to long. Promise." He smiled.

Sue Ellen turned, walked away toward the truck. Billy Joe made his way through the crowd to the stage where Red Avery sat on a folding metal chair next to the stage. Several other men were seated at the long folding table. They were handing out books and literature about the Klan.

"Hey, Red. It's me, Billy Joe Martin. Remember?"

"Oh Yeah. I see you made it. Where's your wife?" He asked, as he darted his eyes as if to see Sue Ellen nearby.

"She's waiting for me back at my truck."

"Well what did you think about my speech?" Red asked.

"I thought it was great, especially that part about the Mudd people." Billy Joe stated with enthusiasm in his voice.

"What about the little woman? What did she think?" Red smiled.

"Oh, I don't know. You know how women are. I think she liked what she heard. I know I did." Billy Joe said, shoving one hand in his pocket.

"You want to join us?" Red asked.

"Maybe. I would like to know a little more about everything. I need to know more about the government and their Mudd people." Billy Joe said as he thumbed through some of the literature on the table.

"I understand, Billy Joe. Here take some of these pamphlets, and here, take this book. It's our bible, it's our bylaws. Read everything very carefully, and then you can decide. We have a meeting every Sunday night at our headquarters at the old church on Fifth street.0ver in COTTENWOOD. You know the one I'm talking about?" Red asked.

"Yes I do." He answered. He took the literature and books that Red had given him, shook hands with everyone, and left.

Billy Joe returned to his truck where Sue Ellen patiently waited for him. They left for home; Billy Joe attended the next meeting where he became a Klan member. Sue Ellen never went back because she did not approve of Red Avery, or the Klan and especially what they stood for. But she never interfered with Billy Joe becoming a member. She figured that all Red's members did was just hold meetings and talk bad about coloreds and Jew's. She figured all they did was play dress up in their white sheets, and make a lot of noise at the rallies. She didn't think they ever really hurt anyone. She just considered it was a hobby for Billy Joe.

But as time went by, it seemed like Billy Joe was drinking more, and was becoming more violent with her over anything that he didn't like. Sue Ellen had become pregnant the night her and Billy Joe made love in the park by the lake Fourth of July. He became very upset the night she told him.

Sue Ellen was waiting up for Billy Joe. She was sitting on the couch when he came home from his Klan meeting. He was never four hours late getting home from a meeting before. But she didn't jump on him for being late. She didn't want to fight with him about being so late. She just wanted to share her joy about being pregnant with him.

"Hi Honey," Billy Joe said as he came in. "Before you start let me explain."

"Billy Joe," she interrupted him. "I don't care why you are late. I have something I want to tell you."

Billy Joe looked at her with a puzzled look on his face. "What?" He said trying to be patient. "Is something wrong?" He asked.

"Come over here and sit next to me, and I will tell you." She said sheepishly.

"OK I'm sitting," he said as he sat down next to her .She gave him a kiss.

"You remember when we made love on the Fourth of July?"

"Yeah. Why you want to do it again?" He asked grinning big.

"Yes, I would but that's not it." She grinned.

"Well, what?" He asked.

"I'm pregnant." Sue Ellen squealed with delight.

Billy Joe's smile faded, and he turned to a scowl. "How could YOU!" He shouted at her.

"How could I? Well, in case YOU didn't know, sometimes that happens when two people make love." She pointed out, tears starting to well up in her eyes. "And besides I didn't do it all by myself." She said, anger starting to build.

At that moment, before she could finish, Billy Joe slapped her. "Get rid of it!" He shouted at her. "I told you I never wanted to have any DAMN KIDS."

"I will not!" she shouted back at him. "It's your own flesh and blood too."

"I don't care. Having a kid will take our freedom. It will make everything change." He went on to say. "We won't' be able to go out when we want, and it will mess up the house and cry all the time; and you will never have time for me. We will never be able to be alone again."

"Billy Joe, you can't really believe that. I will always have time for you, and babies only cry if they're hungry or wet. And as for making a mess, well, I'm the mother; I will clean them up till the baby is old enough to clean up for itself. That is what mothers and fathers are for to teach their children to do things right." Billy Joe, I know you will feel differently once you hold your son or daughter for the first time. You will see that nothing will change between us, except we will have another little person in our life to love us, and for us to love back."

"Ok you go ahead and have it, but I will have nothing to do with it. Not ever. And you better keep your promise that nothing will ever change. Because if they do, I swear, I will get rid of it for you. Is that clear?"

"Yes it's clear. But you will see I'm right. You will come around."

Billy Joe went off to bed. Sue Ellen slept on the couch that night. All through her pregnancy Billy Joe had no compassion for Sue Ellen, only contempt. The first five months of Sue Ellen's pregnancy Billy Joe demanded sex with her every night. Then when she began to show, he stopped. He began staying out late and sleeping on the couch. After Sissy was born, things weren't getting better for Sue Ellen. Billy Joe started putting extra demands on her, trying to make her give him more time than the baby got. But Sue Ellen kept up. He never gave her any help. But she didn't care. She enjoyed Sissy as much as she could. Then one Saturday night, Billy Joe came home wanting to go out dancing with Sue Ellen.

"Sue Ellen, remember when you told me things wouldn't change for us?"

"That's right. But you seem to be the one that has changed." She pointed out.

"Yeah, I guess your right. I have been so jealous of the baby I forgot about the things we used to do together. So tonight we are going out. Call your Mother and have her baby-sit. Ok?" He smiled his boyish smile.

Sue Ellen began to melt inside. She was thinking maybe Billy Joe was finally coming around. "Ok, I will call her right now." She said happy to know Billy Joe and her were finally on the mend. Sue Ellen called her Mother.

"Hi Mom. Mom, I was wondering, could you come over around seven and baby sit?"

"Why of course, Dear. I will be more than happy to see my darling grandbaby. But it will have to be closer to seven thirty. Your father won't be back with the car till then."

"That will be fine Mom, I'll see you then, and Mom, thanks again."

"That's all right, I always like to have more time with that sweet little baby." Her mother said. "Happy to do it."

Sue Ellen stood looking at herself in the full length mirror thinking to herself that she still had her petite figure as she ran her hands down her hips and tummy smoothing the lines of the low cut black dress she had on. She put the finishing touches on her make up and put her long golden blond hair in an upsweep, it was held in place with black and silver sequined butterfly pins. She could have passed for Debbie Reynolds or Sandra Dee. She checked the clock on the dresser. "Seven twenty, come on Momma, please don't be late she thought to herself. Just then she heard the phone ring.

"I got it Billy Joe said from the living room."

"Ok, I'm just going to put the baby down," she called back to him picking up the baby from her bed. Sissy was sound asleep. She gently layed her down in the little crib in the corner of the hallway just outside the bedroom. She could hear Billy Joe talking low on the phone, she couldn't quite make out what he was saying.

"Billy Joe, I'm sorry to call at the last minute, but I can't baby-sit tonight. Rodger has been in an accident. He is ok but they took him to the hospital anyway." Sue Ellen's mother told Billy Joe over the phone.

"Do you want us to come to the hospital?" He asked, concern in his voice.

"Oh no, he is ok. He called me himself from the hospital. Just let Sue Ellen know, and not to worry. Her father is fine, and that I am sorry I couldn't baby-sit tonight. I feel so bad that I messed up your plans for tonight." She said apologizing.

"That's ok, Mom. You just go take care of Pop, and I'll take care of Sue Ellen. I won't let her worry, although she will. I will have Sue Ellen call you tomorrow. Ok?" Billy Joe said trying to lighten the subject.

"Good bye Dear, I better go."

"OK Mom, don't worry now. Talk to you tomorrow, bye now." Billy Joe hung up the phone just as Sue Ellen came in the room.

"Who was it?" Sue Ellen asked.

"Your Mom, she's going to be a few minutes late." He lied.

"Why?" Sue Ellen asked.

"It's your Dad. He had a fender bender. No one got hurt. It just made him late getting home, that's all. She called from the gas station four blocks away. She told us to go on to the club and to leave the key in the mailbox. She should be here in ten minutes. So come on, let's get going or we won't find a table." Billy Joe insisted.

"Can't we just wait till Mama gets here? You said just ten minutes." Sue Ellen tried to protest.

"Look, if we don't go now, we might as well not go at all. What in the hell is the big deal? The baby is asleep, and your mom will be here shortly. Do you think the baby is going to wake up and walk out of the apartment?" Billy Joe said, anger starting to build in his voice.

"All right, Billy Joe. You made your point. I don't want us to end up fighting. I just don't like leaving till someone is in the apartment with her."

"Ten minutes alone. Nothing is going to happen in ten minutes." He said.

"All right, all right. Let's go. If Mom said ten minutes I know she won't be late.

Billy Joe and Sue Ellen had a nice dinner and then they danced almost every dance together. Things were almost like before they got married. Sue Ellen thought to herself that she had the old Billy Joe back. It was the perfect evening.

"You look so beautiful tonight." Billy Joe told her as he held her close to him on the dance floor.

"You look pretty sexy yourself." She answered as she snuggled closer to him.

"You know, I been thinking, how bout we make this our night?"

"What do you mean?" She asked puzzled at what he had in mind.

"Well I was thinking, I'll call your mom and have her stay at the apartment and you and I can stay in a motel tonight. What do you say?"

"Oh Billy Joe, I don't know if Mom wants to stay overnight."

"I bet she will, and besides, we will be home by tomorrow noon. Come on. Let me call her. I promise it will be the Fourth of July. But you won't get pregnant this time. I will make sure of that." He begged with that boyish grin of his.

"Ok. You win, but only if Momma says it's ok with her."

"She will. I know she will." Billy Joe said sounding very confident. He led Sue Ellen by the arm to their table. He pulled her chair out for her so she could be seated. He leaned down and kissed her.

"I will be right back sweetie." Then he walked to the front of the club were the phones were located. But he didn't go to the phones. He went outside and lit a cigarette. He leaned against the building thinking as he took a puff. Then he tossed the cigarette and went back inside. He picked up the phone, dropped in a dime, and dialed. It was after eleven now. Sue Ellen's mother answered the phone.

"Hi Mom. It's me. I'm sorry for calling you so late. But I have to go to work at six in the morning, and Sue Ellen really needs a break from the baby, so could I bring the baby over, say about five? I know it's early, but Sue Ellen really needs to get some rest. I'm worried about her."

"Of course you can, I wish I could have came over tonight."

"How is Dad by the way?"

63

"He is just fine, the car isn't so good; but he is.

"Thanks Mom. I will bring the baby in the morning." Billy Joe said as he hung up.

"Excuse me, Mam, but may I have this dance?" Billy Joe said to Sue Ellen as he approached her sitting at the table. She looked up at him as she smiled back at him.

"Why I don't know if my husband would approve." She kidded.

"Don't worry about him, I'll take care of that wimp." He smiled.

She took his hand and they went out on the dance floor. The band was playing an old Hank Williams tune, "I'm So Lonesome I Could Cry".

"How about going to a motel with me lady? You won't regret it."

"Momma said yes?" She asked.

"Yes she is going to take the baby home with her tonight, and I will pick the baby up at six o'clock tomorrow night. So we have all night and all day tomorrow together."

"Momma agreed to that?" Sue Ellen said with disbelief in her voice.

"Hell it was her idea." Billy Joe lied. "You know she's crazy about the baby. It will be good for her and for you. And most of all for us" He soothed her, making her melt as he looked into her eyes. The club closed at two A.M. They went to a motel at the edge of town called the Night Light Inn. Billy Joe checked them in and they went to room 104. Once inside they undressed and made love. It was two thirty A.M. when Sissy woke up, she was wet and hungry. She started crying, but she was all alone. She cried till after three. She cried herself to sleep. Billy Joe made love to Sue Ellen five times that night. She was so exhausted, she fell sound asleep by four. Billy Joe called to her in a low voice, making sure she was asleep. When she didn't respond he eased out of bed got dressed and went to get the baby.

He came into the apartment, went to the kitchen, gathered her formula and some bottles. He put them in the diaper bag that was on the counter. He checked to see how many diapers were in it, then he went down the hall to Sissy's crib. She was asleep, but soaking wet. He looked down at her.

"You are more trouble than your worth. I should just drown you."

He picked her up, like someone would pick up a puppy. Sissy was dripping wet. He wasn't going to change her, but he knew he couldn't show up with the baby so wet. So he changed his first and only diaper. He stuck Sissy with a diaper pin. She cried. "Shut up you little bastard." He yelled. He pulled off her gown roughly and replaced it with a dry one. He grabbed some clean neatly folded gowns and jammed them into the diaper bag, and then he grabbed a few blankets. He tucked the crying baby under his arm like a football and took her down to the truck; he flung the diaper bag on the seat and then the baby. He threw the blankets on the floor of the truck. He went to the driver's side and got in. He started the truck and drove off.

Sissy was now sucking on her fist and fretting. Billy Joe came to a stoplight. The baby rolled off the seat onto the floor of the truck. She landed on the blankets that cushioned her fall. She let out a little cry. Billy Joe screamed at the baby to shut up, but the baby kept on crying.

Billy Joe pulled up in front of Sue Ellen's parent's house with the crying baby. Her mother was up and waiting. He carried the baby inside.

"I think she needs a bottle." He said as he handed her the baby and the diaper bag. "The bottles and milk is in the bag and I will go get the blankets. Then I got to go before I'm late." He said as he went out the door. Billy Joe made it back to the motel room before six A.M. Re-undressed and climbed in beside the sleeping Sue Ellen who was unaware of what Billy Joe had just done to her child. She never knew her baby spent the night alone.

Sue Ellen and Billy Joe had a great day together, she thought. She was in good spirits when her and Billy Joe picked up the baby from her mother that evening. She was never the wiser nor was her mother as to what really took place.

Sue Ellen took another sip of her coffee as she snapped back to were she was. Her thoughts came back from remembering the past to the present. She got up from the table and went into Sissy's room. She stood over Sissy as she slept soundly in her new bed. She bent down and kissed Sissy's forehead. She whispered, "Someday your Daddy will accept you, and come to find that he really does love you. He just hasn't grown up enough yet. But someday I know he will." A sigh was in her voice as she turned and went back into the kitchen. She put a few more things away then she turned off the light and went to bed.

The next morning, Sue Ellen got up about ten. She woke Sissy up and checked her arm and leg. She changed Sissy's bandages and washed her up in the kitchen sink. She combed her hair and dressed her in a pink flowered blouse and pink peddle pushers. Sue Ellen lifted her down from the counter.

"Ok, Sissy you can go out and play for a little while until your Daddy gets up, then we are all going to Dairy Queen. Doesn't that sound like fun?"

Sissy dropped her eyes to the floor as she meekly answered. "Yes Mommy."

"Hey what's this? You don't sound to happy about going." Sue Ellen said as she cupped her hands under Sissy's chin raising her face up to look at her.

"Can I go play now?" Sissy asked.

"Sissy don't you feel well. baby?" Sue Ellen asked concerned.

"My arm still hurts and my leg too." Sissy answered.

"I know baby, it's going to hurt for a few days. I wish I could make the pain go away, but I can't." Sue Ellen said sorrow in her voice. "OK, Honey you go play and I will call you when we are ready to go."

"Can I go see if my friend is playing today?" Sissy asked as she clutched tightly to her doll.

"Yes you may, but make sure your Daddy can't see you where you play, OK?"

"Oh no Mommy, I promise." Sissy said as she shook her head from side to side. Sissy turned and slowly headed for her secret place. She couldn't move as fast as she usually did because her leg and arm really hurt her. Sissy arrived at her secret spot in the field. Marcy and her brother William was already there playing. Sissy limped over to them and sat down next to Marcy.

"Hi Marcy." Sissy said with a sad voice.

"Hi Sissy. What happened to your arm?" Marcy asked.

"My Daddy threw a jar at me last night and it broke. I got a big piece of glass in my arm." Sissy said.

"That must hurt a lot." Marcy said putting her arm around Sissy to comfort her. "I hate your Daddy." Marcy said.

"I hate my Daddy too. He is always hurting me. He is so mean." Sissy said as a tear rolled down her pale cheek.

"You want a piece of fudge?" Marcy asked as she held out a piece for Sissy.

"My Mama made it last night." Sissy put the fudge in her mouth.

"Is that good?" Marcy asked.

"Mmmm, it tastes very good." Sissy answered her, cheeks bulging with the fudge.

"Does your Mommy make fudge?" Marcy asked.

"No. She sometimes buys some from the store. It don't taste nothin like this does." Sissy said with a smile of delight.

"You want to come over to my house?" Marcy asked.

"I can't, I want to, but my Mommy will be calling pretty soon. I have to go to the Dairy Queen."

"Dairy Queen, I wish William and I was going." Marcy grinned big. "You going to get ice cream?" Marcy asked.

"I guess so." Sissy said in a non-caring voice.

"Don't you like ice cream?" Marcy asked after Sissy gave such a depressed answer.

"I do. But I have to go with Mommy and Daddy is taking us. He probably won't let me have none." Sissy sighed.

"I bet your Mommy will." Marcy said trying to lift Sissy's spirits.

Suddenly Sissy snapped her head up as she heard Billy Joe's voice calling her name and coming closer. Quickly she stood up in the tall grass.

"I'm coming Daddy." Sissy began to have panic in her voice.

"Don't stand up till I'm gone." Sissy whispered to Marcy.

Marcy looked a little frightened as she stayed crouched down low with her little brother in the tall grass. Sissy took off and went as fast as she could with a sore leg.

Billy Joe started to go through the hole in the fence when Sue Ellen called to him. What she said got his attention. Just as he was started back to the house, Sissy crawled through the hole in the fence.

"I'm here Daddy." Sissy said soberly.

He turned back to her, "Get your ass in the yard. We are ready to go. What the hell you doin out there anyway?"

"Playin." Sissy said timidly.

"With who?" He asked.

"With my Dolly." She lied.

"I should have known, you and that stupid thing. I should take that thing and throw it away." He snarled. "What the hell. It fits you; you're as stupid as that thing is, come on, hurry up." He said as he walked ahead of her. Sissy trailed slowly behind feelings of fright and despair, that her father just might take away her doll. She fought back the tears that welled in her eyes.

Sue Ellen was standing on the porch with Carl and Margie from across the street. Billy Joe approached the end of the porch. "Hey." Billy Joe smiled as he came on over to the steps to greet Carl and Margie.

"Hey, yourself." Carl grinned.

"Margie," Billy Joe nodded to her. "We just came over to ask if you and Sue Ellen and Sissy would like to come over tonight about six for a Bar B Que? I make a mean steak." He smiled at Billy Joe.

"Why not? I'll bring the beer." Billy Joe said as he patted Carl on the back.

"Hey. I was just gettin ready to take Sue Ellen and Sissy to the Dairy Queen, you guys want to come along?" He asked.

"Sure I could go for some ice cream." Carl said grinning wide."

"My treat." Billy Joe said. "After all you helped me move, and you are offering us steaks. So that's the least I can do." Billy Joe said rubbing his tummy.

"Let's take our car, its a wagon, I don't think we will all fit in your truck." Carl suggested.

"Oh yeah. I get your point. We could make the women ride in the back." He kidded.

"I don't think so." Sue Ellen interrupted, smiling. "We will ride in your car, and us women, as Billy Joe so well put it, will ride in the back. And you men can feel important by riding in the front."

Everyone laughed. Sue Ellen picked up Sissy and went with the others across the street; where they loaded up in Carl's car and went to Dairy Queen.

CHAPTER SIX

April 26th

The Tall muscular framed Doctor Davis walked down the hallway of Chicago General, stopping in front of the nurses' station. He was in his late fifties, with slightly graying hair. He was very handsome as a young man, and he still had sex appeal. All his female patients had a crush on him. He looked a lot like James Garner.

"Nurse, could you please give, Mrs. Andrews' chart to Doctor Green?"

"Why yes Doctor Davis, I will give it to him as soon as he comes in."

Doctor Davis glanced up at the clock on the wall, a look of surprise on his face as he replied. "He is not in yet? Doctor Green was supposed to be here at six."

"Yes, I know, but he hasn't come in as of yet. It's not like him not to call in if he is going to be late." The nurse informed Doctor Davis.

"Maybe he had car trouble someplace where there isn't a phone." He replied. "Maybe I should just go ahead and see his patients until he gets here."

"Yes Doctor." The nurse agreed.

Doctor Davis turned to walk away when he suddenly stopped and turned back to the nurse. "Auh, wasn't he going to visit his parents in Mississippi?" He asked with concern on his face.

"Why yes, I believe so, Doctor." The Nurse replied.

"Did he leave a phone number for them if the hospital needed to reach him?" Doctor Davis asked.

"Yes Doctor, I'm sure he did." The nurse replied.

"Why don't you give them a call and ask them what time Doctor Green left?" He told the nurse.

"Yes Doctor Davis, that's a good idea. I will put a call in right away."

"Page me when you find out what time he left." Doctor Davis said as he turned and walked away.

"Yes Doctor Davis. I will page you just as soon as I find out." The nurse replied as she reached for the rolodex in front of her containing phone numbers for doctors on call, or out of town. She thumbed through it, "Auh, there you are, got it."

"Got what?" A young dark haired nurse said as she sat down next to the older nurse, Patty Dale.

"Doctor Green's parents' phone number." She said as she stated dialing the number.

"Doctor Green isn't back yet? Its after eleven, he was due in at six."

Nurse Dale held up her hand to jester a hush as the phone rang. Mrs.. Green answered. "Hello."

"Hello, is this the Green residence?" Nurse Dale asked.

"Why yes it is." Mrs.. Green informed.

"This is nurse Dale. I'm calling from Chicago General Hospital. Could you please tell me if Doctor Green has left yet?"

"Doctor Green? You mean my son? Lord, child, he and his wife left a week ago. He's not back yet?" She asked with deep concern in her voice.

"No Mam, he was due in at six A.M. this morning. You said he left a week ago? Was he headed home or was he going someplace else?" Nurse Dale asked.

"Yes Mark said they had reservations at a resort. A place called, oh my, give me a moment. My memory ain't what it used to be." She told the nurse as she pondered trying desperately to remember the name.

"You just take your time dear." Nurse Dale said soothingly as she sensed the worry in the woman's voice over the phone.

71

"It was Lake something, Auh, Lake Pleasant, no, Lake Plaster, no no, auh, Lake Placid. Yes that's it. Lake Placid. They said that was going to be the Honeymoon they never had." Mrs.. Green said.

"Oh well then that explains it, they are probably just taking an extra day." Nurse Dale said, trying to make light of the conversation.

"Its not like Mark to not just call if he going to be late. Do you think everything is all right?" Mrs. Green asked nervously.

"I'm sure he is fine, Mrs. Green. He may be trying to call in now, and maybe all of our lines have been tied up. I'm sure he has a good reason why he hasn't got in touch. Now don't you worry yourself. I will call this Lake Placid, and if he is still there I will tell him to call you right away. I promise." Nurse Dale said reassuring Mark's mother.

"Thank you dear. I would really appreciate that. I'll hang up now so you call. Goodbye now." Mark's mother said as she hung up the phone.

"Goodbye Mrs. Green." Nurse Dale said as she hung up the phone. A worried look came over her as she dialed information.

"Is there anything wrong?" The young nurse sitting next to nurse Dale asked.

"I don't know. I hope not: Hello operator, could you please give me the number for a Lake Placid Resort? I think it's in Lake Placid, Indiana."

The operator gave her the number. Nurse Dale wrote the number down. As she started to dial the number, she turned to the other nurse as she said, "Doctor Green left his mother's house a week ago. He and his wife were supposed to be taking a honeymoon at this resort. I hope they are there." She said sounding concerned.

"Lake Placid." A woman's voice answered.

"Hello. This is Chicago General Hospital; my name is Patricia Dale. I'm a Nurse and I need to speak to a Doctor Mark Green. He and his wife are guests there."

"One moment, please, and I will look at the guest list." The clerk said. She put Nurse Dale on hold while she went to the guest registry. She came back to the phone a few moments later. "Hello, Nurse Dale. Doctor Green had a reservation for the 20th of April. That was a week ago. He never checked in. I'm sorry, that's all I can tell you. I wish I had more information I could give you." The clerk told her.

"Thank you for your help." Nurse Dale said as she hung up the phone. She looked over to the young nurse, a puzzled worried look on her face.

"Doctor Green and his wife never checked in. I don't know where they could be."

Before she could go on to say another word about Doctor Green the phone rang. Nurse Dale answered, "Third floor, this is Nurse Dale speaking."

"Yes, my name is Tom Crandel, I own the Crandel Kennels, I need to speak to Doctor Mark Green." The voice on the phone said.

"I'm sorry, Doctor Green hasn't come in yet. I have been trying to reach him myself." Nurse Dale said.

"Well, when he comes in have him call me, I need to know when he wants us to return his dog to his house." Mr. Crandel said.

"Mr. Crandel , have you called his house yet ?" Nurse Dale asked.

"Why Yes, I have even been over there, and no one was home yet." Crandel said.

"Well I will tell Doctor Green just as soon as he gets in." Nurse Dale answered, saying goodbye as she hung up the phone.

"I am worried now, Mary. I think I should call the police, they might have had an accident somewhere. I'll call the police and you page Doctor Davis."

"I will do it right now Pat." Mary answered.

Doctor Davis' was having his lunch in the cafeteria, when he heard the nurse's voice calling his name over the loud speaker. "Paging Doctor Davis. Please report to the nurses' station on the third floor."

"Well now maybe Mark finally decided to come to work." He thought to himself. As he stood up from his table, he took a quick sip from his coffee cup before leaving. He went to the elevators and headed on up to the third floor. As he approached the nurses' station he noticed the two policemen standing in front of the desk at the nurses' station. Nurse Dale looked up as, "Oh there's Doctor Davis now," she nodded in the doctor's direction.

The policeman turned towards the approaching Doctor Davis. "What's the problem?" He asked.

"I called the police Doctor Davis. It's Doctor Green."

"Doctor Green? Has something happened to him?" Doctor Davis asked.

The policeman spoke before Nurse Dale could. "Well maybe nothing yet, nurse Dale called us. Seems that one of your doctors hasn't showed up."

"Oh you must mean Doctor Green." Davis answered.

"Yes. Doctor Markus Green, is that correct?" The officer asked.

"Yes, that's correct." Davis replied.

"Is he in the habit of being late or missing days?" The officer asked.

"Why no, Mark Green has never missed a day in all the years he's been here. This is the first vacation he has taken in nine years." Davis recalled.

"When was the last time you saw him?" The officer asked.

"He left here two weeks ago, he was due back here at six A.M. this morning. Davis answered."

"Well maybe if he hasn't had a vacation in nine years, he just decided to take a few more days." The officer said.

It was Nurse Dale who spoke up. "He and his wife were supposed to check in last week at a resort in Indiana. I called there they never made it."

"Well we will call the state police there and in the states they may have drove through to see if their car has been seen, or if they have been involved in an accident. In the meantime if you hear from him just give us a call, or have him call us." The officer said as he held out his hand to Doctor Davis. Doctor Davis shook his hand, said goodbye, then turned to Nurse Dale. "I do hope they're OK, you know his wife is due to have a baby soon. Maybe that's what happened, maybe the trip was too much for her, and she is in a hospital somewhere, and Mark just hasn't had time to call us yet."

"I hope you're right Doctor Davis. I hope you're right." Nurse Dale said worriedly.

"I hope so too." Doctor Davis replied. "Well I must get back to my rounds."

"I guess I will do Doctor Green's rounds too. Call my wife; tell her I'm going to be a little late tonight getting home."

"Yes Doctor I will do that right away." Nurse Dale smiled, but still looking very worried about Doctor Green and his wife.

Doctor Davis was worried too, but was trying hard not to show it.

She stared down at her son's photo as tears streamed down her cheek. Mrs. Green whispered softly to herself. "Lord if you are listening. Please let my baby boy and his lovely wife be found safe. And if they're with you in heaven, as I think they might be, I hope you didn't let them suffer before you took them to be with you. I know you will take care of my little baby grandson too. I know in my heart I will never know the joy of seeing and holding him. But if they aren't with you, then please let them be found safe and sound very soon." She sat next to the phone clutching the photos of her son and daughter-in-law holding them close to her heart. Tears streaming down her face, rocking back and forth in her chair, praying, waiting for the phone to ring, hoping that it will be her son calling to say they were all right.

"Attention all units. I have an all points bulletin for two missing persons last seen driving a blue 1957 Cadillac convertible, white top, Illinois plates 879 Doc. Person number one. Male six foot, one inch tall, 195 lbs. Hair black, eyes brown, date of birth 9-18-21. Light skin Negro, name Doctor Markus Thomas Green. Person number two. White female. Height 5-foot 6inch tall. Hair blond, eyes blue, 145 lbs., pregnant. All units be advised that the missing persons were headed back to Chicago from the state of Mississippi. Last seen by husband's parents eight days ago as they were leaving Mississippi heading back to Illinois. Boys let's keep a sharp eye out for them. The A.P.B. was sent out to all southern and Midwestern states.

    The next day the police checked the Greens house and took a photo of Mark and his wife Jane. The photo was released to all the newspapers and law enforcement offices throughout the south and Midwest in hopes that someone may have seen them, and may have information on their whereabouts.

CHAPTER SEVEN

"Sissy." Billy Joe snapped. Sue Ellen looked at her. "She got chocolate all over her. Do something." He demanded.

"Oh, she's just a little girl, they're supposed to be a little messy." Margie said with a little laughter in her voice as she helped Sue Ellen wipe the chocolate from Sissy's face with a napkin. "Excuse me Margie, I'll just take her into the restroom and wash her up a little." Sue Ellen said as she scooted Sissy out of the booth, as Margie stood up to let them out.

"Oh sure, I will go with you." Margie replied.

Sue Ellen and Margie took Sissy by each of her little hands and led her to the restroom.

"Damn kid. She always makin a mess." Billy Joe mumbled to Carl as he sat next him in the booth. Carl dropped his head as he stared at his root beer float.

"At least you got a kid to be a little messy. Marg and I lost our little boy, and she can't have any more babies. So count yourself a very lucky man." Carl said as his voice sounding a little choked up. Billy Joe shrugged as he said, "Sorry," then tried to change the subject.

"Hey, about tonight, should I pick up anything from the store?"

"Na. We got everything we need at home. Just bring the beer." Carl grinned.

"You got it, pal." Billy Joe replied with a wide grin.

"Sue Ellen, I meant to ask you earlier, what happened to Sissy's arm?" Margie asked as she stroked Sissy's hair.

"She dropped a mason jar and it broke. A piece of glass flew up and cut her arm." Sue Ellen lied.

"Oh my, did you take her to the doctor?" Margie asked, concern in her voice.

"No, I cleaned it well and put antiseptic on it. I been changing the bandage every day, and it looks fine." Sue Ellen explained as she wiped Sissy's face with a paper towel. "There now, all clean again except for the stains on your blouse." Sue Ellen said as she tried wiping the front of Sissy's blouse.

"It will all come out in the wash." Margie said smiling at Sissy as she gave her a little hug.

"I guess your right." Sue Ellen replied. "Come on, we better get back to the guys. They are probably wondering what happened to us by now." Sue Ellen said as she picked Sissy up from the sink and stood her down on the floor. The two women and Sissy came out of the restroom and back to the booth where Carl and Billy Joe sat waiting for them to return.

"Well it's about time. You took long enough." Billy Joe growled.

"Everybody ready to go?" Carl spoke trying to make light of the conversation.

"Ready if you are." Sue Ellen smiled.

They left the Dairy Queen getting into Carl's car and headed home. "Margie and I will see you about seven?" Carl asked as he pulled into his driveway.

As he turned the car off Billy Joe answered. "Seven it is, pal. Oh, and by the way, I like my steak medium well." He grinned as he got out of the car.

"You got it. Just bring the beer." Carl added.

Billy Joe and Sue Ellen, carrying Sissy, crossed the street to their house.

Sue Ellen put Sissy down as they climbed the steps onto the porch.

"Come on Sissy, let's get your clothes changed." Sue Ellen said as she started to go in to the house.

Billy Joe called out to her as he went to his truck, "Sue Ellen, I'm going to get the beer, then I'm going to meet the guys. I'll be home about six." Billy Joe said as he climbed into his truck.

Sue Ellen said, "All right. I will see you at six." Her voice sounding annoyed. She went on into the house as Billy Joe back out of the driveway and left.

All the men were sitting on the benches inside the church as Billy Joe walked inside. "Glad you could make it." Red Avery said as Billy Joe took a seat next to one of the other men.

"Ok. Looks like every body is here. So let's bring the meeting to order. Now the first thing on the agenda."

Sue Ellen was changing Sissy's clothes, "There now you're all clean now." She smiled down at Sissy. Sissy looked up at her mother as she clung to her doll.

"Mommy can I go out and play now, with Angel?" She said with a pleading look.

"Sure." Sue Ellen said smiling, as she went on to say. "But you need to stay close. You know we are going to Carl and Margie's tonight."

"OK, Mommy." She called back as she opened the screen door to go out.

Sissy scurried down the steps and headed off to her secret place, hoping her friends Marcy and William would be there.

Sissy stood in the middle of their favorite spot. No one was around. She decided to go find Marcy and William. She headed off in the direction she always seen them come from. She found a path of worn out grass; she followed it. It seemed like she had been walking a long way. Sissy stopped and sat down for a moment. She began to feel cold and have chills, although she was sweating a lot. She stood up, feeling a little dizzy as she started walking again. Her vision was a blur as she saw the fuzzy outline of a tall lanky black boy heading towards her. She heard him call out. "Mama," then every thing went black as she fainted.

"MAMA, come quick. There's something wrong with a little white girl."

His Mother hurried off the front porch of her house. "Don't touch her till I get there." The heavyset black woman panted heavily as she tried to hurry over to where her son, who was now kneeling down by Sissy.

She bent down on one knee to look at the little girl. "Oh my, what a tiny little thing she is. Ben, go get a washcloth and a pan of cold water."

"OK, Mama." He stood and ran back to the house. The black woman brushed back Sissy's hair from her face as she felt Sissy's forehead.

"You poor little baby, you're burning up with fever. Where on earth did you come from?" She said aloud to herself.

"I know Mama." It was Marcy, Sissy's friend, she sat down next to her mother and Sissy as she went on to say, "She's my friend. Her name is Sissy. She lives over yonder on the other street." Marcy informed her mother.

"Is this that little girl you been telling me about?"

"Yes Mama." Marcy answered.

"You didn't tell me she was white." She said with a worried frown on her face.

"I didn't think that mattered, Mama." Marcy said, feeling like she did something wrong.

"baby, it shouldn't matter, but some white folks don't want their childrens playing with little black children. This little child is sick and she is on our land, her Mama and Daddy might make trouble for us."

"Here Mama." It was her older son, Ben, back with a pan of water and washcloth.

Marcy's mother dipped the cloth in the cold water, then she wiped Sissy's forehead and face. Sissy murmured and slowly opened her eyes. The sun was behind Ben, Marcy, and their mother's back, making it appear to Sissy a round glowing light around their faces.

"Are you Angels?" Sissy murmured in a tiny little voice.

"No baby, I'm Mrs. Johnson, Marcy's mother, and this is Ben, her brother. Honey, what you doing over here?"

"I came to play with Marcy and William. But I got sick and fell down. My arm hurts so bad and I'm cold."

Mrs. Johnson looked at Sissy's arm, it was beginning to swell with a red streak running upward. She unwrapped the bandage.

"Oh my goodness, honey, this cut is all infected. You may have blood poisoning in it. How did you do this, baby?"

Before Sissy could answer Marcy cut in. "Her Daddy did it. He threw a jar at her, and it broke, and a piece of glass stuck in her arm." Marcy said with a scowl on her face.

"Is that true, baby?"

Sissy shook her head yes. "What about your Mommy? Didn't she take you to the doctor's?"

"No she didn't want Daddy to get mad anymore."

"Oh Lord child, come on, I'm going to carry you home. Marcy, you show me the way."

"OK, Mama."

Mrs. Johnson stood up, then pulled Sissy up by her hands, then gently picked her up in to her arms and carried her to the back of Sissy's house. Mrs. Johnson looked at the hole in the fence.

"Oh my. I'm way to fat to squeeze through there. Marcy, you crawl through and go up to the door and get her Mama."

"OK." Marcy bent down and crawled through the fence.

Marcy knocked on the screen door. Sue Ellen was in the kitchen wiping the counter when she heard the faint knocking on the door. Her head turned towards the sound. She saw the little black girl through the screen. She went to the door opening it a little as she looked down at Marcy.

"Yes can I help you?" She said with a puzzled look.

Marcy looked up at her, a little scared, as she said, "I'm Marcy, Sissy's friend. She is sick."

"Sick? Where is she?" Sue Ellen said worried.

"Out there in back. My Mama brought her home." Marcy pointed to the backyard fence. Sue Ellen stepped out onto the porch to look. She saw Mrs. Johnson holding Sissy in her arms. She ran down the steps to the backyard to were Mrs. Johnson was holding Sissy.

"Hi. What's wrong with her?" Sue Ellen said as she took Sissy from the black woman's arms.

"My boy found her collapsed by our house. She's got fever, and a bad infection from the cut on her arm, it looks like blood poisoning." Mrs. Johnson said sternly.

"BLOOD POISONING!" Sue Ellen shouted.

"That's right. You see that red streak going up her arm? She needs to see a doctor." Mrs. Johnson said, pointing to the red streak on Sissy's arm.

"It looked fine this morning. I don't understand it." Sue Ellen said worriedly.

"That's how the poison works, it hits you all at once. You probably didn't get all the fine glass out. That's why a doctor should have cleaned it."

"Well I will take her now. And I want to thank you for being concerned."

"No thanks needed. I don't mind helping someone when they're in trouble."

"I don't even know your name. I'm Sue Ellen Martin." Sue Ellen held out her hand.

"I'm Ida May Johnson." She smiled as she shook hands with Sue Ellen.

Sue Ellen took Sissy over to Carl and Margie's house.

"Margie." Sue Ellen called out as she went to the front door.

Margie came to the door. "What is it Sue Ellen?"

"It's Sissy. You think you and Carl could run me over to the emergency?"

"Of course we will." Margie said as she called out to Carl. Carl came to the door. Margie filled him in. They went to Carl's wagon and drove off to the emergency room.

Carl stopped the car in front of the emergency room doors. Sue Ellen got out of the back seat, Sissy in her arms, she hurried in.

A young blond nurse approached her, taking Sissy from Sue Ellen's arms as she said, "What is the problem?"

Sue Ellen answered, a little panic starting to rise inside her, "She fell on a piece of glass the other day. I Cleaned the cut, and put medicine on it. I thought it was OK."

The nurse took Sissy to an examining room where she then layed Sissy on the exam table. She looked at Sissy's arm, then her eyes met Sue Ellen's.

"I will get the doctor to see her right away. Just keep her calm." The nurse gave her a brief smile then hurried out of the room.

A few moments later the nurse came back in to the room, she had a tray in her hand, she sat it down on a small rolling table. She began preparing needles when the doctor appeared in the doorway.

"Hello, I'm Doctor Gains. You say she fell on some glass?" He asked as he went over to Sissy, started examining her arm. "Oh my," he sighed, "This should have had stitches and a thorough cleaning. Why didn't you bring her in right away?" He said as he looked up at Sue Ellen.

Sue Ellen stammered, "I thought I could take care of it myself. I didn't think it was too bad of a cut." She lied.

"Well my dear, it's very bad. I'm going to have to drain it and clean it and put her on an I.V. She is going to have to be admitted to the hospital. She will have to be here for a while; this little girl is going to need around the clock care. She has blood poisoning, and it could possibly turn into gangrene. It could cost her her arm."

Sue Ellen started to cry. "I didn't know." She sobbed.

The stern doctor softened a little. "Now. Now. You just made a bad judgment call. We will take good care of her now. At least you cared enough to bring her in before it got any worse. Now you just go out into the hall for a moment and the nurse and I will get her fixed up and send her up to a room on the children's ward. You can see her when we have finished in here. Then you can come back in and be with her when we take her upstairs. Someone will be out there shortly, to take you down to the admitting to do the paperwork." He put his arm around her shoulder and led her out the door to the hall where he motioned to another nurse to come over to them. The nurse led Sue Ellen to a waiting room and gave her some paperwork to fill out.

Carl and Margie had parked the car and found their way to the waiting room, where Sue Ellen sat tearfully filling out the admitting forms.

"Sue Ellen. How is Sissy?" Margie said putting her arm around Sue Ellen's shoulder as she sat down next to her.

Sue Ellen broke down into loud sobbing sounds as she tried to tell her. "She, she has blood poisoning, and maybe gangrene setting in her arm. She could loose her arm AND IT'S ALL MY FAULT." Sue Ellen sobbed as she buried her head in Margie's shoulder.

"Shhh, now, honey, it's not your fault." Margie soothed.

"OH, but it is. I should have brought Sissy here as soon as I got the first piece of glass out. I shouldn't have tried to take care of it myself."

"Mrs. Martin, we are ready to take your little girl to the children's ward now." A young nurse said as she came towards Sue Ellen, outstretched hand, "Are you finished with the paperwork?"

"Yes." Sue Ellen said, handing the nurse the clipboard.

Margie stood up taking Sue Ellen by the hand. "Come on, honey, Carl and I will go with you. Let's get Sissy settled in."

Carl stood up and took Sue Ellen's other hand in his and they all walked through the waiting room doorway out into the hall were Sissy was being wheeled out of the exam room.

"There's our little Angel." Carl said as he patted Sissy's little foot with his free hand. The three of them followed the orderly pushing Sissy onto the elevator.

They got off on the second floor where all the children were cared for. Sissy was moved into a crib like bed. She was hooked up to IV bottles, and put on oxygen. Sue Ellen stared down at her tiny little girl.

"She looks so helpless," Sue Ellen spoke softly as tears streamed down her cheeks. Carl put his hand on Sue Ellen's shoulder.

"She's going to make it through this, you'll see."

"I'm praying she will." Sue Ellen whispered.

Just then a nurse entered the room. "I'm sorry folks, but only two of you can stay in the room. Usually that means Mothers and Fathers, are you the Father?" The nurse asked Carl.

"No Mam, I'm just a neighbor and friend, this lady is my wife," he took Margie's hand.

"Oh I see. The Father is on his way?" The nurse asked.

"Oh my." Margie spoke up, "Billy Joe. He doesn't know yet. Sue Ellen you want I should go back to the house? He is probably there wondering where we are."

"I guess so." Sue Ellen murmured.

Carl looked at Margie, looking a little puzzled, "I'm sure he wants to know." Call said.

"Don't be to sure about that." Sue Ellen answered as she turned to them as they even looked more puzzled. "Look, Billy Joe just hasn't resigned to the fact that he is a father, and he is probably going to be more upset over the fact he missed out on the cook out. I keep hoping he will change and accept that he is Sissy's father. Billy Joe has a lot of growing up to do."

"Well maybe this will make him change a little." Carl said, trying to raise Sue Ellen's hope.

"Maybe." Sue Ellen replied.

"Well I guess all we can do is go home and tell him, and hope for the best." Carl said as he and Margie headed for the door.

"Thanks guys." Sue Ellen said as she waved goodbye.

"No thanks needed." Carl smiled.

"That's right, honey. You call us if you need anything. Anything at all." Margie broke in as she threw a wave to Sue Ellen. "Promise." Margie begged.

"I promise." Sue Ellen gave a faint smile back to them.

Carl and Margie left and Sue Ellen pulled a chair next to Sissy's bedside and sat next to her holding her hand. She silently said a prayer for Sissy.

It was nearly seven thirty when Carl and Margie pulled into their driveway. Billy Joe was sitting on their front porch, a case of beer next to him.

Billy Joe had just took a swig from the bottle of beer he was holding, he stood up as he tossed a cigarette out of his other hand.

"Some host you are. Late for your own party." Billy Joe said, as Carl got out of his car.

Carl took a deep breath, blew out, as he said." Billy Joe. We just came from the hospital. It's Sissy, she is real sick. Sue Ellen is there with her. They admitted her." Carl said, as he searched Billy Joe's face for a reaction.

"What's wrong with Sissy?" Billy Joe calmly asked.

"Blood poisoning. Maybe gangrene." Margie said worriedly.

"How? From what?" He asked.

"I guess from that glass cut Sissy had." It was Carl who answered.

"Well I guess the steak dinner is out. Guess I better go to the hospital."

"I guess so. Maybe when Sissy's better," Carl said, as he was surprised at how calm Billy Joe was taking the news.

"Hey look, can you put the beer on ice? Go ahead and help yourself to some if you want." Billy Joe smiled.

"Yeah, sure, I'll just hold it till we can have our cook out." Carl replied.

Billy Joe left Carl and Margie with a puzzled look on their face.

He walked across the street and climbed into his truck, started it and backed out into the street. He squealed his tires and headed off towards the hospital.

Billy Joe pulled into the parking lot of the hospital. He pulled into a parking place, turned off the truck engine. He just sat there staring at the entrance to the hospital. He grit his teeth, then slammed his fist against the steering wheel. "DAMN THAT KID." He said out loud to himself. "She is always messing things up. I hope the little bitch dies." He lit up a Lucky, took a long puff off it, then finished the beer he still had with him. Then he took off the cap of the pint bottle of whisky he kept under his truck seat. It had a few swallows left and it was empty. He sat there for a few more moments. Then he started the truck up once again and pulled back out of the lot. He decided to go to a bar and have a few more drinks before returning to the hospital.

Sue Ellen had left Sissy's room. She went out into the hallway to the nurses' station. "Excuse me, but do you have a restroom nearby?"

"Why yes," the nurse answered as she pointed down the hallway.

"Thank you." Sue Ellen said as she headed towards the restroom.

As she started to go in, a poster on the wall caught her eye. She stopped to read it. The poster had a photo of a man and woman. Sue Ellen was staring at the lovely woman standing next to the man. The woman's hand was resting on the front of the man's lapel. She was looking closely at the ring on the woman's finger. Sue Ellen then looked at her hand as she compared the ring she was wearing with the one in the photo. The rings were identical.

The poster read, "Missing, Has anyone seen or know the whereabouts of this man and woman. The man's name is Doctor Markus Green; the woman is Doctor Green's wife, Jane Green, last seen leaving Tupelo, Mississippi on April 18th. It went on to give their dates of birth, and descriptions. Anyone with information of their whereabouts, please contact this number at the Chicago police department, or the Illinois state police.

Sue Ellen stood there stunned, as she remembered back at how she got her ring and the date she had got it. She shook her head, saying to herself, "Sue Ellen Martin, get hold of yourself, it's just a coincidence," She turned and went into the restroom. Sue Ellen came out of one of the stalls of the restroom, she went to the sink to wash her hands. She stared down at the ring on her pinky finger, she couldn't stop thinking of the photo of the lovely woman wearing the same kind of ring on her little finger.

Then she looked at herself in the mirror. She shook her head. "It can't be the same ring." She murmured. "There are probably lots of rings like mine. Hers was probably real and mine is just a cheap copy. That's it. I'm just being silly." She turned the faucet on, washed her hands, trying to put it out of her mind. She dried her hands and returned back to Sissy's room.

She sat down next to Sissy's bed. She took Sissy's tiny little hand in hers. Sue Ellen sat by Sissy's bedside holding her little hand. Sissy started mumbling in a faint little tone.

"Angel. Where's my Angel?"

Sue Ellen spoke softly to her. "Angel is fine Honey. She's at home, Mommy will bring her to you to tomorrow."

"You promise?" Sissy murmured.

"Yes, sweetie, I promise." Sue Ellen said soothingly, as she kissed her little hand.

"Mommy, what color are Angels?"

"Color?" Sue Ellen asked surprised at the question. "Honey, I don't know exactly what you mean." Sue Ellen said.

"You know, Mommy, do they look like me and you, or like Marcy and her Mommy?"

Sue Ellen thought for a moment , then she went on to say. "Well, I think they are all colors. They are very beautiful, you know, just like a rainbow."

"I saw three of them today Mommy." She said with a little smile.

"You did? You Sure you didn't just dream of them?"

"No, Mommy. They were just like Marcy, only they had this real bright golden lite all around them. And they were leaning over me when I was lying on the ground."

Sue Ellen Smiled at her as she said. "Well Honey, you just may have seen real Angels at that."

"Oh our little patient is awake." A nurse's voice broke in as she entered the room. Sue Ellen looked up at the nurse. She knew what she was there for as she saw the needle on the tray she was carrying.

"OK Sweetie. You have to roll over towards your Mommy. I have to give you a shot. It will only hurt for a second. I promise."

Sue Ellen held on to Sissy's hand as the nurse rolled her onto her side, quickly sticking the needle in Sissy's hip. Sissy gave out a little whimpering cry as the needle went in.

"There, all done." The nurse said as she swabbed her hip with a cotton ball. She rolled Sissy back onto her back.

"This will make her sleepy. You can still set with her if you like."

"Yes, thank you." Sue Ellen replied.

As Sissy began to drift off to sleep Sue Ellen sat by her bedside holding Sissy's hand. Her thoughts went to wondering if Billy Joe was ever going to show up. Then the photo of the missing Doctor Green and his wife flooded her mind.

CHAPTER EIGHT

"Mama." Marcy called out as she ran up on the porch where her mother sat on a porch swing knitting.

"What is it baby?" She asked.

"Look Mama. It's Sissy's dolly, she must have dropped it." Marcy said as she held out the doll for her mother to see. Marcy's mother looked up from her knitting.

"Dolly," she took the doll from Marcy to look at it more closely. "Child, this ain't no doll, it's a Christmas tree topper."

"No Mama, it's Sissy's Angel dolly, she loves her, Sissy is gonna be so lonely without her."

"Hush your mouth, child. Look at this old thing. It ain't even got any legs . See?" She said as she flipped back the dolls dress. "Just this old rusty spring. Something no child should be playing with."

"But Mama, please don't throw Sissy's dolly away. Sissy loves her, and it's the only thing she has. Please, Mama." Marcy begged. She looked at the pitiful plea. Her little girl was pleading for her little friend's only possession. Her heart went out to her little girl and to Sissy.

"Go fetch me your daddy's wire pliers from the barn. I will just fix this doll up for your little friend. I'm even going to give this doll some legs. Now scoot. Get me them cutters."

"Oh thank you Mama, Sissy will be so happy." Marcy squealed with delight. She kissed her mother's cheek and scrambled off the porch for the barn. She smiled as she saw the happiness on her child's face.

"You gonna give Sissy's baby legs?" Her little boy William asked as he climbed on the porch swing and sat beside her.

"You like that little white girl, don't you?" She asked her little boy.

"Yessum." He answered. "Sissy my friend." He gave her a big grin.

"William, you go in the house and get Mama her sowing basket. Can you do that for me?" She asked cupping her hand under his little chin

"Yes Mamma." He said as he slid himself down from the swing. He scrambled towards the front door to get his mother's sewing basket.

Marcy brought her mother the wire cutters she asked for. Little William brought the sewing basket. Mrs. Johnson had moved from the porch swing to a card table and four chairs on the other end of her large porch. She took the cutters from Marcy, she turned the doll upside down. She very carefully cut the spring from the doll.

"There." She said pleased. "Marcy, give Mama that satin pink ribbon in the basket."

"Yes Mama." She pulled out a wide roll of flesh colored pink ribbon.

"Is this the one, Mama?" Marcy said as she handed the ribbon to her.

"Yes baby, now get the pink thread and the scissors. Be careful not to stick yourself with the needle that's in the thread."

"I will be careful." Marcy replied as she pulled out the thread and scissors. William sat with his knees on the chair, his little hands closed into fists, elbows propped on the table, his chin resting on his fists as his big dark eyes watched his mother's every move.

"Mama, you gonna make the other half of the baby's body and give her some legs?"

"Yes, Honey."

"You gonna put feet on her to?" William asked curiously.

"Yes baby." She answered her son as she cut a pattern for the ribbon.

"You gonna make underpants and shoes too?" William asked.

"Hush up, William. You ask to many questions." Marcy snapped.

"Marcy, you mustn't snap at your little brother that way. He has to ask questions so he can get answers. That's how you learn. You should always remember that. You won't know anything unless you ask questions. Understand?" She looked over to Marcy as she started sewing.

"Yes, Mama." Marcy answered.

"Good. Now tell your brother you're sorry."

"Yes Mama. Sorry." Marcy said in a low voice to her little brother.

"I think you're right William. She needs some shoes, and most definitely underpanties. Marcy, you know were Mama keeps her cotton balls?"

"Yessum. Want I should get them?" Marcy asked.

"Yes child, now hurry, I'm almost ready to stuff the body."

Marcy got up from her chair and hurried into the house for the cotton balls.

"What's ya need the cotton for?" William asked.

"Well you see, baby, I got to put the cotton in the body and legs I just made to give it shape."

"Oh, Sissy is going to be so happy, her baby doll's got some legs. She used to pray with us. We all prayed her baby doll would grow some legs. But she never did. Still had that old spring on her." William said wistfully.

"Well she going to have legs now." Mrs. Johnson chuckled.

Marcy returned with the cotton balls. Her mother went to work to finish. Marcy and her brother William watched their mother intensely as she worked gracefully on the doll.

"Oh Mama, she looks just like a real doll now. Sissy will be so happy." Marcy smiled happily.

"Yeah. She gots underwear and shoes." William grinned wide.

"What's you doin?" Mr. Johnson said as he came up on the porch.

"Mama fixed Sissy's dolly." Marcy beamed.

"Sissy, who's that?" He asked.

"You know, that little white girl we helped today." His wife answered.

"You know, Ida May, you shouldn't get involved with those white folk. They will bring us nothin but trouble." He scowled. "Mark my word. Nothin but trouble." He opened the screen door, he looked back at his wife.

"What's for supper? I'm hungry."

"I got a roast in the oven, it should be done in twenty minutes." She replied. He turned and went inside. Mrs. Johnson turned to her two children. "Don't you mind your daddy, we'll give the doll to Sissy's mama tomorrow."

"OK, Mama. But Daddy seemed awful mad." Marcy said.

"Oh, he ain't mad, he just don't trust white folks, that's all."

"Does that mean me and William can't be friends with Sissy anymore?" Marcy asked as tears welled in her eyes.

"Of course not, child." Mrs. Johnson said as she took her little girl in to her arms hugging her. "Come on now, you dry your beautiful eyes, and let's get your daddy's dinner on the table."

"OK Mama." She sniffled as she rubbed her hand across her face.

Marcy and her big brother Ben, set the table while their mother prepared the dinner. Mr. and Mrs. Johnson, and their three children, sat around the table.

"Marcy, would you like to say grace?" Her father asked.

"Yes sir." Marcy answered.

They closed their eyes and bowed their heads as Marcy said the Lord's Prayer.

CHAPTER NINE

Billy Joe left the bar a little drunk. He staggered a little as he bent down to pick up his truck keys, he dropped on the sidewalk. As he picked up the keys he lost his balance, falling forward to the cold cement sidewalk. Billy Joe skinned his nose. He laid there spread eagle for a moment. Then he pushed himself up on his knees, Billy Joe shook his head, then collected himself and got to his feet and slowly walked to his truck. He managed to get himself behind the wheel. Billy Joe just sat there staring out the front window. Then he thought of Sue Ellen, She must be wondering where I am. He mumbled to himself. "I guess I better get me some coffee and go get her." He said aloud to himself as he turned the key starting his truck. He shifted to first gear, squealing his tires as he drove off.

Sue Ellen sat there watching Sissy sleep. She looked at her watch. "Billy Joe, where are you?" She thought to herself. She stood up bent over her sleeping little girl, she kissed Sissy on the forehead. As she left her little girl's bedside, stopping in the doorway pausing to take another look back at the sleeping child. She then went out in to the hallway heading towards the restroom. Sue Ellen paused in front of the poster on hallway wall. She stared at the Green's photo as she turned the ring on her little finger .She couldn't get the woman's gentle face out of her mind. She stared at the ring on Mrs. Green's finger, then she looked at the ring she was turning on her finger. Tears filled her eyes as she remembered the time she got the ring from Billy Joe.

It was the Monday night after her and Billy Joe had a fight. She remembered how apologetic he was, and how he held up his hand, swearing he would never hit her again, then reaching in his pocket of his shirt, Billy Joe pulled out the ring and slipped it on her little finger.

"I got this for you Honey. I wanted to get a box for it and have it wrapped before I gave it to you. It's my way of saying I'm sorry." Billy Joe smiled.

"Oh Billy Joe. It's so beautiful. It looks so expensive. How could you afford it?" she asked. "Oh Honey, it isn't really. I only paid twenty bucks for it." He grinned.

"Twenty dollars? From where did you get it at that price?" She asked, admiring how the ring looked on her finger.

"I got it from Melvin Gum." He told her.

"Melvin Gum? How did he come by something this nice?" Sue Ellen asked.

"You know how Melvin and his brother are always trading for stuff, besides it probably ain't real. It just looks pretty" Billy Joe said smiling. Sue Ellen looked back to the poster as she read the value of Mrs. Green's ring. Then she looked at the ring on her finger. Then it hit her.

"Oh God, what if I'm wearing her ring? That means that Melvin Gum is somehow involved with the Green's, worse yet maybe even Billy Joe." She thought.

Sue Ellen wiped the tears from her eyes, went back down the hall to Sissy's room. She had a surprised look on her face as she saw Billy Joe standing at the foot of Sissy's bed. She thought she heard Billy Joe saying something to Sissy, but she couldn't hear what he was saying for his voice was so low. But her heart leaped as she thought he was starting to show some concern for Sissy.

"Where have you been?" She asked as she came in to the room. Billy Joe.

"I was out in the parking lot." He said as he quickly spun around to face her.

"Why didn't you come in?" Sue Ellen asked.

"Well I did. I went to the emergency and I didn't see you anywhere, so I went back outside to see if maybe you were outside waiting for me. When I didn't see you, I just waited outside in the truck for a while. Then I went back home to see if you took a cab home. When you weren't there, well, I came back here. I asked the front desk if they had seen you, and they told me Sissy had been admitted. So here I am."

"Billy Joe, have you been drinking?" Sue Ellen asked as she observed him swaying.

"I had a few beers while I was at home waiting for you." He answered.

Sue Ellen looked at him. She didn't say anything more. She just felt he was lying.

"Well how is she?" Billy Joe asked. Sue Ellen looked at him as she frowned at him saying, "Do you really want to know?"

"Of course I do. I am her father," Billy Joe said, trying to sound sincere.

"Well Sissy has blood poisoning and gangrene is starting to set in her arm. And she may loose her arm. Maybe even her life." Sue Ellen said tears starting to stream down her face. "AND IT'S OUR FAULT. YOUR TEMPER, MY STUPIDITY." She gritted her teeth in a low shout.

Billy Joe dropped his head. "You're right." He murmured. "I don't know what else I can say. I said I was sorry. You know how she gets me so mad at her sometimes." He said trying to convince Sue Ellen it was all Sissy's fault.

"Look, Sissy needs her rest, and so do I. So just take me home and I will come back in the morning." Sue Ellen said as she brushed by Billy Joe to stand next to Sissy's bedside. She bent down and kissed Sissy goodbye. Billy Joe went out into the Hall.

Sue Ellen pushed a lock of Sissy's hair from her little face. "Goodnight my little Angel. Mommy loves you." She left Sissy's room and joined Billy Joe in the hall. They left the hospital. Sue Ellen sat in the truck next to Billy Joe, they were both silent 0n the trip home. Once they were in the house.

"You coming to bed?" Billy Joe asked.

"Later. I need to do a few things, then I will be in."

Billy Joe fell silent as he started to protest. He just went on into the bedroom and went to bed. Sue Ellen went into Sissy's room where she sat down on Sissy's bed. She fell back onto the bed where she cried herself to sleep. Her dreams were of Sissy, then only to turn into nightmares of Doctor Green and his wife.

CHAPTER TEN

Sue Ellen woke around five A.M. She got up and went into the kitchen. She packed Billy Joe's lunch, then made his breakfast. Billy Joe got up a short time later, the smell of the bacon Sue Ellen had frying in the skillet woke him. He got up showered, dressed and went into the kitchen. He poured himself a cup of coffee and sat down at the table.

Sue Ellen put down a plate of bacon and eggs in front of him. It was Billy Joe who finally broke the silence in the room.

"You want me to drop you at the hospital before I go to work?" He said taking a bite of his food.

"Yes, that would be fine, except I can't get in till eight o'clock. Visitor hours start at eight." Sue Ellen said curtly.

"Here." Billy Joe said as he pulled out his wallet. He pulled out a ten-dollar bill, putting it down on the table in front of Sue Ellen. "Take a cab." Billy Joe said as he put his wallet back into his hip pocket. "Do you want me to pick you up?" He asked, taking another bite of food.

"Don't you have to work a double shift tonight?" Sue Ellen asked.

"Auh, shit. I forgot about that. Look, want me to see if I can get somebody to cover for me?" He said trying to sound sincere.

"No, Billy Joe. You can't afford to do that just now. It's OK, I can catch a cab home." She said starting to warm up to him a little more.

"What do you mean I can't afford to?"

"You did. You told me when you first started there, the bosses don't like giving anyone time off or early off days." Sue Ellen remind him.

"Yeah, I guess your right. But I will if you want me to." Billy Joe said.

"No, it's OK. Really. You need that job." Sue Ellen patted the top of his hand.

"OK, I guess you're right." He stood up went over to her side of the table. He bent down, gave her a quick kiss. "I am sorry for all this, Honey. I will try harder, I promise. Tell Sissy I said Hi." He gave her one of his big smiles, picked up his lunch bucket, and left for work.

Sue Ellen sat at the kitchen table twisting the ring on her finger. "If only you could talk," she said to herself staring at the ring. She felt a great sadness in her heart as she thought of Mrs. Green.

"I just have to know. Are you worth twenty dollars or thousands of dollars?" She said aloud as she got up to clear the table.

"ANYBODY HOME?" Margie called through the screen door.

Sue Ellen looked up. "Yes, I'm here. Come on in." She said happy to see her.

"How's Sissy?" Margie asked.

"She was OK last night. I'm going to go see her in a little while." Sue Ellen replied.

"You need a ride?" Margie asked.

"Guess I will take cab." Sue Ellen answered.

"I don't have to be at work until ten thirty. I can drive you." Margie offered.

"That would be great, if it's not out of your way." Sue Ellen smiled. "I could use the company. Want some coffee? It's still hot." Sue Ellen asked.

"Sure. And it's not out of my way. What are friends for? We are friends aren't we?" Margie said as she took the cup of coffee Sue Ellen handed her.

"Yes I feel that we are very good friends." Sue Ellen smiled as she sat down at the table across from Margie.

"Nine OK?" Margie asked.

"That's fine. It gives me time to change and take a shower. I might even have enough time to find Sissy's doll." Sue Ellen said as she took a sip of coffee from her cup.

"OH, that's right. Sissy didn't have her doll with her." Margie said. "I don't think I ever seen her without it." She added.

"No, she clings to that doll as though it's a part of her. She dearly loves that thing. This is the first time it's been out of her arms since she found it." Sue Ellen said as she went on to say. "That's why I have got to find it."

"She didn't leave it here?" Margie asked.

"No, I think she might have dropped it in the field. That's her favorite place to play. She loves the wild flowers."

"Why don't the two of us go out and look for it now? I'm finished with my coffee." Margie suggested.

"That would be great. It will save time with the two of us looking. You don't mind, do you?" Sue Ellen asked.

"Why of course I don't." Margie said smiling.

"Well then, let's go." Sue Ellen laughed.

Sue Ellen and Margie's eyes scanning the ground searching for the doll. "Watcha doin?" A tiny voice came from behind Sue Ellen. She spun around a little startled. She looked down to see the very small black boy, hands shoved deep into the pockets of his bright blue bib overalls, his tiny body swaying back and forth as he shuffled one of his bear feet in the grass. Sue Ellen stooped down in front of him.

"We are looking for a doll, it's a special doll, it has wings. Have you seen one around?" She asked.

"You mean Angel, she's Sissy's Dolly." He said with a big grin.

"Yes, you know Sissy?" She asked smiling at the little boy.

"Yessum, Sissy me an Marcy friend."

"Oh I see." Sue Ellen said. Just then Margie walked up beside her and the boy.

"Well who do we have here?" She asked smiling down at the little boy.

"Well it seems that he and someone named Marcy are friends of Sissy."

"Marcy's my sister. My name is William." He informed them.

"Well William, have you seen Sissy's Doll?" Sue Ellen asked.

"Yes Mam. My Mama got her. She made legs for Angel." He beamed.

"Oh my, that has to be a big improvement." Sue Ellen smiled. "Where might your mother be? I would like to talk to her." Sue Ellen said.

"She at home." The boy answered.

"Can you take us there, Honey?" She asked.

"Yessum." He took Sue Ellen by her hand and led her towards his house.

Sue Ellen and Margie followed the little boy down the path that led to a big white house. Sue Ellen saw his mother sitting on the porch swing centered on the full wrap around front porch. Sue Ellen thought to herself how lovely the place was with all the pretty flowers and well-manicured yard.

"Hi. This your little Boy?" Sue Ellen said, then as she got closer to the woman on the porch. "Oh, you're a Mrs. Johnson. Am I right?"

"And you're Sissy's mother?" The black woman nodded her head smiling as she spoke.

"Margie this is Mrs. Johnson, the lady I told you about. Mrs. Johnson, this is my friend Margie Holt, she lives across the street from me. Your little boy here tells me you found Sissy's old doll. And that you gave it some legs?" Sue Ellen smiled.

"Yes Mam. My children begged me to fix it. I hope that's OK. And how is Sissy?"

"Sissy isn't out of danger yet. She could loose her arm." Sue Ellen sighed with tears starting to well up in her eyes.

"Oh that's terrible. Child come up on the porch and sit." Mrs. Johnson said with sympathy in her voice.

Sue Ellen and Margie went up the steps onto the porch where they sat down in the big wicker chairs facing Mrs. Johnson. Sue Ellen wiped her eyes with a hanky she took from her purse.

"I sat with Sissy till the hospital made me go home. Sissy was asking for her doll, I promised I would bring it today. This is the first time she and that doll have been apart. She takes it everywhere with her." Sue Ellen said a slight laugh, trying to cover her sadness.

"William, baby, go in the house and get Sissy's doll." Mrs. Johnson said.

"Yes Mam." William said as he scurried into the house to get the doll.

"Can I get you two ladies anything?" She asked.

"No thank you, Mrs. Johnson, it's most kind of you to ask." Sue Ellen smiled.

"Child, you can call me Ida May, Mrs. Johnson sounds to formal." She giggled.

"You can call me Sue Ellen." Sue Ellen smiled at her.

"I got her Mama." William said as he ran out the door holding the doll under his arm.

"Take it to Sue Ellen, baby." Ida May said.

Sue Ellen took the doll. "Oh my, I can't believe this is the same doll." Sue Ellen said in amazement. "Oh, Sissy will just be so thrilled. "She loves this doll so much. Thank you. Whoever thought that old Angel could look so good?"

Margie smiled with amazement.

"You even put pretty little ribbons in her hair, and she got little white satin slippers. Oh Ida May, you did such a remarkable job." Sue Ellen said very pleased.

"Yes, she even has legs now instead of a spring. By the way, how did you hide the spring?" Margie asked.

"Oh, I just cut that old thing off." Ida May smiled.

"Ida May, I just don't know how I can ever thank you enough for this." Sue Ellen said.

"Just knowin that it will make that sweet little child happy is thanks enough." Ida May replied.

"Well, it's getting late. Margie has to go to work and I need to go to the hospital and take the doll to Sissy. I know this is going to cheer her up."

"Oh, before you go, the children made Sissy a get well card, I'll get it for you."

CHAPTER ELEVEN

Betty Flint was a buxom thirty-six year old blond who was the supervisor over the forty colored workers in her department of the textile mill where Red Avery and Billy Joe worked. She was walking out of the building to take her morning coffee break when the tall gangly sixteen-year-old black boy, named James Hooker, ran up from behind her calling to her.

"Miss Flint. Miss Flint, wait up."

She stopped and turned to see the young boy carrying a basket of fresh cut flowers.

"Yes, James." She answered.

"Miss Flint, I'm glad I saw you. Here Mama told me to give you these. They are from her garden." He said trying to catch his breath from running.

"Why James they're just lovely." She said leaning in to smell the flowers.

"Mama wanted you to have them. She said it was her way of thanking you for that wash machine." He smiled.

"You tell your Mama I was glad to give it to her. I appreciate the flowers."

Betty took the flowers from James, then gave him a kiss on his cheek.

"Ahu shucks, Miss Flint, you didn't have to do that." He said shuffling his feet.

"Why James Hooker. If I didn't know better I say your blushing." She giggled.

"I best get back to work now, I still got a lot of sweepin to do."

"OK, darlin, you run along now. Don't forget to tell your Mama I love the flowers."

"Yessum, I be sure and tell her. I sure will." He said as he scampered off.

Betty took another whiff of the flowers. She walked out to her car smiling.

Red Avery, Billy Joe and several other men were sitting on a cotton wagon taking their break. Billy Joe lit up a Lucky, took a puff, blowing smoke out his nose.

"Look at that." Red said as he nudged Billy Joe.

"Look at what?" Billy Joe said looking around.

"At that Betty Flint. She just kissed that BUCK"NIGGER."

"Are you sure?" Billy Joe asked.

"I saw it with my own two eyes." Red glared in Betty's direction.

"I always thought she was to fond of the niggers. That bitch needs to be taught a lesson, and THAT YOUNG NIGGER BUCK, TOO."

Betty walked out to her car, she opened her trunk taking out an old coffee can to use to put water in for the flowers as she shut the trunk lid. She turned around to find Red Avery standing no more than two feet in front of her.

"OH, you startled me." She said dropping the coffee can on the ground.

"Sorry about that. Maybe you wouldn't be as startled if I was that NIGGER BUCK you was bein so friendly with." Red sneered at her.

"What on earth are you talking about?" She gasped.

"You know perfectly what I'm talking about. I saw you kiss that nigger."

"WHY HE IS JUST A BOY. And besides, what business of yours is it anyhow?" Betty said annoyed with his accusations and starting to become very angry.

"I'm making it my business, Missy. You should stay in your place." Red snapped.

"And just what do you mean by my PLACE?" She glared at him.

"You stay with the white folks. You don't go round kissin on young buck niggers." He said in a threatening voice.

"Well let me tell you, Mr. Red Avery, you can't tell me where my place is. You are not my husband. You can't intimidate me like you do the poor colored folks in this town. You and that bunch of KLUKERS you run with." She said hatefully.

"WHY I SHOULD PUNCH YOU." He raised his fist as if he was going to hit her.

"GO AHEAD, HIT ME, AND MY HUSBAND WILL KICK YOUR DUMB REDNECK ASS." She dared him. He lowered his fist as he went on to say.

"You better watch yourself, maybe if your husband knew how you been messin with the nigger boys around here, he just might kick your ASS." Red warned.

"Get the hell out of my way. Break time is over." She said as she pushed her way past him.

"You better watch your ASS." He yelled at her as she walked across the parking lot.

Betty was about to go into the building when she remembered the flowers lying on top of her car. She turned around and went back to her car. Red Avery was gone. He went back into the building to work with the rest of his men in his department. Betty picked up the coffee can from the ground. She swooped up the flowers from atop her car with her free hand and hurried back to her department where she filled the coffee can with water, put the flowers in the can, and set the can of flowers on her desk.

"Billy Joe," Red Avery called out to him. Billy Joe was about to go into shipping office.

"Yeah, man, what's up?" Billy Joe said as he paused in the doorway.

"We gotta talk." Red said as he approached Billy Joe.

"Yeah, sure. Let's go into the office."

"No not here. At lunch. Meet me at your truck. Just pass the word to the guys to meet us there at lunch. I'll fill you in then." Red said, licking his lips.

"OK man. I will see you then." Billy Joe said as his voice was full curiosity as to what Red Avery was up to.

Betty sat at her desk. She was going over some paper work. The fragrant smell of the flowers on her desk filled the room.

"Hey, beautiful, how bout lunch?" The tall man in his forties graying side burns said as he leaned in the door way smiling. Betty looked up surprised that her husband had drove to her work place to ask her to lunch.

"Hi honey. What a nice surprise. Can you make it back to your job site if we go?" She asked.

"Yep. We finished the job this morning, so I have the whole day off." He said with a wide grin on his face.

"Just give me ten minutes to finish up here and then we can go." She smiled back at him.

"Nice flowers, where did you get them?" He asked.

"Oh, Mrs. Hooker sent them with her son James this morning. It's her way of saying thanks for that old washer we gave her."

"That was a nice gesture. I'm glad we gave it to her." He said sincerely.

"Greg that Red Avery might try to make trouble. He tried to make out like I did something wrong by taking the flowers from James. Him and I had words over it." She confided.

"Red Avery is a jerk and a blow hard." Greg said.

"I don't know honey, he's Klan." She said a little worry in her voice.

"So what? Anyhow, how did he know James gave the flowers to you?" Greg asked.

"He saw James give them to me, and I gave James a little kiss on the cheek."

"So what? He is just a kid" Greg answered.

"Well Red Avery doesn't see it that way." .She answered.

"The hell with Red Avery. Let's go to lunch, I'm hungry. He gives you any shit, I will clean his clock. I'm not afraid of his dumb ass."

Sue Ellen and Margie had arrived at the hospital around nine. Sissy was still sleeping. Margie stayed till about ten, then she had to leave for work. Sue Ellen put Sissy's doll on the bed next to Sissy. She gently tucked the doll under Sissy's arm.

A nurse came in to the room. She checked Sissy's vitals.

"How is she?" Sue Ellen asked.

"She is doing just fine." The nurse answered.

"But it's after eleven and she is still sleeping." Sue Ellen said full of concern.

"It's the medication. I'm afraid she won't wake up for at least four more hours. Maybe you would like to get you some lunch or something." The nurse answered.

"Yes maybe I should. I just don't want her to wake up and think she is all alone." Sue Ellen said with concern.

"Trust me. The medication she is on will keep her asleep, like I said, for at least four hours." The nurse assured Sue Ellen.

"OK, I do have a couple of errands I need to do."

"Go ahead, dear. And when you get back, she should be waking up. But it won't be for too long, she is going to be heavily sedated for a few days. That's the doctor's orders, she won't feel as much pain this way." The nurse said.

"Ok I will be back before she wakes." Sue Ellen said, then she left Sissy's room.

Sue Ellen walked out of the hospital. The sun felt warm on her face. She went down the steps that lead to the street. She walked about six blocks to downtown Main street. She stopped in front of Kramer's Jewelry store. She stared down at the ring on her finger. "I have just got to know." She said to herself as she got up her nerve to go inside.

The Elderly man with silver hair and gold rim glasses was standing behind the showcases. "May I help you?" He asked.

"Well I don't know, maybe." She stammered, "I would like to know just how much my ring is worth?" She said nervously.

"You looking to sell it?" He asked.

"Well, I don't know." She answered.

"Well, take it off and let me have a look."

Sue Ellen slipped the ring off and handed it to him across the counter. He put the jeweler's scope to his eye, held the ring up to it.

"Where did you buy this ring?" The jeweler asked as he studied the ring.

"It was a gift." Sue Ellen replied.

"Oh. Someone must think a lot of you." He smiled.

"My husband. He bought it for me a while back. I just wanted to know if he spent to much for it, that's all." Sue Ellen explained.

"Well my dear, I don't know where your husband bought this ring, but I do know that he must have had it made special. I would say it came from a very well known jeweler. He had to of paid anywhere from seven thousand, to maybe even ten thousand dollars for it."

Sue Ellen's mouth dropped as she felt her heart skip a beat. She turned a little pale as she searched for the right words to say.

"Are you all right Miss?" The jeweler asked concerned.

"Aw, yes, I just felt a little faint, that's all. I'm OK now." She lied.

"Would you like to sit down? I'm sorry I forgot your name." He asked.

"Oh no. I'm fine, really. I don't recall giving you my name, but I'm Sue Ellen Martin."

"Well Mrs. Martin, if you're sure you're OK, I guess names aren't important. Not unless you would want to sell your ring. I could give you five thousand."

"Oh no, I could never sell it. Like I said, it was a gift. I just needed to know how much he paid for it, that's all." She said her voice still shaky.

"Well now you know. And if I was you, I would get it insured." He informed.

"Yes, I think you're right. I'll look into it. How much do I owe you?"

"Not a thing. Like the sign says appraisals are free." He smiled.

"Well, thank you for your time. I must be going now." Sue Ellen shook his hand and left the store.

The Jeweler walked to the window and watched Sue Ellen as she walked down the street. He went to his office; he started rummaging through some papers on his desk, then on top of his filing cabinet.

"Mildred." He called out to his wife.

"What dear?" She answered as she wondered what on earth he could be so frantically looking for. "What are you looking for Dear?" She asked.

"That poster. You know the one that policeman gave us to hang up. I laid it on my desk I thought. Where did it go?" He said getting impatient.

"I hung it on the front window." She replied.

He rushed back out to the front of the store. He took the poster down from the window. He turned it over to look at the photo on the poster.

"Mildred, bring me the magnifying glass."

His wife brought the glass,

"What is it Harry?" She asked as she handed him the glass.

"I knew it. It's the same ring." He said excitedly. "That young woman that was just in here has the ring. The ring this Mrs. Green has on."

"Are you sure?" His wife asked.

"As sure as I'm standing here." He replied. "I need to call this number for the F.B.I. That young woman may know something about this Doctor Green and his wife."

"Oh my." Mildred gasped. "Do you really think that young woman is involved?"

"Well she has the ring. She said her husband gave the ring to her. Maybe he did. He may have bought it from someone who was involved. I don't think they could have paid a lot of money for it. So he either bought it or stole it. Let the F.B.I. find out."

He sat down at his desk, picked up the phone, and began dialing the number. "Hello, my name is Harry Kramer. I may have some information for you on those two missing people, Doctor and Mrs. Green."

"What kind of information?" The agent on the other end of the phone asked.

"I saw the ring Mrs. Green has on her finger in the photo." Harry said.

"The ring? How can you be sure it was the same ring?" The Agent asked.

"Because I am a jeweler and the young woman by the name of Sue Ellen Martin brought it in for me to appraise it for her."

"Did she give you an address?" The Agent asked.

"No just her name." Harry replied.

Sue Ellen sat on a bus bench in front of the hospital. Tears filled her eyes, running down her cheeks, as she tried to sort out all the bad feelings and thoughts she was having about Billy Joe.

She slipped the ring off her finger; she stared at it for a moment then put it in her purse. Taking a hanky from her purse she dried her eyes and wiped her face. She then stood up and walked towards the front door of the hospital. All she wanted to do now was be by Sissy's bedside.

Sue Ellen stepped onto the elevator, as she turned to press the button for her floor. She stood frozen for a moment, staring her in the face was the poster with the Green's photo. The elevator doors closed. Sue Ellen reached up and removed the poster from the wall; quickly she rolled it up and stashed it in her purse. She pressed the button number that took her to Sissy's floor. Her heart raced as she felt a rush of guilt. Her face became flushed. But in her heart she felt she just had to have the poster. She stepped off the elevator and walked down the hall to Sissy's room. Sissy was still sleeping. Sue Ellen pulled up a chair next to the bed and sat down taking Sissy's tiny little hand in hers. Sue Ellen sat silently watching Sissy sleep.

She closed her eyes, leaned her head on the back of the chair. Her mind flooded with images of Mrs. Green wearing the ring.

"Mommy, I'm thirsty." Sue Ellen opened her eyes as she quickly leaned forward. She smiled at Sissy who was awake and asking for a drink of water.

"Hold on, baby. Mommy will get you some water." Sue Ellen reached for the pitcher of ice water that sat on the food tray next to her bed. Sue Ellen poured Sissy a glass of water. She slipped her hand behind Sissy's head and shoulders giving her support so she could drink. She held the glass for with her free hand, "You were thirsty." Sue Ellen said as she lay Sissy's head back on the pillow.

The noon whistle blew at the textile mill, all the white workers hurried out the front door, some going to their cars and trucks. Some just sat down in front of the mill with their lunch pails and brown bags. The colored workers had to go out back by the cotton bales to eat. Red Avery and his little Klan group sat on the old cotton wagon out front.

He stood on the ground next two the wagon. "OK, I see you're all here." He said as he took a bite of his bologna sandwich. "OK, now listen up. We got us a nigger lovin white bitch working here, and we need to put her in her place. We got to teach her a lesson on staying in her place. So I need a couple of you boys to go with me tonight after work."

"What you plannin on doin to her Red?" A skinny looking man asked.

"Well we are going to kick her ass a little." Red said with a cruel grin on his face. The skinny man took a bite from his chewing tobacco as he laughed with the others.

"Hey Red, what time tonight?" Billy Joe asked.

"She goes to the market about seven, so we will be there when she comes out."

"I want to go, but I have to be back here by ten. I'm pulling swing tonight."

"Oh you will be back in plenty of time. Shit it ain't going to be more than twenty minutes to show her the way." Red sneered.

"OK, I'll go." Billy Joe said. Three others agreed to go also.

"OK, we will all meet at six forty-five at the PigglyWiggly parking lot." Red instructed. The whistle blew once again. Lunch break was over. It was time for everyone to return back to work.

"Remember, Piggly Wiggly, six forty-five." Red called out as they all hurried back to work.

CHAPTER TWELVE

Billy Joe drove his truck into Piggly Wiggly's parking lot. He pulled in next to Red Avery's blue sedan; it was six thirty. Ray Parks, Tom Sweeny and Bobby Taylor were sitting in the back seat of Red's sedan. Billy Joe got out of his truck, and leaned in Red's window.

"Where's Pete and Mike?" Billy Joe asked, lighting up a Camel.

"They couldn't make it. We really don't need them. The five of us can take care of her." Red said as he puffed on his cigar clenched between teeth. "Billy Joe, I want you and Ray to approach her when she gets here. She don't know you two cause you're new at the mill. A better yet, Ray, you approach her first. Then Billy Joe you get behind her and throw the pillowcase over her head, then shove her into the back seat of her car. Ray you take her keys and drive her car out to the old nigger cemetery road. We will follow you. Then we will settle with Miss Betty." Red said with a snide grin.

7:10 P.M.

Betty Flint pulled her car into Piggly Wiggly's parking lot. She parked three cars down from Red Avery's car. Billy Joe hurried around to the back of Betty's car. Ray approached from the driver's side. Betty turned the car's engine off as she opened her car door to get out. Ray was standing by her door.

"Excuse me, Mam, but could you maybe give my car a jump with yours?" He said smiling.

Betty looked at him for a moment. The she relaxed. "I would but I don't have any cables." She smiled. "Do I know you? You look familiar." She looked at him as if she was trying to recall where she had seen him before.

"I have some cables, Mam." Ray said nervously.

"OK, where's your car?" Betty asked.

Ray pointed to a white Mustang parked next to the street. "Over there." He smiled.

"Nice car." She said as she started to get back in to her car. Suddenly she felt the pillowcase thrown over her head. She tried to scream, she couldn't. The pillowcase tightened around her throat. Billy Joe was twisting the pillowcase tighter and tighter. Betty struggled for air as she tried to fight back, dropping her purse and car keys to the ground. Billy Joe was too strong for her. She began to lose consciousness.

"Hey Man, we don't want to kill her. Ease up." Ray said to Billy Joe as he pulled at his arm. He bent down picking up the car keys and Betty's purse. "Put her in the back seat." Ray opened the door and Billy Joe shoved Betty's limp body in to the back seat of the car. He slid in next to her. Ray jumped into the front seat, started the car and sped out of the parking lot. Red Avery, Tom Sweeny, and Bobby Taylor, followed Betty's car out of the lot.

Ray headed for the old cemetery road. Billy Joe's heart was pounding in his chest as his blood was pumping very fast. He felt very excited. They arrived at the cemetery road at seven forty P.M. Ray pulled the car onto a dirt road that ran thru a wooded area. He stopped the car about a half-mile in. Betty was coming to; she was coughing and gagging. It was very difficult for her to breath in the pillowcase. She started crying. Ray got out of the car. He opened the back door.

"Get her out." He said to Billy Joe. Red Avery and the other two men got out of his car. They approached Betty's car as Billy Joe drug Betty from the back seat onto the ground. She hit hard as Billy Joe drug her across the gravel on the road. Betty felt the stinging pain from the scrapes on her body from the gravel. She sobbed and pleaded for her life as she thought she was about to die.

"Shut the hell up, BITCH. We ain't gonna kill you. We just gonna teach you about staying with your own kind. You are just to friendly with all them niggers. So you got to learn to stay with the white folks."

Billy Joe shoved Betty's face in the gravel, then he ripped off her skirt and under panties. She was lying on her stomach. Hold her down." He yelled.

Red and Ray dropped on their knees as they held her down, pushing hard on Betty's shoulders. "What you gonna do?" Red asked excitedly.

"I'm going to FUCK HER IN THE ASS." Billy Joe yelled with excitement in his voice as he pulled a rubber from his pants pocket. He unzipped his jeans and dropped them to his knees. He opened the rubber packet and slipped it over his penis that was very large and very hard. He was totally out of control. He dropped to the ground and forced her legs apart. He pulled her hips up to him putting her on her knees in a doggy position. Then as hard as he could he thrust his penis inside her rectum, ripping and tearing the soft tissue. Betty screamed, she tried to wiggle free. But Red punched her in the side. Billy Joe went wild as he pumped faster and faster. He bent over her biting her back drawing blood. He let out a howl like a dog as he came. Then he went limp as the sweat poured from his brow.

"Hey Man you got any more them rubbers?" Ray asked.

"Yeah. Here." Billy Joe panted as he took several from his pocket.

"Shit. The bitch bled all over my dick." Billy Joe complained as he grabbed her skirt to clean himself.

"YAHOO." Ray yelled. "I ain't never done it like this before." He slipped the rubber on and he mounted Betty the same way Billy Joe had.

"I'm next." Red called out. All five men took turns sodomizing Betty. Then Billy Joe flipped Betty over on to her back. He began violently kicking her. The others joined in. Betty lost consciousness. Billy Joe went wild again as he dropped on top of her. He forced her legs apart as he began raping her again. He thrust his penis into her as hard as he could, ripping and tearing her vagina with his large penis and violent thrusts. After he was finished, Red Avery, and Tom Sweeny took a turn at raping her. Then the others beat her some more. They couldn't get aroused again, so they just beat on her after they were done with her.

They all got into Red Avery's car whooping and howling as they drove off. They were all very proud of themselves as they left Betty lying in the middle of the gravel and dirt road. She was all broken up and unconscious.

"You are some kind of stud, Billy Joe. You must have fucked her six times." Red said laughing.

Billy Joe just snickered. "I just got a big appetite."

"Yeah, and a big DICK to go along with it." Tom said laughing.

"Hell Man, she ain't never gonna look at no nigger dick. She probably done fell in LOVE WITH YOU." Ray chided.

"Yeah, right. Hey Red don't forget to drop me back at my truck. I still got to go to work." Billy Joe said becoming more serious.

"Don't worry. I'm on my way now. I will get you there in plenty of time." Red went on to say. "Look guys, we got one more thing to do. Everybody is off from work on Saturday night, so all of us are going to pay that NIGGER BUCK, HOOKER a little visit. Hell, I think we will just cut his nuts off and hang him. How's that sound to you boys?" Red said.

"That sounds good to me." Billy Joe said as the others shook their heads agreeing with Red and Billy Joe.

"Great then we will all meet at nine thirty Saturday night at the meeting hall. Everyone should be at the meeting. We can discuss the details then." Red said as he pulled into The Piggly Wiggly parking lot. Billy Joe got out of Red's car and went to his truck.

"Saturday night." Red remind Billy Joe.

"Saturday night. Nine thirty." Billy Joe replied as he waved at Red. He got into his truck, started it up and drove out of the lot, headed for his job. Red Avery and the others headed in the opposite direction. None of them felt the slightest bit of remorse for what they had done to Betty Flint.

When Betty hadn't returned home by ten thirty, her husband called the police. Betty wasn't found till seven the next morning by a black man and his wife who were on their way to work. They used the gravel road as a short cut to the main road from their house to work every morning.

Billy Joe got off work at two thirty A.M. He pulled his truck in to his driveway at two forty five. He saw the kitchen light on as he got out of his truck to go in to his house. Billy Joe came in the kitchen door. He saw Sue Ellen sitting at the table drinking a cup of coffee. On the table in front of her was the poster of the missing doctor and his wife and her ring was lying on top of the poster.

"Why are you still up?" Billy Joe asked with a surprised look on his face.

"Waiting for you. We need to talk." Sue Ellen replied.

"Talk about what?" He said as he sat his lunch bucket on the kitchen counter. He poured himself a cup of coffee, went to the table joining Sue Ellen.

"What's all this?" He asked as he sat down across from her.

"This is what we need to talk about." Sue Ellen said with a serious look on her face.

"Your ring or a picture of some nigger with a white woman?" He sneered.

"Both." Sue Ellen replied.

"I don't know what you are trying to say." He growled.

"Look at the photo." She said as she pointed at the ring on Mrs. Green's finger.

"So?" Billy Joe shrugged.

"Look at the damn ring she is wearing and look at this one." She snapped.

"All right. So she's got a ring like yours, so what's the big deal?" He answered sounding annoyed at her question.

"Like my ring? It is my ring. I had it appraised today. And you know what? It has the same value. Six to ten thousand dollars, Billy Joe, not the lousy twenty dollars you claim you paid for it. Now what's the real story behind the ring?" She demanded her voice escalating to a shout.

Billy Joe just sat there for a moment, his jaw twitching as he clenched his teeth. "What are you saying, Sue Ellen? You think I stole the ring?"

"I'm saying maybe you know what happened to these people." She said angrily.

"That's nuts. I bought that ring like I told you. I didn't buy it from Gum. There was these two nigger boys driving a blue Cadillac parked out by the alley that runs next to the Mobil station. One of them called me over to the car. He said he bought the ring for his girl, but she broke up with him before he could give it to her, said he would take twenty bucks for it. I looked at it. I knew you were going to be mad at me for being late. I knew you would like it, so I bought it. I thought it might be stolen, but I figured it was probably taken from another town or even another state. I thought it was just a cheap dime store ring. And that's the truth. I Know nothing about these people that's missing." Billy Joe said looking Sue Ellen directly in the eye as he lied to her. He gave her his famous look of innocence on his face. "Honest. That's what really happened." He pleaded.

"Oh, what are we going to do Billy Joe?" She moaned, tears starting to stream down her cheeks.

"Honey, come on now. We aren't going to do anything. No one knows we got the ring."

"The jeweler knows. How long do you think it will take him to figure it out?" She cried.

"So? He doesn't know who you are, does he?" Billy Joe asked.

"He knows my name." She answered.

""Did he write it down?" Billy Joe asked.

"No." She answered.

"Well there you go then. He probably won't even remember who you are." Billy Joe assured her. "Anyway if the cops happen to find us, well, I will just tell them where I got the ring and give it to them, that is, if it's the same ring. Although I really don't think it is." Billy Joe said as he put his hand on Sue Ellen's, giving it a little squeeze. "Don't worry. It's going to be all right, you'll see. By the way how is Sissy doing?" He asked trying to sound concerned.

"She's doing OK. Thank you for asking." She answered, surprised that he did ask.

"Tell you what, I don't have to go to work until five tomorrow, so how bout I go to the hospital with you to see Sissy? How's that sound?" He smiled.

"Great." She said a little stunned.

"Come on, Honey, let's go to bed."

"I need to take a shower."

"How bout we take one together like we used to?" He asked smiling.

"Why not?" Sue Ellen said feeling happy and relieved all at once. Billy Joe went into the shower before Sue Ellen. He wanted to make sure he was clean of any blood that might still be on him from Betty Flint. Sue Ellen joined him in the shower a few moments later. He slipped his arms around her slim waist, he ran his hands up and down her back, working one of his hands to cup her breast. He kissed her plump full round breast. He ran his tongue around the tips of her nipples, causing them to become hard. Reaching down he put his hands on her perfectly round cheek bottom. He lifted her up so that he could gently insert his hard penis. Sue Ellen wrapped her legs around his hips as she felt his large very hard penis slip slowly inside her. She moved in a slow rhythm with him as the warm water rained down on them.

Still inside her Billy Joe carried her out of the shower into the bedroom. Their bodies dripping wet, as he layed her down on the foot of the bed. Sparks of electricity shot thru their bodies as they thrust against each other in perfect rhythm. Sue Ellen hadn't felt this kind of passion since that Fourth of July night by the lake. The night she conceived Sissy.

This was the first time Billy Joe has given her this kind of sexual tender passion in nearly four years. She felt the sexual passion and love flow thru her entire body. She really thought she had her loving husband back, who was even starting to be concerned about their little girl. Sue Ellen closed her eyes as her body trembled, she moaned, panting heavily as Billy Joe thrust hard inside her. They both moaned as they reached a climax together. Billy Joe went limp on top of her.

"Oh baby, that was the best it's been in a long time. I love you, Sue Ellen." He said as he raised himself off of her.

"I Love you too, Billy Joe." She smiled. They climbed into bed and fell asleep in each other's arms.

The next day Billy Joe kept his promise. He went to the hospital with Sue Ellen. Billy Joe even read a storybook to Sissy. Sue Ellen was bubbling over with happiness of the sudden change in Billy Joe.

CHAPTER THIRTEEN

Mark Green stood by his car as he watched the approaching headlights coming closer to him on the dirt road. He opened the driver side door. He poked his head in.

"It's OK Honey, there's another car coming. I will try to flag him down. Maybe they can help me get the car out of the mud."

"Should I get out of the car?" Jane asked.

"Oh no, Honey. You stay right where you are. I don't want our baby to be born out here on a dark country road." He said smiling at his very pregnant wife. Suddenly the headlights shined brightly on Mark. It was a pickup truck. Mark waved as the truck came to a stop. Mark held up his hand to block the light, then he noticed the lights were so bright because two more cars had approached and stopped. A tall figure stepped in front of the headlights of the truck.

"Looks like you got yourself stuck pretty good. You need some help?" The voice came from the other man who now stood beside the taller man.

"Yes sir. I sure could use a hand." Mark said with a friendly smile. The two men approached him, then suddenly there were four more men crossing in front of the lights. Mark began to feel a little uneasy as the men approached him. One of the men bent down looking at the rear tire of Mark's car. The taller man was now standing close to the passenger side looking thru the window at Jane.

"Nigger, you sure did get this big fancy car stuck good. Now what's a nigger boy like you doing with such a nice car? Did you steal it?" He laughed as he spit tobacco on the ground, then looking up at Mark. "WELL NIGGER BOY, did you steal it?" Mark felt instant fear grip the pit of his stomach.

"Look fellows, I don't want any trouble." Mark said as he started backing away from them.

"Boy, you got trouble the minute you came down here with your white trash NIGGER LOVEN WHORE."

"BOY, you should have stayed up North." The voice belonged to Red Avery. Red pulled out his gun, aimed it at Mark. He pulled the trigger, shooting Mark in the stomach. He felt the bullet as it invaded his body with its hot burning painful path as it passed thru his stomach and exited out his back. Mark was bent over clutching his stomach. Jane was screaming as she saw the man shoot Mark. She frantically tried to reach across the seat, hoping to open the car door. She was pleading for his life.

"Please don't kill him. Mark please get in the car. Mark."

As she saw Mark fall to his knees, she suddenly felt herself being pulled from the car by her hair. As she looked up at her attacker, she pleaded with him to let them go.

"Please, let us go. Don't hurt my baby, PLEASE. I BEGYOU. PLEASE DON'T DO THIS. OH GOD, PLEASE HELP US." She felt herself being drug across the gravel, thru the mud. The man let go of her hair as he threw her to the ground. She now realized she was lying on some grass. Jane saw Mark being drug and then thrown to the ground next to her. Mark was still conscious. His eyes met hers as he lie there bleeding.

"I love you, darling." She said to him. Tears filled her eyes as she tried to stay focused on Mark. Tears streamed down his face as he tried to speak.

"I Love you too." Mark whispered trying to smile. Then suddenly the man that drug her from the car pulled her head up by her hair. He put his gun to her head and fired. Jane went limp as he let go of her hair her head hit the ground with a thud. Her cold dead stare was facing Mark. He tried to scream from the horror and pain he felt as he saw his wife murdered before him. He knew they were about to finish him off, but he did not realize they had just castrated him. He could not feel anything from the waist down. He could hear them laughing and talking.

It was Elvin Gumm. "I saw her belly move." The others just ignored him. Elvin took out his hunting knife, he carefully cut Jane's stomach open. He reached his hands in and pulled out the baby. The baby coughed and then it started to cry. Elvin became very excited

"Look. It's a boy." He smiled, very pleased with himself. Mark slowly reached his hand over to Jane's hand.

"Now why and the hell did you go and cut that half breed out of her?" Red Avery yelled at Elvin.

"It's mine, I saved it. I want it." Elvin protested.

Mark could see his baby son being held up by Elvin. He gently squeezed his wife's hand. His last words were "We have a son, Jane. He's beautiful. I love you both." Then he lost consciousness. He took his last breath, then he died.

It was Billy Joe who walked up to Elvin holding the crying baby. He bent down, snatched up the baby holding it by one arm like a rag doll. He put the muzzle of his gun to the baby's head and fired. The baby died instantly.

"No. You had no right. That baby was mine." Elvin cried out.

"Fuck you, Gumm." Billy Joe snapped as he threw the baby down. Its tiny little body landed across its mother's legs. Elvin jumped to his feet aiming his gun at Billy Joe.

"Tweren't right. I saved it. It was mine, not yours." He sobbed.

Red Avery looked over to Melvin. "You best calm your brother down."

He nodded. Melvin walked over to his brother. He put one arm around his brother's shoulder, lowering the gun barrel with his other hand. "Come on now, Elvin. You know that baby couldn't live, cause it wasn't its time to be born.

"I raised that rat coon, didn't I?" Elvin protested.

"Elvin, that ain't the same." Melvin tried to reason.

"Look Elvin, we came out here to kill us a nigger and a nigger lovin whore. And that baby was nothin more than their mongrel offspring. Have you forgotten that is what we are all about?" Red Avery exclaimed to him.

"I know but I wanted it for a pet." Alvin protested.

"Elvin, don't you think that someone might wonder where you got a half-breed kid from?" Red said, trying to reason with him.

"Ah, shucks, I guess you is right. But look at him. He looks white." Elvin pointed out.

"He is now, but if it was to live it would get nappy hair and turn dark as it grew older." Red exclaimed.

"OK, but Billy Joe, you ever take somethin from me again without askin, I will put a bullet RIGHT THRU YOUR FUCKIN HEAD. YOU GOT THAT?" Elvin said still angry with him.

Billy Joe just shrugged and walked away.

"Come on, let's get the hell out of here." Red said, as he kicked at Mark's head.

"Hell that nigger is dead." Melvin said as he walked away. Red agreed and left.

As the men went to their truck and cars Billy Joe stopped.

"Wait a minute, Red. I got to go back, I need to get somethin." Billy Joe said as he quickly turned and went back to Mark and Jane's bodies.

"Billy Joe. What the hell you doin?" Red called out to him.

Billy Joe bent down by Jane, he snatched her rings from her fingers. He stood up and walked to where Mark's trousers were lying on the ground a few feet away from his body. Billy Joe picked the trousers up, he reached into the back pocket, pulled out Mark's wallet, opened it and took out his money. He tossed the trousers and wallet back onto the ground.

"You took that nigger's money." Red said scratching his head.

"Hell yes. It all spends the same. Besides, it ain't gonna do him any good." Billy Joe grinned. "Hell, the way I figure it, we can split it up between us." Billy Joe said as he started counting the money. "Holy shit. You know how much is here?" Billy Joe said excitedly.

"Can't be much. niggers don't ever have much money." Red said.

"Well that nigger did. There is three thousand dollars here." Billy Joe said smiling wide.

"Hey fellas. Hold up." Red called the other men back to Billy Joe's truck. The other four men got out of their cars and joined Red Avery and Billy Joe beside his truck.

"It seems that the old nigger boy over there was a rich nigger boy." Billy Joe said as he went on to say, "He had three thousand dollars in his wallet. So I figure that's five hundred for each of us. Oh, and Elvin, here, you take the wedding rings. You can either sell em or just keep them. You know, in case you find a wife."

Elvin gave him a hard glare, then he snatched the rings from Billy Joe. He examined them very close. He put the rings between his teeth and bit down.

"They is real gold. I reckon I'll keep em. Don't think this makes us even. It don't. What you done to me twern't right. I ain't likely to forget for a very long time."

Elvin spit a wad of tobacco out, nearly hitting Billy Joe's shoe tops. Before Billy Joe could say or do anything Elvin turned and walked back to his brother's car. Melvin took his cut of the money.

"Don't worry, Billy Joe. You know how he is. He will get over it. Just give him a little time.

Billy Joe and Red Avery went to Billy Joe's truck after splitting the money between themselves and the other two men.

"One of these days I'm going to put a bullet in that fucking retard's head." Billy Joe snarled as he got into his truck.

"Ahu, you don't mean that, Billy Joe. He is a little stupid, but he stands up for our cause. He has always been loyal." Red defended.

"Well maybe so, but he better not fuck with me ever again." Billy Joe said.

Melvin Gumm turned his car around and headed back to the main road. Elvin Gumm sat next to his brother in the front seat. He finally spoke as his brother turned onto the main road back towards town.

"I'm gonna get even with that son of a bitch one day. You just wait and see." Elvin vowed to his brother.

"Ahu come on, Elvin, just let it go." Melvin tried to sooth.

"No sir rebob. I ain't gonna just let it go. I'm gonna get him for this." Elvin said, anger in his voice.

Billy Joe stopped his truck in the alley that ran next to the Mobil gas station. Red opened the door to climb out. He looked over to Billy Joe.

"That little gal of yours going to be pissed?" Red said grinning.

"Probably, but she will get over it when I give her this." He grinned as he held out the ring for Red to see.

"I thought you gave the rings to Elvin?" Red said surprised.

"I gave him the wedding rings, but I kept this one for Sue Ellen." He said smiling slyly.

"Well you better get on home now, so you can smooth things out with her. If it doesn't work out there's always my couch." Red laughed.

"Don't you worry. I can handle Sue Ellen" Billy Joe assured him.

Red closed the passenger door. Billy Joe pulled out of the alley and headed for home.

CHAPTER FOURTEEN

Harvey Hines and his wife Bessy were driving down the old cemetery road on their way to work. They were both in their mid sixties.

"Harvey, STOP THE CAR." Bessy cried out to him.

"What for, woman?" He said startled as he slammed on his brakes.

"That's what for." She said pointing to the bloody white woman's body lying in the road. Bessy opened her door, she climbed out.

"Bessy, what you gonna do?" Harvey said in a worried voice.

"I'm gonna see if I can help her." She said as she slowly walked her small frail body towards the woman lying on the gravel road in front of her.

"Bessy, you need to get back here. We shouldn't get involved." He called out to her as he got out of the car.

"Hush up old man. This little girl needs help." Bessy said as she bent down to look at the injured white woman.

"Oh My God, who done such an evil thing to you, child?" She said as she felt sadness and pain for this helpless woman flood over her.

"You just hold on child. We gonna get you some help. Harvey, fetch me the blanket from the back seat" Bessy called out to him.

Harvey opened the back door of his old Buick, reached in and pulled off the blanket that was covering the ragged back seat.

"Lord, Lord. We ain't gonna find nothin but trouble get involved with white folks." He grumbled to himself as he lumbered his tall thin arthritic frame slowly carrying the blanket to Bessy. He handed the blanket to Bessy. She covered the woman's naked body with it. Harvey looked down at the injured woman with shock and horror on his face.

"Good Lord. What kind of monster did such a thing to her?"

"I don't know, but she needs to be in a hospital. You drive down to that little store at the crossroads. I will stay here with her. Hurry. And you best call the sheriff too." Bessy told Harvey. Harvey nodded his head and went to his car to go get help. Bessy sat on the ground next to the woman.

"What's your name, Honey? Can you hear me?" Bessy asked. The woman moaned and then a faint whisper. "Betty, Betty Flint. Myyyy..." Then she passed out.

Sheriff Bill Combs pulled his car to a stop. He saw Bessy Hines sitting next to the covered body of Betty Flint. She was holding Betty's hand trying to comfort her. Bill got out of his car and went over to Bessy. He looked down at Bessy, her silver hair glistened in the sunlight. Her chocolate brown wrinkled face looked up at him, tears streamed down her frail bony cheeks.

"Mornin, Miss Bessy." He said tipping his hat.

He bent down on one knee as he gently pulled the blanket back. "Ah No. Not you." He groaned.

"You know her Sheriff?" Bessy asked.

"Yes, her name is Betty Flint, her and her husband belong to our church. As he pulled the blanket all the way exposing her body, he quickly put it back over her.

"What kind of animal done this?" He said anger in his voice.

"I think it was more than one, Sheriff." Bessy replied.

"What makes you say, Bessy?" He asked.

"Take a look around on the ground." She motioned with her head. Bill looked on the ground. He stood up.

"My God, Bessy, you're right, there must be at least a dozen rubbers. They gang-banged her." He said angrily. "Bessy, did she say anything?"

"Just her name and then she passed out." Bessy said. "Sheriff, she has been out for such a long time. She don't look good at all." Bessy said very worried.

"I got an ambulance coming, it should be here soon. Bessy, you and Harvey can go now if you want. I can stay with her till they get here." Bill said.

"Sheriff, I would like very much to stay with her if you don't mind. I feel sort of a connection to this poor girl. It's like God led me to her. Harvey wanted to go the long way to work today and I wouldn't let him. It was like somethin kept tellin me I should go this way. So can I please stay?" Bessy pleaded. Bill smiled at her.

"Sure you can, Bessy. You're a good woman, Bessy. I think Betty would be glad to have you stay by her side."

"Thank you Sheriff, you're a good man too." She smiled at him.

Just then two more Sheriff cars pulled up. The first car had two men in it. They got out and approached the Sheriff.

"What you got, Sheriff Combs?" Deputy Jackson asked as he hitched up his pants adjusting his gun belt.

"A rape and assault." Bill answered.

"What's with the old colored woman?" Jackson asked.

"That's Bessy Hines. She and her husband Harvey found Betty on their way to work this mornin." Bill informed him.

"That's Harvey sitting in the old Buick." Bill nodded.

"You called the victim Betty. Do you know her?" Jackson asked.

"Yes I do. I know her and her husband." Bill answered.

"Her husband? You want me to inform him?" Deputy Jackson asked.

"No I will do that myself when the ambulance gets here." Bill said.

"What do you want us to do?" Jackson asked.

"Get your camera out and take photos of this whole area." Bill instructed.

The ambulance arrived a few moments later. They loaded Betty's broken bloody body onto a stretcher taking her in the ambulance to the hospital.

"Sheriff Combs, over here." One of the Deputies called out to him from behind Betty's car.

Sheriff Combs went over to the deputy. "You got something?" He asked.

"Well, it looks like two men got out of the victim's car by the footprints and it looks like something was drug, more than likely the victim. Then it looks as though another car pulled in behind hers, and four more got out of that car. The Deputy pointed out.

"Get photos of all of it." Combs told him. "I what to find these bastards. They are worse than animals." Combs said as he went to his car. "You boys finish up here. I got to go break the bad news to her husband. I will see you back at the office, later.

"Yes sir." The Deputy answered.

Sheriff Combs drove off, his heart was heavy with the task before him. But he knew it would be better if he told Betty's husband instead of a stranger.

The emergency doors swung open as two ambulance attendants pushed the gurney, with Betty Flint's limp body.

"Put her in room two." A young blond nurse said as she led the way. Two more nurses came into the room to assist. Doctor Norman Cole entered the room.

"Give her some ringers, and an I.V. push. Nurse Trent, you can put in a chest tube. It looks like a rib or two may have punctured a lung. Nurse James, call Doctor Webster. I need to incubate. Damn, somebody did a number on this poor woman." He said shaking his head.

"Doctor, she is hemorrhaging" The nurse said as she covered Betty with a sheet.

"Pack her off. She's bleeding internally also. Call X-ray and tell surgery to stand by, we need to operate right away. Come on people lets work faster here. This woman's life is in our hands." He said as he worked on Betty.

They rushed Betty into surgery, she was in the operating room for over six hours. It took that long to make all the repairs.

Sheriff Combs arrived at the hospital with Betty's husband. They were wheeling Betty out of the room, headed to surgery. Betty's husband ran to her side.

"Betty, Honey, it's me. I'm here, darling." He cried, trying to hold onto her hand.

"Please, sir, you have to let go now. Your wife needs to get up to surgery. She needs to go now. Nurse, take this man to the waiting room." The doctor said as he motioned to the nurse. Sheriff Combs and the nurse took Mr. Flint by the arm, leading him away from Betty, to the waiting room.

"Come on now, let the Doctors do their job. I will stay here with you till she comes out. Is their anyone we can call for you?" Sheriff Combs asked.

Flint looked up at him, he answered between sobs. "Betty's mother. She lives in Jackson." His hands shaking as he reached in his back pocket for his wallet. He took out a small piece of paper, handed it to Sheriff Combs. "Her name is Pat Bower."

"You wait here and I will go down the hall and call her. They're taking good care of your wife. She's in good hands. God will guide the doctors." The Sheriff smiled at him.

"Sheriff, you will get those bastards that did this to my Betty, won't you?" He said crying.

"You bet I will." Sheriff Combs assured him. Sheriff Combs went down the hall to call Betty's mother. Two reporters approached him at the end of the hall.

"Sheriff Combs can you tell us anything yet?" One reporter from the Cottonwood News asked.

"No. Only that Mrs. Flint is in surgery." He said as he tried to get past them to the phone.

"Sheriff, do you have any suspects? Did Mrs. Flint tell you who her attackers were?"

"Fellas, come on. Give me a break here. When I know something for sure I will let you in on it. OK? But right now it's to early in our investigation. So please just wait like the rest of us, OK?" The Sheriff said as he pushed his way past them. He called Betty's mother and he posted a deputy down the hall to keep the pesky reporters from bothering Mr. Flint.

At four P.M. Doctor Cole entered the waiting room. Mr. Flint and Sheriff Combs stood up.

"How is she doctor?" Mr. Flint asked worriedly.

"Right now she is stable. She's in recovery and soon she will be moved to intensive care."

"What were her injuries, Doc?" Sheriff Combs asked for his report.

"Well first off, she has a severe head concussion, fractured jaw, broken nose, three fractured ribs; two of them punctured her left lung. A fractured collarbone, right and left wrists are fractured as well as her left hip. We had to remove her spleen, sew up her uterus, as well as her vaginal and rectal area. There was a lot of tearing in those areas. Did you know your wife was three months pregnant?"

"Yes, she told me the night she disappeared. We were so happy about having a baby." Flint said.

"I'm sorry to have to tell you this, but your wife miscarried. That's why she was hemorrhaging so badly. I'm sorry, Mr. Flint. Your wife is lucky to be alive. It might have been a different outcome if she wasn't found when she was. At least now she has a fifty-fifty chance of surviving. She is in a coma right now, but that should only last a few days. When she wakes up, she is going to need all the love and support you can give her. Come on, I will take you to see her for a few moments." The doctor said as he patted Mr. Flint on the back.

Doctor Cole lead Sheriff Combs and Betty's husband to the recovery room. Mr. Flint turned ashen gray as the shock of seeing his wife so battered and bruised. He stared at her swollen face. His entire body began to shake. "Look what these animals did to her, Sheriff. You better get them before I do, because I swear, I will kill them. Look at her. They tortured her." Mr. Flint sobbed.

"Doc, what are those round circles from?" Combs asked.

"They are burns. It looks like when they got bored with biting her they burned her with cigarettes, cigars, and a car cigarette lighter. They also bit off her nipples from her breast. I am so sorry for your wife and for the pain you must be having. I promise you I will do everything in my power as a doctor to get her through this. Right now she needs rest, and so do you." Doctor Cole said with sympathy for Mr. Flint. "Come on, you can see her again later when she is moved to intensive care." The three of them left the recovery room. Sheriff Combs and Mr. Flint returned to the waiting room. Sheriff Combs stayed with Betty's husband till her mother arrived. Then he left the hospital and returned to his office.

When he walked into the station, he was informed by one of his deputies that two FBI agents were waiting in his office for him. Combs removed his white hat, hung it on a pole rack standing by the door just inside his office. The two well-groomed agents stood up from where they were seated on the two leather-overstuffed chairs. They both were wearing well-pressed dark gray suits with black mirror shined shoes.

"I'm Agent Fred Wells, and this is Agent John Wallis. The older of the two held out his hand to Sheriff Combs to greet him.

"I'm Sheriff Bill Combs. What can I do for you?" He asked.

"We are working on a missing persons case." Agent Wells said as he sat back down in one of the leather chairs.

"Would that be that Doctor and his wife from Chicago?" Combs said.

"Why yes." Wells answered a little surprised.

"I read the bulletin you fellas sent us." Sheriff Combs smiled.

"Well we received a phone call from one of your local merchants. He has a jewelry store in town. He said that a young woman came into his store. Said she wanted an appraisal on a ring she had and according to him, he says it's the same ring that Mrs. Green is wearing in the photo that's on all the flyers we sent out." Wells said handing the photo of the Greens to Combs.

"And you think it's somebody local who has the ring?"

"Yes." Agent Wells answered.

"You got a name?" Combs asked.

"Sue Martin." Wells answered.

"Never heard that name before but I will have one of my Deputies run a check on the name. I wish I could be of more help to you, but I have got a very gruesome case of rape I'm working on. I need to put all my attention and resources on that right now." Combs said.

"We understand. We want to thank you for whatever help you can give us." Agent Wells said as he shook hands with Sheriff Combs. Agent Wallis shook hands, then the two agents went to one of Sheriff Combs' Deputies who could help them run the name they had by looking in several books containing names of everyone who had a driver's license, the state of Mississippi.

"Well fellows, take off your jackets, roll up your sleeves and have a seat. This could take a while." The deputy said as he gave them each a very large book containing thousands of names. The agents looked at each other. They shook their heads and took off their jackets and began looking through the pages in the books

CHAPTER FIFTEEN

Sue Ellen was getting ready to go to the hospital to see Sissy. She was brushing her hair when she heard a faint knocking sound. The sound was coming from the back door. Sue Ellen came to the door. She looked down to see Marcy and her little brother William.

"Well Hi there. What can I do for you two little Angels?" Sue Ellen asked smiling

"We come to asked how Sissy is and when she gonna get better and come home."

"Oh how sweet of you both for your concern. You really like Sissy, don't you?"

"Yes Mam. She is our friend." Marcy replied.

"Yessum. She our friend." William said as he wiped his nose with his shirtsleeve.

"Did she like her Dolly and the card we made?" Marcy asked.

"Oh Sissy was thrilled. She can't hardly wait till she gets home to play with you both."

William stared up at Sue Ellen, "Here. You give this to Sissy." He said as he handed her a box neatly wrapped in white tissue paper with a bright red ribbon and fancy tied bow. "It's cookies, Mamma made em." He said smiling."

"Why thank you darlin. Now you be sure to thank your mother too." She smiled.

"Yes Mam." William smiled.

"We picked some flowers too." Marcy said as she held out a hand full of flowers "You can keep some of them for you, and give some to Sissy at the hospital."

"Thank you sweetie. I will put these in water, and I will be sure to take some to Sissy." Sue Ellen said as she took the flowers from Marcy.

"We got to go now. Don't forget to tell Sissy 'Hi' for us." Marcy said as she took her little brother by the hand to go down the steps.

"Oh I almost forgot, you asked me when Sissy might be home. Well the doctor said maybe one day next week." Sue Ellen said.

"Well who do we have here?" It was Margie; giving William a little pat on the head as she stopped on the steps to the porch, as the children came down. "This is William, and his sister Marcy. They are Sissy's little friends." Sue Ellen said smiling.

"Oh how nice. Bet you came looking for her, didn't you?" Margie asked. "We brung Sissy a present for her Mama to take to the hospital." William said.

"Oh how sweet. They are just adorable." Margie said admiringly.

"Yes they are." Sue Ellen said as she waved to the children as they hurried off the porch for home. "I couldn't help overhearing. You said Sissy might get to come home next week?" Margie said as she went up the steps.

"Yes come in I will fix us a cup of coffee." Sue Ellen answered.

"I'm glad to hear Sissy's doing better." Margie said as she sat down at the table.

"You're glad, I can't even begin to tell you how worried about her I was." Sue Ellen said as she poured Margie a cup of coffee.

"One of the reasons I came over is to asked about Sissy first, and Carl wanted me to asked if you and Billy Joe would like to come over tonight and have that cook out we never got to have last Saturday." Margie asked.

"I think we can do that. Billy Joe gets off work at five today. He stops at the hospital and picks me up. He spends about a half hour with Sissy. So we will probably be home by six." Sue Ellen said sipping on her coffee.

"Oh, you mean to say Billy Joe is actually taking an interest in Sissy?" Margie said looking very surprised.

"Ever since Monday night. I think he is beginning to grow up." Sue Ellen said with a look of real happiness written on her face. She went on to say proudly. "This has been the greatest week of my life together with Billy Joe. It's like it was when we were first married." A warm glow in her eyes as she spoke.

"Sue Ellen, I am very happy for you." Margie said with a friendly smile.

"Oh my, I'd better call a cab." Sue Ellen said as she look at the clock on the wall.

"You will do no such thing. I will drive you; I haven't seen that little Angel of yours for a few days, so this will be my chance. I will go in with you and visit a while, then I will go do my shopping." Margie said happily.

"Fine, thank you. Just let me grab a few things and I will be ready to go." Sue Ellen said as she put her cup in the sink.

"I will bring the car over here." Margie said heading for the back door.

Billy Joe sat a case of bottled Budweiser beer on the picnic table.

"Hey, Billy Joe. You still have that case you left the last time we planned this." Carl said as he threw some steaks on the grill.

"That's OK. We are having a party aren't we?" Billy Joe grinned wide. "So I figure between the four of us, we can down most of it. Whatever's left we can have another time. If there is any left." Billy Joe laughed.

"OK, Pal. Just put the bottles in that tub of ice over there." Carl pointed with the big barbeque fork. The steaks sizzled on the grill.

"Oh that smells great. My husband the chef." Margie laughed.

"Well at least your husband cooks." Sue Ellen kidded.

"I don't need to know how to cook, I'm a great lover." Billy Joe said sheepishly.

"OOOH" Carl, Margie and Sue Ellen chided.

"Steaks are ready. Grab a plate and come and get em." Carl called out.

Everyone fixed their plates and sat down to eat at the redwood picnic table covered with a bright red and white checked tablecloth.

"Wasn't that just awful what happened to that woman the other day?" Margie said, making conversation, as she cut her steak.

"Oh yes. I was at the hospital when they brought her in. She is just around the corner from where Sissy was in I.C.U. I was walking down the hall, I had to go to the bathroom when they wheeled her right by me. God, I couldn't believe how bad her face looked. I thought it was a traffic accident till I heard the nurses talking. Those men who done that to her had to be animals, actually worse than animals." Sue Ellen said thoughtfully.

"The paper said she works at the mill where you work, Billy Joe. Did you know her?" Margie asked.

"No, it's a big plant and I have only been there a short time." Billy Joe answered, then he took a bite of his food.

"Hey you two. This is supposed to be a happy time, and you two are telling horror stories. Come on, lighten up." Carl remind the girls.

They sat around drinking beer and having fun, enjoying one another's company. It was about ten thirty when they decided to call it a night and started cleaning up and putting things away.

Billy Joe emptied the ice from the tub on to the grass. "Hey Carl, where you what me to put the tub?" Billy Joe called to Carl who was cleaning his grill.

"In the garage, there's a hook above the workbench, just hang it there." Carl said as he scrubbed harder with his wire brush.

Billy Joe went into the garage. He was looking for the hook above the workbench. He reached up to hang the tub, as he did he knocked off a stack of papers to the floor. "Shit." He said as he bent down to pick them up. As he shuffled the papers together, the heading on the papers caught his eye. A dark clouded scowl came over his face as he read the top paper. "What the fuck," Billy Joe said out loud to himself." I can't believe this. Carl another nigger lover." Billy Joe straightened the papers and put them back on the workbench but not before he took one for himself. He folded it and put it in his back pocket.

He lit up a Lucky, took a drag from it and went back to were Carl was still scrubbing the grill.

"Did you find the hook OK?" Carl asked looking up at Billy Joe.

"Yeah, I found it." Billy Joe said quietly. He stared at Carl as He scrubbed the grill.

"You really believe that niggers have a right to vote, Carl?" Billy Joe asked.

Carl stopped scrubbing and looked at Billy Joe surprised at his question.

"I believe everyone should have that right." Carl answered with a serious sounding voice.

"So you are really a part of that civil rights bunch?" Billy Joe said starting to sound angry.

"Yes, I guess I am. I'm Jewish too, Billy Joe. Does that mean we can't still be friends?" Carl asked.

"I don't know I don't believe the same things you do." Billy Joe answered as he was a little taken back by what Carl had just told him.

"Look, Billy Joe. We don't have to believe in the same things, to be friends. That's what makes this country great." Carl explained.

"Billy Joe, are you ready to go home?" Sue Ellen said as she and Margie came out the back door.

"Yeah, I guess so." He answered as he stared intensely at Carl.

"Billy Joe, I hope this doesn't change things between us?" Carl asked.

"I gotta go." Billy Joe said as he turned and walked away. Billy Joe took Sue Ellen by the arm. "Let's go." He said somberly.

"Billy Joe, what's wrong?" She said taken back by his tone.

"Nothing. Now let's go home." He said as his tone raised and his grip on her arm tightened.

"I'll talk to you tomorrow, Margie." Sue Ellen called over her shoulder to Margie as she walked faster to keep pace with Billy Joe.

"Yes, I will see you tomorrow." Margie said as she waved to her, looking very puzzled. Margie looked over to Carl as he just stood by the grill, a very perplexed expression on his face. Margie walked over to Carl.

"What happened between you and Billy Joe?" She asked.

"He found the voting forms when he went into the garage to put the tub away." Carl said.

"Is that all?" Margie asked.

"No. I told him we were Jewish." He said as he closed the lid on the grill.

"Oh Carl, you know Billy Joe is such a strong bigot What on earth were you thinking?" Margie said worriedly.

"I just thought our friendship could over ride our difference of opinions." Carl said.

"I don't know, dear, Sue Ellen told me Billy Joe is a Klan member and you know how deep their ignorance is rooted." Margie pointed out.

"Oh Honey. You worry to much. Billy Joe will come around, you'll see." Carl said sounding very confident. "Come on now.." He gave her a hug and a kiss on the cheek. "Let's go into the house and have some coffee." Carl added as he put his arm around her waist and they went in to the house.

Billy Joe and Sue Ellen were already in their house. Billy Joe was very silent. Sue Ellen was very puzzled at his mood change. "Well are you going to tell me what's going on?" Sue Ellen said breaking the silence.

"Nothing." Billy Joe answered.

"Nothing? OK, then why the big rush to come home and then you sit here with such a solemn look on your face?" Sue Ellen said as she poured them both a cup of coffee.

"They are Jews and nigger sympathizers." Billy Joe blurted out.

"Who?" Sue Ellen asked.

"Carl and Margie, that's who." Billy Joe snapped.

"Now who told you that?" Sue Ellen asked in a serious voice.

"Carl, that's who." Billy Joe said angrily.

"So? Look, they are good people, and they have been nothing but good friends to us. So I can't see why it should make such a difference on our friendship with them." Sue Ellen said.

"Well it does. Look I got to go. You know I have to work tonight." Billy Joe said as he got up from the table.

"Oh yes, I forgot." Sue Ellen said.

Billy Joe picked up his cigarettes from the table and headed for the back door. "It's only for a few hours. I should be home by three or four." He said as he went out the door. Sue Ellen sat at the table with a bewildered look on her face.

Billy Joe wasn't really going to work. He just told Sue Ellen he was. What he really had to do was meet Red Avery and the rest of the group for a Klan meeting. Billy Joe walked into the meeting hall a little after eleven o'clock. Most of the men were there. There was still a few who hadn't made it yet.

"Well boys we will wait another ten minutes or so. If the others aren't here by then, well, we will just have to start the meeting without them." Avery said as he was putting on his robe. Six more men came in five minutes later. Red Avery went to the pulpit. "Let this meeting come to order." He said. "I see that we are all here. Now as you know we took care of the business of teaching a white whore how to keep her place with her own white race. Now tonight we are going to teach a nigger buck the same lesson." Avery preached.

"Who might that be?" One of the men asked.

"That nigger boy who cleans up at the mill." Avery answered. "He stepped over the line by being a little to friendly with the white women who work with him. He has been keeping company with one whore who has been taught what happens when she crosses the line with niggers." Avery said as the men cheered him on with his every word. "Now are you men ready to go out and do God's work?" Avery shouted.

"Yes sir. Let's get us some niggers." One man shouted back. Everyone sounded out. "We gonna castrate him or just plain hang him." A man named Perry Weeks said as tobacco juice ran down the corner of his mouth sticking to his scruffy unshaven beard.

"No I think we will just give him a good whippen." Red said smiling. "OK, now some of you guys make sure you make up at least a couple dozen cocktails, cause after we finish with the nigger boy we got us a nigger meeting place to burn down. Them white trash nigger lovers been holding meetings there encouraging the niggers to vote. So we are going to give them a taste of what happens when they step over the line. OK, guys, let's mount up." Red called out.

The men all piled into five pickup trucks. Three and four men rode in the cabs and seven to eight men rode in the truck beds. They drove off whooping and howling, heading to James Hooker's home. The Men arrived in the five pickups at midnight in front of the Hooker home. They were all clad in their white robes and hoods. The men jumped out of the trucks. Four of the men carried a make shift cross soaked in gas. They stuck it upright in the front lawn and lit it on fire. The cross blazed giving off a bright glow. It lit up the front yard like a bright neon light.

"James Hooker," Red shouted. "Hooker, you best get your nigger ass out here," Red called out again.

Mrs. Hooker jumped from her bed. She ran down the hall to her son's room. "James, Honey, wake up." She said shaking her sleeping son. "Waa...What is it Mama?" James asked startled as he wiped the sleep from his eyes.

"You got to get up now. Get dressed and go out through the basement." She said urgently.

"What for?" James asked.

"It's the Klan, and they are calling for you. Now Honey, you listen to your Mama, and you go out the back way. Go through the woods and make your way to Mr. Jones' house and be careful that they don't see you." She told him. "Mr. Jones will hide you and Granma and I will come for you in the morning." She said.

She then went to the bedrooms of her other sleeping children. She woke them and hurried them down to the basement. Her mother, May Bell Brock met her in the hallway.

"You get the childrens down to the basement. I will try to stall them." May Bell said as she headed to the front door.

"Mama, you be careful" Mrs. Hooker called out.

"What you men want?" May Bell said as she stepped out on the front porch.

"We want that nigger grandson of yours." Red yelled out.

"He ain't here." May Bell answered.

"Now, old woman, you wouldn't be lying to us, would you?" Red said.

"I don't lie. It's the gospel." May Bell answered.

"Well where is he?" Red demanded.

"He went to Nashville to visit his aunt." She informed him. "Now you men get off my property. Go home I don't want no trouble." She said.

"You gonna let that nigger bitch talk to you like that?" Perry Weeks said as he spit out some tobacco juice on the ground.

"Come on boys. We can come back later. Old woman you best not be lyin." Red said as he started to back down.

"I say we go in the house and see for ourselves." Weeks said angrily.

"Now you all listen here." May Bell said as she stepped off the porch into the yard to confront the angry men. "This is my home, and I know almost all of you, and you all knows me. You all might be coverin yourselves with them there hoods over your faces, but I knows who ever dang one of youse is. Mike Parks, I nearly raised you, I changed your diapers and rocked you to sleep when you was a baby. And you Mr. Red Avery, I helped your wife do her spring cleanin. Now you all gonna do me like this? What's wrong with all youse?" She asked as tears of anger and disbelief ran down her cheeks.

Billy Joe stepped forward. "You want that nigger boy? Then I say we go get him. He raised his gun, walked up to May Bell and fired, shooting her in the head. She fell backwards and hit the ground, with a thud. The others stood there for a moment stunned at what just happened before their eyes. "Hell with going in." Billy Joe said as he took a cocktail out, lit it, and threw it through the front window.

Billy Joe grabbed another bottle filled with gas, lit the rag that was hanging out the end of the bottle. He tossed it through the front door.

Mike Parks walked up to Billy Joe. "Why did you do that?" He demanded.

"What? Kill some old nigger woman?" Billy Joe laughed.

Mike Punched Billy Joe in the jaw, knocking him to the ground. "That old nigger woman, as you put it, never hurt anybody in her life. Besides that she was my Mammy. She took great care of me when I was a kid." Mike said as tears filled his eyes. "Don't even think about pulling your gun on me, cause I ain't no defenseless colored woman." He said angrily. He turned and headed back to his truck. "I'm leaving. Anyone else want to come?" He looked at the men who rode with him. Six of the men jumped in the back of his truck. Mike pulled off his hood and through it out the window. "Tonight you went too far, Red, I'm out. No one was supposed to get killed. You want to run with that crazy bastard, you go right ahead, but count me out. I don't hold with murder. I don't care what color they are. Murder is murder." Mike said as he drove off.

The house was fully engulfed by the flames, the outline of May Bell's body lie on the front lawn like a shadowy bush in the glow of the flames.

"Come on guys, let's get the hell out of here. We got us a meetin place to burn down. They went to the trucks and drove away, leaving May Bell's burning house to lite up the night sky.

Mrs. Hooker was huddled in the basement with her three young girls and three young sons. The girls were ages eight to twelve. The boys were the youngest, being four, and twins age six.

"Mama, what's that popping and cracking sound?" The twelve year old asked.

"I don't know baby." She answered fearfully.

"Oh Mama, I think the house is on fire." She screamed out.

Mrs. Hooker went to the steps that led up to the kitchen. She screamed as she saw the fire glowing through the cracks around the door. "OH GOD. COME ON, CHILDREN, WE GOT TO GET OUT OF HERE." She went to the cellar door that went to the outside.

Mrs. Hooker went up the three steps that the two closed storm cellar doors were above her head. She pushed on them to open them. But they wouldn't budge. Panic began to set in as she tried again with all her strength. The doors wouldn't open because debris from the burning house above had fallen on the doors. They were trapped. She and the older girls kept trying to push open the doors. Out of breath and out of strength, she sat down the steps. She pulled her children close to her. They wrapped their arms around each other. "Lets pray children." .She said as she closed her eyes. "Oh God, hear my prayer. Please help us. Give me the strength and the power to save my children. Amen." One of her twins looked at her. "Mama, we gonna die?" He asked.

"Not if I can help it, baby." She stood up and began pushing on the cellar doors again. Then suddenly one door flung open. She saw her son James, and Mr. Jones. She lifted the smaller children up to them. They brought them out one by one. As she crawled out she saw what had been holding the door. A beam from the roof had fallen on to the doors. Mr. Jones and her son James had managed to move it over enough to open one side of the cellar.

"James, baby, you shouldn't be here." She cried.

"They're gone, Mama. I went over to Mr. Jones' house. He came back with me when we saw the flames from the house. We was at the edge of the woods when we saw them leave. They killed Granma, Mama. They just shot her dead in the front yard." He sobbed.

"Why they have to do that, Mama? Why?" He cried. His whole body shaking with each painful sob.

"I called the Sheriff." Mr. Jones said tearfully. "Sheriff Combs, he is a fair man. He will get them who done this, and he will put them in jail." He assured her.

"Ain't no white man ever going to go jail for killin a colored person. You know that Mr. Jones." She said angrily.

"Sheriff Combs is a good man, but he is a white man. And besides," She went on to say, "There ain't never been no Klan member ever been put in jail."

"Things is changin, Mrs. Hooker. Maybe not before, but you'll see. They is gonna pay this time. Mark my word. They will pay." He tried to say with a confident tone of voice.

Sheriff Combs was kneeling next to May Bell Brock's body. He tilted his hat back with his thumb. "Who and the hell would want to ever hurt you?"

He said aloud, shaking his head. He motioned to one of the firemen who was going back to the fire truck. "Hey, buddy, you got something on your truck to cover her body with?" The Sheriff asked as he stood up.

"Yes sir, I got a small tarp. We use it for car fatalities. I'll get it for you." The young fireman said.

"Thanks." Sheriff Combs said.

As the firemen helped him cover May Bell's body, a car pulled up. He recognized the two men who got out and walked over to him. "What are you two doing here?" He asked surprised to see them.

"We were in the neighborhood." One of the well dressed men answered.

"In the neighborhood, you say? Why would the F.B.I. be doing in this neighborhood this time of morning?" The Sheriff asked curiously.

"Well it seems that their was a meeting hall burned also tonight." It was Agent Wells speaking as he lifted the edge of the tarp that covered May Bell's body. He looked at the dead woman's face. "Shot in the head. At least she didn't know what hit her." He said as he covered May Bell back up. "I see this is the work of the Klan." He said.

"What makes you so sure it was the Klan?" Combs asked.

"That." Wells said pointing to the smoldering charred cross laying on the ground a few feet away in the yard.

"You're right." Sheriff Combs said as he lit up a cigarette. "You got the call for the meeting hall?" Combs asked.

"Actually, your radio calls crossed over our radio. So we thought we would lend you a hand." Agent Wells said.

"Thanks. I could use some help. I was going over there after I finished here." Combs said as he blew out a puff of smoke. "Klan?" Combs asked. Agent Wells shook his head yes. "The little bastards have been real busy tonight." Sheriff Combs stubbing out his cigarette with disgust in his voice. "Did you guys find your girl yet?" Combs asked as he kicked the smoldering cross angrily.

"No not yet. We still got a lot of pages to go through." Agent Wells said.

"What makes them hate the coloreds so bad?" Sheriff Combs asked as he looked at Agent Wells, tears welling up in his eyes.

"I don't know, Sheriff." Agent Wells said putting a hand on the Sheriff's shoulder.

"Well I'm going to do everything in my power to find out who did this. That poor woman lying dead over there never hurt anyone in her life." Sheriff Combs said angrily.

"Look, my partner and I will help you anyway we can. We been trying to break these kinds of hate groups for years." Agent Wells said sounding reassuring as he went on to say, "They are starting to get too bold, and sooner or later they will make a mistake. And tonight I think they made a mistake. A big one." Wells said.

"You think that maybe your missing people and this are all tied to the Klan?" Sheriff Combs asked.

"I don't know if they are all tied to the same group, but I do know that they all have Klan written allover them." Wells said.

Sue Ellen was still up when she heard the fire engines speed by her house. She stepped out on to the porch to have a look. She saw the fire truck make the turn up the street from her house as she looked in the direction of the field behind her house. She could see the bright glow of the fire above the woods. She could smell the smoke as the breeze gently blew in her direction.

"It woke you too." Margie called out as she walked across the yard to where Sue Ellen stood on the porch.

"No I was still up." Sue Ellen said.

"Oh my, that looks like a pretty big fire." Margie said as she came onto the porch to stand next to Sue Ellen.

"Where's Carl?" Sue Ellen asked.

"Oh, he's sound asleep. A bomb could go off right next to him and he wouldn't hear it. He sleeps like a rock." Margie laughed.

"I just made a fresh pot of coffee, you want to come in and have a cup with me?" Sue Ellen asked.

"Sure, why not? It will either keep me up or make me sleep." Margie giggled. They both went in to the house. Margie spent an hour drinking coffee and visiting with Sue Ellen. Then she went home to bed and Sue Ellen started to wait up for Billy Joe. But after a while she began to get sleepy; so she turned in for the night. Billy Joe came home around four. He didn't bother to wake her. He just went to bed and fell asleep.

CHAPTER SIXTEEN

The red haired boy of twelve named Skeeter Miller was playing in the woods with his friend Leroy Jackson. Leroy was a tall skinny Negro twelve year old a foot taller than his white friend Skeeter.

"Watcha wanta play now?" Skeeter asked Leroy as he tossed a pebble to the ground.

"Auh, I don't knows." He said as he bent down picking up a pebble giving it a toss.

"Hows bout we go swimming at Cutter's Pond?" Skeeter said as his big blue eyes twinkled and a big smile lit up his freckled face.

"Yeah. That's a good idea , Skeeter. We could play fox and the hound on the way."

Leroy grinned wide. "OK, you be the fox and I be the hound." Skeeter said.

"You should be the fox cause you gots the red hair." Leroy kidded.

"Auh, shucks, Leroy, I was the fox last time. Come on, let me be the hound." Skeeter said kicking at the dirt with the toe of his shoe.

"OK, but youse got to give me a head start." Leroy said.

"OK, I will count to fifty, so you best get going." Skeeter grinned as he started counting. "One, two, three..."

Leroy took off running. He ran for the eadge of the woods. He could hear Skeeter baying like a hound not far behind him. The closer he came to the clearing, the stronger a horrid odor hit his nostrils. Leroy's stomach started to churn. He stopped dead in his tracks as his breakfast started to come up. He started vomiting.

"Some fox you are." Skeeter said as he caught up. "Hey, what's the matter?" Skeeter asked as he saw his friend heaving. Then the odor hit him.

"EEGADS. What's that smell?" Then he heaved.

"Look over there." Leroy pointed as something caught his eye.

"What is it? Dead animals?" Skeeter said covering his nose.

"I don't think its animals." Leroy said as he walked over to get a closer look.

"They is people. Dead people." Leroy said his hand covering his nose.

"Is that a baby?" Skeeter asked as he pointed at the rotting body of a small baby.

"Lets go tell our folks." Leroy said.

"Yeah. My house is closer." Skeeter said.

"Well let's get out of here. I ain't never seen no dead peoples before." Leroy said as he turned away.

"Me either." Skeeter said.

The boys took off running as fast as they could. Their hearts were pounding so fast they felt like they were going to just jump out of their chest. Skeeter's father was working on his tractor when he heard the boys screaming as they ran across his cornfield. He looked up. He went for his rifle hanging on a rack in the barn. He thought the boys were being chased by a bear or some other animal.

"Daddy, daddy." Skeeter screamed.

Leroy was screaming right along with Skeeter. "Mr. Miller, Mr. Miller."

Mr. Miller ran towards the boys, calling out to them. "I'm coming boys. What's the matter?"

Skeeter threw his arms around his father as they met in the cornfield. Leroy grabbed onto him too.

"What's chasing you boys?"

"Nothing, daddy, it's, it's..." Skeeter and Leroy panted out of breath as they both were talking at the same time.

"Hold on, slow down. One at a time. Now, Skeeter what you boys all riled up about?" Mr. Miller said as he looked very puzzled at the two boys behavior.

"Daddy. Dead people in the clearing the other side of the woods." Skeeter blurted out.

"Yeah, they is three of them; one is a little baby." Leroy said still catching his breath.

"Are you boys sure?" Miller asked. "You better not be foolin around." Miller said sounding serious. "You boys go wait for me in the barn. I best go to the house and call the Sheriff." He said, then went to his house to make the call. The two boys sat in the barn on some bales of hay.

"Leroy, you think the Sheriff gonna make us go back there?" Skeeter asked.

"I don't knows, but I sure hope he don't. I sure don't wants to go back." Leroy said sounding scared.

"Leroy, what you think happened to those people?" Skeeter asked wide eyed.

"Don't know. Maybe a lion or tiger gots them." Leroy said.

"There ain't no lions or tigers in the woods. They are in Africa." Skeeter answered.

"Well maybe it was a bear." Leroy said.

"That could be." Skeeter said. "Although I ain't never seen one." Skeeter said.

"Me either. And I don't wants to. Leroy answered, all wide eyed, and scared at the thought.

Sheriff Jack Maxwell was the Sheriff of Tupelo. He was in his early fifties, very overweight and balding. He pulled up at the Miller farm about an hour after Mr. Miller called him.

"Howdy, Jed." He said as he got out of his car.

"Afternoon, Sheriff." Jed said.

"Now just what you think your boy and his playmate think they saw?" He smiled.

"Well they came runnin home about an hour or so ago, yellin and cryin their fool heads off. They kept saying they saw some dead bodies." Jed informed.

"Well, let's go talk to them." The Sheriff said as he lumbered towards the barn with Mr. Miller. The boys were still sitting on the hay when the Sheriff and Skeeter's father entered the barn.

"Howdy, boys. I hear you two had yourself some kind of day." He grinned.

"Yes sir." The boys answered nervously.

"Now. Why don't you boys just tell me what you think you saw." The Sheriff asked.

"We saw three dead people." Skeeter spoke first.

"Now are you sure it was people you saw, and not some dead cow or horse?" The Sheriff asked.

"No sir, there was a man, a woman, and a little baby." Leroy said earnestly.

"Why don't you boys go with the Sheriff and show him?" Mr. Miller said.

"Oh daddy, please don't make us go back there." Skeeter begged.

"That won't be necessary right now." The Sheriff said as he mussed Skeeter's hair. "I tell you what. Maybe you can show me were this clearing is Jed, that is if you know." The Sheriff said turning to Jed.

Jed looked at the boys as he asked. "Skeeter, are you talking about that clearing that leads to Cutters Pond?"

"Yes, daddy, that's the one." Skeeter said.

"Yes sir, youse will smell them before youse see them." Leroy said all wide eyed.

"OK, let's go, Jed. You show me." The Sheriff said as he turned to leave.

The Sheriff and Jed Miller got into the Sheriff's cruiser and headed down the dirt road towards the woods.

It was a little after one in the afternoon when they reached the clearing. The sun was high in the sky and it was very warm.

"Did the boys mention anything about a car?" The Sheriff asked as he approached the parked car.

"No, they didn't, Sheriff." Jed said as they stopped behind the big blue Cad.

As they opened their car doors to get out. "Oh my. We must be in the right place." Sheriff Maxwell said as he took out his hanky and put it on like a robber's mask. Jed did the same. Sheriff Maxwell walked over to the bodies. "Well the boys were right. A man, woman, and a baby." The Sheriff said.

"What do you think happened to them Sheriff?" Jed asked.

"Well, from what I can see, looks like they were all shot, except for the male, looks like he was castrated, and shot." The Sheriff said grimly. "And some one just cut that little baby right out of the woman." He said with a disgusted tone.

"My God, who would do such a horrible thing?" Jed said as he looked away.

"Most likely the Klan. It looks like something they are known to do." He said shaking his head.

"But why? What makes them so damn bloodthirsty?" Jed asked.

"Who knows what makes those crazy bastards tick? But I think I know who these people are." The Sheriff said.

"Who do you think they are?" Jed asked wondering.

"I'm very sure they are that missing doctor and his wife from Chicago."

"Are you sure?" Jed asked as he remembered the posters he had seen.

"Well the Cadillac has Illinois plates and it's a blue convertible. Jed, I'm sorry the boys had to see something this grizzly," the Sheriff said. "Well, let me call it in and I will drive you back home. I hope those poor boys don't have to many bad dreams over this." The Sheriff said, concern in his voice for the boys.

Sheriff Maxwell drove Jed home then he returned back to the clearing. He stayed with the bodies until the F.B.I. agents arrived. He knew this was in their hands now. He would still be working with them to help solve the case. But deep down he wondered if they ever would find the ones responsible for the Greens' murder. The Klan was very good at never being brought to justice for their crimes.

Sheriff Maxwell was leaning against the trunk of his cruiser up wind of the dead bodies. The black '57 Ford pulled up to him. The two F.B.I. agents got out of the Ford.

"You must be Sheriff Maxwell." Agent Fred Wallis said as he held out his hand to the Sheriff.

"that's right." He said shaking hands.

"I'm Agent Fred Wells, and this is Agent John Wallis." Wells said as the Sheriff shook hands with Wallis too.

"You boys sure did get here fast." The Sheriff said amazed at the time.

"We got the call in Cotton Wood. We been there for the last week and a half."

"Oh I'm surprised that you guys would be located over there." The Sheriff replied.

"Oh we just happened to be there running down a lead." Agent Wallis said.

"So what you got? Fill us in." Agent Wells said.

"Two young boys were playing in the woods when they came across three dead bodies. They ran home scared stiff. One of the boy's daddy called me. I came out, then I put a call in to your main office in Jackson and now here you are." Maxwell told them.

"Sheriff, you said you have three bodies?" Wells asked.

"Yes, three. A man, a woman, and a little baby." Maxwell said, then added. "Look, why don't you fellas just have a look for yourself? But first you better put a hanky over your face They been dead a while. The smell is pretty bad." Maxwell said as he tied his hanky around his nose. The two agents followed suit. Then they followed the Sheriff to where the three bodies were.

"Good God. What kind of sick bastard could have done this?" Wells said as he shockingly stared down at Jane Green's mutilated body.

"Some one cut that baby right out of her." Wallis said as he was about to become sick to his stomach.

"Get the camera, John. We need to photograph everything." Wells said looking a little peaked himself.

"Gladly." Wallis replied as he hurried back to the car.

"Don't forget to bring some evidence tags too." Wells called out to Wallis.

He turned back to the Sheriff. "Sheriff, has anybody else been around the scene?" He asked.

"No. Just the boys. I don't think they came too close. Then the one boy's daddy, but we didn't get too close, either." The Sheriff assured Wells.

Sheriff Maxwell and agents Wells and Wallis spent the rest of the afternoon collecting evidence and preserving it on film, and in plastic bags. They were joined by more F.B.I. agents and four more of Sheriff Maxwell's deputies. They were in charge of making plaster casts of all the different footprints and tire tracks. The Cadillac was dusted for prints inside and out. Agent John Wallis was walking towards the Cadillac as he was looking at all the spots where the poured casts were, being careful not to step on any. He noticed one of the Sheriff's deputies dragging one of his feet like he was trying to wipe something off his shoe. The Deputy locked eyes with him for a moment. Then he turned and walked over to his cruiser. He put his casting kit into the trunk. Wallis walked over to where the deputy had been. As he looked down, he saw a faint set of tire tracks that had partially wiped out by the deputy.

"Hey, Fred, you got a minute?" Wallis called out to Wells.

"Yeah, John. I will be there in a second." He said as he jotted something down in his notebook. Putting the notebook back into his pocket as he went over to Agent Wallis. "What did you find John?" He asked as he came up to stand beside him.

"I'm not sure Fred. But I saw one of Sheriff Maxwell's deputies drag his foot across these tire tracks. It was as though he did it on purpose.

"What do you think?" John asked.

"I think we need to find out a little something about that deputy." Fred said seriously.

"You think he's Klan?" John asked.

"Could be, won't be the first time one of these redneck deputies belong to the Klan." Fred said, as he looked in the deputy's direction.

"Lets get one of our guys over here, have them photograph this spot. Then see if they can get a cast off what's left. Don't let that deputy near this spot. I'm going to see what I can get out of Maxwell." Fred said as he turned and walked over to where Sheriff Maxwell was.

"Hey Sheriff, can I have a word with you?" Agent Wells asked as he approached him.

"Sure, what about?" The Sheriff asked curiously.

"What's that young deputy's name?" Wells said, pointing in the deputy's direction.

"Oh that's Deputy Otis Macky. Why you askin?" The Sheriff said a little on the defensive side.

"Oh just like to know who I'm working with, that's all." Fred lied.

CHAPTER SEVENTEEN

Sue Ellen and Margie brought Sissy home from the hospital. Sissy spent two weeks there.

"Mommy, can I go play?" Sissy asked as they went into the house.

"Sissy we just got home." Sue Ellen said surprised that Sissy wanted to go out of the house before she even got into the house.

"Please, please, Mommy, I want to go see Marcy and William. Please, can I?" Sissy begged.

"OK, just for a little while. I don't want you to get yourself sick." Sue Ellen said, letting Sissy go out.

Sissy went hurriedly to her favorite spot. She couldn't hardly wait to see her little friends. Sissy stood in the middle of her secret spot in the meadow. She looked all around no one was there. Then she thought to herself. Marcy and William must be at their house. Her sad face turned quickly to a happy one. She skipped off singing a little song heading to her friends' house. Marcy and William were sitting on the front steps of their house. They were drawing pictures and coloring them with crayons. Their heads snapped to attention as they heard the sound of singing.

"Do you hear that William?" Marcy asked as she strained to listen.

"I hear it. There's somebody out there." William said, standing up so he could see better. His eyes lit up with excitement.

"It's Sissy. Look Marcy, Sissy back." They both squealed out with joy as they scrambled off the steps. They ran the rest of the way through their yard to meet Sissy. Marcy and William threw their arms around Sissy. Sissy gave them a big hug.

"What's all this yellin?" Marcy's mother said as she walked out on the porch.

"Mama, look. Sissy is back." Marcy and William said at the same time, joyous smiles on their lit up happy faces.

"Well, MY MY. Come over here baby. Let me give you a big hug and a kiss." She said with outstretched arms.

Sissy ran over to the steps where Ida May now stood. She bent down embarrassing Sissy with a big hug and a kiss on her rosy cheeks.

Sissy, Marcy, and William were inseparable. They spent every afternoon together playing in the meadow. Sometimes Marcy and William's mother would bring them lemonade and cookies. Sue Ellen and Margie would come out and set in the field with the children, just to talk and watch them play. It wasn't long before Sue Ellen and Margie became good friends with Ida May. Sue Ellen really liked Ida May. But she knew she would have to keep their friendship a secret. So when she would visit with Ida May she always made sure she got home before Billy Joe. Things were running smoothly between her and Billy Joe, so she didn't want to do anything to change that. Although Billy Joe hardly spoke to Carl and Margie anymore. Sue Ellen was very surprised that he didn't forbid her to associate with them.

Summer was almost gone now, and fall was in the air. Sue Ellen had not been feeling well. She was having problems keeping food down. She felt nerves almost every day. Margie suggested she see a doctor. Sue Ellen left Sissy with Ida May, and Margie drove her to the doctor's office.

"Well, Mrs. Martin, congratulations. You are about to be a mother in, I would say, in the next five and a half months." The doctor said after his exam.

"Are you sure?" Sue Ellen said nervously.

"You're not happy about your pregnancy?" The doctor asked, as he read the look of dread and disappointment on her face.

"Oh doctor, I am. It's just, well it's not the right time, that's all." Sue Ellen said looking down at the floor.

"Well, it's never the right time for these kinds of things, but they have their way of working out." The doctor said to Sue Ellen with a smile.

"Thank you doctor." Sue Ellen said as she slipped off the exam table.

Margie was waiting for her in the waiting room. "Well, what did the doctor say was wrong?" Margie said impatiently as Sue Ellen came back into the waiting room.

"I'm pregnant." Sue Ellen said quietly.

"Oh that's wonderful." Margie said as she hugged Sue Ellen.

As they left the doctor's office Margie was talking excitedly about planning a baby shower for Sue Ellen.

As they got to Margie's car, "Stop it, Margie." Sue Ellen snapped. "Don't you understand I have to go home and tell Billy Joe. I remember how crazy he went when I told him about Sissy. Things have been pretty good so far. He hasn't yelled or got mad at Sissy for a long time. I think he is finally accepting the fact that he is a father. But me telling him I'm going to have another baby...I don't know. He has never wanted kids. I just don't know." Sue Ellen broke down crying.

Margie came to her side of the car, putting her arms around Sue Ellen to comfort her as she sobbed uncontrollably on Margie's shoulder.

"Oh Sue Ellen, Honey. I'm sure he might be a little upset at first. But once he gets used to the idea, I'm sure he will come around." Margie said soothingly.

"I don't know, Margie You have never seen Billy Joe when he loses control.

"Well, then just wait a little longer before you tell him. Wait till he is in a very loving mood, then break it to him." Margie said.

They got into the car and Margie drove Sue Ellen home.

Sue Ellen went over to Ida May's house to get Sissy after Margie dropped her off.

"Hi Mommy." Sissy said as she stopped with her picture she was coloring.

"Hi baby, what are you coloring?" Sue Ellen asked as she sat down on the steps next to Sissy.

"I'm coloring it for you. Marcy drew the Angels and I'm coloring them." Sissy smiled a big smile as her blue eyes sparkled with proud delight.

"Oh, they are lovely." Sue Ellen said as she held the picture in front of her.

"That Sissy of yours really loves Angels." Ida May broke in as she stood at the top of the steps.

Sue Ellen looked up at her. "That she does." Sue Ellen replied. "She has all the Guardian Angels, and every one of them is a different color." Ida May pointed out with a loving smile.

"The color of Angels are like the colors of the rainbow, Mommy. See?" She pointed to her picture.

"Yes, baby, I see." Sue Ellen smiled. "Well, baby, we have to go home now. Thank you, Ida May for watching her." Sue Ellen said as she stood up.

"My pleasure" She is a very good little girl." Ida May said as she came down the steps.

"Bye Sissy." William said looking up from his coloring.

"Bye Sissy. We will see you tomorrow." Marcy said.

"Bye. See you tomorrow." Sissy said waving.

Sue Ellen took Sissy's hand and walked down the path for their house. Sue Ellen knew Billy Joe would be home soon. She began making dinner. Sissy went to her room to play with her doll. Billy Joe came home at six thirty. Sue Ellen had dinner on the table when he walked in the door.

"Hi Honey." Sue Ellen said cheerfully.

Billy Joe leaned down kissing her on the cheek. "Smells good. Let me wash up and I will be right out to eat." He said as he gave her a little playful slap on her rear.

"All right you." She laughed. Then she fixed Sissy's plate. She took it in to Sissy's room. Although Billy Joe was beginning to get better with Sissy, he still didn't allow her to eat at the table with him and Sue Ellen.

Sue Ellen had found an old card table that had been left by the former tenants. She had found it in the old garage out back, so she cleaned it up and put it in Sissy's room along with one of her kitchen chairs.

"Time to eat baby." She smiled at Sissy as she sat the plate of food down.

"Thank you, Mommy." Sissy said as she got up from the floor with her doll in one hand.

"There you go." Sue Ellen said as she pushed the chair close to the table with Sissy in it. Sue Ellen went back to the kitchen where she fixed Billy Joe's plate. Billy Joe came in to the kitchen and sat down at the table. Halfway through their meal Sue Ellen was wondering to herself if she should tell Billy Joe about her pregnancy.

"You still not feeling good?" Billy Joe asked as he took a bite of food.

"A little." Sue Ellen answered.

"Then how come you ain't eating?" Billy Joe pointed at her plate with his fork.

"I'm just not very hungry I guess." Sue Ellen answered as she moved her full plate of food around.

"What do you say we go out Saturday night?" Billy Joe said as he chewed a mouthful of food.

Sue Ellen thought for a moment. "Where do you want to go?" She asked.

"There's a new band playing down at the bar. I thought maybe we could go there." He said as he leaned back in his chair. That was pretty good, Hon." He said as he lit up a cigarette pushing his plate away.

"Sounds nice. I will ask Margie if she can sit with Sissy." Sue Ellen said.

"Why?" The kid will be asleep by the time we go. Besides she stayed here before by herself. We don't need a Jew watching our kid." Billy Joe pointed out.

Sue Ellen wasn't happy about it but she agreed with him to keep him happy. She thought to herself that maybe she could have Margie check on Sissy without Billy Joe knowing about it.

That night, Billy Joe was in the mood to make love. As bad as she was feeling she didn't make any excuses, she went ahead and let him as long as he didn't get rough like sometimes he did. She was a little puzzled as to why he was being so gentle lately. She was glad that he was being so loving like he used to be when they were first married. She just hoped and prayed he would continue to stay this way. She thought she would wait and break it to him about having another baby, if his mood was good on Saturday. Maybe even while they were on the dance floor.

CHAPTER EIGHTEEN

"Hi. Sheriff Combs here." The Sheriff said as he answered his phone.

"Yes, Sheriff, this is Fred Wells. I'm the agent that was in your town a while back." Wells said as he twiddled with a pencil at his desk.

"Oh yes, the F.B.I guy." Sheriff Combs answered as he wondered what the agent wanted.

"The reason I'm calling you is, remember that homicide you had?" Wells asked.

"Which one? We have had six homicides in the past three months." Combs asked.

"You know, the one that happened the night we were there. I think the name was Brock." Wells informed him

"You mean the colored lady, May Bell Brock." Combs answered.

"Well you know we found the Greens." He said sadly.

"Yes I know, but why are you asking about Mrs. Brock?" Combs said curiously.

"Well you remember the bullet you sent to our office in Jackson?"

"Yes." Combs replied.

"We got a match. It seems that the same gun killed the Greens and Mrs. Brock. The killer either lives in Tupelo or Cotton Wood." Wells said.

"What makes you so sure it,s Tupelo or Cotton Wood? Hell the Klan is everywhere. Combs said with a little sigh.

"I'm almost positive because number one, the girl who had the ring appraised and two, we have two sets of tire tracks that were cast at the murder scene of Mrs. Brock's house. The meeting hall fire and at the scene where the Greens were found." Wells said very sure of himself.

"You know, I think you just might be right. Now all we got to do is find the one with the gun and the car or truck those tire casts match." Combs said.

"I think if we find out who this Sue Ellen Martin is, she will lead us to the shooter." Wells said with confidence."

"I know you're right, but we haven't had any luck locating her either. She may not even be from here." Sheriff Combs said as he leaned back in his chair.

"Well, I think Agent Wallis and I are going to start asking questions in Tupelo." Wells said.

"I think I might do the same here. We might get lucky." Combs replied.

"We will stay in touch." Wells said.

"I will do the same." Combs said as he hung up.

Sheriff Combs sat at his desk thinking about his conversation with Agent Wells. "I think Wells might be right." Combs thought to him self. "I sure wish I could find the bastard before Wells does. I would like to put a bullet in his brain, just like he did to poor May Bell. His face lit up as he thought of something. He got up from his desk and went to the front desk.

"Sam." Combs said excitedly as he went on to say. "You remember that artist fella? What's his name?" Combs waved his hand.

"Oh yeah, Sheriff. His name is Matt Wendel." The deputy answered.

"Yes that's his name, Matt Wendel. Try and get him on the phone for me. I'll be in my office. Buzz me when you reach him." Combs said smiling.

The deputy shook his head wondering what had the Sheriff so fired up with excitement over some big city artist.

"OK Sheriff, I will call him now."

Sheriff Combs turned and went back to his office. A few moments later Sheriff Combs' intercom buzzed.

"I got Wendel on line one, Sheriff." The Deputy's voice said over the intercom. Sheriff Combs picked up his phone pressing the button on the phone for line one.

"Hello, Mr. Wendel, Sheriff Combs here. I need to ask you something."

"Sure, Sheriff, what is it?" Wendel asked a little puzzled.

"Can you draw a person's face from someone giving you a description?" Combs asked.

"Well I don't know. I've never done that before, but I'm willing to give it a try." Wendel said.

"Great. Can you meet me at the jewelry store over by the hospital, say in an hour?" Combs asked.

"Sure I can." Wendel answered.

"Great. Here, I will give you the address." Sheriff Combs said as he started to read him the address.

"I don't need the address, Sheriff, I know where it's at."

"Fine. Then I will see you there." Combs answered, they both said goodbye and hung up the phone.

Sheriff Combs pulled up in front of the jewelry store. Matt Wendel was already there standing in front of the store. He walked over to the Sheriff's cruiser. Wendel was a very thin small framed man in his early thirties. He had jet black hair combed straight back. He had a widow's peak that made him look very thin in the face, almost bony with his pencil thin eyebrows, milky white skin and very dark brown eyes and hook nose. He could have been mistaken for a vampire.

"Matt Wendel?" The Sheriff asked as he got out of his cruiser.

"Yes sir that would be me." Matt said grinning as he shook hands with the Sheriff.

"I hope you can do what you say you can." Combs said looking a little skeptical.

"I sure can. I can draw anything and anyone. Not that I'm bragging or any thing. But I am good at what I do." Matt stated.

"I'm sorry. I didn't mean to sound skeptical, but this case is so important to a lot of people. This is the first lead we have had. I want to thank you for your help." Combs said.

"I haven't done anything yet. Thank me when I show you what I can do. Besides, I hope I can be of help to you." Matt said with an honest smile on his face.

They went into the jewelry store where they found Albert and his wife Rosie, the storeowners waiting for them. Sheriff Combs introduced them to Matt. Then they got started on the sketch. Sheriff Combs stood there patiently as he listened to Albert describe Sue Ellen, as he watched Matt's hand quickly moving on the sketchpad. Matt stopped and turned the sketchpad to Albert.

"Does this look anything like her?"

Albert took the pad in his hand. "That's her." Albert said excitedly.

"My that does look like that lady that was in here." Rosie said as she looked at the sketch.

"That's her, Sheriff. I can't believe how good this looks, it's as if she posed for this." Albert said to the Sheriff.

"Well, thanks, folks, this has been a great help." Combs said as he shook their hands. "And most of all, thanks to you. Without your talent we would never know for sure what this woman looks like." Combs said giving Matt a pat on his back.

"Glad I could help Sheriff." Matt said smiling.

"Well, I better take this to the newspaper and get copies.

CHAPTER NINETEEN

It was Friday afternoon; Sue Ellen was sitting on her porch steps waiting for Margie to come home from her job. She had been working on her courage all week to tell Billy Joe about her pregnancy. She kept telling herself that maybe Billy Joe would take the news better than he did for Sissy. Sue Ellen stood up when she saw Margie's car drive into her driveway. Sue Ellen called out to Margie as she got out of her car.

"Margie, you got a minute?"

Margie waved at Sue Ellen as she answered. "Yes, I will be right over." She closed her car door and crossed the street to go over to Sue Ellen standing on her steps.

"Hi, what's up?" Margie asked as she stopped in front of Sue Ellen.

"What are you doing tomorrow night?" Sue Ellen asked.

"Carl and I are going to hear the Reverend Martin Luther King speak over in Jackson." Margie smiled as she answered Sue Ellen.

"Oh." Sue Ellen said with a disappointed sound in her voice.

Margie searched her face puzzled at Sue Ellen's tone. "Sue Ellen, you sound very down. What's the matter?" Margie asked.

"Oh nothing. I just wanted to know if you could keep an eye on Sissy for me tomorrow. I'm going to tell Billy Joe about the baby." Sue Ellen sighed.

"Oh you know I would be glad to do it. But we made plans for this weeks ago. Why don't you just wait till Sissy goes to bed?" Margie suggested.

"Yes, I guess I will. I hope you guys have a good time." Sue Ellen smiled.

"You worry too much. You tell Billy Joe, it will turn out OK. You wait and see." Margie said, trying to reassure her.

"I hope you're right." Sue Ellen said.

"Trust me, I'm your friend, every thing will turn out OK. Now I hate to run off on you, but I got to go pack. We will be back late Sunday night. I don't have to work Monday, so I will see you for coffee. Then you can tell me all about it. OK?" Margie smiled.

"OK. Have a good trip." Sue Ellen said as they gave one another a hug goodbye.

Sue Ellen felt uneasy as she tucked Sissy into bed. She didn't like leaving Sissy alone in the house. But she knew she had to if she was going to get along with Billy Joe. She kissed Sissy on the cheek giving her a big hug goodnight. She turned out the lamp by Sissy's bedside and went to her bedroom to get dressed to go out with Billy Joe. He was in the shower. He came out as Sue Ellen was putting the finishing touches on her make up.

Billy Joe came up behind her as he rubbed his naked body against her. He kissed the nape of her neck. He placed his hands on her thighs as he raised her dress. She could feel him getting very aroused as he pressed his hard penis against her buttocks. He ran one hand between her legs, and with his other hand he slipped his hand in her bra gently taking hold of her breast. Sue Ellen knew she had to give in to him.

"Billy Joe, we are going to be late." She said as he was now unzipping her black party dress.

"So we will be a little late. I just got to have you. baby, you just drive me crazy." He said taking off her bra dropping it on the floor where her dress was now lying. He turned her towards him. He began kissing her breast, then he lead her over to the bed and gently layed her down, slipping off her panties. He parted her legs and was inside her. They made long passionate love together. Billy Joe rolled off her onto his back, still breathing hard.

"Oh baby, that was great." He said as he reached for his pack of Luckys on the nightstand. "Let's take a shower together." He said as he lit his Lucky up.

"OK, you still want to go out?" She asked hoping he would say no.

"You bet your sweet little ass I do. It's only nine now, so if we hurry we can get there before ten o'clock." He said as he stubbed out his cigarette .Sue Ellen got up off the bed, thinking to herself, at least Sissy would only be alone for just a couple hours instead of four or five hours. She figured since Billy Joe was in such a good mood, this would be a good time to tell him about the baby. They showered together and quickly got dressed. They arrived at the bar, nine forty-five. They were on the dance floor a little after midnight when she got up her nerve. She waited till they were dancing a slow dance. Billy Joe was holding close. He was kissing her neck, she nuzzled his ear, then she said timidly." Billy Joe, I have something to tell you. But first you must promise not to get mad."

"Mad? Mad about what?" He said as he looked her in the eyes.

"Promise me." She looked at him pleadingly.

"OK, I promise." He sighed with an annoyed sound in his voice.

"I'm pregnant." Sue Ellen blurted out. She felt his muscles tighten up, and that dark look come over his face. He was silent for a moment. Then he relaxed and moved her around on the dance floor till the song ended. He looked down at her, then he said, giving her the shock of her life. "When?" He said.

"When what?" She asked puzzled.

"When are you having the baby?" He asked.

"I'm almost four months." She said blankly.

"Having another kid going to change anything between us?" He asked.

"Why no." She answered.

"Well then I guess I will have to get more overtime at work." He said calmly. "Maybe this time you will have a boy." He said, then he kissed her.

They went back to their table and sat down. Billy Joe ordered another round of drinks.

"You're not mad?" She asked.

"No I'm not mad, that's what happens when two people make love like we do." He smiled at her.

Sue Ellen sat there numb from disbelief of how he was taking it. She was happy, but deep down inside she just didn't believe him. For now she breathed a sigh of relief.

Sue Ellen checked on Sissy as soon as they came home, a little before two. After making sure Sissy was all right, she went to bed. Billy Joe made love to her three more times that night. She didn't care as long as he was not mad about the baby.

CHAPTER TWENTY

Cora Green's arthritic hands clutched firmly to the broom handle as she slowly swept the front porch of her house. A shiny glint caught her eye. She looked to see what was now a shiny glare from the sun's bright reflection. She squinted her eyes as she held up one hand using it to shield the glare. She could see that it was the glare from a car. She started to go back to sweeping, then suddenly she stopped as she realized the car was turning into her driveway. She felt her heart leap as she hopefully thought it might be her son. But as the car came closer she got a sick feeling in the pit of her stomach. The car came to a stop. Tears began to well in her old tired eyes as she saw it was a Sheriff's car.

Sheriff Maxwell got out of his car, walked up the steps to the porch were Cora stood frozen.

"Howdy, Miss Cora." He said solemnly as he tipped his hat to her.

"Hello, Sheriff. You bring me some news about my boy and his wife?" She asked as her voice began to choke up. "Did you find them? Are they all right?" She said as she began to shake.

Sheriff Maxwell took her by the arm to steady her. "Miss Cora come sit down over here." He said as he steered her to the wicker chair on the porch. "I'm sorry to have to bring such bad news to you. But we found your son, his wife and their baby."

Cora broke in. "baby? Jane's baby isn't due for another two weeks." She said.

"Well, Miss Cora , I don't want to tell you all the grizzly details. But it looks like they were murdered, and some one took the baby from the mother by cutting her open. We found the baby lying by her. I'm sorry, Miss Cora." The Sheriff said with deep sympathy in his voice.

Cora covered her face with her hands as she sobbed, unable to hold back her tears of pain and grief.

"Is there anything I can do for you? Do you want me to call someone to come be with you?" The Sheriff asked, trying to sooth her pain.

"Sheriff, tell me, was the baby a boy?" She asked.

"Yes." He answered.

Cora looked up at the Sheriff, her eyes red and still full of tears. "Sheriff, can you take me to see them?" She asked still sobbing.

"Auh, Miss Cora, you don't want to see them this way. There was a lot of decomposition. You want to remember them the way they were when you last seen them." The Sheriff said, trying to console her.

"I guess you are right, Sheriff." She whispered in a soft choking voice.

"Look, I'm going to call your sister over in Jackson. You need her to be with you and the Mr. right now. She's still in the same place isn't she?" The Sheriff asked.

Cora shook her head yes, then took the Sheriff's hand in hers as she wrapped her wrinkled bony fingers around his large muscular hand. "You're a good man, Sheriff. You have always been kind to everyone. You have never treated us colored folks any different than the white folks. I just want to thank you for comin out here and tellin me yourself."

"You're welcome, Miss Cora. I felt this was something you needed to hear in person, not over the phone. You just take it easy for now and I'm going to go call your sister." The Sheriff said as he patted her hand, then turned to leave. He looked back at her one more time before he got into his car to leave. "You take care, Miss Cora, and once again, my condolences for your sorrow." She looked his way nodding her head.

The Sheriff backed out of her driveway heading back to his office.

Cora sat on the porch, eyes closed as she tried to picture her son Mark's face and his wife Jane. She recalled that last happy night they spent together. Tears of deep grief streamed down her face as she called out their names. "Oh Mark, my sweet baby boy, and my sweet darling Jane. Why did these evil people take you from me? Oh Lord, God, Why? Why?" She cried.

Cora's Sister Martha came that night when she received the Sheriff's phone call. Martha was preparing lunch for Cora and Henry. She looked out the kitchen window. She was saddened at the sight of Henry's garden. The weeds were overtaking the lawn and Henry's flower garden.

Henry had become very withdrawn ever since Mark and Jane's disappearance and now with the knowledge of their deaths, all he does is read his Bible. Cora just cries and stares at the photos of Mark and Jane.

"Cora, Henry lunch. You need to come and eat." Martha called out to them. "Please Cora, we have to go to the funeral home to make the arrangements" She remind.

"You don't have to shout." Cora said as she came into the kitchen.

"Where's Henry?" Martha asked.

"He's sleeping." Cora said, her voice solemn.

"Oh, well, don't you think he should be awakened?" Martha asked.

"No, we can go with out him. He needs to rest." Cora said.

"And you don't?" Martha said as she put a plate in front of Cora's place at the table. Just then the phone rang.

"I'll get it." Cora said getting up from the table.

"Hello." Cora said as answered the phone.

"Hello, Mrs. Green." It was a man's voice.

"Yes, this is she." Cora answered.

"Mrs. Green, this is George Moesly, I'm the director of the funeral home." He informed.

"Yes, we were coming down after lunch. Is something wrong?" She asked, feeling something wasn't quite right in his tone of voice.

"Well, yes, there is, Mrs. Green." He said dryly.

"What is it?" She asked nervously.

"I have your son's body, and the baby's body. But the City Morgue, well, they won't release your daughter-in-law's body because she is white. They tell me it's a law. She has to go to a white funeral home. You know it will be the same rule at the cemetery." He said.

"Thank you Mr. Moesly. I will take care of it. My son will be with his wife and baby." Cora said firmly.

"Not in the State of Mississippi." He said.

"Then I will just have to take them where they can be together." She said.

"I wish you luck, Mrs. Green. Goodbye now." He said.

"Thank you. Goodbye." Cora replied, then they hung up.

"What was that all about?" Martha asked.

"It seems that the State of Mississippi has a town with a law that says if a man and his wife are of different colors, they can't share the same funeral home or graveyard." Cora said, anger in her voice.

"That's terrible. What are you going to do Cora?" Martha asked.

"I don't know just yet. I got to think about this." Cora answered with a tired sigh in her voice.

"Cora, you expecting anyone?" Martha asked as her attention was on the big black Buick she saw through the window pulling to a stop in the driveway.

"No, I wonder who it could be?" Cora said as she went to the front door. Martha followed Cora out to the porch. They stood together as they watched the four men get out of the car.

"Oh that's Reverend Barns. He's the Reverend from my Church. I don't know who the other gentlemen are though." Cora said wondering.

"Well, I know who that one man is." Martha squealed excitedly with a whisper in Cora's ear as she clutched Cora's arm.

"Hello, sister Green." The Reverend called to Cora.

"Hello yourself Reverend, what brings you out here?" Cora said.

"I came because I heard about your loss, and I brought someone who wants to meet you." He said as he climbed the steps to join Cora and Martha.

"Thank you Reverend. I was going to call you later today." Cora said.

"Well, I saved you the trouble of a phone call." He smiled. The other three men came on the porch with him.

"Reverend, I don't think you met my sister Martha." Cora said.

"No, but I have the pleasure now." He said shaking Martha's hand.

"Cora, Martha, I would like to introduce you to Reverend Martin Luther King." He smiled as both women's eyes widen.

"How do you do, ladies?" King said as he shook both their hands. "I'm sorry to hear about your son and his wife." Reverend King said with sincerity in his voice.

"Thank you. We were about to have lunch. Won't you join us?" Cora invited them.

"We would be happy to, if it's not to much of a bother?" Reverend Barns said.

After the introduction of the other two men; a Reverend Joe Simms and the Reverend Tom Hall, they all went into the house to have lunch in Cora's kitchen. Martha went to Henry's room and woke him. He came down to the kitchen to join them. First time in weeks he showed any interest in anything. Henry was very honored to meet the Reverend King, and very honored to have him as a guest in his home. Cora told them about what Mr. Moesly told her about Tupelo not allowing Mark and Jane to be together with their child at the funeral home or in the same cemetery. Reverend King listened intensely to Cora's dilemma. He saw the pain in her heart and the tears that filled her eyes as she told him her story.

"Sister Green, Brother Green, I shall see to it that your loved ones are buried together as a family. I promise you, you have my word on it. And now I must be going. It was a very good lunch. I thank you for your gracious hospitality. I will call you tonight and let you know what is to be done about this. The Lord shall show me the way. Now let's join hands and thank God, and ask him for his help in doing this." They all joined hands and the Reverend King led the prayer. Cora and Henry felt a little better after Reverend King and the others left. She and Henry were very thankful that they now had some one who could help them through their time of pain and sorrow.

That evening Cora and her sister Martha sat on the sofa. They were reminiscing through an old photo album. It was close to nine P.M. when the phone rang. Cora got up from the sofa to answer it.

"Hello." She answered.

"Is there a Mrs. Green there, please?" A woman's voice asked.

"This is she." Cora said.

"Mrs. Green, my name is Sarah Myer, I'm Jane's mother." She said as she broke down crying over the phone.

"Oh, I'm so glad you called." Cora said as she too began to cry.

"They won't let our children be together here." Cora sobbed.

"I know. Your Sheriff Maxwell called me, he gave me the news they were found. But Reverend King called me to tell me that Markus and Jane could not be put to rest with each other." She said crying.

"I know, and it's not right. They loved each other so much." Cora cried.

"That is one reason I'm calling. My husband Seth and I are flying out. We are going to take Jane's body home. And we would like for you to consider letting Markus' body come back here too. At least here they can be put to rest together. We can make arrangements at the cemetery here. That is if it's all right with you and your husband. Sarah said, a little more composed now.

"God bless you child. I have been praying for a way our two children, and our grandson could be together." Cora said delighted.

"Grandson?" Sarah said surprised.

"Yes, didn't the Sheriff tell you?" Cora asked.

"No, he didn't mention that Jane had the baby." Sarah said sounding sad.

"Jane didn't just have the baby. Those murdering bastards who took our children's lives cut Jane's body open and murdered our grandbaby too." Cora cried.

"Oh my poor Jane." She gasped in a horrified voice.

"Mrs. Green, did they suffer before they died?" Sarah asked as she sobbed.

"I don't know. I hope they died quick." Cora answered sadly as she went on to say, "You know, the only way Markus and Jane can travel together is by train."

"Yes, I know. I thought maybe we could all take the train back together." Sarah said.

"We can, except we have to ride in separate cars." Cora informed.

"You mean to tell me we can't ride on the train together?" Sarah gasped.

"That's right. We have to ride in the coloreds only car, and you and your husband will have to ride in the whites only car." Cora said.

"Why that is terrible. I never knew such a thing existed." Sarah said stunned.

"That's how it is down here. I won't even be able to meet with you. Not until we get to Illinois. I hope we can there?" Cora added.

"We don't do things like that here. Everyone is treated the same way here." Sarah said.

"I wish it was that way here, but it's not." Cora said.

"I want you to know, Mrs. Green, we were very proud to have Markus as our son-in-law. We loved him as much as we love Jane." Sarah said sincerity in her voice.

"Thank you for telling me that. We felt the same way about Jane. She was a wonderful person." Cora said.

"Did Jane tell you what she was going to name the baby if it was a boy?" Sarah asked.

"Yes, she told me she was going to name the baby David Markus, if it was a boy and Sarah Jane if the baby was a girl." Cora said. "That's what Jane told me the last time we talked." She said as she started to cry again.

Two days later Mark and Jane's bodies were put on a train along with their son. Mark's coffin was put into one baggage car along with the baby's tiny coffin. Jane's coffin was put into another car because she was white. Everyone from the Green's family rode in the passenger car reserved for coloreds only and Mr. and Mrs. Myer road in the whites only car. When they arrived in Chicago both families finally got to meet. They hugged one another as they waited at the platform for the bodies to be unloaded. Two hearses from the funeral home were parked nearby waiting to take the bodies to the funeral home, then to a church where services would be held for the families and friends. Nearly two hundred people came to the church service. Reverend King officiated the funeral ceremony. The church was full with friends, other doctors, their families as well as nurses and their families. Even some of Mark's patients attended. The Green family stayed three days after the funerals with Jane's family. The Myers took Mark and Jane's little dog Toby to live with them. Mark and Jane's home was sold and all the money from their estate was donated to the hospital and to Reverend King's cause for freedom. Ten thousand of it was offered as a reward for the arrest and conviction of those responsible for the deaths of Mark his wife and baby.

Their deaths touched a lot of people in Chicago as well as in the state of Mississippi. There was some people in the state of Mississippi who thought the Klan should be brought to justice for their crimes against colored people and that things should change in the south. Sheriff Jack Maxwell and Sheriff Bill Combs being two of the many who felt that way.

CHAPTER TWENTY-ONE

Margie came over to see Sue Ellen for coffee on Monday morning as she had promised on Friday. She sat across the kitchen table facing Sue Ellen. Sue Ellen was giving her all the details from the weekend as they sipped on their coffee.

"That sounds wonderful, Sue Ellen, you should be happy that Billy Joe is finally coming around."

"I don't know, Margie, I just can't see him changing towards having children overnight." Sue Ellen said with a shrug as she took another sip from her coffee cup.

"Well there's an old saying, honey. Don't look a gift horse in the mouth." Margie chided.

"Yeah, well the only reason they say that is because the damn horse just might bite you." Sue Ellen laughed. They both kidded about Billy Joe's new attitude towards being a father.

"Where's Sissy? Is she still asleep?" Margie said as she missed seeing Sissy.

"Oh no, Sissy left out the door a half hour before you came over. She went to see her playmates, Marcy and William. According to Sissy they had a lot of flower picking to do today."

"Sissy really does love her flowers." Margie said smiling.

"That she does." Sue Ellen said as she went on to say, "I'm just glad Sissy has someone to play with. She was so lonely when we lived in Tupelo. There weren't any children her age in or near the apartments we lived in. She use to play all by herself under an old tree. That was her special place. She would play under that old tree all day long. She just loves the outdoors. And here she has the outdoors as well as two dear little friends to play with."

"You know, Sue Ellen, I think it is just great that you let Sissy play with Marcy and little William. Not to many white people let their children play with colored children." Margie said as she poured herself another cup of coffee.

"Color has never been an issue with me. I don't care what color someone is as long as they are a good person. I have never understood why there is so much hatred for colored people by white people. I have met a lot of nice colored people. Ida May and her children are among them." Sue Ellen said.

"Billy Joe being one of those white folks who hate coloreds." Margie said taking a sip of her coffee.

"Billy Joe wasn't always that way, Margie. He didn't get that way till he met that damn Red Avery." Sue Ellen said defensively.

"Oh, who's Red Avery?" Margie asked curiously.

"He's a Klucker." Sue Ellen said sounding cynical.

"You mean he's a Klu Klux Klan member?" Margie asked wide eyed.

"Yes, if you want to give him an official title. Far as I'm concerned he is nothing more than white trash to me. I don't like the man, I never have and I never will. He gives me the creeps. I wish Billy Joe would have never met him. He made Billy Joe change." Sue Ellen said bitterly.

"You really believe that one man made Billy Joe change?" Margie asked.

"Yes, I do. Billy Joe used to be a kind, sweet, loving and gentle man, till he met Red Avery." Sue Ellen said.

"Have you tried talking to Billy Joe about your feelings on this matter?" Margie asked.

"Oh hell, yes, many times. But he just shuts me out, so I found it best to just not say anything on the subject." Sue Ellen said.

"Oh my look at the time." Margie said as she looked at the clock on the wall. "I hate to run dear, but I have to be over to the church on First Street, I have to help people fill out there voter forms today. Would you like to come along?" Margie asked as she got up to leave.

"I would, but I have got to do laundry today." Sue Ellen said as she followed Margie to the door.

"Well, maybe next time." Margie said going out the door.

"Yes, next time I would like very much to go with you." Sue Ellen said cheerfully.

"Bye now, see you later." Margie said waving as she went across the street to her house.

"Bye." Sue Ellen replied waving back as she stood on the porch watching Margie as she went into her house. Then Sue Ellen went back into her house to get started on her laundry.

Sissy, Marcy, and her brother William were playing in the meadow happily when suddenly William started to cry. "What's the matter, William?" Marcy asked.

"Look my wheel broke on my truck." He whimpered.

"Don't cry, William, we can take it to Mr. Jones. He will fix it. He can fix anything." Marcy stated.

"Who's Mr. Jones?" Sissy asked.

"He is our friend. He fixes broken toys." Marcy answered. "Come on, William. Let's go to his house." Marcy said taking William's hand.

"Can I go to?" Sissy asked.

"Yes Sissy. You need to meet him, cause if you get a toy broke, he will fix it." Marcy said.

Sissy stood up taking Marcy's other hand in hers and the three off them went happily through the meadow to Mr. Emmitt Jones' house.

Emmitt Jones' house was located behind Sissy's house. His fence line joined the far corner of Sissy's fence line. His house sat at the far end of his twenty acres. Emmitt lived alone, his wife and son died of a flu epidemic twenty years earlier. He was a stocky built colored man in his late sixties. He was balding, his hair was nearly snow white that seemed to frame his round face, making his very dark skin nearly glow with the kind smile he always had. He spent his spare time fixing and making toys for the neighborhood children. At Christmas time he was like a Santa Claus for all the poor. It didn't matter if they were colored or white. To him they were all of God's children.

Emmitt was in his garden when the children came up to his fence. "Mr. Jones. Oh Mr. Jones." Marcy and William called to him.

He looked up from his late beans he was picking. He stood up from his kneeling position. "Hello there, children." He called back to them as he walked over to where they were standing.

"Mr. Jones, can you fix William's truck?" Marcy asked.

"Well let me see it." He smiled down at them. William handed him the truck. "OK you three come around to the gate and go to my barn. I will meet you there." He started to walk away then he stopped. "Hold on there. You forgettin your manners? Who is your little friend there." He pointed to Sissy.

"Oh, I'm sorry. This is my friend Sissy. She lives over there." Marcy said pointing towards Sissy's house.

"Well, I'm glad to make your acquaintance, Miss Sissy." He said bowing to her. The children giggled with delight.

"You're funny." Sissy said snickering with laughter.

"What's your dolly's name?" He asked Sissy.

"Her name is Angel cause she is a real Angel. See , she has wings." Sissy said holding up her doll so he could see.

"MY, MY. I guess she really is an angel." Mr. Jones said smiling. "Well, now that we know each other, I got a truck to fix. I will see you all at the barn, now scoot." He said with a kindly smile.

The children ran down the fence line to Emmitt's front gate. They were waiting in the barn by the time Emmitt slowly walked to his barn.

"You sure is fast." He said as he came inside the barn. "I guess I'm slow because I'm an old man." He said wiping his brow. He took William's truck over to his workbench and began the task of repairing it.

"There. Here you go, William." Emmitt said as he handed the truck to him.

"WowWee. It's good as new." William said hugging his truck.

"OK, where's my payment?" He looked down at William looking serious.

"I don't gots no money, Mr. Jones." William said as his big brown eyes looked up at Mr. Jones sadly.

"Money? Who said anything about money? I think you should pay me with a big hug." He grinned widely down at William. William put his little arms around Emmitt's neck as he bent down for William.

"Thank you, Mr. Jones." William said, hugging Emmitt.

"You're very welcome, child. Now you all better get along home, it's gettin late. Your daddies and mamas will be worried about you all."

"Goodbye, Mr. Jones." They called back waving to him as they left the barn heading for home.

"Goodbye, children. You come back and see me again soon." He said smiling as he waved back at them.

"We will." They said as they went down the path leading to his front gate.

Billy Joe pulled his truck up to the old garage behind his house. He had gotten off work early so he decided to change the oil in the truck. As he got out the sound of childrens' laughter drew his attention to the field. He walked over to the back fence. He scanned the field with his eyes focused in the direction of the laughter. He saw two colored children waving and who they were waving at. It was Emmitt Jones. He started to shrug it off, then he saw Sissy as she trailed behind the two children. His whole body tensed up as he grit his teeth at the site of his little girl happily running with the little colored children. He climbed through the hole in the fence. He walked through the field taking off his belt as he walked towards Sissy.

"SISSY." He yelled. Sissy froze in her tracks as her face turned pale. "SISSY"YOU GET YOUR ASS OVER HERE NOW" He yelled again at her. Sissy just stood there, her body trembling with fear. Marcy and William stood beside Sissy, too afraid to move as they saw Billy Joe coming closer and closer to them yelling at the top of his lungs at .Sissy.

"Sissy, WHAT THE HELL ARE YOU DOING WITH THESE NIGGERS?" He demanded. He stopped in front of the children. "ANSWER ME." He screamed down at her.

Sissy started to cry as she tried to answer him. "We were just playin daddy."

"You nigger kids go back to wherever it is you came from. And don't let me catch you ever again near my kid. Now git." He threatened Marcy and William. They looked up at him with frightened eyes. Then they ran as fast as they could for home.

Billy Joe's yelling had got Mr. Jones' attention. He came to his fence line to see what all the commotion was. Billy Joe raised the belt in his hand, striking Sissy in the face, knocking her to the ground. He grabbed her by the hair pulling her up. He struck her repeatedly with the belt. The blows hitting her back legs, buttocks. He didn't care. He was too enraged with anger. Sissy screamed out in pain with each hot stinging blow with the belt.

Emmitt called out to Billy Joe. "Hey, Mr., there ain't no need to beat that little child like that."

"NIGGER, YOU GO BACK IN TO YOUR HOUSE AND MIND YOUR OWN BUSINESS." Billy Joe yelled shaking the belt at Emmitt.

"You don't stop hitting that baby, I'm going to make it my business by callin the Sheriff, you HEAR?" Emmitt yelled back at Billy Joe as he turned and went to his house to call the Sheriff. Billy Joe turned his attention back to hitting Sissy. Then he reached down grabbing her by the hair again. He began dragging her across the field towards his fence line. Once he reached the hole in the fence he dragged Sissy through the fence. Sue Ellen could hear Sissy screaming and crying as she begged her father not to hit her again. Sue Ellen ran to the porch then down the steps to the back yard were she saw Billy Joe standing over Sissy. She could see the rage in his face as he screamed down at Sissy. "I DON'T EVER WANT TO SEE YOU WITH ANY OF THOSE NIGGERS AGAIN, YOU HEAR ME?" He said as he stuck her once more.

"BILLY JOE, STOP IT." Sue Ellen yelled out as she grabbed Billy Joe's arm to stop him from hitting Sissy again. Billy Joe jerked his arm hitting Sue Ellen with his elbow. She fell backwards against Billy Joe's pickup. She caught herself by grabbing hold of the truck's bed. Billy Joe turned to her.

"What the hell do you do all day long? Don't you watch what this damn kid does?" He demanded.

"I don't know what the hell you're raving about." Sue Ellen snapped back at him.

"I'm talking about the fact that you spend to much time having coffee breaks with that Jew bitch nigger lover from across the street. You don't see what our kid is doing with niggers in that damn field out there. That's what I'm talking about." He yelled.

"They are just children." Sue Ellen gasped.

"You knew about this?" Billy Joe said angrily.

"Yes, children need playmates." She snapped.

"Not nigger ones." He answered.

"Well in case you haven't noticed, there aren't any white children Sissy's age to play with around here." She said as she pushed by Billy Joe to pick Sissy up into her arms to carry her to the house.

"You have been around those Jew bastards across the street so long you are starting to think like them." He said with anger in his voice.

"I don't believe you, Billy Joe. Margie and Carl have been friends to us. You're the one who has a poisoned mind. I thought I was getting back the man I married. But ever since you got involved with Red Avery, all you have is nothing but hatred in your heart. He has turned you into some kind of monster and if you ever beat our child again like this, I swear, Billy Joe, I will call the cops on you and have you arrested and I will take Sissy and you will never see either of us again. I'm not afraid of you anymore, Billy Joe. So don't even think about beating me. Now I'm going to the house to take care of Sissy." She said as she left Billy Joe speechless as she headed towards the house. Billy Joe stood by his truck for a long time. Then he started to change the oil in the truck.

Sue Ellen took Sissy into the bathroom were she put her into a tub of cool water. Sissy had welts covering nearly her entire body. Tears streamed down Sue Ellen's face as she sponged Sissy's wounds with the cool water. Afterwards she put salve on the welts, dressed Sissy and left the house.

Billy Joe was under his truck when the Sheriff's car pulled into his driveway. Billy Joe rolled out from under the truck when he saw the Sheriff walk onto the porch to knock on the door. He stood up. "Can I help you?" Billy Joe called out to the Sheriff.

Sheriff Combs stepped down off the porch and went over to Billy Joe. "You live here?" Combs asked.

"Yes, I do." Billy Joe answered cautiously.

"I got a call about a man beating a child. Do you have a child?" Combs asked searching Billy Joes face.

"Yes, I do." He answered.

"Where is the child?" Combs said as he hitched up his gun belt.

"She is with her mother. They left a few minutes ago." Billy Joe answered.

"Did you beat your child?" Combs asked bluntly.

"No, I spanked my child for not staying in the yard." Billy Joe answered trying to stay calm.

"What's your name, sir?" Combs asked suspiciously.

"Billy Joe Martin." He replied.

"Well I have to check out all the calls, you know. Someone probably mistook the spanking for a beating. I would like to see the child for myself. But if you say she isn't here, well, I guess I will have to take your word for now. Your sure your wife took the child with her?" Combs asked.

"Yes, would you like to go into the house and see for yourself?" Billy Joe offered.

"No, I will take your word for it. But if I get another call, well, then I will have to see the child. I'm not going to get another call, am I?" Combs said sternly.

"I don't know, Sheriff, are you telling me I can't spank my kid if she's doing something wrong?" Billy Joe said sounding sarcastic.

"Yes you can spank your child, but you can't beat your child." Combs said firmly.

"Sheriff, I don't beat my kid or my wife." Billy Joe said smugly.

"That's good. I wouldn't want to have to put a nice looking young fella like you in my jail." Combs replied. "Well I got to go, you have a nice day. Give my best to your wife and little girl." Combs tipped his hat.

"I will do that, Sheriff." Billy Joe answered as the Sheriff turned to go back to his car. Billy Joe watched the Sheriff drive away relieved as the Sheriff's car was out of sight. He crawled under the truck again to finish the oil change.

Sue Ellen had went down the street to the bar to call a cab. She took Sissy into town with her to the Dairy Queen where she bought them both some ice cream. Sissy could hardly sit in the booth because of the pain.

"Mommy I lost Angel." Sissy said as tears streamed down her cheeks.

"Don't worry, Honey. Mommy will find her for you later." Sue Ellen said reassuringly.

"Daddy said I can't go in the field no more." Sissy said sadly.

"Don't you worry about what daddy said." Sue Ellen said.

"I can't see Marcy and William no more?" Sissy asked.

"Honey, you listen to me. Yes you can. We just have to make sure your daddy doesn't find out. I'm going to make sure I come and get you home before your daddy gets home. OK?" She patted Sissy's little hand.

"OK, Mommy." Sissy tried to smile.

"Sissy I don't want you to grow up thinking that colored folks are bad people. Your daddy doesn't understand that all people are the same. They just look different It will take time to change him, if that is even possible. But Mommy is going to try. But I want you to grow up with love in your heart like you have now. I don't want you to grow up with a heart full of hate. Do you understand what I'm trying to tell you baby?" Sue Ellen said as she looked deeply into Sissy's big soft blue eyes. One of her eyes was turning black at the corner where the belt hit her.

"You want me to love everybody like the Angels do." Sissy answered innocently.

"Yes, baby, like the Angels." Sue Ellen smiled at her.

Sissy sat silent for a moment. Then she looked up at her mother, a very serious look on her face. Then she said innocently. "Mommy does that mean I have to love daddy too?" She dropped her chin on her chest.

Sue Ellen took Sissy's chin in her hand, raising her face to look at her. "Sissy, look at me, yes honey, that means daddy too. I know he makes it hard for you when he gets mad at you. But honey, he needs all the love and forgiveness we can give him. It's going to take time honey, but he will soften up. You wait and see. You just keep being the sweet little Angel you are and I will keep your daddy in line. Now lets go home." Sue Ellen said as she slid out of the booth.

"OK, Mommy." Sissy said as she took Sue Ellen's hand to leave.

When Sue Ellen and Sissy arrived home by cab Billy Joe was not at home. She was relieved that he wasn't home. When Sue Ellen and Sissy went into the house Sue Ellen's jaw dropped as she saw the big basket of red roses sitting on the kitchen table. Next to the roses was a pink teddy bear. Sue Ellen walked over to the table, a puzzled look on her face, as she picked up the large envelope that was in front of the teddy bear. She opened it. It contained a card.

The card read on the front "I Love You". Inside as she opened it, it read "I'm sorry, Please forgive me. The bear is for Sissy, tell her I'm sorry. I Swear I will never hit Sissy or you ever again. I don't want to lose you Sue Ellen. You are my life. I can't live without you. I want us to be a family. I don't know what comes over me, I just get mad and I don't think. But I'm going to try to do better, I promise. I won't be home tonight. I went fishing. I thought it will give us time to sort things out. I will see you in the morning. Love, Billy Joe.

Sue Ellen had to sit down, she couldn't believe what she was reading. Feelings of shock, happiness, and wonder flooded over her. Could this mean that Billy Joe is really going to try to change? She thought to herself. She held the card against her chest and smiled. She reached for the Bear.

"Sissy, this is for you. It's from daddy. He said to tell you he is sorry for hitting you today." She said handing the Bear to Sissy.

Sissy took the Bear, she stared at it blankly.

"What are you going to call the Bear?" Sue Ellen asked.

Sissy put the Bear back on the table. "I don't want it. I want my Angel." Sissy pouted, then she turned and ran to her room crying. Sissy threw herself on her bed burying her face in her pillow sobbing.

Sue Ellen followed her into the room; she sat next to Sissy on the bed. "Don't cry, Honey. I told you we would look for your doll, and we will."

"Can we go now?" Sissy said rolling over to face her mother.

"I can't see why not. Only if you stop crying, then we will go look. OK?" Sue Ellen said softly. Sissy sat up rubbing her eyes with her palms. "Thank you Mommy. I love you so much." Sissy said giving Sue Ellen a big hug around her neck.

"Well we better be going if we want to find her before it gets dark." Sue Ellen and Sissy started out the kitchen door just as Margie was coming up the porch steps.

"Hey girls, where you off to? Margie said smiling.

"Sissy lost her doll in the field. We were just going to look for it. Want to come?" Sue Ellen asked.

"Sure. I know how important Angel is to Sissy." Margie replied.

The three of them headed for the field in back of Sue Ellen's house. They searched the field for about thirty minutes with no luck finding the doll.

"Oh Mommy, she's gone. Where could she be?" Sissy cried.

"Oh Honey, don't cry, she has got to be here somewhere, let's just keep looking. We will find her, I'm sure of it."

"Sue Ellen, look on the fence. Isn't that the doll?" Margie said pointing at the doll hanging on the fence by a red ribbon tied around her waist to the fence post.

"ANGEL!" Sissy cried out with delight.

"Well, I'll be." Sue Ellen said as she took the doll down, giving it to Sissy.

CHAPTER TWENTY-TWO.

Billy Joe, Red Avery and Ray Ray Smith got out the truck at the lake. They took out their fishing poles from the back of Billy Joe's truck.

"Ray Ray, you get the gear and the bait. Billy Joe and me will get the beer." Red said as he grabbed a case of beer off the truck.

"Billy Joe this was a great idea you had. I ain't been fishin in a coon's age." Ray Ray said as he picked up the poles and bait bucket.

"I just needed to relax and fishin helps me do that." Billy Joe said as he put a case of beer on his shoulder.

They headed down the path to Billy Joe's favorite fishing spot. They walked through the tall grass that stood waist high on each side of the path. About a quarter of a mile to the fishing spot Billy Joe stopped abruptly. He sat the case of beer he was carrying on his shoulder on the ground.

"What's wrong, man? I almost ran over you." Red said as he too dropped his case of beer down off his shoulder.

"Over there." Billy Joe nodded his head in the direction of his fishing spot.

"I'll be damned. Them fucking niggers think they can go anywhere a white man goes." Red said spitting tobacco juice out the side of his mouth to the ground.

"Well what you want to do? Run them off?" Red asked Billy Joe who seemed frozen where he stood. "Well?" Red asked again.

"Yes I am. They ain't never comin back." Billy Joe finally spoke as he took his gun from his waistband of his jeans. He then walked up quickly behind the colored man who was sitting next to his twelve year old son, fishing in the lake. Billy Joe fired his gun into the back of the man's head. Then he shot the boy who had turned to look at Billy Joe with horror and disbelief as he saw his father fall forward in to the lake. "Daddy!" The boy screamed. Then Billy Joe shot the boy between the eyes. The boy fell backwards, he died instantly as did his father whose body was now floating in the lake. Billy Joe picked the boy up and tossed his body into the lake with his father. Billy Joe turned to Red. "Lets go upstream, I ain't sittin where a nigger has sat."

Billy Joe, Red and Ray Ray went to a clearing upstream a few hundred yards from where the man and his son's bodies were still floating in the Lake. The three of them sat on the bank fishing and drinking beer.

"Damn, I didn't know a nigger could float that long." Billy Joe said as he took another swig from his beer. He could still see the two bodies floating in the lake, as they bobbed up and down like a cork.

"You know we been here three hours and we haven't had one bite. I think those two niggers you shot, Billy Joe, are scarin the fish away." Red said lighting up a cigar.

"Ray Ray, hand me another beer." Billy Joe asked.

"Sorry Billy Joe, I gave you the last one a while ago." Ray Ray answered.

"Shit, I need another beer. Hell, let's go to the bar, the fish ain't biting anyway. Whatayou say, guys? You wanta go?" Billy Joe suggested.

"Hell, why not?" Red said pulling in his pole. They gathered up their empty beer bottles, putting them back into the cases to be returned for a refund. They headed back to Billy Joe's truck. They drove to a little bar called the Spot out on old Highway Thirty. The three of them spent a few hours drinking in the bar then they decided to buy a couple more cases of beer and go to another lake to fish. It was dark when they came out to Billy Joe's truck. Ray Ray was pretty drunk so they left him climb into the bed and sleep it off. He passed out on his sleeping bag. Red rode up front with Billy Joe. Billy Joe squealed his tires as he drove onto the highway. Billy Joe drove about seven miles down the highway; he turned off onto a dirt road that was a short cut to Hunter's Point. He knew the fishing was good there. He had fished the lake many times before. As they turned down the dirt road they passed by a church that sat nestled in the trees just off the road a half mile down. Billy Joe slowed down as his headlights shined on two dark figures on the side of the road.

It was a fifteen year old colored boy named Ernest Polke, and his twelve year old sister Amanda. Ernest was walking his sister home from choir practice at the church.

"Hey Red, let's have us some fun." Billy Joe said.

"Yeah, why not? You wanta play with the nigger kids?" Red jested.

Billy Joe pulled his truck alongside Ernest and Amanda. "Hi kids, you want a ride?" Red asked smiling at them through the truck window.

"Thank you, sir, but we just live up the lane there." Ernest said smiling back at Red.

"Well, my friends and I are going fishing and we aren't sure if we are going the right way." Red said as Billy Joe got out of the truck quickly walking around the back coming up behind Ernest as he grabbed Amanda by the wrist. Amanda screamed, Ernest turned to his screaming sister, a surprised look on his face as he saw the gun in Billy Joe's hand. Before he could utter a word Billy Joe shot Ernest in the stomach. He dropped to his knees, then fell forward face down on the grass. Red opened his door and Billy Joe shoved Amanda at Red who pulled her into the truck. Billy Joe jumped back into his truck and drove off with the crying, screaming Amanda. Leaving Ernest for dead alongside the road. Billy Joe drove past the lake, then turning onto a dirt road that led to the highway. He then drove another five miles to a dirt road that led to an old shack in a woods. Ray Ray was still passed out in the back of the truck unaware of what had occurred. Billy Joe stopped the truck in front of the old run down shack. He got out and helped Red drag Amanda inside.

They threw her down on the dirty floor. She was sobbing and begging them not to hurt her and to let her go home. Billy Joe looked down at her as he unbuckled his belt taking off his shirt and jeans after removing his boots. He stood there naked except for his socks.

"Shut Up Bitch." He yelled at the girl as he ripped off her clothing. "Red, hold her down so I can fuck her, or do you want to go first?" He asked Red.

"Na, you go ahead. I got sober up a little more before I can get it up." He grunted.

Billy Joe got on his knees between her legs forcing them apart. Then he thrust himself violently, ripping and tearing her vagina as he made his way inside her. She cried out with screaming pain. That only excited Billy Joe more. He began biting her on her undeveloped breast. She began going into shock. Her cries became gurgling sounds. Her eyes had a glazed look as she just layed there not moving.

Billy Joe climaxed. He went limp for a moment, breathing heavy as he got off the top of Amanda. He looked down at his penis as it dripped with her blood. "Shit. Look at this. That bitch bled all over me." He said as he picked up his pants taking out his hanky to clean himself. "I thought all nigger bitches were well broke in by the time they're nine." Billy Joe commented as he wiped himself off.

"Well, I guess you got a cherry." Red joked.

"Well, it's your turn, I'm going out to the truck and get me a beer." Billy Joe said as he headed for the door.

"Hey wake up Ray Ray. He might want a piece of this." Red said as Billy Joe went out the door still naked.

"Hey, Ray Ray, wake up." Billy Joe said as he shook the sleeping Ray Ray.

"Wha... What? Come on, man, let me sleep." He said rubbing his eyes, then folding his arms as he started to snuggle back in to a sleep position. Then suddenly he opened his eyes and sat upright looking at Billy Joe. "Hey man. What the hell. Why are you naked?" He asked with wonder on his face.

"We got pussy, man. That's why I woke you up. You want some?" Billy Joe asked as he opened a bottle of beer.

"You guys got a woman?" He asked surprised.

"Yeah, come on before Red gets it all." Billy Joe laughed.

"I don't know, man. I got pretty drunk. I will give it a try." He said as he climbed out the back of the truck.

He followed Billy Joe into the shack. Red was just finishing with the girl when they walked in. Ray Ray stood there staring at the lifeless little girl on the floor.

"She ain't nothin but a little girl. She can't be more than eleven or twelve." Ray Ray said with disgust in his voice.

"So what?" Billy Joe snapped. "She ain't nothin but a nigger, that's the only thing they're good for anyway." Billy Joe added.

"I'm going back to the truck, I ain't havin nothing to do with raping a little kid." Ray Ray said angrily.

"What makes the difference? A pussy is a pussy. Not unless you're just a little soft on niggers." Billy Joe snarled.

"I'm not soft on niggers, but a kid is a kid, what if that was your kid lying on the floor? You wouldn't be doing this, now would you?" Ray Ray said.

"Hell, yes I would. I would do mine now if I could." Billy Joe said.

"Your Sick. I'm going back to the truck." He turned and walked out.

Ray Ray heard Billy Joe and Red laughing as he walked off the porch. He stood by the truck trying to clear his head. He took out his sleeping bag and went to the back of the shack. He knew that Billy Joe might kill the little girl when they were finished with her. He frantically tried to think of what to do as he looked around the shack outside. He could hear Red and Billy Joe inside.

"Hey Red, you ever fuck someone in the ass?" Billy Joe asked.

"No, I was going to do it with Betty the Pig. But I ran out of staying power."

"Well, here's your chance." Billy Joe laughed.

Red pulled the girl's buttocks up to him. He frantically pumped, but he couldn't penetrate her. "Damn this is hard to do. I can't get my dick in." Red growled.

"Want me to get it open for you?" Billy Joe grinned.

"Auh, what the hell? Why not? I sures hell can't do it." Red said as he gave up trying.

Billy Joe grabbed the girl's waist forcing buttocks apart, then with a hard thrust he penetrated her rectum. He went wild as he pumped fast as he could. "Hell, yes, I'm coming! Auh, oh, fuck this is great. Come on, Red, get ready. I got her hole open for you." He said as he let go of her.

Red took his turn, he was able to slip his penis in more easily as he pumped. He came fast with a shout. "Oh man, Billy Joe, you're right, ain't nothin like fucking like this. Wow." He groaned as he went limp. Billy Joe was dressed when Red finished with girl.

"You done with her?" Billy Joe asked as he pulled out his gun.

"Yeah, man. I don't know how you do it. You came four times to my two. How do you do it?" Red asked.

"I don't know, I just like to fuck, I guess." He answered.

"Well now what?" Red asked.

"I will shoot her, and then we can go fishing."

"Why can't we just leave her here?" Red asked.

"Because she can identify us, that's why." Billy Joe answered seriously.

"Yeah, I guess you're right." Red answered.

Billy Joe raised his gun to take aim. At that moment Ray Ray came in. "Wait. It's my turn." He said.

"I thought you said you didn't fuck kids." Billy Joe said mockingly.

"I changed my mind. "I can't do anything in front of you guys, though. I got to be alone with her." Ray Ray said nervously.

"OK. Red and I will wait outside. I need a beer anyway. Don't take too long." Billy Joe laughed as he and Red went outside.

Ray Ray bent down on one knee to look at the little girl. "You hang on, darlin, I'm going to get you some help." He went to the back door of the shack. He picked up his sleeping bag that he stashed there moments before. He took it back to Amanda. He picked her up and gently slipped her lifeless body in to it. Tears welled in his eyes as he saw what they had done to her. He stood up and went out to the truck. "You fucking assholes. You left me a dead body." He said trying to sound offended.

"You sure?" Billy Joe asked, surprise in his voice.

"Yes, I'm sure. She wasn't breathing and her heart wasn't beating and she was stone cold." He lied.

"Let's go make sure." Billy Joe said.

"I'm telling you she is dead. I know dead when I see it." Ray Ray said. "Save your bullets."

"Billy Joe. I believe Ray Ray. Lets get the fuck out of here." Red said.

"Yeah, I guess you're right. Let's go have some fun." Billy Joe said as he got into his truck to leave.

"Let's go back to the bar out on the highway." Ray Ray said.

"Yeah, that sounds good." Red said smiling.

"OK. We are on our way." Billy Joe said, putting the truck in gear, heading back to the highway.

It took Billy Joe less than fifteen minutes to get to the bar. The three of them got out of the truck and went into the bar. Ray Ray stopped by the payphone just inside the door.

"Hey guys, I'll be in in a minute, I need to call home. MaryAnn has been sick, I just want to check on her to see how she's feeling. OK?" He said holding the receiver in his hand as he dug in his pocket for change with his free hand.

Billy Joe gave him a hard stare for a moment. "You want us to order for you?" Billy Joe asked.

"Yeah, order me a Blue Ribbon." Ray Ray said trying not to sound nervous.

"Come on, Billy Joe, I'm thirsty, let him call his mommy. You know he's pussy whipped." Red chuckled as he tugged on Billy Joe's arm.

"Just don't take too long." Billy Joe said seriously. Then he went inside the bar with Red. Ray Ray watched to make sure Billy Joe and Red went inside.

Once they were out of sight, Ray Ray dropped his dime in the phone, then dialed the operator. "Hello, operator. This is an emergency. Connect me with the Sheriff's department please." The operator put the call through.

"Sheriff's department. How may I help you?" A mans voice said over the phone.

"Yeah, listen. You need to send someone out to an old shack in the Coonridge Woods. It's the first dirt road five miles in, off old highway 18. There is a little girl about eleven or twelve inside. She has been raped."

"OK, what is your name, sir?" The man asked.

"Never mind my name, just get someone over there to help her. She is bleeding badly. She needs help now." Ray Ray yelled, then he hung up the phone. He felt sick to his stomach. He couldn't get the sight of the little girl out of his mind. In his heart he wanted to kill Billy Joe and Red for hurting the little girl. He was a member in Red's Klan, but he couldn't see the honor in raping and killing children. He knew in his heart that he was leaving the Klan and that he didn't want anything more to do with Billy Joe or Red.

He went in to the bar. He saw Red and Billy Joe sitting at a table. He went over to them. He sat down. "This beer mine?" He asked as he picked up the bottle of Blue Ribbon.

"Yeah, man." Red said.

"Look guys, I need to go home. Ann is feeling worse. I need to be there to take care of my girls."

"Can't you get someone to stay with her?" Billy Joe asked.

"No, I need to be there. I called a cab, no need for you guys to change your plans." Ray Ray said as he took a drink from his bottle.

"Hey, buddy. We can take you home. Ain't that right, Billy Joe?" Red said.

"Yeah. We can take you." Billy Joe said.

"NO, NO. You guys go ahead and have some fun. The cab is on it's way." Ray Ray insisted.

"Fun, hell, we been havin nothin but fun." Red laughed.

"Someone call a cab?" The bartender yelled out.

"Yeah, I did." Ray Ray said, getting up from the table. "Look guys maybe we can do this again sometime." Ray Ray said starting to walk away.

"Yeah, next time." Billy Joe said coldly.

Billy Joe watched Ray Ray as he went out the door with the cab driver.

"I don't trust that little son of a bitch." Billy Joe said leaning over the table to Red so Red could hear him.

"Auh, he is OK. He is just young and hen pecked by his wife." Red said in a slurred voice. "Come on, Billy Joe, lighten up. What do you want to do now?" Red said as he lit his cigar.

"I want to kill me some more niggers." Billy Joe snarled.

"DAMN, boy. You already killed four of them today." Red replied.

"So I want to get me a few more, that all right with you?" Billy Joe said vengefully.

"Hell, it's OK with me. But where are we going to find us some?" Red asked.

"I know just the place." Billy Joe said with excitement in his voice.

"Well let's go then." Red said, swigging down the last of his beer.

Billy Joe and Red left the bar. Billy Joe drove down the highway to a crossroad that led to Route 59. On that corner was an Esso gas station. He pulled his truck up to the gas pump. An old skinny man with grey hair came over to the pump.

"You want I should fill her up?" He asked.

"Yeah, do you have a pay phone here?" Billy Joe asked.

"It's over there on the side of the building." The old man pointed.

"Thanks." Billy Joe said as went to find the phone.

Ten minutes later Billy Joe returned to the truck where Red sat patiently waiting for him.

"That will be three dollars." The old man said as Billy Joe got in his truck.

Billy Joe reached in his wallet and handed the old man the money for the gas. Billy Joe drove his truck across the road and parked.

"Why we stoppin here?" Red asked.

"We are stopping here to wait on a few of the guys I called." Billy Joe grinned wide.

"What the hell for?" Red asked raising an eye brow.

"You said you wanted to have some more fun, didn't you?" Billy Joe asked.

"Well, yes. But what do we need the guys for?" Red asked sounding even more curious now.

"I got me a plan." Billy Joe smiled.

"You gonna let me in on this plan?" Red asked.

"Well, how would you like to get twenty or thirty niggers at one time?" Billy Joe asked being mysterious.

"Hell, yes. What you got in mind?" Red asked sounding anxious.

"Well, I called the Gum brothers, Perry Weeks, and Jimmy Parks and his two brother's Ray and Ricky. Jimmy is bringin an extra twelve gauge for you." Billy Joe said excitedly. "Now when the guys all get here we are going to drive over to that road house nigger bar. You know that one they call the Sugar Shack just outside old nigger town." Billy Joe explained to Red.

"Yeah, yeah. Then what?" Red said with excitement.

"We are going to walk in and scare them a little, you know, play with them. Then we will kill them all. It's perfect. No one will never know what's going on because it sets out off the road about a mile from anything. So there won't be any pain in the ass do gooder calling the Sheriff on us. It's perfect." Billy Joe said excitedly. His eyes lit up like a little kid at Christmas time.

Jimmy Parks and his brother's were the first to arrive thirty minutes later.

"Hey, Billy Joe. What's up man?" Jimmy said as he came up to Billy Joe's truck.

"We are going nigger hopping. Did you bring the gun?" Billy Joe said smiling.

"Yeah, it's in my car's trunk. So where we going?" Jimmy asked.

"Out to that old nigger bar called the Sugar Shack." Billy Joe answered him as he looked to see Red crossing the road coming towards him and Jimmy. Red had went to buy himself some cigars from the gas station where they had bought their gas earlier.

"Hey, Jimmy glad you could make it. Where's Ricky?" Red asked as he shook hands with Jimmy.

"He's in the car." Jimmy answered.

Just then Perry Weeks pulled up in his Ford truck with Melvin Gum sitting on the passenger side. Billy Joe got out of his truck and walked back to Perry's truck who was now parked behind Jimmy's car.

"Are you ready to have some fun?" Billy Joe said with a big grin on his face.

"Hell, yes. I'm always ready to go nigger huntin." Perry laughed.

"Hey Melvin, where's your brother?" Billy Joe asked looking in to the truck.

"He wouldn't come. He's still mad at you, man". Melvin said with a serious tone.

"He's still mad at me?" Billy Joe said.

"Yepp. He will get over it. Just got to give him some time. You know how he is." Melvin said.

"Well, fuck him. I don't give a shit if he never gets over it. Who needs him?" Billy Joe said angrily. "Well let's get going. We got us a little over three hours to get this done. So you guys just follow me." Billy Joe said, then he turned and went to his truck.

CHAPTER TWENTY-THREE

The Reverend Ike James was standing on the steps of his tiny church. He was saying goodnight to the remaining choir members as they left. He was a balding, short, heavy-set black man, in his late fifties. Deacon John Hinkel was standing next to him. It was a little after seven P.M. Suddenly the sounds of crickets chirping in the woods and the chatter of the children and their parents leaving was overtaken by a loud cracking sound. Everyone became silent as their eyes were focused in the direction of the loud noise. Even the crickets were still.

"That sounded like gun fire." Reverend James said with concern in his voice.

"Maybe not Reverend, it could be a backfire from that old pickup that passed by a few minutes ago." Deacon Hinkel said.

"Didn't the Polke children walk that way a little while ago?" Reverend James said even more concern in his voice now.

"John, let's you and me take a ride in my car." Reverend James said as he went down the steps.

"Yeah sure. But where we goin'?" The deacon asked.

"I want to make sure the Polke children got home all right." The Reverend said as he opened the car door of his forty-nine Buick. Deacon Hinkel who was tall and thin, and very dark skinned climbed in next to the Reverend on the passenger side front seat. They drove down the road in the direction of where they heard what could have been a backfire or a gunshot. They could see taillights in a far distance ahead of them.

"See what I tell you, that's probably that old pickup I saw. It probably just back fired." The deacon said.

Then suddenly the Reverend's car lights shined on something lying in the ditch alongside the road.

"There. What's that?" The Reverend said pointing to the side of the road as he stopped his car.

"Oh My God." He moaned as he got out of his car and walked over to the ditch. He could see it was a young boy lying face down.

"Oh Lordy Lordy." The Reverend cried out as he knelt down beside the boy, rolling him over. "Its Ernest Polke, and he's been shot." He yelled out to John who seemed to be frozen in the front seat of the car.

"JOHN, help me. John, please get out of the car and help me."

John numbly got out of the car. He went over to kneel down by the boy and Reverend James who was holding the boy in his arms.

"Help me get him into the car, he needs a doctor now." Reverend James said.

Ernest was barely conscious. He was mumbling his sister's name. "Amanda, they took Amanda." He kept saying, then he passed out completely.

"John, help me get him to the car, he's lost a lot of blood."

"Doc Jacob's place is the closest. We can take him there." John said as he lifted the boy by the legs.

"We need to call the Sheriff when we get there and get somebody to get back out here to find Amanda." The Reverend said as he carried the boy by the shoulders.

"John, you take him to the doctor's, and I will stay here and look for Amanda." John said as he helped put the boy in the back seat of the old Buick.

"OK, but you be careful, I will get some men together to come out here and help you. You might want to go up the lane over there and let the Polke's know what's happened to their children."

"I will do that Ike, now you just get him to the Doc's." John said closing the car door.

The Reverend turned the old Buick around in the road and sped off heading for Doctor Jacob's house. Doctor Jacob was an old country doctor who took care of most of the colored folks in the valley. Doctor Jacobs was just settling down in his easy chair to read his newspaper. He and his wife had just finished dinner moments before when suddenly he heard the honking of Reverend James's old Buick's horn. Doctor Jacobs got back up from his chair to go to his front door. He ran his fingers through his thick white hair as he went to open the door. The Reverend James stopped his car in the driveway. He jumped out leavin his car door open. He ran to the front porch screaming out the Doctor's name. "DOCTOR JACOB, PLEASE HELP ME, DOCTOR JACOB." The Reverend called out as he ran up the front porch steps.

Doctor Jacob opened his front door. He flipped on the porch light to see Reverend James nearly out of breath, fear written on his tear streaked face.

"Reverend James, is that you? Are you hurt?" He asked as took hold of the Reverend as he was gasping hard to catch his breath.

"NO, no, it's it's the Polke boy. HE, HE'S been SHOT." The Reverend said still gasping pointing at his car as he pulled on the doctor's shirt.

"The Polke boy, how did he get shot?" He asked the Reverend as he started towards the car, then he called to his wife. "ANNA, come quick. I may need some help, get a wheel chair." He opened the back door of the Buick. He looked inside at the Polke boy's ashen face from the loss of blood.

"I need to operate right away, I don't know if I can save him. He has lost a lot of blood."

"Oh my, isn't that Ernest Polke ?" Anna asked as she stopped the wheelchair to see who was lying on the back seat.

"Yes. Anna, do we have any plasma on hand?" The Doctor asked.

"Yes I think we have at least ten units. If that's not enough, I could call the hospital for more." She said as she helped her husband move the boy to the wheel chair.

"There's no time. I need you to assist. Reverend, you can call for me. Tell them who it is for and tell them to send it over by ambulance. The number is on my desk in the office. Has the boy's parents been notified?"

"I left the Deacon Hinkel to do that. I need to call the Sheriff too." The Reverend said as they hurried inside with the boy. The three of them lifted the boy onto a table in one of his exam rooms in the rear of his house where his office was located.

"Lets get his clothing off, Anna."

She cut off his clothes with scissors, then she irrigated his wound with a sterile wash, then covered him with sterile sheets. Her and her husband washed with the antiseptic and gloved and gowned up. Doctor Jacobs gave the boy a spinal, and began operating on him. It took Doctor Jacobs four hours to repair the damage Billy Joe's bullet had caused.

"Anna, after I finish here, I want you to cross match his blood and get some here right away.

Anna entered the office to find the Reverend James holding hands with the Polke boy's parents. They were encircled kneeling in prayer.

"Lord please hear our prayer. We wants to ask you to please let Curtis and Esther Polke have their child Ernest live through this. Lord we ask you to keep their other child, little Amanda safe and bring her back to the loving arms of her mother and father. We are your humble servants who are asking you to help us through these troubled times. Amen."

The three of them stood up after the Reverend finished the prayer. Esther saw Anna. Their eyes met. Anna could see the pain and worry in Esther's red tear filled eyes.

"Miss Anna, my boy, is my boy gonna be all right? Please tell me." She asked in a broken voice.

"I hope so, Esther. The doctor is doing everything he can to keep him alive. I have to call the hospital now, he has lost a lot of blood. I need to check on his blood type and have the hospital send some to us." Anna said taking Esther's hands in hers. "We all need to pray to God to help us. My husband is doing everything in his power to save your son. But it also has to be God's will to help too. He helps through our prayers. I must go now I have to hurry I need to help my husband."

"I know you and the doctor will do your best to save my Ernest." Esther said as her husband came up putting his arm around her shoulder steering her back to the sofa to sit down. Suddenly the office door opened.

Sheriff Combs stepped inside. "Esther, Curtis, Reverend." He said as he took his hat off.

"You found our baby girl?" Esther asked as she stood up.

"I'm sorry, Esther. Not yet but we are still looking. I have all my men out there and there must be a hundred of your neighbors out there looking for her. We will find her, I promise." He said putting his arm around her shoulder.

"Is there any word on Ernest yet?" He asked with deep concern in his voice.

"He is still in the operating room with the doctor." Reverend James answered.

"Sheriff Combs, can I help you?" Anna said as she noticed him standing in the doorway.

"Has the Doc removed the bullet yet?" He asked.

"Far as I know he hasn't found it yet." She answered.

"Tell him to keep it for me when he does."

"I will tell him." Anna answered. She started to say something else when the phone rang. "Excuse me," she said as she went to answer the phone.

"Doctor Jacob's office. Yes, hold on, he is in the outer office, I will get him. Sheriff Combs, it's your office." Anna called out.

She handed him the phone as he came in. "I have to get back in with the doctor."

He took the receiver from her. "Sheriff Combs here." He said as he spoke into the receiver.

"Sheriff, we just got a call from a man. He wouldn't give his name. He said there's a little girl up at the old hunter's shack in the woods just off the old highway. He said she has been raped." The dispatcher's voice said with a touch of anger.

"Is she still alive?" Combs asked.

"Don't know Sheriff." He said she was when he called, but said she was in a bad way."

"OK I'm on my way, send out another car and see if you can get an ambulance out there."

"Right away Sheriff." Combs hung up the phone. He went back into the waiting room. "Reverend James, would you mind taking a ride with me?" Combs asked.

"I don't mind, but I think I'm needed here." He replied.

"I don't think Mr. and Mrs. Polke would mind, I really need you."

"Well Sheriff, since you put it that way."

"Curtis, Esther, you gonna be OK till I get back?"

"Of course Reverend. If the Sheriff needs you, you go on."

"We be OK." Esther said smiling.

"OK, don't forget to knock on the door to let Miss Anna know when the blood gets here." He remind Esther.

"I will, now you better get going."

"She is right, Reverend." Combs said trying to hurry the Reverend.

They left the doctor's office. As they got into the Sheriff's car Combs looked over to Reverend James.

"I didn't want to tell you in front of them, but I think we may have found their little girl."

"That's wonderful. But don't you think they should know?" The Reverend said with a puzzled look.

"I didn't want to tell them, because it may not be Amanda, and this little girl has been raped, according to an anonymous caller. I needed you to come to identify her. I don't know if she is alive or dead." The Sheriff said grimly.

"I see, you're right, it would only have upset them. They are going through enough pain right now." Reverend James said as the Sheriff drove down the road, headed for the place where the girl was.

The rusted hinges creaked as the door to the old shack slowly swung open. "Hello. Anybody in here?" Sheriff Combs said shining his flashlight inside the shack.

"Shine the light back." Reverend James said as he spotted the sleeping bag on the floor. Sheriff Combs shined the light on the bag. As he approached the bag he bent down pulling the top back. He looked down to see cold dead stare of the little girl's brown eyes. Her face was swollen, her skin color was gray. "Oh Lord God Why?" What kind of man could have done such a thing to a sweet little child?" Reverend James moaned as he choked back the tears.

"Not a man, Reverend, it took a real animal to do something like this." Combs said, anger building in his voice.

"Can we move her out of this wet stuff on the floor, Sheriff?" The reverend asked as he felt his shoes slide as he lifted his feet.

"It kind of feels like oil."

"I'm sorry, Reverend. We can't move her yet. The wet stuff your standing in, its her blood. I'm afraid she bled out. Whoever did this must have ripped a main artery. It looks like she bled to death. Maybe it would be better if you waited outside. I need to examine her body closer, and take photos. Come on, I need to get my camera anyway. I will stay with you for a little while. My deputies should be here in a few moments. They will be leading the ambulance in." Sheriff Combs said as he put his arm around the Reverend's shoulder leading him outside. They went outside to Sheriff Combs' car. He went to the rear of the car, opened the trunk, taking out his camera and a set of portable battery operated floodlights. He looked up as he saw the headlights coming down the dirt road towards them. It was the deputy's car and the ambulance following close behind with its red lights flashing. They came to a stop behind his car. The deputy got out. "I got here as quick as I could. Is it that little girl?" The Deputy asked.

"Yes, I'm afraid so. Have the ambulance boys wait here. Then you come inside with me. But first you rope off the area." The Sheriff instructed.

"Sheriff, is the little girl dead?" The deputy asked.

"Yes. Now let's get this over with." He said in a low voice.

The room of the shack was illuminated with bright light from the portables. The room was stifled with the smell of blood. The deputy came in as Sheriff Combs pulled the sleeping bag back exposing Amanda's entire body. The deputy became violently sick as he ran back out the door to vomit.

"Butler. Get back in here. Put your hanky around your nose." Sheriff Combs called out to him as he loaded his camera with film. The deputy came back in. He tied his handkerchief around his face, with his western style hat on he looked like an old time cowboy bandit.

"The smell, how can you stand it?" He said trying to choke back the queasy feeling in his stomach.

"You get used to it after a while. It will get worse if we take longer than two hours to get this done and get her to the morgue." Combs said as he snapped a photo.

"Are those bite marks on her?" Butler asked as he looked closer.

"Yep. Do they remind you of another victim we had a while back?" Combs said as he took another picture.

"Yes, now that you mention it. That lady we found out on the old road. Augh, what was her name,? Flin, no it was Flint. Betty Flint, that was it. Betty Flint. Sheriff, you think this is the work of the same person or persons?" Butler asked.

"Yes I do. There is more than one involved, but only one that is really a violent animal. We have got to find this guy before he rapes and kills again. And he will." Combs said.

"What makes a man do something like this?" Butler asked shaking his head in disgust as he stared at the little girl's body.

"I don't know. All I do know he has to be stopped." Combs answered.

"You know he likes to rape his victims, but why torture them by biting and burning them with cigarettes?" Butler pointed out.

"Don't forget he likes to beat them to a pulp and then shoot them. But why didn't he shoot this little girl, or Mrs. Flint?" Combs said thoughtfully.

"Maybe he just likes to see them suffer." Butler added.

"Maybe, well, lets hurry up and finish here so we can get this little girl out of here." He began to finish taking crime scene photos and his deputy searched for any clues that might have been left behind by the men responsible.

CHAPTER TWENTY-FOUR

Ossie Peaters, seventeen, and his younger brother Jeffry, sixteen, along with Monroe Helms, and Josh Hamsy, both seventeen, went into the Sugar Shack Bar. The four hundred pound bartender Sugar Brown sat on a stool behind the bar, arms folded, puffing on a big Havana cigar. He was also the owner of the bar.

"Now what in the hell you young fools wants?" He said in a gruff voice.

"We come in to gets us a beer, sir." Ossie said smugly.

"Is that a fact? I tells you what, you best get your young asses on out here. You's come back for beers whens you ens old nuff to grow hair round them peach fuzz lips. Now you gets your asses on out here, don't make me comes over this bar and come upside your head with my club." He said firmly as he laid a baseball bat on the bar. The boys knew he meant every word, so they turned and nearly ran out the door to their car. The boys got into the car and kicked back, smoking cigarettes and listening to the car's radio. They were hoping they would see someone they knew so they could get them to buy some beer for them. Monroe flicked his cigarette out the car window.

"Man, let's get out of here. Ain't nobody we knows gonna come. Let's just go cruzen."

"Shhhh. Someone's comin." Jeffery said pointing to the headlights turning into the driveway.

"Think it Jack or Marty?" Ossie asked.

"Na. They don't gots pickups." Josh replied as he watched them pull in and stop.

"Shit, man. Everybody get down." Monroe said in a panic as he crouched down, turning off the radio.

"What the hell you doin, man?" Ossie said wondering what was going on.

"Quiet, man." Monroe said in a loud whisper. "It's the Klan Man and they goin into Sugar's."

"What you think they goin in there for?" Jeffry asked.

"Well you can bet it ain't to go dancing." Monroe answered. All the men went inside wearing hoods. Suddenly the boys heard a shot gun go off.

"Shit, man, start the car let's get the hell out of here." Jeffry said in a panicky voice.

"Na, man, wait." Monroe said.

"You crazy, man? They are shooting folks in there and I don't want to be one of them." Ossie said as he fumbled with his car keys. His hands shook uncontrollably as he tried to turn the ignition. Monroe grabbed his hand to stop him from starting the car.

"NO, man. If you start this car those two Klansmen standing over there will shoot us, and if they miss they will chase us till they catch us."

"Then what we gonna do, man?" We can't stay here, they might walk over here, find us and still shoot us." Ossie said crying now with fear.

"Look we can't open the door. They might see the overhead light, so we need to very quiet, climb out the windows on your side of the car and maybe we can sneak out through the woods there and go somewhere for help.

"Sounds good to me. Anything is better than stayin here waitin to get shot." Josh said nervously.

"OK, let's do it." Ossie said.

"Quietly." Monroe cautioned.

Ossie very quietly slithered out his window to the ground. Then his brother did the same out the back seat window, followed by Josh. Then Monroe climbed out the front window Ossie had exited just moments before. They could hear the screams of some of the women as they heard more gunshots. One by one they ran for the woods and slipped away into the darkness of the night.

In the distance they could hear women screaming and the loud sounds of the gunshots being fired. They ran blindly through the dark woods, their hearts beating faster and faster. Ossie suddenly found himself falling down a hill as he stumbled trying to keep himself upright. He found himself suddenly lying face down in a muddy ditch. For a moment he just laid there the only sounds he could now hear was the loud pounding of his heart, as his blood pumped wildly with the fear he felt.

The other three boys fell down into the ditch with him. Monroe fell on top of Ossie.

"DAMN, man, get off me." Ossie said as he pushed Monroe off him.

"Hey you two, quiet! You want them guys to hear us? You knows if they do they will comes after us and kill us all. Josh said as wiped the mud off.

"We needs to get to somebody to gets them folks and us some help." Josh whispered to the others.

"How? The closest place is five miles from here. I think we needs to stay put till them Klan guys are gone." Jeffry whispered back to Josh.

"By that time those folks back there will be dead." Ossie said in a low whispering voice.

"They are probably dead already." Monroe spoke up in a low sorrowful tone.

"You know if we's get to the road, we can cut through the field at the curve and that will take us to old Mr. Jenks' farm. We can't be seen by anyone and we save at least a mile, maybe even two. And he even gots a phone. We could call the Sheriff from there." Josh said.

At that moment the boys' attention went back in the direction of the bar as they heard more shots being fired. The look of fear and sadness for the people inside the bar was written on the expression on their faces.

"What are we waitin for? Let's get the hell out of here." Monroe said as he stood up. The boys made their way to the road, they stayed close to the edge of the woods just in case they had to hide and not be seen by anyone like the Klan that might drive down the road.

Once they made it to the open field they felt relief from some of the fear they felt inside them. The farther they walked the better they felt. They knew they were headed in the direction of safety. But the sounds of the screams and gunshots still rang out in their ears and the thoughts of what was happening to all the people inside the bar was like a living nightmare for them.

The boys finally made it to the Jenks' farm. It seemed like they had been walking for five or six hours. But in reality it had only been close to two hours. As the boys approached the back porch of the old two story saltbox style house, with its peeling paint. The floorboards creaked when they stepped on to it. Monroe began pounding with hand on the back door. All the boys began calling out Mr. Jenks by name. "MR. JENKS, MR. JENKS, HELP US, PLEASE, MR. JENKS COME TO THE DOOR."

Billy Joe and Red Avery were the first to enter the Sugar Shack Bar. Sugar looked up startled at seeing the hooded men. "We's don't wants no troubles, man." Sugar said as he tried to reach for a gun he kept under the bar.

"We ain't here for trouble, you old fat nigger. We are here for fun. Show him, Red." Billy Joe said smiling under his hood as he hunched Red on the arm.

Red raised his twelve gauge and fired at Sugar. Sugar tried to duck behind the counter but he wasn't fast enough because of his weight. The blast from the gun caught Sugar in the face and throat. He fell back to the floor behind the bar. Billy Joe went up to the bar, leaned over it looking down at Sugar. He shot him in the head three more times. Then he reached in the cooler and took out two bottles of beer. He tossed one of the beers to Red. Some of the people in the bar just stood frozen in place. Others were screaming, and some tried to run out the back door hoping for safety, only to run into Jimmy and his brother's Ray and Ricky Parks. They opened fire on them as they came out the back door. Perry Weeks and Melvin Gumm stayed out in front of the bar as lookouts.

"I don't think I like this." Perry said to Melvin as he stubbed out his cigarette on the ground with his shoe.

"Me either, that fucking Billy Joe. He's a crazy son of a bitch. This ain't right, man. He gonna get us in trouble, killin all these niggers." Melvin said spitting out a plug of tobacco on the ground.

"You is right, man. Killin one or two don't gets much attention. But they in there killin a whole bar full." Perry said.

"I tell you what, if I see a police car comin I will give them dumb asses inside a holler, then I'm gettin the hell outa here. You with me?" Gumm said.

"You bet your ass I am." Perry replied, as they heard more gunshots go off and more screams and crying.

Billy Joe and the other three men had all the people inside the bar lined against a wall on the far side of the dance floor. Billy Joe paced up and down behind them, poking his gun against their heads as he went one by one down the line. He was glad only with his cowboy boots and his hood.

Billy Joe singles out a heavyset woman in her late forties. He pulls her by the hair away from the wall. She falls down on her knees. She is crying as she looks up at Billy Joe. Fear written on her face as she knew she was about to die. Billy Joe stood in front of her his cold eyes staring down at her. He was smiling under his hood as he waited for her to plead for life. But to his surprise, she didn't, she just sat there on her knees praying.

"Please Mr. don't hurt my Netty." It was her husband speaking up, begging for her life.

"Shut the hell up, nigger." Billy Joe snapped as he hit the man in the face with the butt of his gun. He turned back to Netty, facing her with his naked body. "Suck it bitch." He said as he pushed his penis in her face. Netty looked up at him with contempt as she said to him coldly.

"Mr. you best go on and shoot me, cause there ain't nothin gonna make me suck your filthy dick." She said defiantly.

"You tellin me no, nigger?" He snapped back at her. "Well we will see about that. Ricky, go out to my truck, in the back of the bed you will find a bunch of rope. Bring it in." Billy Joe ordered.

"You got it man." Ricky said as he headed for the door.

"What you got in mind Billy Joe?" Red asked, as he drank from a bottle of Black Velvet.

"We are going to have us a party." Billy Joe said excitedly. "And you and your hubby here are the guests of honor." He said slyly, almost giddy.

Ricky went to Billy Joe's truck to get the rope. "Hey Ricky, what's going on in there?" Melvin Gumm asked.

"Well Billy Joe wants this rope. I think he's going to hang a nigger. Right now he is in there stark naked. He is going to make some fat nigger woman give him a blow job. That Billy Joe, man, he somethin else." Ricky laughed shaking his head. "Hey why don't you guys come in one at a time, and get some of that black pussy before Billy Joe gets it all."

"If it was a more private place I might. But, man, I don't think so, not like this." Melvin said in a serious voice.

"What about you, Perry?"

"I don't think so. Melvin's right. This is too risky. This is gonna make trouble for all of us." Perry said rubbing his chin.

"Well suit yourself, I need to get this rope into Billy Joe." Ricky said as he slung the rope over his shoulder and went back inside.

"You know what? I say we give them fools inside another hour. If they don't come out by then, I say you and I get the hell out of here." Melvin said firmly.

"I agree, you go, I go with you." Perry said in full agreement with Melvin.

"I got the rope, Billy Joe." Ricky said as he came back in.

"Bring it over here." Billy Joe said still holding the gun on Netty. Ricky brought the rope to him. "You know how to make a noose?" Billy Joe asked him.

"You bet. You want me to make one?" Ricky asked.

"Yes there should be eight ten-foot pieces, make them all in to nooses." Billy Joe instructed. "When you get them made throw them over those beams up there." Billy Joe pointed at the big open rafter beams overhead.

It took Ricky only ten minutes to make the hangman's noose. He slung the ropes one by one over the rafter beams.

"Good Job, now pull up a chair under each one." Billy Joe instructed Ricky. "Now lets start with this one." Billy Joe said as he shoved Netty's husband to Ricky.

Netty looked into her husband's tear filled eyes. "I Loves you Netty Brown." He said as Ricky forced him up on a chair, then putting the noose around his neck.

"I love you to Malcom Brown." Netty said as tears streamed down her round dark brown cheeks.

Billy Joe turned back to Netty, coldly stared down at her. "Now it's like this. You said you would rather I shoot you. I could do that right now. But I want something from you and I'm going to get it. If you don't give me the blow job I asked for, well then, I guess I will just have to kick that chair your hubby is standing on right out from under him. Now what's it gonna be?" Billy Joe asked smugly.

"Please don't hurt him." Netty begged tearfully.

"I won't if you do as I ask you to." Billy Joe said as he brushed his penis against her lips. Netty flinched her head back, she saw her husband nod his head then he shut his eyes tight so he wouldn't have to watch.

Netty reluctantly took hold of Billy Joe's penis, she closed her eyes tightly, gagging each time Billy Joe shoved himself deeper into her mouth as he grabbed her hair tightly in his fingers, forcing her head to move the way he wanted. Suddenly he stopped, he pulled away from her.

"Ricky, you want some of this?"

"Hell yeah, man. Hey, you other guys you want to get in on this after she does me?" Ricky called to the others as he undone his jeans as he went over to Netty forcing himself on her.

"You go ahead, Ricky. She's all yours. Your brother and I are going to get it on with this little gal here." Red said as he ripped the clothes off one of the young waitresses. He had hit her so hard with his fist that she lost consciousness. She lie sprawled out on the floor, as Red pushed himself between her legs and was now inside her. Meanwhile Billy Joe was about to rape the other waitress when she had tried to resist him. He hit her upside her head with his gun but she fell backwards striking her head once more on the steel leg of the pool table. Her body convulsed for a moment, then she stopped breathing. She died instantly. Billy Joe angrily picked up her limp body trying to shake her awake. Then he realized she was dead, so he tossed her lifeless body against the wall were it landed in a heap on the floor in a corner. He grabbed another woman in her late twenties. Her name was Viola Watson.

"Shucks, baby, you don't have to grab ole Viola so hard. Sugar Viola takes good good care of you. I really wants to have a nice big white cock like yours. Viola do anything you wants her to do." She cooed to him in a teasing voice. Billy Joe pushed her on her back on top of the pool table. She spread her legs willingly for him as he climbed on top of her. She had already pulled up her dress over her head dropping it to the floor, as Billy Joe thrust himself harder and harder inside her. She wasn't wearing anything under her dress. She was completely naked on the pool table as she stroked Billy Joe's back with her long thin fingers. "Oh baby, for a white boy you sure do knows how to give it to ole Viola. Oh baby, do it to me harder. Her breasts were perfectly round like grapefruits, her nipples stood up becoming very hard.

Billy Joe is pumping faster and faster. Then he starts biting her shoulder.

"Ouch! DAMN, baby you don't has to bite ole Viola. Come on baby, I will come with you. OOH baby bring it on home"

"Shut the fuck up, bitch." Billy Joe said breathing hard as he took her wrist slamming her arms down on the table. Then he began biting her nipples. She screamed out in pain as he bit down as hard as he could. He reached his climax as he bit her nipple off. Then he spit it out in her face. She lie there, screaming and crying, as he climbed off her. She grabbed her bleeding breast. Billy Joe grabbed a beer from behind the bar. He opened it took a swig, then spit it out on the floor. He leaned his back against the bar, then took another drink. Then he noticed Sugar's baseball bat lying on the bar next to him. He picked it up. "WOW. This is a real Louisville slugger. I think I will keep it. Thanks, fatso." He said to Sugar who lay dead on the floor behind the bar. Then one of the men he had standing on a chair next to Netty's husband was laughing out of control. He was laughing so hard tears ran down his cheeks.

Viola was still lying on the pool table crying from the pain in her breast. "Hey nigger. What's so fucking funny?" Billy Joe asked as he stood naked in front of him.

"You man." The man said looking down at Billy Joe still laughing.

"Me? Now what do you find so funny about me?" Billy Joe asked as he leaned on the bat.

"Well you just had ole Viola over there. Around here we calls her Typhoid Mary. I garen'tee you in three days your dick is going to start dripping and running nonstop and you will be climbing the walls when you got to take a piss. She just gave you the clap, man" He started laughing again.

Billy Joe's face turned beet red. Anger building as his veins bulged on his forehead. He sat his beer down on one of the tables. He turned and walked over to the pool table where Viola was now sitting up and crying as she held her breast. Billy Joe held the bat with both hands and swung with all his strength hitting Viola in the forehead. She fell backwards onto the table. He just kept on hitting her head. Billy Joe kept on swinging the bat again and again until Viola's skull and face were so crushed that it turned to a mush like substance. Brains and blood oozed out on to the green felt on the table. Violas face was no longer her own. She was unrecognizable. Finally Billy Joe stopped hitting her. He took a pitcher of beer from one of the tables. He dipped his penis in the beer, then poured the rest on the front of himself. He took a bar towel and wiped himself dry. Then he walked over to the eight men standing on the chairs with the hangman's noose around their necks. Quickly one by one he kicked the chairs out from under them. Netty clenched her teeth as she saw her husband's body jerk and convulse as he hung from the rafter. She jerked her head back and wailed as she got up and tried to hold her husband's body up, so he wouldn't choke from the noose.

"Fuck, man, she bit me." Ricky howled.

Billy Joe grabbed his gun and shot Netty in the head.

"Look what she did. She nearly bit the end of my dick off." Ricky cried out in pain as he held his bleeding penis cupped in his hand. Billy Joe put on his clothes.

"Let's just finish all of these niggers off. I'm bored with all of them."

Red was just finishing up with the waitress for the second time. He and Jimmy Parks, Ricky's brother, had took turns on the waitress.

Billy Joe Started shooting the rest of the people against the wall.

Red and Jimmy fired their shotguns killing the remaining people Billy Joe hadn't killed.

Melvin and Perry came in the front door just as the firing stopped. The bar was filled with the smell of gun smoke and blood. Melvin saw Viola's body lying on the pool table. He saw the bodies of the eight men hanging. To him it looked like a battlefield filed with bodies. He turned around and ran for the door, Perry was right on his heels. They both got sick, puking in the parking lot. Melvin looked at Perry. "I told you that Billy Joe is a crazy son of a bitch. I ain't never seen anything like that in my life."

"Me either." Perry said, still feeling sick.

"Let's get the hell out of here." Melvin said. Then he hollered out to the others still in the bar. "We are leaving." Perry honked his horn as Melvin jumped in beside him and they drove off. Billy Joe was standing in the doorway as he saw Perry and Melvin spin out of the parking lot.

"Fucking chicken shits." Billy Joe said as he went back inside. "Red you and the other guys take all the money from their wallets. Rings and watches too. I will get the money from the till." Billy Joe said as he hopped over the bar. After cleaning out the till he went into the cooler and took two cases of beer. That's when he noticed a large metal box sitting on the floor. It had a padlock on it. He carried the beer out and set it down on the bar. He pulled his gun out of his waistband and went back into the cooler where he shot off the lock. Red called out to him. "Everything OK, Billy Joe?"

"Yes, I just killed a lock." Billy Joe answered as he opened the lid on the box. "Man, that old nigger was loaded." He said to himself as he took out bundles of cash. He threw the money back in the box and carried it out to the bar. Red was standing by the bar, stacks of money and jewelry laying on the bar in front of him.

"Here. You can throw it all in here." Billy Joe said as he sat the box on the bar.

Red's eyes widened as he looked inside the box. "Holy shit. There must be a few thousand in there." He said with a big smile on his face.

"Let's take it to the meeting hall and we can count it and divide it up there." Billy Joe said as he handed the box to Red. Jimmy and Billy Joe carried out the cases of beer. His brother Ricky hobbled bent over from his pain out behind them. They put everything in the back of Billy Joe's truck. Then they headed for their headquarters, where they divided everything between all of them. Melvin and Perry didn't get any of the money because Billy Joe didn't think they earned it. Billy Joe, Red, Jimmy, Ray and Ricky all got over six thousand dollars apiece. They figured that was their pay for ridding the world of thirty-six niggers, as they put it. In reality they massacred thirty six people and robbed them of their life and money and their jewelry.

"Dispatch to Sheriff Combs. Come in, Sheriff."

"This is Sheriff Combs. This better be important." Sheriff Combs answered his radio call as he was leaving Doctor Jacobs' office in his car.

"Sheriff we just got a call from a Mr. Jenks, said he's got some boys there scared to death, said they seen some Klansmen shooting up the Sugar Shack Bar just off the old highway.

"Is that place in our jurisdiction?" The dispatcher asked over the radio.

"Yes, I'm afraid so." Combs answered. "Notify all the deputies that are on call, tell them to meet me there." Combs sighed at the news.

"Right away Sheriff. Dispatch out."

"What the hell is going on tonight?" Combs said out loud as he pulled his car to the side of the road. He got out and opened his trunk. He bent over and reached in pulling out a double barrel shotgun. Closed his trunk and put the gun on his front seat, then got in his car and drove back onto the road headed for the old highway for the bar.

"Car 12 this is car 24, do you read me? Over." Combs reached for his mike to answer.

"This is car 12. Deputy Conners is that you? Over."

"Yes, Sheriff, I have Deputy Mills with me. What's going on Sheriff? Over."

"I wish the hell I knew. When we get there I want everyone to go in without lights. Is that clear?"

"Yes Sir." The deputy answered.

Combs looked in his rearview mirror. He saw the headlights of his deputies' cars fast approaching. He was soon joined by four more cruisers. As they approached the Sugar

Shack Bar they all turned out their headlights. They drove in the driveway parking lot as quietly as they possibly could. They came to a stop, got out of their cars fully armed with shotguns. There were eleven men altogether. They carefully went up to the doorway of the bar. Five of the men went to the back door. Guns aimed, they rushed inside only to find they were the only ones that were alive. It looked like a war zone inside. The smell of gun powder and blood still lingered in the stale air inside the bar.

"OH MY GOD! This was a massacre." Conners said in disbelief at what he was seeing.

"This is the work of madmen." Combs cringed at the sight. "Bobby, call it in. Tell them to send out some trucks. They got a lot of bodies to move."

The sun was starting to rise, bringing in the dawn with a purple and pink glow, pushing the night slowly away, to bring on a new day.

Sheriff Combs and his deputies had been at the Sugar Shack Bar all night. "Well, thank God that's the last of them." Sheriff Combs said to Deputy Conners as they watched the last three bodies being loaded on a refrigerated box van.

"Yeah, I ain't never seen that many bodies at one time in my life. Where do think the Coroner got all them body bags from Sheriff?" Conners asked as he tipped his hat back with his thumb.

"He sent one of his men out to the army base. He got them from the supply sergeant. They keep them on hand for the entire state in case of a major disaster. You know, like a flood or a twister." Combs answered.

He went to his car to load up his camera and the ten rolls of film he shot of all the victims and the crime scene. As he was about to get into his car, the dispatcher's voice came over his radio.

"Dispatch to Sheriff Combs."

"Go ahead, dispatch." Combs answered through his mike.

"Sheriff, there has been two more bodies found at the lake. A young colored boy and an older colored man. They were found floating in the lake. Looks like they were both shot in the head."

"Who took the call?" Combs asked over the radio.

"I sent Harley, sir. There wasn't anyone else cause you had everyone out there with you, Sheriff."

"I guess you're right, after all he is a deputy Sheriff, even though he's been a desk sergeant for the past ten years. He still can investigate a crime scene." Combs replied.

"Oh, one more thing, Sheriff. I thought you might want to know, the Polke boy died about an hour ago."

Combs dropped his head and sat there silent for a few moments.

"Sheriff, Sheriff, are you there? Sheriff, can you hear me? Sheriff."

"I'm still here, Ben. I was just thinking about the boy's parents. They just lost two children in one night. All because of some crazy son of a bitch who likes to kill." Combs said with anger welling up inside him. "Look Ben, call Harley and tell him to be sure he gets photos of the scene as well as the bodies and take casts of any tire tracks he might find."

CHAPTER TWENTY-FIVE

Billy Joe drove his truck into his driveway. The house was dark. Sue Ellen and Sissy where sound asleep inside when Billy Joe let him self inside the back door. He went straight to the bathroom to take a shower. After he showered and shaved he went in to the bedroom and quietly climbed into bed next to Sue Ellen. She never stirred once. He turned on his side and went to sleep.

"Wake up sleepy head. You're going to be late for work." Sue Ellen said as she gently shook Billy Joe on the shoulder. He slowly opened his eyes as he drowsily opened his eyes to see Sue Ellen sitting on the edge of the bed smiling down at him. "What time did you get home?" She asked."

"I don't know, eleven thirty or twelve, I think." He said rubbing his eyes with his palm.

"How many fish did you catch?" Sue Ellen asked."

"A bunch. We ate some of them and what was left Red and two of the other guys took them home. I didn't bring any home cause I know you don't like fish." He said in a kidding voice.

"Well thank you for remembering that. But I would have cooked some for you." She said lovingly to him as she kissed his forehead. He slapped her on the butt as she got up from the bed.

"Coffee hot?" he asked as he threw the covers back, getting out of the bed. His lean naked body glistened in the sunlight shining through the gold sheer curtains over the window. He went into the bathroom. Sue Ellen went into the kitchen to fix his breakfast and pour his coffee. Billy Joe held his penis in his hand examining himself, wondering to himself what he was to look for in case Viola really did have gonorrhea. He couldn't see anything different, so he shrugged his shoulders and held his penis over the toilet bowl to urinate. As he did he started to feel a slight burning sensation.

230

"DAMN." He said out loud as he bit his lower lip. "I am glad I bashed that bitches' heads in. I wish I could do it again." He thought to himself.

After breakfast Billy Joe kissed Sue Ellen on the cheek and headed out for work. But he decided he wasn't going to work that morning. Instead he called in sick from a pay phone in front of the Piggly Wiggly. He decided to drive down to Jackson where no one knew him. He also knew that Jackson, being a large city, there would be a lot of medical clinics. If he was infected he could get the medicine he needed and no one would be the wiser.

He arrived in Jackson at ten that morning. As he drove down a street he was given directions from a gas station attendant where he had stopped to gas up his truck. After a few blocks he spotted a sign. Jackson Medical Clinic, walk-ins welcome. He pulled his truck into the parking lot and parked. He went inside. He looked around at the three people that were sitting in the waiting room. That made him feel a little better. He figured he wouldn't have a long wait.

"May I help you?" A nurse said from behind the counter.

"Yes I need to see a doctor, if I can." Billy Joe said nervously.

"Your name?" The nurse asked.

"What?" Billy Joe stammered.

"Your name, sir, I need a name for our records. And your name is?"

"Auh, uh, Joe Taylor." He answered as he lied about his name.

"Your date of birth Mr. Taylor?" She asked as she looked up at him thinking to herself that he seemed very nervous.

"January tenth, 1933." Billy Joe answered.

"Do you have insurance?" She asked.

"Insurance? No, I will pay cash." Billy Joe answered starting to get a little agitated.

"OK, then what's the reason for your visit today?" The nurse asked as she filled out a chart.

"What?" Billy Joe asked.

"Why do you want to see the doctor, are you sick or hurt?" She asked again.

"It's a man thing, I can't tell you, only the doctor." Billy Joe said firmly.

"Just take a seat and I will call you when the doctor can see you." The nurse answered, a little sarcasm in her voice. Billy Joe sat down in one of the empty chairs and waited to be seen by the doctor.

The nurse called Billy Joe from the waiting room and led him to an exam room.

"The doctor will be with you shortly, Mr. Taylor. Just have a seat on the table there." She said curtly as she left the room leaving Billy Joe to stare at sterile white walls with a stainless steel sink against one wall. Billy Joe sat there wishing he could light up a Lucky Strike cigarette. He was getting very fidgety and impatient. He felt like he had been in the exam room for an hour, in reality it had only been fifteen minutes. Finally a short heavy-set balding man in his late fifties entered the room.

"Mr. Taylor, what seems to be the reason for your visit with us today?" He asked with a big friendly smile.

Billy Joe sat there trying to grab the right words to answer him. "I'm not sure doctor. Well you see it's like this. I got drunk over the weekend and I picked up some girl. I don't even know her name. Anyway it hurt me this morning when I went to the bathroom." Billy Joe said with an embarrassing tone in his voice.

"Hurt you in what way?" The doctor asked.

"It burned a little when I made water." Billy Joe answered.

"Well let's get a urine sample. It might be you just have a little bladder infection. I will send the nurse in. Don't worry, if it does turn out to be something more, well, a good shot of penicillin and some pills will fix you right up. Relax. You're not the first young fella who has made the mistake of being with the wrong woman." He chuckled.

Billy Joe left the clinic about noon with a prescription and a sore arm from the penicillin shot and instructions not to have sex for ten days. He got into his truck very angry that Viola had given him gonorrhea. He wanted to kill her allover again if he could. Now he had to figure a way not to have sex with Sue Ellen and not get her suspicious. He had a lot to think about on his drive home.

Sissy, Marcy, and William were playing tea party on Marcy and William's front porch. Sue Ellen was doing the laundry at her house. Margie was helping her sort the clothes.

"Sue Ellen, look at this shirt." Margie held up the blue shirt so Sue Ellen could see the red stains on the sleeves. "It looks like blood." Margie remarked.

"It probably is. Billy Joe wore it on his fishing trip over the weekend, it's probably fish blood." Sue Ellen explained to her.

"What did he do, massacre the fish?" Margie joked as she threw the shirt into the washer. "That's men for you. It's either blood from some dead animal, or oil stains from their dead cars." She said with a laugh.

"How bout some coffee?" Sue Ellen asked Margie as she closed the lid on the washer, starting it.

"You bet. I thought you'd never ask." Margie said as she and Sue Ellen headed for the kitchen.

They poured their coffee and sat down at the table. Margie had brought over a coffee cake she had made the night before. As they drank their coffee and nibbled on the cake chatting about the new baby Sue Ellen was going to have.

Sue Ellen and Margie spent the afternoon together. Sissy played with Marcy and William till three o'clock, then she headed for home where she found her mother in the kitchen ironing clothes.

"Hi Mommy." Sissy smiled as she clutched her doll in one hand and a small pink box tightly tucked under her arm, trying very hard not to crush the big white bow attached to it.

"Hi sweetie. What you got under your arm?"

"It's a present for the baby from Marcy's mommy." Sissy said as she set her doll down on the floor, then went over to her mother to hand her the box.

"Oh, how nice of her. Shall we open it?" Sue Ellen said smiling as she set her iron down on the metal plate at the end of the ironing board. Sue Ellen took the box and sat down at the table. Sissy was very excited as she climbed on the chair next to her.

"Hurry, mommy, open it. I want to see."

"Ok honey, just give me a minute. I want to save the pretty bow. I wonder what it could be." Sue Ellen said as she very carefully opened the pink wrapping paper.

"Oh my, its beautiful. It's a sweater set."

"Gee." Sissy said.

CHAPTER TWENTY-SIX

"Sheriff. Agent Wells is on line two." A deputy's voice said over Sheriff Combs' intercom."

"Yes, Agent Wells, what can I do for you?" Combs said with a smile.

"I think it's what we can do for each other. That sketch you sent me paid off. I found our gal. Mrs. Sue Ellen Martin.

"Oh, that's great, where did you locate her?" Combs asked as he straightened up in his chair, eager to hear more.

"She was raised in Tupelo, she married a Billy Joe Martin, also from Tupelo. They both reside in your town. The husband works at the textile mill and they live at 409 Oak Street."

"Did you say Oak Street?" Combs asked as a memory flashed in his mind of the address.

"Sheriff. You still there?" Wells asked.

"Yes I'm still here. I was just thinking about a call I had a few weeks ago at that address. I talked to this Billy Joe. His wife, however, wasn't home at the time." Combs told him over the phone as he tapped his pencil on the edge of his desk.

"Listen, I'm on my way down there. I should be at your office, say, in an hour and a half. Then we can pay a little visit to Mrs. Martin."

"I would like that very much. I got a gut feeling about this Billy Joe Martin." Combs said thoughtfully.

"You think you got something?" Wells asked.

"Maybe. Look, I will fill you in when you get here. I need to check on something before you get here." Combs said as his mind was in deep thought.

"Till then. I will see you in a little while. Bye for now."

"Yes, see you in a while. Bye." Combs said as he hung up the phone.

After hanging up he pushed his intercom button. "Are those crime scene photos back from the lab yet?" Combs asked the deputy on the other end.

"Not yet Sheriff, but they should be here in a half hour or so. Do you want me to call them and see if I can hurry them up a little?" The deputy asked.

"Yes, why don't you do that, I need the tire photos and while you're at it, get me the photos from the Flint case and the Brock case as well as the Polkes' murder case." Combs said, very serious tone in his voice.

"Yes sir, right away." The deputy said as he clicked off the intercom and picked up the phone to call the lab. A few moments later the deputy brought the case file photos into the Sheriff. After the deputy left the room Combs spread the photos out on his desk. He took a large magnifying glass from his desk drawer.

"I'll be a son of a bitch. The same bastard has been at every crime scene." He said out loud to himself. He walked over to the large chalkboard that hung on the wall behind his desk. He began writing the victim's names on the board with chalk, starting with the Greens' name first, along with the dates and place of their deaths. Then in the center of the board he wrote down the caliber of the gun they where all murdered with.

"Sheriff Combs, the photos are here from the lab." The deputy's voice said over the intercom.

"Thank you, would you please bring them to my office?"

"Yes sir, right away. A few moments later the deputy knocked on the office door as he opened it and came in. "Here they are, Sheriff." The deputy said as he laid them on the desk.

"Thank you. Also I'm expecting Agent Wells. Just send him on in when he gets here." Combs instructed as he studied the crime scene photos from the Sugar shack.

"Yes sir." The deputy answered as he left the office.

Sheriff Combs read the report as he looked at photos. There where ten people shot with the same gun, a 45 caliber. He wrote their names on the board too. Then he came to the photos of Viola, Amanda and Betty Flint. All three had been raped and all had the same bite marks on their bodies. The only difference was that Betty Flint was still alive. Viola Watson and little Amanda Polke weren't so lucky. He wrote their names on the blackboard also. He knew that somehow they where all tied together and that one man was responsible for all the deaths and rapes. Now all he needed was a name and a face to go with a gun of the same caliber as proof of the killer responsible for all the murders that were taking place in the two towns.

Sheriff Combs was sitting at his desk reading over the lab results. Agent Wells was knocking on his door as he poked his head in.

"May I come in?" He smiled as he opened the door to enter the office.

"Of course you can, have a seat." Combs said motioning with his hand for Wells to come in and sit down.

"Hey, I like that, I'm very impressed the way you laid it all out." Wells commented, looking at the blackboard as he sat down in a chair in front of Combs' desk.

"Thanks. That's my way of linking all this together." Combs said as he stood up and wrote another name on the board.

"So you think this is the work of one group of men?" Wells asked curiously.

"A group, maybe, but most of them where murdered by just one man. And whoever that man is, is the owner of the colt forty-five and I will bet we find him, we find the gun, and he will be the one whose teeth will match all the rape victims also." Combs said with confidence in his voice.

"Did you ever think about joining the Bureau?" Wells ask smiling.

"Not really, you guys move to slow for me." Combs kidded.

"Well maybe we can speed things up for you. You might change your mind and join up." Wells kidded back.

"Well let's speed things up by paying this Billy Joe Martin and his wife a little visit." Combs said as he stood up to get his hat from the hat rack standing in the corner.

"I'm ready when you are." Wells answered.

"I'm ready now, shall we go?" Combs said coming around his desk.

"You said you met this Billy Joe?" Wells asked.

"Yes, I got a call that he was beating his little three year old a few weeks back." Combs answered.

"And you didn't arrest him?" Wells asked, surprised that Billy Joe wasn't in jail.

"I couldn't, the wife and child weren't at home when I got there. There wasn't any evidence to prove he beat the child, so I had to let it go." Combs said as they walked out the door.

"You think this Billy Joe might be involved in any of these murders?" Wells asked.

"I think he is in it up to his eyeballs. You will see what I mean when you meet him." Combs answered.

"What about the wife?" Wells asked.

"That I don't know because I have never met her." Combs answered as he got into his car.

"Mommy can I go to play with Marcy at her house?" Sissy asked as she put her empty milk glass down on the table.

"Well I guess it will be all right only if her mother says it's OK, and you must be home before four o'clock."

"OK mommy, but how will I know when it's four o'clock?" Sissy asked with a perplexed look on her insistent little face.

Sue Ellen smiled at her little girl. "Well why don't you just tell Marcy's mother to make sure she sends you home at ten minutes till four."

"OK, mommy." Sissy beamed.

"Wait a minute honey, so you won't forget, I'm going to give you a note to give to Marcy's mother. Just let me go into the bedroom and get a piece of paper and pen." Sue Ellen said as she went towards her bedroom. Sissy waited in the kitchen for her mother to return with the note. She was sitting on a chair swinging her feet happily back and forth as she hummed a little tune to her doll she held in her lap. Suddenly she jerked her head up as she heard a knock on the door. Sissy slid off the chair and scrambled to open the door. As she opened the door her eyes opened wide as she saw Agent Wells and Sheriff Combs at the door.

"Well hello there, little Miss. Is your mother home?" Sheriff Combs asked smiling down at her. Sissy stood there silently shaking her head yes as her blond curls danced about her head. She quickly turned and ran towards her mother's bedroom.

"Mommy, mommy." Sissy called out as she ran into Sue Ellen as she was coming out of her bedroom. "Mommy there's a big policeman at the door with another big man.

"What? Oh honey what? A policeman?" Sue Ellen said with a surprised look on her face. Then she went to the door. "Oh you are a policeman." Sue Ellen said. "What can I do for you?" Sue Ellen said with a curious look.

"Is your name Sue Ellen Martin?" Combs asked politely.

"Yes I am. How did you know my name and why are you asking? Oh has something happened to my husband at the Mill?" Sue Ellen asked worriedly.

"Mrs. Martin, my name is Sheriff Combs and this is Agent Wells with the F.B.I. We just need to ask you some questions, and nothing has happened to your husband. If it's all right with you, we would like to come in and have a little talk with you."

"Well, yes I guess that will be OK. I don't understand what you could possibly want to talk with me about." Sue Ellen said looking very puzzled as she opened the door for Combs and Wells to let them in. She led them to the kitchen table.

"Won't you please have a seat? Would you like a cup of coffee?" Sue Ellen asked politely.

"Thank you Mam, I don't mind if it's not too much trouble?" Combs said as he and Wells sat down at the table.

'Not at all, I just made a fresh pot." Sue Ellen said as she went to the cabinet taking down coffee cups.

Sissy followed close behind her. "Mommy." Sissy whispered.

"In a moment, Sissy." Sue Ellen answered.

"But mommy, can I go now? Please." Sissy begged.

"Yes, honey, you go on over to Marcy's. Got your note? Don't forget to give it to Marcy's mother."

"I won't mommy." Sissy said as she kissed her mother back.

"Bye Bye." Sissy said as she ran out the door.

"You have a very pretty little girl, Mrs. Martin." Combs said.

"Thank you." Sue Ellen said as she sat a cup of coffee down on the table in front of him and Wells.

"I couldn't help wondering what happened to your little girl's arm. It has an awful big scar." Combs said wistfully.

"Oh, she fell on a piece of glass a while back and she got a bad case of blood poisoning." Sue Ellen answered as she sat down at the table with them.

"Mrs. Martin, I'm going to get right to the point. We are here because a while back you went into a jewelry store in town to have a ring appraised, in fact the one you have on your finger now." Combs said, pointing to the ring on Sue Ellen's finger.

"Yes I did. I just wanted to know if my husband spent too much money for it, that's all." Sue Ellen said defensively as her eyes dropped to the ring on her finger she was now turning nervously on her finger.

"So you got the ring from your husband?" Wells asked.

"Yes. He gave it to me as an anniversary present. But it was really a present to get me over being mad at him." Sue Ellen said in an honest sounding voice.

"Do you know where your husband got the ring from?" Combs asked.

"He just told me he bought it from some guy for twenty dollars." She answered.

"Twenty dollars? Are you sure about that?" Wells said with a raised eyebrow.

"Yes that's what I said. Twenty dollars." Sue Ellen said, starting to get a little agitated that Wells sounded like he didn't believe her.

"Mrs. Martin, what Agent Wells is trying to say, well look at it the way we are seeing it. You had the ring appraised so you must know how much its worth. If your husband got that ring for twenty dollars like you said, then he got one hell of a deal. That ring cost ten thousand dollars. You must have felt it was stolen." Combs said sternly.

"I thought the jeweler was mistaken. The thought did cross my mind, but I know my husband didn't steal it. If that's what you're implying." Sue Ellen replied defensively.

"Mrs. Martin, we aren't implying anything yet. All we want to know is where and from whom he got the ring from. That's all." Combs said.

"That's something you will have to ask Billy Joe." Sue Ellen said.

"We intend to, Mrs. Martin. What time do you expect him home?" Wells asked.

"He should be here a little after four." She answered.

"That's fine, we will come back then. For now Mrs. Martin, I'm afraid we will have to ask you to give us the ring. We will have it examined and if it's not the ring we are looking for, well, then you will get it back with our apologies. But if it is, well then it will become evidence and your husband will have to prove where he got the ring." Combs said.

Then he and Wells got up from the table. Combs held out his hand to Sue Ellen for the ring. She took the ring off her finger and handed it to Combs.

"Thank you. We will see ourselves out. We will return about five. Please tell your husband to be here." Combs said as he put the ring in his shirt pocket.

He and Wells went out the door. Sue Ellen sat at the table feeling numb. She wanted to cry, but the tears didn't come. Just memories of the day Billy Joe gave her the ring. They came rushing through her mind like waves from the ocean flooding her with all the little details of that day in question. "Where did you get that ring Billy Joe?" She said out loud to herself.

Sheriff Combs and Agent Wells sat parked across the street in Combs' car watching and waiting for Billy Joe to come home.

"There goes the little girl." Combs said to Wells as he watched Sissy scramble up the steps to her house. "Right on time. Her mother told her to be home by five till four, and it's now five till four." Wells commented.

"She sure is a pretty little girl. I wonder if her father loves her as much as her mother does?" Combs said to Wells as he opened his thermos to pour himself a cup of coffee.

"What makes you say that?" Wells asked as he held out his cup to Combs for Combs to fill.

"Like I told you, I met this Billy Joe Martin a while back. I got a call that he was beating that little girl. I couldn't prove it because the little girl and her mother weren't here when I arrived, but he was. Just looking in his eyes sent a shiver up my spine. The man is cold. I believe he is mean through and through. I think he beats the child and the mother." Combs said.

"I think you're right. I noticed a lot of bruises on the little girl's legs." Wells answered.

"Well I want to really find out if this guy is involved with all the murders. If he is I want to see him get the death penalty." Combs said as he sipped on his coffee.

"And if he doesn't have anything to do with them?" Wells asked.

"Then hopefully I can get him for assault on a child. Because I know deep down in my gut, he is hurting that sweet little girl." Combs said firmly.

"There comes our boy now." Wells said as Billy Joe turned into his driveway. Billy Joe got out of his truck and went inside his house. Combs tossed his coffee out his car window to the ground. He started to get out of his car. Wells grabbed his arm.

"Wait a minute, let's give him a little time to relax before we go in."

"Relax? You think his wife isn't going to tell him we are coming?" Combs said a little agitated at Wells' request.

"That's right. He will relax then she will tell him. Then he will start thinking, and then we show up. Now how do you think he is going to answer all are questions? Will he be direct and to the point or will he trip himself up?" Wells grinned wide.

"I got you." Combs grinned back.

Billy Joe came into the house just as Sissy was finishing eating some cookies. Sue Ellen had given her there was a little milk left in her glass as she accidentally tipped the glass spilling the milk onto the table then on to the floor.

"Sissy." Billy Joe yelled at her.

Sissy's head jerked up, her body tensed up as her eyes widened with fear, as to what was to come from her father.

"You stupid little bitch. Can't you do anything with out making a mess?" He demanded.

Sue Ellen came into the room as Sissy sat frozen to the chair; her rigid little body shook with gripping fear of her father.

"Billy Joe stop yelling. You're scaring her to death. It's just a little spill. It only takes a second to wipe it up." Sue Ellen said defending Sissy.

"That's right, defend her. She ain't nothin but a spoiled little brat." Billy Joe spat angrily at Sue Ellen as she wipe up the spill.

"Sissy go to your room." Billy Joe snapped.

Sissy quickly slid off the chair and ran to her room.

"Well you came home in a cheerful mood." Sue Ellen said snidely.

"I had a crappy day, so don't you start." Billy Joe snapped.

"Well my day hasn't been roses either. The Sheriff and the F.B.I. was here today." Sue Ellen told him.

Billy Joe turned a little pale in the face.

"What the hell for?" He demanded.

"They took the ring you gave me, and they said they were coming back to talk to you about it." Sue Ellen said a little coldly.

"What did you tell them?" Billy Joe said sounding a little nervous.

"I told them the story you told me. Why? Is there more to it than you told me?" Sue Ellen asked curtly.

"HELL NO. It happened just the way I told you." Billy Joe said defensively. "I got it off two nigger guys." He said, suddenly the nerves in his neck jumped as he heard the knock on the door.

"That's probably them now." Sue Ellen said as she went to answer the door.

"Hello Sheriff, Mr. Wells. Come on in, Billy Joe is waiting for you.

"Hello Mr. Martin. Remember me?" Combs asked as he walked over to Billy Joe sitting at the table. He held out his hand to shake with Billy Joe.

"Mr. Martin, this is F.B.I. Agent Fred Wells. We need to ask you a few questions.

Combs shook Billy Joe's hand then sat down at the table next to him. Agent Wells sat across the table from Billy Joe. Wells stared intensely searching Billy Joe's facial expressions for any signs of guilt. Wells made Billy Joe start to feel very uncomfortable. Sweat beaded on his forehead. Billy Joe kept twitching in his chair. Then suddenly he stopped. He took out his pack of Luckys from his shirt pocket. He lit one up and took a deep draw, then blew the smoke out his mouth and nostrils.

"Look. I told you I bought the ring in Tupelo one night on my way home." Billy Joe said firmly.

"From two colored guys?" Wells asked as he wrote in his note pad.

"That's right. I got it from two niggers. They pulled up next to my truck as I was ready to pull out of the gas station. One of them asked me for directions out of town. Then one of them got out of the passenger side of the car and showed me the ring. He said he bought it for his girlfriend and they broke up, he offered it to me for fifty dollars. I told him I only had twenty. He took my twenty gave me the ring. Thanked me and they drove off heading out of town. I bought it because I thought my wife would like it and not stay mad at me for coming home so late.

"Why where you so late coming home?" Combs asked.

"I told you I went out with my friends to a bar. We shot pool and I got a little drunk and I just lost track of time. I knew I was in the doghouse when they called out last call. So I left the bar and walked across the street to the gas station to get in my truck to go home." Billy Joe said as he took another puff from his Lucky.

"Why did you park at the station?" Wells asked.

"Because the bar's parking lot was full." Billy Joe answered stubbing out his butt in the ashtray.

"What kind of car were they driving?" Combs asked.

"I already told you, a blue Caddy." Billy Joe groaned.

"What year?" Wells asked.

"Hell man, I don't know. All I know is that it was a hell of a lot newer than my old truck." Billy Joe said as he lit another Lucky.

"OK, I'm going to show you some photos of some Cadillacs. You tell me if it is like the one you saw." Wells said as he laid out some photos of different year Cadillacs. Billy Joe looked at the photos, then he pointed to one with his finger.

"This one." He said.

"Are you positive?" Wells asked.

"Yes I'm sure. The only difference was it was a convertible, blue with a white top." Billy Joe said being very precise.

"You know you picked out a brand new 57. Didn't you wonder how two coloreds could be driving a new car and have an expensive ring to sell so cheap?"

"No. I know a lot of those niggers from up north drive new cars." Billy Joe said smugly.

"How did you know they were from up north?" Wells asked.

"I saw their plates, they were from Ohio or Indiana or maybe Illinois. Hell I don't remember for sure where they were from. It's been a long time ago." Billy Joe answered sounding a little agitated at the question.

"What about the ring? Didn't you think twenty dollars was a little suspicious?"

"No. I thought it was just a cheap dime store ring. In fact I thought I paid to much for it." Billy Joe said curtly.

"Didn't your wife tell you how much it was worth when she took it to the jewelers?" Wells asked.

"I never told him." Sue Ellen spoke up before Billy Joe could answer. Lying to protect Billy Joe.

"That's right. She never told me." Billy Joe said smugly.

"Why didn't you tell your husband Mrs. Martin?" Wells asked.

"Oh I don't know, I guess because I thought the jeweler was wrong, and I felt a little guilty for wondering about the worth of it. After all it was a gift from the heart." Sue Ellen said.

"Well I guess we have all we need for now." Wells said as he closed his notebook.

"If you think of anything else that might be helpful, call my office." Combs said as he stood up from the table.

"You know the ring belonged to a Mrs. Green. Her and her husband and baby were brutally murdered. Mr. Martin you may have been the only one who saw the men responsible." Wells said as he held out his hand to shake Billy Joe's hand. Billy Joe felt relieved they where finally leaving. He stood in the doorway and watched Sheriff Combs and Agent Wells get in to the Sheriff's car and drive off.

Sue Ellen came up beside him putting her hand on his arm. Billy Joe turned towards her. "You stupid bitch." He snarled at her as he punched her in the face. The blow sent Sue Ellen reeling backwards, falling to the floor.

"You just had to get the cops involved. You couldn't just keep the damn ring and trust me that I bought the damn thing for you in good faith." Billy Joe yelled at her as he kicked her on her hip as she lay on the floor crying in pain. He reached down and grabbed her by the hair, hitting her in the face once again. "No, you had to think I killed somebody to get it." he shouted as he hit her again. Sue Ellen fell back striking her arm on the edge of the table as she fell to the floor again. She curled her body into a fetal position, as she begged him not to hit her again. Billy Joe stared down at her coldly with his hands balled into fists as if he was going strike her again. He stopped himself short of hitting her, turned and went out the door to get into his truck and leave. Sue Ellen heard the truck start up and pull out of the driveway. Sissy came running out of her room.

"Mommy, you OK?" Sissy asked as tears streamed down her cheeks. Sue Ellen looked up at her with blood gushing from her nose and split lips. both eye's which started to swell nearly shut.

"Run across the street to Margie's and Carl's and tell her I need her. But you be careful when you cross the street." Sue Ellen said in a gurgling voice.

Sissy stood up and ran out the door as fast as her little legs could carry her. Sissy looked both ways for cars, then she ran across the street to Margie's house.

"Aunt Margie!" Sissy cried out as she banged on the door with her tiny fist.

There was no answer. So Sissy ran around the house to the back door. Sissy frantically banged on the door hysterically crying and calling out for Margie. She suddenly realized there was nobody at home, so Sissy ran back across the street and passed her house. She was headed to her only real friend's house. Sissy ran through the field down the path to Marcy's house. She was crying uncontrollably all the way to Marcy's house. Sissy made it to Marcy's house .She stumbled her way up the steps.

"Marcy, Mrs. Woods, somebody help me." She cried out as she banged on the door. Marcy's mother Ida Mae came to the door as she heard Sissy's urgent crying for help.

"What is it child? What's wrong?" She asked very concerned as she opened the screen door for Sissy.

"Its, it's my, my Mommy, she's hurt real bad. She gots blood allover her. Please come." Sissy begged her as she sobbed.

"Come child, you show Ida Mae where your mama is." She said as she took Sissy by the hand. Together they went down the path to Sissy's house.

Ida Mae went up to the back door of Sissy's house. She saw Sue Ellen curled in a ball lying unconscious on the kitchen floor. She came inside and knelt down next to her. Sue Ellen was covered in blood from her wounds.

"Sissy, honey, get me a towel." She said as she stood up and went to the sink. Sissy ran into the bathroom and brought out a towel to Ida Mae.

"baby, where does your mama keep her pans? Ida Mae asked as she searched the cabinets.

"Over there in that closet." Sissy pointed to a skinny door.

Ida Mae went over to it and found a small metal washbasin. She went back to the sink and filled it with warm water. She went back over to Sue Ellen and began washing the blood from her face.

"Lord, child, did that man of yours do this to you?" Ida Mae asked as she was trying to wake Sue Ellen.

"Daddy did it." Sissy said still crying.

"Yes I know, baby. Your mama needs to be in the hospital. She needs a doctor. Sissy, where is your phone?" Ida Mae asked looking very worried.

"We don't gots a phone." Sissy answered. "Mommy goes to Margie's house." Sissy said still teary eyed.

"OK, honey, you go over to her house and tell her to call for an ambulance."

"Aunt Margie ain't home." Sissy answered.

"Then I'm going to have to go back to my house and call. baby you will have to stay here with your mama." Ida Mae said as she got up to go get help.

As she started for the door she saw someone coming up the steps to the porch.

"Sue Ellen, you home?" It was Margie who called out.

"Oh, Miss Margie, I'm so glad to see you." Ida Mae said as she opened the door.

"Ida Mae, what's wrong? Where is Sue Ellen?" She said looking surprised to see her at Sue Ellen's.

"It's Miss Sue Ellen, she needs a doctor." Ida Mae said as Margie came onto the porch.

"Oh my God. What happened to her?" Margie asked as she saw Sue Ellen lying motionless on the floor.

"That evil man of hers beat her up." Ida Mae said, anger in her voice.

Margie ran over to Sue Ellen. "Sissy go get Uncle Carl."

"OK." Sissy said as she scrambled for the door.

"How long has she been like this?" Margie asked.

"I don't know, Sissy came crying over to my house about a half hour ago. I came straight over and found her like this. I got the bleeding to stop, but she won't wake up." Ida Mae said worriedly.

"She might have hit her head. My husband and I will take her to the hospital. Can you take Sissy over to your house?" Margie asked.

"I sure will." Ida Mae said.

Carl came in the door with Sissy. "What the hell?" He said as he hurried over to his wife who was holding Sue Ellen in her arms. "Did Billy Joe do this?" He asked as he stared at Sue Ellen's swollen face. "Where is he?" Carl asked angrily.

"We don't know." Margie answered.

"That little bastard, just wait till I see him. Look honey I will bring the car over, and we will take her to the hospital. But what we going to do with Sissy? She can't stay here."

"Ida Mae said she will take her home with her." Margie said.

Carl looked over to Ida Mae who was comforting Sissy. "Ida Mae, you are an angel, you know." Carl said with a smile as he got up to go get his car.

"She is a beautiful Angel, she's my Angel." Sissy said as she hugged Ida Mae.

"And you're my little golden Angel. Now lets go baby." Ida Mae smiled hugging Sissy back.

"I want to stay with Mommy." Sissy cried.

"Honey, they got to take your mama to the hospital and they won't let little childrens go in with their mamas." Ida Mae said trying to make Sissy understand.

"Sissy go with her." A faint whispering voice of Sue Ellen said to Sissy.

"Mommy!" Sissy squealed as she ran over to her mother.

"You go with Ida Mae. Mommy will be all right. I will come get you later." Sue Ellen said slowly.

"You scared the hell right out of us. I'm so glad you are awake. Carl is bringing the car over. Can you stand?" Margie asked.

"I...I don't know, I hurt so bad." Sue Ellen said in a low tone.

"Don't you worry, missy, I will take good care of your baby girl. You just go get yourself looked after." Ida Mae said with a smile.

"I know you will." Sue Ellen squeezed Ida Mae's hand.

"You get yourself well, don't you worry none about your baby, I will take good care of her." Ida Mae assured her again.

"Great. She came around I see." Cal said as he came in the door.

"She can't stand up, Carl, I think her arm is broken." Margie said worriedly as she and Ida Mae had tried to get Sue Ellen to her feet before Carl had come in.

"I will carry her, you get the door." Carl said as he slid his arms under Sue Ellen and picked her up like he was picking up a child. She was as light as a feather to Carl as he carried her out to his car. He laid her down in the back seat. Margie got into the front passenger seat. Carl got in on the driver's side. He already had the car running. He put the car in gear and backed out of the drive.

"Bye, mommy." Sissy said, waving from the porch as they drove off.

Ida Mae closed the door to the house. "Come on baby, let's go to my house. Your mama is gonna be all right. You just wait and see." She said as she took Sissy's hand and led her down the steps. Her and Sissy went through the backyard and through the fence heading to her house.

Carl and Margie arrived with Sue Ellen at the hospital twenty minutes later. Carl pulled the car up to the emergency room door. He went inside to get someone to bring out a. stretcher and take Sue Ellen inside. Once inside they took Sue Ellen straight up to X-ray. Margie and Carl waited for word on her condition in the waiting room.

"You want some coffee?" Carl asked Margie, as they waited.

"Yes, honey. I think I could use a cup about now. How could he do that to her?" Margie asked Carl bewildered.

"I don't know Hon, Billy Joe has just got a short fuse, I guess. Look, you wait here in case there is some word of her condition, and I will go get us some coffee." Carl said as he kissed Margie on the forehead before he went for coffee.

"Well, what did you think of our Mr. Billy Joe Martin?" Combs asked Wells as they drove back to the Sheriff's office.

"He's one cool individual. He is either very naive and innocent, or he's the most cunning cold-blooded son of a bitch I ever met." Wells answered.

"Well I think he is the latter. I think he is very deeply involved with everything here. All we have to do is find his gun and get an impression of his teeth and we can nail that son of a bitch." Combs grinned sheepishly at Wells.

"Well, we can't nail him without evidence. He says he doesn't own a gun. We need a search warrant to search his house, and I don't think we can get a judge to give us one on what we have." Wells said grimly.

"Well, I know one that will." Combs said thoughtfully.

"That will be great, are you sure he will give us one?" Wells asked sounding a little skeptical.

"Yeah, his name is Adam Hains. He hates the Klan as much as I do." Combs said as he turned in to the parking lot at the station.

"Wait a minute. We don't know if Martin is Klan." Wells said with caution in his voice.

"I'm sure that little bastard is Klan. I'm willing to bet my children's life that he is." Combs said confident with his statement.

"I think before we go to this judge, we need to find out a little more about this Billy Joe Martin. We need to find out about his friends, and where he hangs out. You know? We need a little background on him." Wells said trying not to sound like he was quoting the law to Combs.

Combs looked over at Wells thoughtfully for a moment as he said, "Maybe you are right. Where do you want to start first?" Combs smiled.

"I will check out Tupelo, you check out his workplace and find out who he hangs with, and I will check back with you in a few days. Then we will compare our notes. Hopefully we can find out just where he was when all of the murders took place. Hell, who knows we might even get lucky and find a witness or two that will either clear him or hang him." Wells said firmly.

"That sounds like a plan to me." Combs said as he opened his car door to get out.

"I will check back with you on Friday, maybe sooner if I find something concrete." Wells said closing his car door as he set his briefcase on the car hood.

"Want some coffee before you start back?" Combs asked.

"No, I better get on the road back to my motel. The sooner I start checking things out the sooner we get closer to a warrant for our Mr. Martin." Wells said as he shoved his notebook into his briefcase.

"You're right. See you Friday." Combs said.

The two men said their goodbyes. Wells went to his car and left for Tupelo. Sheriff Combs went to his office and began making calls. Combs or Wells were unaware of Sue Ellen's beating by Billy Joe after they left the Martin house.

Ida Mae went into her house with Sissy. Her husband met her at the door. "Woman, where's you been?" He asked sounding agitated.

"I went to help Sissy's mama. Didn't Ben tell you?" She said defensively.

"What kinds of help?" he asked.

"Her husband beat her up and she had to go to the hospital." Ida Mae said.

"There you goes again, meddlin in white folks troubles." he said grumpily.

"I ain't meddlin. I will help anyone that needs it. Just cause she is white makes no never mind to me. That baby girl's mama has treated me and our childrens right. So if she needs help I am gonna give it. That damn man of hers needs to be put in jail and have the key throwed away." She said angrily.

"See. That's what I's been tryin to tell you. You go messin in them folks troubles, and that will cause us trouble. I heared he is Klan. And we don't wants Klan comin to our farm. They could burn us out and even kill us all. Is that what's you want?" he said seriously.

"Well I'm keepin Miss Sue Ellen's child for her till she gets better. God tells us to look out for one nother and he don't say nothin about what color they should be. Now I'm going in to the kitchen and fix supper, and you need to open your heart and do God's work." She said stubbornly.

"You better hope God helps us when the Klan come callin." he called out to Ida Mae as he left the house to go finish his chores.

Billy Joe turned his truck in to Red Avery's driveway to his home. Red was sitting in his garage, drinking a beer and cleaning one of his hunting rifles. Red looked up as he heard Billy Joe's truck. "Over here." Red called out to him as he closed his truck door. Billy Joe walked up to the open door of the run down shabby garage.

"Hey man, what you doing?" Billy Joe asked.

"Now what the hell does it look like I'm doing?" Red grinned. "What brings you out here?" Red asked.

"I think we got trouble." Billy Joe said with a serious look on his face.

"Trouble? What kind of trouble?" Red scowled.

"When I went home from work, the sheriff and an F.B.I. agent came. They where asking me about that damn ring I gave Sue Ellen."

"Ring, what ring?" Red said looking puzzled.

"You know. The one I took from that white slut with her nigger husband." Billy Joe said refreshing his memory.

"Oh Yeah, I remember. That's the one old Gumm got all pissed off at you for killin that half breed kid. Hey, wait a minute. How did they know to come to you?" Red asked, curiosity in his voice.

"Well, it seems that Sue Ellen got it in her head to take the ring to a jewelry store to find out what it was worth." Billy Joe answered.

"What did that stupid wife of yours tell them?" Red said sounding angry.

"The same story I told her. That I bought it from a couple nigger boys. But they were asking where I was this weekend and who I was with."

"Yeah, and what did you tell them?" Red asked listening intensely to Billy Joe's story.

"I told them that you and I and Ray Ray went fishin over in Alabama at Potter Lake. You know the one I mean. We went there last summer." Billy Joe said explaining his alibi to the law.

"You know they will be back and they will come back with a warrant to search your place and probably my place and Mike's place too. We need to get rid of our guns." Red said even more serious than before.

"You mean destroy em?" Billy Joe asked.

"Well, yeah, you don't want them to trace our guns back to us, do you?" Red answered.

"Aha, man, I don't want to get rid of my gun. It was my grandaddy's. Why can't we just hide them somewhere for a while?" Billy Joe said.

"Yeah, I guess we could. I kinda like my old gun too. I think I know just the place and we better warn the others." Red said seriously as he got up and went over to a big metal locker. He opened the rusting door, its squeaking hinges made a loud sound. Red took out a twelve-gauge shotgun and another one that was a thirty-thirty, lever action, Springfield rifle.

"Here take these. You know how to break these babies down?" Red asked as he handed the guns to Billy Joe.

"Wow. They are real beauties." Billy Joe said as he admired the guns.

"Well do you or don't you?" Red said impatiently.

"Hell yes, I can do it with my eyes closed." Billy Joe grinned.

"Well do them with you eyes open on the table over there." Red motioned with his head. "After you break them down, wrap them in that oil cloth on my workbench."

Billy Joe took the guns over to the table and began breaking them down.

"I got to go in the house for a minute. I will be back. I got to get somethin." Red said as he headed out of the garage. Red returned a few moments later with a flower box. It had plastic flowers with wire stems stuck in to a Styrofoam block.

"What's the flower box for?" Billy Joe asked looking at the box.

"I will show you. Watch." Red said as he lifted out the Styrofoam block holding the flowers. "Put the guns inside. Go get your gun, wrap it in another oilcloth, and put it with them." Red ordered Billy Joe.

"But I need my gun, man." Billy Joe protested.

"Look the law is snoopin around now and if they catch you with your precious gun they will hang your ass right along with the rest of us. Now get your damn gun." Red demanded angrily.

"OK, man, don't get pissed, I will get it. Just give me a minute, I got to get it from my truck. Relax, OK?" Billy Joe said as he backed up from the table holding up his hands as to gesture a stopping motion to Red.

Billy Joe went to his truck. He pulled his seat back forward, he reached behind the seat back, and detached a holster holding his gun. He pushed his seat back into position. Closed his door and took the gun to Red. Red took the gun from him and put it in the box with the other two.

"Now what?" Billy Joe asked.

"We put the flowers back and we go get the other guy's guns." Red said as he picked up the box from the table.

"Let's take my truck. They might be watching for yours." Red said as Billy Joe followed him. Red and Billy Joe drove off in Red's truck. They went around to all the Klan members' houses that where involved in all the killings they had anything to do with. Red then drove to a little town called Cedar Falls. He went to a cemetery just out side of town. He and Billy Joe got out of his truck. Red took the flower box from the back of his truck. Billy Joe took out another flower box, just like the one Red had. It was also filled with guns. Billy Joe followed Red to a stone mausoleum. Red sat the box down on the steps, reached in his pocket for the key to unlock the door. The steel rusted door made a hollow creaking sound as he opened it. They went inside to the damp musty smell, a soft amber color of light shown dimly through the stained glass window. Once inside Red slid back one of the marble covers to one of the crypts.

"Who is buried in here? Billy Joe asked.

"My great granpappy, General James Avery. He was one of the South's greatest Generals, that is, except for General Lee." Red said proudly.

"Wow, I'm impressed. I feel like I'm in the presence of a king." Billy Joe said feeling honored to be there.

"Yeah, does kinda make you feel that way, don't it? Now come on, let's get the guns out and put them in here." Red told him as bent down to take the guns from his box.

"Won't they get rusted in here?" Billy Joe asked concerned about his gun.

"No. That's why I had you wrap them in the oilcloth. Hell, we could leave them in here for years and they won't get a speck of rust on them." Red informed.

They put all the guns in the crypt and slid the marble slab back in place.

"Now lets get out of here." Red said after locking the steel door back with the padlock.

Red looked at Billy Joe. "I hope you got that little woman of yours under control now." Red said to him as they started down the steps.

"Don't you worry none about Sue Ellen. I kicked her ass a little. She ain't going to be talkin to anybody about anything from here on out." Billy Joe assured him.

"I'm glad to hear that. You know we got to knock our old ladies around once in a while. It keeps them in line. They got to know who is the boss." Red said with a chuckle.

"You got that right." Billy Joe agreed.

"Come on, let's go get your truck. We need to play it cool for a while." Red said as they left.

CHAPTER TWENTY SEVEN

The tall young doctor came down the hall to the waiting room where Carl and Margie patiently sat waiting for word on the condition of Sue Ellen.

"Hello. I'm Doctor Porter. Are you related to Mrs. Martin?" he asked with a friendly smile. He had a very kind face with very soft brown eyes. His dark wavy hair made him look much younger than his forty years.

"No, we are just good friends with her." Carl answered.

Margie cut in, we also live just across the street from her. "Please doctor, how is she?" Margie asked with great concern.

"She is fine under the circumstances. She has a broken arm, a concussion; I had to sew four stitches in her lip and she has two cracked ribs. The baby seems to be fine. But I want to keep her here for a few days just to be on the safe side. She has suffered a lot of trauma. I wanted to call the police. But she refused to press any charges against whoever did this to her." He said shaking his head.

"It was her husband." Margie spoke up.

"I thought that might be the reason. Would you like to see her now?" he asked.

"Yes, thank you, doctor." Margie said as she stood up.

"Fine. She is in room 104, that's just down the hall and to your right. Oh, and when you talk to her, see if you can't convince her to do something about her husband. You know if a man beats his wife like he beat her, he will most likely do it again. Next time she might not be so lucky." he said in a serious tone.

"You are so very right, doctor." Margie agreed.

Carl and Margie left the waiting room to go see Sue Ellen. Carl had called Sue Ellen's parents. They were on their way. They were hoping her parents would be at the hospital before Sue Ellen was placed in a room. Margie gasped as she saw Sue Ellen's face.

Margie fought hard to hold back the tears and anger that was welling up inside her when she saw how swollen Sue Ellen's face was. Her face was three times it size. She could barely see out the slits of her eyelids that were now nearly swollen shut.

"Sissy, where's Sissy?" Sue Ellen murmured low.

Margie went to her bedside. She took Sue Ellen's hand in hers. "She is fine. Sissy is with Ida Mae. Carl and I are going to pick her up when we leave here. She can stay with us till your mother and father get here."

"You called my mother?" Sue Ellen whispered.

"Yes, honey, I thought they should know. Besides, I think Sissy will be happier staying with them. With Carl and I both at work, she would have to stay at Ida Mae's. I know she would be happy there too. But if somehow Billy Joe ever found out it could be an ugly situation for Ida Mae's family." Margie said seriously.

"You're right. I never know how he's going to react to anything. Look at me." Sue Ellen tried to make a joke.

"Are you going back home when you get out of here?" Margie asked.

"I don't think so, I think I will stay at my mom's for a while. I need time to think and sort things out. I need to be away from Billy Joe for a while." Sue Ellen whispered.

"You need to rest now." Margie said as she was interrupted as Sue Ellen's mother and father entered the room.

"Oh my baby. What happened?" Sue Ellen's mother asked in an upset voice.

"Did Billy Joe do this to you?" her father asked angrily.

Sue Ellen nodded her head yes.

"That son of a bitch. Did you call the cops on him? He needs his ass thrown in jail for this."

"No daddy, please just let me work it out for myself." Sue Ellen said with a groan.

"I'm sorry, honey. We will discus Billy Joe later. You just rest." Her father said, patting her hand.

"I'm sorry. Are you the folks who called us?" He asked Margie who was now standing at the foot of Sue Ellen's bed.

"Yes, we live across the street from Sue Ellen." Margie replied.

"Thank you, where is our grandbaby?" he asked concerned.

"We were just on our way out to go get her. Sissy is with another neighbor who was kind enough to keep her while we brought Sue Ellen to the hospital. She is in good hands, believe me." Margie said.

"You said you live across from Sue Ellen?" Sue Ellen's father asked.

"That's right." Carl answered.

"Fine. We will be by to get the baby after we visit Sue Ellen for a while."

"518, that's our address." Carl said.

"Got it. 518. We will see you later then." Sue Ellen's father replied.

Billy Joe stood in the doorway; his eyes scanned the kitchen. He saw the bloody towel draped over the edge of the sink. The overturned chair on the floor next to a dried pool of blood.

"Sue Ellen." he called out as he started searching from room to room. His stomach began to knot up. Fear and panic began to run through his mind. Images of what he did to Sue Ellen filled his heart with shame and guilt. "Oh, Sue Ellen, what have I done?" he said out loud to himself. He knew that she must have went to the hospital. He ran out the door and jumped into his truck. He spun out of his driveway and onto the street. His truck tires squealed loudly as his engine roared taking off at a high rate of speed on his way to find out if Sue Ellen was there.

Carl and Margie had only missed Billy Joe by five minutes. They were over at Ida Mae's house to pick up Sissy so her grandparents could take her to their home to stay until Sue Ellen could get out of the hospital.

Billy Joe drove into the hospital parking lot. After parking he sat in his truck. He lit up a Lucky, took a long draw, leaned his head back against the rear window glass. He blew out the smoke. He stared up at the full moon shining brightly in the night sky. He thought to himself, wondering why he would get so angry at the one person he loved so much. How could I hit her? He thought to himself. She didn't mean to get me into any trouble with the law. But I just get so mad. She is probably going to leave me after this. Maybe she already has. Maybe she isn't here. Maybe I really didn't hurt her too bad. Fuck, I know I did from all that blood on the floor.

Well I got to find out and I can't do it sitting here. He thought to himself as he tossed his cigarette and got out of his truck. He walked into the hospital. As he went in the front door he ran into Sue Ellen's mother and father. He now knew positively she was there.

"You got some nerve coming here." Sue Ellen's mother snapped at him.

"Look, I'm sorry, I just lost my temper. Please tell me, is Sue Ellen OK? I need to see her. Please tell me where they have her. Please, I'm so sorry for what I've done." Billy Joe begged as tears rolled down his cheeks.

"You SON OF A BITCH. How could you hurt our little girl like that? If I was twenty years younger, I would beat the hell out of you, just like you beat our baby." Sue Ellen's father said angrily.

"Please, dad, I'm so sorry. If it will make you feel better go ahead and hit me." Billy Joe said as he stuck out his chin to him.

"Don't tempt me. I'm going to the car. Elizabeth, are you coming?"

"In a minute, Charles. Go home Billy Joe. Sue Ellen doesn't want to see you right now." Elizabeth said firmly.

"Wait, please just tell me. How bad did I hurt her? Please, mom, please." He begged holding onto her arm as tears streamed down his face.

"Do you really want to know? Do you?" She said choking back her own tears as she went on to say. "Let's see, where do I start? How bout I start with the fracture on her jaw, and the two ribs on her right side. Oh, and how about the two broken molars, and all the stitches in her tongue that she nearly bit in half. Not to mention her split lips that have stitches along with the head concussion, two black eyes, and you want to know how bad you hurt her? Well let me tell you this. You hurt her. You hurt her bad. I thought I knew you, but I guess I really don't know you at all. How could you?" She said angrily as she broke down into tears.

She shrugged from his grip and hurried out the door to the car where her husband was patiently waiting. Billy Joe stood in the doorway crying as he watched his in-laws drive out the parking lot. He wiped his face with his shirtsleeve. He started to go into the hospital to find out where Sue Ellen was. He stopped short as he saw two deputy sheriffs coming down the hall towards him. He turned around and went back out the door for his truck. Once back in his truck he just sat there. He sat there all night.

The dawn was breaking when Billy Joe went back into the hospital. He found out where her room was. He stared at her swollen face as she slept. Then he left.

CHAPTER TWENTY EIGHT

Billy Joe left the hospital and went straight to his job at the mill. After work he went to his house. Margie was sitting on her porch when he pulled in to his driveway. He looked over to her as he got out of his truck. He was about to say something to her, but she gave him a cold stare, got up from her porch swing, and went in to her house. Billy Joe dropped his head with a heavy sigh and went on into his house. As he came into the kitchen his eyes were fixed on the dried red bloodstain on the yellow block linoleum floor. He went to the closet taking out a mop and a bucket. He filled the bucket with hot water; he began mopping up the blood from the floor. He mopped the floor four times, but the bloodstain was still there. Finally he gave up. He carried the broken chair out to the garage. Then he went back into the house. He took a shower, and shaved. Got dressed and went to the hospital. This time he was determined to see Sue Ellen.

He arrived at the hospital around seven thirty. Sue Ellen's Mother had left only minutes before he went in to her room. Billy Joe pulled up a chair next to her bed. Sue Ellen turned away from him.

"Sue Ellen, please listen to what I have to say. Please, honey. I'm sorry. Oh God I'm so sorry I hurt you like this. Sue Ellen, please, honey, forgive me. I promise you I will never ever lay a hand on you as long as I live. Honey, please talk to me."

Sue Ellen rolled over to look at Billy Joe. She saw the tears running down his cheeks. Her heart went out to him for a second but a pain shot through her arm. Then she felt nothing but contempt for him.

"I'm through, Billy Joe. You made the same promise to me before. And the minute you loose your temper you take it out on me or Sissy. I can't take living like this anymore. You drink too much, and you run too much with your drinking buddies. I hate the fact you joined up with that Red Avery and his Kluckers. I hate everything they stand for. I wasn't raised to hate people because their skin color or religion is different than mine. I just can't deal with that any more. I can't deal with you. As soon as I'm released, I'm going to stay with mom and dad's. I need time to think, I need time away from you."

"Please, baby, don't leave me. Please, honey, I will do whatever it takes. I love you Sue Ellen. If you want me to quit the Klan I will. And I will stop drinking. Please honey, we belong together.," he cried as he buried his head in Sue Ellen's lap.

"Go home Billy Joe. You promise now, but you have to prove yourself to me. I want a real home. Hell, everything we got, somebody gave it to us. I'm tired of hand me downs. We could have more than we do. You spend half of your paycheck on beer for you and your friends. That leaves hardly anything for groceries. I would like just once to be able to buy something new. I would like to be able to have new curtains, fix up the house, and make it a real home. But I can't do that because you are content living like a bachelor. So I'm leaving you so you can live that way. I will give you three months. You show me that you can really change and just maybe, just maybe, I remind you. I might take you back. But for now just be thankful I refused to have you put in jail for assault. Now I want you to leave, and don't come back. I need to go to sleep now. I need my rest. Goodbye, Billy Joe." She said coldly.

Billy Joe stood up, his face tear streaked from crying. "All right Sue Ellen. I will prove to you I can change. You'll see. I will do whatever it takes to get you back. I love you Sue Ellen. I will never stop. You are my life. I can't live without you." Billy Joe sadly said as he turned to leave the room.

"You should have thought about that before you put me in here. Goodbye Billy Joe." She turned her head on her pillow as to not look at him.

Billy Joe dropped his head and slowly left the room.

Sue Ellen's words kept flooding through his mind over and over as he drove his truck home.

Billy Joe stood in the middle of his kitchen. He scanned it with his eyes. Sue Ellen is right. I guess this place is really a dump. He said out loud. He went into the living room; it looked just as bad he thought. Then he climbed the stairwell that they never used. He got to the top floor. To his surprise he discovered five rooms he never knew existed for he had never went up stairs before. He walked down the hall, checking out all the rooms. Well, Sue Ellen, if it takes making this place into a fancy house for you. I will make it happen, if that's what it takes to get you back. He said out loud to himself. He went back down stairs. He went outside to his garage. He opened his tackle box where he took out a coffee can. He took off the rubber band that held a cloth in place over the lid. Turning it upside down, he shook out the contents. It was money rolled up with rubber bands. Each roll was a thousand dollars. Billy Joe had nine rolls. He carefully took off the rubber bands on four of the rolls. He straightened them out, then folded them over and shoved them deep into his pants pocket. He put the other five rolls back into the coffee can and put it back in his tackle box. He went back to the house. He sat down at the table with a tablet and pencil making out a list of the things he was going to need to fix up the house. He got up from the table and went to the fridge.

"You are going to be the first thing to go." He said as he took out a beer. He had three left. He sat at the table making out some plans on the house. He downed the last of the three beers. He decided he was going to have one last beer fling, and then he was going to give it up for good. He decided everything he would need to buy in order to start on the house would be over in Jackson. So he decided to call in sick at work so he could spend the night over in Jackson and get what he needed in the morning first thing. He stopped on his way out of town at a phone booth and called in the night shift office to let them know he would be off sick for the next three days.

Billy Joe arrived in Jackson at one in the morning. He decided to go to one of the local bars. All the bars in Jackson had a three o'clock closing. He went in to a place called the Pink Lady. As he walked in he was amazed at the sight of topless girls dancing in cages on each end of a stage. The only light inside was the dimly lit candles on the tables and the colored spotlights shining on the girls dancing.

Billy Joe took a seat at a table in front of one of the cages. He ordered a beer. Billy Joe took a sip from his beer glass; the girl in the cage caught his eye. He licked his lips as the sweat beaded up on her large full rounded caramel colored breasts. He felt a hot flashing surge run through his body as her dark brown nearly black sparkling eyes met his. She flashed a sweet sexy smile at him. He felt himself becoming sexually aroused. He stood up and handed her a twenty-dollar bill. She thanked him then slipped the twenty into her G-string. He smiled at her,

"Hey can I buy you a drink?" Billy Joe asked as he slipped her another twenty.

"Why sure you can, sugar. I got one more song left. Then I will come join you." She said as she wiggled her hips to the music.

"You do that, sugar. I will be right here waitin." Billy Joe said as he gave her that boyish grin of his. Billy Joe thought to himself that she was the most beautiful nigger girl he had ever seen in his life. He couldn't get over how her jet-black silky hair flowed down her back, ending at her perfectly rounded buttocks. She had perfect long shapely legs. And her face he thought, man, she's as beautiful as Elizabeth Taylor. "I got to have her" he thought to himself.

"Hi sugar," she said as she sat down beside Billy Joe at the table.

"What are you drinking?" He asked politely.

"Well I'm not much of a drinker. Just make it a coke." She smiled at him.

"Coke it is. Boy you are going to be a cheap date." He laughed.

"Honey, you won't think that when you get the bill. They charge four dollars for a coke in here." She said seriously.

"Four Dollars, what a rip, but for you darlin, I don't care if its ten. Hell, baby I will buy you Champaign if you want it." Billy Joe grinned.

"Look here sugar, I don't want you to spend all your money in this place on me." She smiled at him.

"Don't you worry your pretty little head about me. I know when I spent enough money. Hey, you haven't told me your name."

"Sonia." She answered flashing him her sweet smile.

"Sonia, that's a pretty name. You can call me Joe." He said as he put his arm around her shoulder.

"Well Joe, what do you do for a living?" She asked as she sipped on her coke.

"I work in textiles." Billy Joe said as he smiled back with warm look in his eyes. God, you're beautiful." Billy Joe said as he looked deep into her eyes.

"You really think so? I've always thought I was just average." She blushed.

"Average? Oh God, no. You could never be average." Billy Joe said softy.

Billy Joe sat with her the rest of the night between her dances. The house lights came on.

"Last call, folks. It's closing time." The bartender called out.

"Well sugar it's been a wonderful night, but it's time I go home." She said as she kissed him on the cheek.

"Let me buy you breakfast. Please." Billy Joe begged her.

"I would love to. But honey did you forget where you are?" She smiled.

"I don't know what you mean." Billy Joe said with a puzzled look.

"A white man and a colored woman eating together. Maybe up North, but not in this state. You're in the south and that just doesn't happen here. Besides the only place open this time of morning is the Country Kitchen, and it's for whites only. They don't serve colored folks." She remind him.

"Well how bout I get us something to go and we go down by the lake and have ourselves a breakfast picnic?" He said giving her his boyish grin.

"I don't think so honey. I don't know you that well." She declined.

"Well, then can I see you tomorrow night?" Billy Joe asked with begging eyes.

"Well sure you can, if that's what you want. I better get going." She said as she got ready to leave the table.

"Can I. drive you home?" Billy Joe said quickly.

"No." She called back over her shoulder.

"I will see you." He said.

Billy Joe had checked in the Star Light Motel, it was just a half-mile from The Pink Lady club. Billy Joe had woke up around eleven that morning. First place he went to was the Jackson Paint warehouse store. He bought thirty gallons of white paint, brushes, and an extension ladder. As he was driving back to the motel, he spotted a for sale sign. He stopped his truck in front of the sign. He got out and walked up the little stone path leading to a little four-room cabin. It was a neatly kept little place. He looked in one of the windows; to his surprise he saw that the living room was all knotty pine board. He went back to his truck where he took out a pencil and paper to write down the phone number displayed on the sign. He drove from there and went back to his room at the motel.

Once back in his room he called the number for the cabin. "Hi, I'm calling about your cabin you have for sale on Lakeview road." Billy Joe said to the man over the phone.

"Yes, what can I tell you about it?" The man said back to him.

"Well, first of all how much you askin for it? And can I see it today?" Billy Joe sounding a little anxious.

"I'm askin six hundred for the place. If you can meet, me there in an hour, I will be happy to show it to you. By the way my name Elmer Coates, and who might you be?" Coates asked.

"My name Billy Joe Martin. I can be there in an hour." He told Elmer Coates over the phone.

"See you in an hour, Mr. Martin." Coates said.

Billy Joe hung up the phone. He decided to take the ladder and paint off his truck and leave them inside his room. He put the last can of paint in his room, then he locked his door, got back into his truck and headed back to where the cabin was to wait for Mr. Coates.

Mr. Coates was right on time. He drove up in his big fifty-six Buick. It was two toned red and black. Coates was a skinny little gray haired man in his late sixties.

"Mr. Martin?" He asked as he shook hands with Billy Joe.

"Yes sir. Billy Joe answered with a big smile.

"Well come on, let me show you the place. I got the key here somewhere. You are going to like it." Mr. Coates said as he fumbled with some keys he had on a big ring. "Ah. Found it." He smiled as he put the key in the lock, turned it and the door opened. Billy Joe followed him inside. The entire house was finished in knotty pine; the floors were matching hardwood. They shined. The whole house was kept very clean. It was even nicely furnished.

"You sellin the leather couch and chair too?" Billy Joe asked as he sat down on the couch.

"I will let all the furnishings go wit the house for a hundred fifty more. The lot is a full acre, you can have it all for seven hundred fifty dollars." Mr. Coates smiled at him.

"Well Mr. Coates, I'll take it. Will you take cash?" Billy Joe grinned.

"You bet I will. Follow me back to my house and we can sign the papers and the place is all yours." Coates said as he and Billy Joe shook hands once more.

After Billy Joe closed the deal on the cabin, he went to town. His first stop was the utility companies to have them turned on. He bought himself a new shirt and jeans, a few groceries. Then he picked up his ladder, paint and the shaving kit he bought that morning, and checked out of the motel. He went back to his new cabin and set up housekeeping. He was feeling very proud of himself for buying the cabin. After he put things away he took a shower and put on his new clothes. He went down to the Country Kitchen and ate dinner. Then he left the restaurant for the Pink Lady so he could see Sonia.

After each show she did, she sat with Billy Joe. They talked and were having a good time enjoying each other's company. Tonight when you get off I'm taking you for breakfast and I won't take no for an answer." Billy Joe grinned.

"I would love to go with you Joe, but we have been all through the reasons why I can't." She said sadly.

"Yes we can. I found the perfect place that will serve us, and I guarantee you that no one will bother us." He beamed.

"I don't know, Joe. I don't know of any place in this state or any state for that matter in the south." Sonia said firmly.

"Well I found one. So you just meet me out front when you get off." Billy Joe said, not giving her a chance to protest as she went up on stage to do her last show. He sat at his table and watched Sonia dance. He couldn't believe how he felt about her. He never thought he could feel so drawn to a colored girl. She made him feel really good about wanting to be with her. He thought he might even be falling in love with her. He hadn't even gave a thought about Sue Ellen. Not one time since he had came into the club and saw Sonia for the first time. Sonia was all he had on his mind since they met.

Billy Joe was leaning against a lamppost smoking a Lucky when Sonia came out of the club. "Wow, you look gorgeous." Billy Joe said to her.

"And you look very handsome." She smiled. "Are you sure we ain't going to get into no trouble?" She asked nervously.

"Trust me, I'm not going to let somebody as beautiful as you get into any trouble." He said smiling at her as he took her arm and led her to his truck. Billy Joe opened the door for her, helping her in, then he went to the driver's side, climbing in next to her.

"It will be all right sweetie. Don't you worry your pretty little head about anything. I will look out for you. I promise." Then he leaned over and gave her a little kiss on the cheek. He started the truck and drove off heading for his new cabin. He pulled his truck in the dirt driveway. He pulled as close to the front porch as he could.

"Why are we stopping here?" She asked.

"This is where we are going to have breakfast." Billy Joe said as he went around the truck to open the door for her.

"whose place is this?" She asked as she got out.

"Welcome to Joe's place. It's mine." He beamed.

"This is your house?" She asked.

"Cabin. It's a cabin, but if you want to call it a house, well I guess you can." Billy Joe said as he walked her to the front door.

They went inside. "Oh it's so beautiful." She gasped.

"You like it?" He said, happy that she liked it.

"Oh my, what's not to like?" Sonia said as she ran her hand over the back of the leather sofa.

"Come in to the kitchen, Madam, and I will put the steaks and eggs on." He said bowing like a nobleman.

After they had finished eating the steak and eggs Billy Joe and Sonia went into the living room. They sat down on a bearskin rug in front of the flagstone fireplace. Billy Joe lit the pilot light under the imitation logs. It gave off a warm cozy glow. Billy Joe had a bucket filled with ice surrounding a bottle of Champaign. He handed two wine glasses to Sonia as he rolled the Champaign bottle between his palms. Then he popped the cork on the bottle. He filled the glasses.

"I told you I don't drink." She smiled.

"Auh, come on just have one with me. I'm celebrating and I don't want to make a toast by myself."

"What are we celebrating?" She asked with a little giggle.

"It's my birthday and I'm celebrating that you are here with me and I'm not alone. And for that I thank you." Billy Joe said giving her one of his boyish grins of innocence.

"Why didn't you tell me? I would have gotten you a present." She said happily.

"You already did." Billy Joe smiled.

"No I didn't." She giggled.

"Yes you did." Billy Joe teased.

"OK, what?" She said as she sat up on her haunches.

"Just being here like this, letting me look deep into your beautiful eyes. Now let's make a toast." He held up his glass to hers.

"OK, a toast." She held her glass to his.

"Here's to the most beautiful girl in the world who has come into my life and made my world perfect."

They clanged their glasses together and drank down the wine. They laughed then Billy Joe looked deep into her eyes as he moved his face to hers. He leaned in and ever so gently kissed her on the lips. She felt the warmth of the passionate fire that was beginning to build inside their bodies. She sat her glass down on the floor next to her. She felt Billy Joe's arms around her. He began kissing her long and hard. Her body responded back. He gently laid her back on the rug, as a wave of electrifying currents ran through her body. Billy Joe had unbuttoned her blouse, then with one hand unfastened her bra. He slowly moved his lips from hers. He kissed her neck. Then ever so slowly he ran his tongue and lips kissing her breasts, her nipples stood up becoming very hard as she moaned low. Still holding her in one arm. With his other arm he slipped off her panties and skirt. He put his hand between her legs, he could feel how soft and moist she felt. Quickly he sat up and removed his shirt and jeans. They were now both naked, lying on the soft furry rug. She could feel his large penis pulsating against thigh.

"Joe we shouldn't be doing this." She moaned trying to fight off her desire for Billy Joe.

"Oh yes baby, we should. It's so right, we are meant for each other." Billy Joe murmured as he kissed her again.

"But I have never been with a man, I wanted it to be on my wedding night." She groaned.

Billy Joe stopped a moment to look into her eyes. "You telling me your a virgin?" He asked, a little surprised.

"Yes, I have never had sex with anyone. I have never even had a boyfriend." She murmured.

"Well I thought that is what I was going to be. Look baby, I'm falling in love with you and someday I want to marry you. So what makes the difference if I have you now or later?" He smiled.

"Don't you think we're moving too fast?" She asked.

"Hell no. I always go after what I want. And baby I want you. I know you feel the same way I do. I want you to be my wife. Will you?" Billy Joe said as he started kissing her breast again. Another wave of passion took over her body.

"Yes I think I want you too. If we are going all the way, please don't let it hurt." She moaned as he kissed her again.

Then he looked deep into her eyes. "Oh baby, I could never hurt you." He said as climbed on top of her. Then slowly but gently he began thrusting inside her. He took his time with her. At first she felt a hot burning pain, but it was quickly replaced by a huge rolling wave of desire, as she clung to him trying to reach the peak of erotic explosion of the fire within her body as they became one. Billy Joe had never felt such passion before. His whole body was exploding with passion and desire. They were both in a slow rocking motion as she reached the first climax of her life. She let out with a panting yell.

"Oh God, I'mmmm cumming. Oh yes, baby keep moving. Yes, Oh that's it. Oh baby."

"I'mmm coming with you. OH YEAH" He howled. Then they both fell limp. He rolled off her, then he took her in his arms where they fell asleep.

They woke up around noon, they made love three more times before they finally decided they were hungry. They got up and took a shower together. They dressed and went out to the kitchen.

"I'm fixin lunch." She said as she opened the fridge door. "Joe you ain't got any food in here." She said to him as she stared at the empty shelves inside.

"There are some eggs in the bottom drawer." Billy Joe grinned a big sheepish grin at her.

"I can sure see you're a bachelor." She giggled, pulling out the eggs.

They where seated at the table eating the eggs Sonia had just made.

"You know I been thinking." Billy Joe said as he chewed his bite of egg. "Why don't you move in here with me?" He smiled.

"Move in? Oh, I don't know Joe." She said a little surprised.

"Why not? You said you hated that roomin house. Look, honey, I'm gone most of the time, I'm only here on weekends. The place would just be empty when I'm gone, and when I come home with you here, well let's just say you would give me a reason to come home." He winked at her.

"Its so far from my job." She said.

"Take a cab." He answered.

"Take a cab? Do you know how much that would cost? I don't make that much at the club." She protested.

"Can you drive a car?" He asked.

"Yes, but do you see me with a car?" She asked.

"You got a license?" He asked.

"Yes." She answered again.

"There you go then. Problem solved." Billy Joe smiled.

"What? How you figure that?" She asked.

"I will get you a car." He smiled big as he leaned his chair back.

"Joe, buy me a car? Oh baby I think we are just moving too fast here." She said in protest.

"Look, honey, we care about each other, right?" He went on to say as she nodded her head yes. "Well there you go. Look, honey, I will buy you a car no strings attached. If it don't work out for us you keep the car as a token of what we have. Now you make out a grocery list and I will go to the store and you can come with me and pick out the car you want.

"What will people say if we are seen together?" She remind him.

"You know what? I don't really care what they say. All right, if it will make you feel better, I will tell them you're my maid." He said sheepishly. She finally gave in to him and they left for town to buy her car.

CHAPTER TWENTY NINE

Billy Joe left Sonia on Sunday night. He talked her into moving into the cabin. He bought her a red Chevy convertible, it was a used fifty-five, but in excellent shape. Sonia was thrilled with it. She had never been so happy in her life. Billy Joe couldn't believe how she had made a change in him. All he knew is he liked how she made him feel. He came down off his cloud as he drove his truck into his driveway. He unloaded the paint and ladder from his truck. After putting them on his porch he went into the house. As he walked into the kitchen the reality hit him. You have a wife, a white wife. He thought to himself. But I have Sonia now, I can't, and won't give her up. I will just have to figure out a way to keep both of them, he thought to himself, as he got ready for bed. It took him a while to fall asleep. But he finally drifted off. His dreams where filled with his and Sonia's lovemaking.

The alarm clock went off at six thirty, Billy Joe woke from the wonderful dream he was having. He got out of bed and dressed for work. Red Avery was leaning against his truck when Billy Joe arrived at work.

"Hey man, where you been?" Red asked.

"I had to go to Jackson. I'm fixin up my house." Billy Joe replied coolly.

"You were in Jackson for four days?" Red asked curiously.

"Yeah, I just needed some time to think, that's all." Billy Joe replied.

"Think about what?" Red asked.

"Well if you must know, how to get my wife back. Sue Ellen left me." Billy Joe said curtly.

"Hell man, just go get her and drag her home where she belongs." Red growled.

"That won't work with her. And besides, that's what made her leave me in the first place. She said I need to change my ways and that is exactly what I'm going to do. I want my wife back home and happy with me." Billy Joe said getting a little agitated at Red.

"You don't have to get so touchy." Red said as he spit tobacco on the ground. Billy Joe started to say something else but the whistle blew for work to begin.

Billy Joe avoided Red the rest of the day. He went straight home and began painting the outside of his house.

Carl and Margie watched through their front window, amazed at how hard he was working on the house. Billy Joe had the house painted by Wednesday night. On Thursday he began on the inside after work. He started by ripping up the old linoleum in the kitchen. On Friday he left work two hours early. He went straight to Jackson where Sonia waited for him to come home to their little cabin in the woods. She took that weekend off from her job so she could be with Billy Joe. They spent the weekend together making love and just enjoying each other's company. On Sunday he kissed her goodbye. He told her he wouldn't see her again until the Friday after next. She wasn't very happy about it, but she accepted it. For he told her he had to be out of state for his job. What he really was going to do is put more time in fixing up his house. He had promised to take her on a trip the first week of Dec. He was planning to fly out to Vegas and he wanted her with him. She was thrilled about the idea of them going someplace they could really be together in public. She didn't know he was planning to ask her to marry him there.

Billy Joe stood on the well-kept front porch of Carl and Margie Holt. He stood there hesitating for a moment. He drew in a deep breath, then knocked on their front door. The door opened.

"You got some nerve coming over here after what you did to Sue Ellen." Margie said angrily to him.

"Please. Wait. Hear me out, please." Billy Joe said as he tried to stop Margie from closing the door in his face.

"Is there a problem honey?" Carl said coming up to stand next to Margie.

"No problem. Billy Joe was just leaving." She said coldly.

"Please. This concerns you both. Just let me say what I came here to say, then I will leave. I promise." Billy Joe pleaded, tears welling in his eyes.

"Save it for Sue Ellen." Margie snapped.

"Wait a minute honey, let's hear Billy Joe out." Carl said as he put his arm around Margie's shoulder,

"Go ahead, Billy Joe let's hear it." Carl said waiting to hear him out.

"Look I know I have been an asshole. I have done a lot of things to piss people off. But most of all I hurt the only people who ever gave a damn about me. I hurt the two closest and dearest friends Sue Ellen and I ever had. I want to tell you I'm sorry and ask you for your forgiveness, I'm trying real hard to make things right between us. I don't know if that is still possible. But I have to try. I'm trying hard to change. I have stopped drinking and I am trying to make a real home for Sue Ellen and Sissy. I promised I was going to do all the things she wants right. But I can't do it alone. I'm fixing the house for Sue Ellen, but I don't have a clue as to how she might want the furniture, curtains, and the colors should be. Margie, I'm here to ask you because you are her best friend." Billy Joe said between sobs, them he dropped to his knees. He buried his face in his hands crying uncontrollably. Carl came out on the porch he knelt down beside him putting his arm around his shoulder.

"Come on buddy. Get hold of yourself. I forgive you. We forgive you, and I want to help. Everyone deserves a second chance. I'm going to help you, and Margie will too. Right Margie?" Carl said looking up at her as tears filled her eyes.

"Yes. I will do it for Sue Ellen." She said feeling sorry for Billy Joe.

"Come on buddy, let's stand up. Every thing is going to be all right. Come into the house we will have some coffee." Carl said as he helped Billy Joe to his feet.

"Bring him into the kitchen, I'll put the coffee pot on." Margie said as she wiped her eyes with her hanky. She rushed into the kitchen to start the coffee. The three of them sat at the table drinking coffee and talking things out. Two hours later Billy Joe went home to work on his house.

CHAPTER THIRTY

Agent Fred Wells walked in to Sheriff Combs office. All the photos of the murdered victims still on his make shift crime board.

"Hey Bill, I see you still have those crusem photos up." Wells smiled, they were now on a first name basis.

"Tell me you got something." Bill said looking up at Fred.

"Well I don't think our Billy Joe is our boy."

"Oh, and just how did you come to that conclusion?" Bill asked, sounding a little agitated.

"Lets just say the tail I had on him tells the tail."

"What? What the hell does that mean?" Bill asked with a look of confusion on his face.

"What I'm trying to say is I have had a tail on this guy for over a month now and all he does is go to work and come home every night five days a week. It looks like he's been working on his house at night, you know, remodeling." Fred said.

"So what's that prove other than he likes to fix up his house?" Bill replied.

"Well fasten your seat belt. He's got a girl friend he goes down to Jackson every Friday night to see her. He comes home on Sunday night and goes to work on Monday morning. I don't think he's our man." Fred said firmly.

"So what? That don't mean because he's banging some other woman that he isn't responsible for killing all those people." Bill said, pointing to the photos behind him on the board.

"His girlfriend is colored." Fred said.

"What?" Bill gasped not believing his ears.

"That's right. I think he just bought the ring like he said he did. He has had every reason to feel guilty with his wife. He's not Klan, that's for sure. They would hang him for having a colored girlfriend." Fred stated a known fact.

"Yeah, but what about his association with Red Avery?" Bill remind him.

"Hell he knows him because he works with him. That don't mean he's Klan because he knows Red Avery." Fred commented.

"I don't know, I still think he's involved in this more than the ring. I feel it in my gut." Bill said with a deep sigh.

"Your feeling in your gut is not hard evidence." Fred said sternly.

"Well maybe he knows your tailing him and he is throwing up a smoke screen." Bill said thoughtfully.

"Well what do you suggest I do? Keep the tail on him?" Fred replied. Asking with a slight bit of sarcasm in his voice.

"Well I think that would be a damn good idea. I know this guy is going to kill again." Bill said sounding very serious.

"Auh, come on, Bill. I don't think my bosses will let me have the man-hours. You're asking a lot for a man we don't have any hard evidence on. And I really think this guy is innocent." Fred tried to reason with Bill.

"OK, if you won't do it, I will on my off hours." Bill said stubbornly.

"Man you can't do that. You haven't jurisdiction in the other counties he crosses. If he did do something, you could not arrest him." Fred pointed out.

"I know I can't arrest him, but I would be a unshakable witness in court." Bill said.

"Look Bill, I will put a tail on him for another month. If we don't get anything on him by then, I have to call it off. In the meantime we will keep digging for hard evidence." Fred said with an honest smile on his face.

"Thanks Fred, I know I'm right about this guy. I feel it in my gut." Fred said with him jokingly.

"Well I better get going if I'm going to sell this to my boss." Fred said as he shook Bill's hand.

Agent Wells left the sheriff's office, leaving Sheriff Bill Combs in deep thought. "I'm going to get your ass, Billy Joe Martin. I know you're the one." Bill said out loud to himself as he leaned back in his chair.

Margie and Carl could see the big change in Billy Joe. They were nearly in shock the day Billy Joe installed a gate where the hole in the fence used to be. To top that off, he saw Marcy and William playing in the field. He called them over to him. "Hey kids come here a minute will you." He called to Marcy and her little brother William.

They looked frightened, but they reluctantly walked over to Billy Joe, not knowing what to expect. "Yes, Mr. Martin?" Marcy said.

"Aren't you Sissy's little friends?" Billy Joe said giving them a big smile.

"Yes sir." Marcy answered.

"You see this gate I just put in?" He said as he opened it, as though showing them how it worked.

"Yes sir." They both said shaking their heads yes.

"Well Sissy's going to be coming home soon and I want you both to know that you can use this gate to come in and play with Sissy. And look over there." Billy Joe pointed. "You see that play house over there?"

"Yes sir." They said eyes wide.

"Well I built that for Sissy and her friends to play in and tomorrow I'm putting up a swing set. So you kids can come over and play on it anytime you want." Billy Joe said smiling.

"Gee, thank you, sir." They replied happily.

"Mr. Martin, what day is Sissy coming home?" Marcy asked.

"I don't know what day, but she will be home very soon. Until she does get home, you can play on the swings and in the playhouse. I'm trusting you to kind of look after them for Sissy till she does get home. Think you can do that for Sissy?" Billy Joe asked.

"Yes, Mr. Martin. William and me we will takes good care of them for Sissy cause she's our friend." Marcy said excitedly.

"Good. Now you two better get on home before your mommy and daddy wonders where you are." Billy Joe said giving them a friendly smile.

"Yes sir. Goodbye Mr. Martin. Tell Sissy we said Hi." Marcy said as they headed home waving back to him. Billy Joe waved back smiling. Then he turned to see Margie and Carl standing by the garage with dropped jaws.

"Billy Joe, that was the nicest thing you just did. I'm really proud of you. I think you really mean it when you said you have changed. Did you really mean what you told those children?" Margie asked.

"I wouldn't have said it if I didn't mean it." Billy Joe answered Margie sounding sincere.

"Oh the reason I came over is to tell you I found the curtains Sue Ellen said she always wanted."

"Great. Why don't you guys go to town with me and help me pick out the furniture and stuff." Billy Joe suggested.

"Sure, Margie and I will be glad to go with you." Carl said.

The three of them left for town in Billy Joe's truck. "You sure have put an awful lot of work in that house for just being a renter." Carl said as they drove to town.

"It ain't a rental anymore. I bought it. It belongs to me and Sue Ellen now." Billy Joe said smugly.

"That's great, man. How much did you have to pay that old tightwad Hanson?" Carl asked with a chuckle.

"Nine hundred. Did I pay to much?" Billy Joe asked.

"No I don't think so. He charged me twelve hundred for ours." Carl replied.

"Yeah, but your house is a hell of a lot better than mine." Billy Joe commented.

"My house was just like yours when we bought it. I put all that work in it. Hell we didn't even have a hot water tank. We had cold water only for three months." Carl said.

"Billy Joe, I don't want to sound nosy or anything. But how are you going to pay for all this stuff your getting?" Asked Margie curiously.

"It's OK, I don't mind telling you. I been saving up for a house ever since Sue Ellen and I got married. Then I got promoted at work, which meant a raise in pay and I have been putting in a lot of overtime and when Sue Ellen left me, partly because she was tired of living in a dump and as you already know about my temper from drinking to much. Well, it woke me up. Instead of waiting another five years to give her all the nice things she wants and deserves I figured now is as good a time as ever to do it." Billy Joe told her.

"Well I think you are doing the right thing for Sue Ellen." Margie said as Carl agreed with her.

They pulled in to Mark's Furniture Store. It was next to a Sears store. Billy Joe gave Margie the money to go in to Sears and buy the curtains and bed linens. He and Carl went in to the furniture store. They would look around till Margie came back to help pick everything-out for the house.

There was a crisp chill in the air as Billy Joe got out of his truck in front of Sue Ellen's parent's house. He walked through the picket fence gate. He had brought a present for Sissy along with some drawings from Marcy and William, they had drawn for Sissy. The crisp chilly November breeze licked at his ears as he walked down the flagstone walkway. With one hand he turned up his jacket collar. Sue Ellen met him at the front porch. She pulled the fuzzy pink sweater front closed, arms folded to keep out the chill. "Billy Joe, you weren't supposed to be here till Friday. This is only Wednesday." Sue Ellen remind him as she wondered why he was two days early.

"I have to pull another double shift on Friday. So I wanted to see you and Sissy. I have some things here for Sissy. I didn't want to wait till next week to give them to her. Look Sue Ellen, I have done every thing you have asked of me. I haven't had a drink in over two months. How much longer are you going to punish me for the past?" Billy Joe asked.

"I am not trying to punish you Billy Joe. I need to know if I can ever trust you again." Sue Ellen said flatly.

"I'm trying honey I really am. Look can I please come in? It's cold out here." He said with a shiver."

"Yes I guess it can't hurt. I'm a little cold myself." She said as she opened the door, to go inside as Billy Joe followed close behind.

"Thanks, burrr. I think winter is almost here. Where's Sissy? I got some stuff here for her." Billy Joe asked trying to smile.

"She's in the kitchen with mom, they're making cookies. You might as well come to the kitchen and have some coffee. It will take the chill off." Sue Ellen said leading the way.

"Sissy, someone is here to see you." Sue Ellen called to Sissy as they approached the kitchen doorway. Sissy was standing on a step stool at the kitchen counter helping her grandmother roll out cookie dough. She looked over to the doorway to see her mother and father who was coming just behind Sue Ellen. Sissy looked up, her big blue eyes widened as she blinked. Her happy smile left her face as she saw her father come in.

"Billy Joe, we weren't expecting you till Friday." Sue Ellen's mother commented.

"Yeah, I know but I have to work. So I came over today. Sissy, I brought you something. I got some pictures Marcy and William made for you too." Billy Joe said as he sat down at the table. Sissy's face lit up when he mentioned Marcy and William.

"Wait a minute, honey. Let granma wipe your hands first." Her grandmother said as she wiped Sissy's hands with a wet cloth. "There. All clean, now go see what your daddy has brought for you." She said to Sissy as she helped her down off the stool. Sissy went over to Billy Joe. He gave Sissy the drawings. Sissy took them excitedly.

"What do the words say, daddy?" She said as she turned the drawings for Billy Joe to see.

"It says We miss you, and love you Sissy, please come back home soon. Love from Marcy and William." Billy Joe read the words on the drawings to Sissy. Then looked over to Sue Ellen. She was pouring the coffee into cups. She had a little disbelief and shock written on her face.

"When did you become friends with Sissy's friends? I thought you hated coloreds." She said surprised that Billy Joe was even talking to colored children.

"I have changed my way of thinking, Sue Ellen. I told you I'm really trying to be the man you want me to be." Billy Joe said sincerely.

"I'm sorry, I'm not used to seeing the new you I guess." Sue Ellen said as she brought the cups of coffee over to the table.

"Sissy this one is from me to you." He handed her the little white tissue wrapped box. "Go on open it." Billy Joe said smiling at her.

Sissy tore the red ribbon off, then the paper. She opened the top of the box. She looked inside, her eyes widened big as she reached inside and pulled out a music box. It had an angel on top of the gold and white porcelain box. "Gee. Oh daddy, its beautiful." Sissy squealed. "Look mommy, it's got an angel on top. Thank you Daddy."

"Turn it over, Sissy. You see that key, turn it." Billy Joe instructed.

"It plays music." Sissy said in amazement.

"Sissy, go show your music box to granma. I want to talk to daddy a minute." Sue Ellen told her.

"You still going to your Klan meetings?" Sue Ellen asked looking into Billy Joe's eyes as he sipped his coffee.

"I haven't been to a meeting in months. I guess you can say I'm not a member anymore. Sue Ellen, I've done a lot of soul searching lately. I don't think that way anymore. I hardly speak to Red anymore at work. Sue Ellen, what do I have to do to convince you to come home? Honey, I want us to be a family again." Billy Joe said taking Sue Ellen's hand in his. "I would like you and Sissy to come home by Christmas." Billy Joe added.

"All right, Billy Joe. I and Sissy will stay here till Thanksgiving, You are invited to have dinner with us anyway, I will have an answer for you then." Sue Ellen said firmly.

"Why can't you answer now?" Billy Joe asked.

"Don't push me, Billy Joe. I still need a little more time to sort things out. I want more from this marriage than you have given." Sue Ellen said in a serious tone.

"OK. What time is dinner?" Billy Joe agreed.

"At one." Sue Ellen answered.

"Is it OK if I come at around nine?" Billy Joe asked.

"I guess that is OK." Sue Ellen said.

"I just wanted to spend a little time with you. I have to work Thanksgiving. I don't have to be there until six." Billy Joe answered.

"You are sure working a lot lately." Sue Ellen said.

"Well we need the money with the new baby and all." He smiled at her.

"You really are thinking about us being a family, aren't you?" Sue Ellen said a little surprised at his statement.

"You just wait till you see how much I'm thinking about our family when you come home." Billy Joe grinned wide.

"Billy Joe, you give me the time I need and I promise I will give you an answer on coming home." Sue Ellen said taking hold of Billy Joe's hand.

"I guess I have to wait. Here, before I forget." He said as he handed a tiny little red box to her.

"What's this?" Sue Ellen asked as she took the box from him.

"It's a little present. I figured I owed it to you after the mess I made of our marriage." He murmured.

Sue Ellen opened the little box, inside was a ring similar to the ring Billy Joe had taken from Jane Green the night he killed her. "You got it back." Sue Ellen said puzzled.

"No, Sue Ellen, take a closer look at it. This time I bought it from a jewelry store. The diamonds are real; the blue stone is a look alike. It's real gold too. But it cost more than twenty dollars and it's a cheap copy of the one I should have walked away from. But I wanted you to have something nice. Something that shows how much I love you." He said earnestly, as he looked deep into her eyes, as his eyes welled with tears. Her heart went out to him. She began to see something in him she had not seen in him in a very long time. She was seeing a gentler, more loving Billy Joe.

"I think I like this ring better. No I don't just like it, I love it and I love you, Billy Joe. No matter what happened, I will always love you." Sue Ellen said as she slipped the ring on her finger. She cupped his face in her hands, and gently kissed him. "Thank you." She whispered.

Billy Joe wiped his eyes quickly and cleared his throat. "I better go, if I'm going to make it to work on time. How bout I call you tomorrow? It's OK if I call you, isn't it?" He asked as he stood up to go.

"I would like that. I'd like that very much." She answered as she smiled up at him. Billy Joe took her in his arms and kissed her long and deep.

"I love you." He whispered in her ear. "I got to go."

"Sissy, come give your daddy a hug and a kiss. He has to go to work." Sue Ellen called out to the living room where her and her grandmother were playing a game. Sue Ellen's mother had taken Sissy to the living room so Sue Ellen and Billy Joe could be alone to talk. Sissy shyly appeared in the doorway. "Come say goodbye to your daddy." Sue Ellen prodded.

Billy Joe made the first move. He went over to Sissy, he squatted down in front of her, and he pulled her close giving her a hug and a kiss on the cheek. "I will see you on turkey day. So you be good now. OK? Mind your mama and granpa and granma." Sissy shook her head yes. Billy Joe stood up, said his goodbyes to his mother-in-law and left. He really wasn't going to work, he was going to Jackson to see Sonia and spend the night.

CHAPTER THIRTY ONE

Billy Joe had had dinner with Sue Ellen, Sissy and Sue Ellen's parents on Thanksgiving Day. Sue Ellen agreed to come home with Billy Joe on December tenth. They had a pleasant dinner, except Sue Ellen's father was very cold to Billy Joe. He hardly spoke to him when they where at the dinner table. He went out to his workshop before and after dinner so he wouldn't have to talk to Billy Joe. After Billy Joe left Sue Ellen and his in-laws, he went to Jackson to have a. late Thanksgiving dinner with Sonia. The next day, Billy Joe and Sonia left for Kansas City on a train. From there they boarded a plane for Las Vegas.

They stepped off the plane in Vegas on Sunday morning. They took a cab from there, and checked in at the Tropicana. No one even noticed that Sonia was colored. She looked like a very beautiful tanned Hollywood starlet.

"Oh Joe, this is so exciting." Sonia said squeezing his arm.

"We are going to have one great week, baby." Billy Joe said to her on their way up to the room. Billy Joe tipped the bellboy. After closing the door he went over to Sonia, she was standing with her back to him. He snuck up to her and wrapped his arm around her, kissing the back of her neck. "Come on honey, put on your best outfit, and we will go out on the town." Billy Joe whispered softly to her, then he spun her around to face him. "But first, I want you to put this on." He said smiling as he stuck a ring box in her cleavage.

"What's this?" She asked with a giggle.

"Will you marry me?" He asked as her eyes lit up as she opened the box to see the diamond engagement and wedding rings inside. She threw her arms around his neck, as she jumped up and down squealing with excitement.

"OH.YES. YES. I will marry you." She said as she gave him a big kiss, then slipped the ring on her finger. She held her hand out admiring the engagement ring on her finger.

"Well, aren't you going to put the other one on?" Billy Joe asked.

"OH, No. darling, it's bad luck. You have to put it on at the ceremony. OH GOD. I don't have a wedding dress. I can't get married till I buy me a dress." She said with a moan.

"So we go get you a dress. What's the big deal?" Billy Joe said, trying to understand.

"What's the big deal? I want my wedding to be with a white gown and a veil. I wanted it to be in a church or chapel."

"Well let's go get you the dress you want, and I'm sure we can find a chapel. In fact I already made us a reservation at one." Billy Joe gave her a sheepish grin.

"Oh you." She said as she playfully hit his chest. "When?" She asked.

"Six P.M. tomorrow." He told her.

"Tomorrow. That only gives me a few hours to find the dress and get my hair done and, and..."

"Relax, honey, you're in Las Vegas. This place never closes. In fact the bellboy told me there are shops right here in the hotel. You can even get your hair fixed. I can't see why you think it needs fixin, I think it is beautiful already." He commented.

"Ain't that just like a man. Men just don't understand how a woman wants to look good for her man." She sighed.

"baby, you will always look good to me. Here, honey, will five hundred be enough to get a dress?" Billy Joe said as he took out a roll of bills.

"That's more than enough. A dress shouldn't cost more than two hundred." She said smiling.

"Well you take this, get whatever you need to buy. Go do your shopping. Then meet me in the lobby, say about four o'clock, and I will take you to dinner. How's that sound to you?" Billy Joe asked.

"That sounds great. But what will you do with yourself all that time?" She said concerned.

"Well, baby this is Vegas. So I'm going to do a little gambling." he answered. "Now hurry up and get changed and I will walk down with you." He said as he gave her a playful smack on her bottom.

"Just give me ten minutes." She smiled as she went into the bathroom to change.

Billy Joe left Sonia at the shops to do her shopping and he headed for the blackjack tables in the casino. He had a thousand dollars in his wallet to gamble with. He won, then he lost. Then he decided to hit the dice tables. He started winning, he had two thousand in front of him. He had a crowd of people around him cheering him on each time he threw the dice. He decided to make a very bold move. "I have four thousand in chips. I want to bet it all on this next roll. Can I do that?" He asked the pit boss.

"The sign says no limit. You sure that's what you want to do Mr.?" The pit boss asked as he pointed out the sign.

"Yeah, let it ride." Billy Joe said as he blew on the dice. Then he shook them in one hand. Everyone around him was cheering him on. He threw the dice. They rolled down the green, as they hit the backboard, they rolled to a stop.

"Seven. The winner." The tableman called out. Everyone broke out in a loud cheering yell. Billy Joe stood there a little stunned.

"Mr., you just won thirty thousand dollars." A man standing next to him said excitedly as if he had just won.

"What you going to do Mr.?" The pit boss asked as he waited on Billy Joe's answer.

"I think I'm going to cash out while I'm ahead." Billy Joe smiled big as he gathered up his chips.

"Wait a second, sir, I will get security to help you cash in your winnings."

"Thanks." Billy Joe said as a waitress handed him a drink.

Billy Joe cashed in, then took his winnings up to the room. They put his money in a little leather pouch. He hid it in his suitcase after he took out another thousand in his wallet.

He was so excited he was about to burst inside. He couldn't have been happier. He had never seen so much money in his life, he felt like a millionaire. He changed his clothes and went down to the lobby to meet Sonia.

She was sitting in the lobby with a dozen or so packages. "Damn, you must have bought the store out." Billy Joe kidded.

"I got all this for two hundred and thirteen dollars. I even got you a tux." She said, pleased with herself.

He helped her carry the packages back to their room. Then they went to dinner.

It was nearly noon on Monday when Billy Joe and Sonia woke up. They showered together, then dressed and went down to the casino for a little while after lunch. It was now three thirty, and Billy Joe was standing in front of a mirror fumbling with a cumber bun to his tux.

"Sue Ellen." He called out. Then he caught himself. "Damn." He said under his breath. Sonia stood in the bathroom doorway, a puzzled look on her face.

"Sue Ellen, who is Sue Ellen? You called me Sue Ellen. Who is she?" Sonia said a little hurt.

"I don't know, I think that was the name the operator told me when I called the limousine service, I guess. Hell I don't know, I'm so damn nervous, I don't know what I'm saying or doing right now." As he yanked cumber bun off. "How and the hell does this thing work?" He said looking bewildered.

"Here give it to me, relax, baby. I forgive you this time." She smiled at him as she took the cumber bun from him and began putting it on him properly.

"I'm sorry, you know it's not like I do this every day." Billy Joe said as he put his arms around her.

"You look very handsome." She smiled straightening his tie.

"And you are the most beautiful girl in the world. Hey, wait a minute. You haven't put your dress on yet." He noticed that she was wearing a pink sundress.

"I know. I'm taking it with us to the chapel. I will get dressed there."

"But I wanted to see the dress on you." He pouted.

"Because it's bad luck for the groom to see the bride in her dress before the wedding." She teased.

"OK, if you say so. I guess I better call to have them pick us up a little early."

"Oh My, Billy Joe, I just thought of something. Don't we have to get a license to get married?" Sonia asked concerned.

"Honey, it's all taken care of. We do all that at the chapel."

"But I always thought you have to get a blood test first, and fill out some kind of application at the courthouse." Sonia said thoughtfully.

"That's in Mississippi, this is Nevada. You don't have to wait in this state." Billy Joe informed her.

"I sure hope you're right." Sonia sighed.

"Trust me." He said, kissing her on the forehead, as he patted her on the bottom. "Now lets get started."

The limo stopped in front of The little white chapel, with a red carpet that led all the way to the chapel double doors. The sign above the church like steeple, read Cupid's Heavenly Hearts Chapel. The driver got out and opened the door of the limo for Billy Joe and Sonia. Billy Joe stepped out first, then he took Sonia's hand helping her out. The driver went to the trunk of the limo, took out the plastic bag that held Sonia's wedding gown. He handed it to Billy Joe. Billy Joe tipped him a hundred dollars, and asked him to wait till the services were over. Then Billy Joe and Sonia went inside the chapel. The Reverend who was to perform the ceremony met them in the hall of the chapel. He was a chubby version of Elvis. His hair was dyed jet black, with long sideburns. He was wearing a white choir robe with red sequin trim. He was probably in his late forties. His bleach blond heavyset wife showed Sonia to a changing room. She was in charge of the music. She played the organ and sang. There was an older gray haired man dressed is a black tux who served as an usher. Sometimes he gave away the brides.

Sonia came out of the changing room. "Oh my, you are such a beautiful Bride." The Reverend's wife said as she put her hands to her red cheeks that showed too much rouge. Sonia blushed as she stood there in her white satin flowing gown with just the right amount of lace and pearl beads. The Reverend's wife picked up the long six foot train of Sonia's gown as she directed Sonia to a little hallway. "Now you just wait here deary, till I get Marty to come back here so he can lead you down the aisle. She hurried off to where Billy Joe waited with her husband and the usher named Marty. "We are ready now." She said with a very cheery excited voice.

"Well then let's get started. You have the ring?" He asked Billy Joe.

"Yes right here." Billy Joe answered as he patted his coat pocket.

"Then just follow me." The reverend said with a hand motioning to him to follow.

Billy Joe nervously stood at the altar of the chapel with the Reverend. The Reverend's wife sat down at the organ. She began to play Here Comes The Bride. Billy Joe turned to see Sonia and Marty holding her arm as he led her down the long aisleway of red carpet between the pews. As he led Sonia to the altar, Billy Joe said out loud with a gasp, "God. She's so beautiful."

"I'll say she is. She has got to be the prettiest bride that has ever walked down that aisle." The Reverend whispered to Billy Joe. "You are one lucky fellow."

"You bet I am." Billy Joe grinned proudly.

Marty approached the altar, giving Sonia's hand to Billy Joe. He was shaking as he held Sonia's hand in his. The Reverend began his wedding speech he must have done thousands of times.

"Do you, Joseph Martin, take this woman, Sonia Banks to be your lawfully wedded wife?" He said as he watched Billy Joe staring into Sonia's eyes.

"I do." Billy Joe said softly.

"And do you, Sonia Banks, take this man Joseph Martin to be your lawfully wedded husband?"

"I do." She answered softly.

"Then by the powers invested in me from the state of Nevada, and the City of Las Vegas, I pronounce you Man and Wife. You may put the ring on her finger and kiss the bride."

Billy Joe pulled back her veil, and lovingly kissed Sonia. Billy Joe shook the Reverend's hand and Marty's hand as they walked back down the aisle together, the Reverend's wife played the traditional wedding march. Marty walked behind them tossing a little rice. They hurried out to the awaiting limo.

"Well Mrs. Martin where shall we go?" Billy Joe asked after they were seated in the limo.

"Anywhere you go." She answered as they kissed.

They went back to their hotel room and made love the rest of the night. They spent the next two days in the room making love and ordering their meals to the room. On their last day in Vegas they stopped by the giant slot machine.

"Oh Joe, please put a dollar in it." Sonia begged.

"This thing takes three dollars." He said.

"Please." She begged.

"OK." He said. He got change. He dropped it in then pulled the handle. Three sevens came up.

Billy Joe stood there frozen, as the red sevens came up. Lights flashed and bells rang as silver dollars clanged in the bottom of the large coin tray. Sonia jumped up and down screaming with delight.

"You won. Oh My God, you won the fifty thousand dollar jackpot." She shouted then flung her arms around Billy Joe's neck. "OHOOOOOWEEEEE! WE ARE RICH, BABY, RICH." She kissed, him as he was still just standing there staring at the machine.

People gathered around them cheering and clapping for their stroke of luck. Finally Billy Joe snapped out of it. "I can't believe it. Honey, you are my lucky charm." He said to Sonia as he gave her a big kiss. After Billy Joe collected his winning they were taken to the airport in a limo furnished by the hotel.

When he and Sonia boarded the plane, Billy Joe had eighty thousand dollars in. his suitcase. When they arrived back in Jackson he stayed with Sonia two more days. He had bought a little safe and installed it the day before he left. He installed it in the floor of the cabin. He had put the fifty thousand in the safe and took the thirty thousand back to his house in Cotton Wood where he had bought and installed another safe. He had installed that one under the main staircase closet floor. He was as happy as any man could be. Everything was going his way; he felt he had a life that every man dreamed of. He had it all. Two women who loved him, and the money to keep them both financially well cared for. He had thought of buying himself a new truck, but he thought it might draw attention to him. So he decided not to. Besides he loved his old truck, he told himself. He was very excited that night, he could hardly sleep because he was going the next morning to bring Sue Ellen home to stay.

He arrived at Sue Ellen's parents house at ten o'clock Sunday morning. Sue Ellen said her goodbyes to her parents as Billy Joe loaded the suitcases in the back of his pickup. A light snow had fallen during the night. It was barely an inch deep. But the temperature was very cold. Billy Joe's ears were red from the cold breeze that made his face and ears sting like a bee. He left his truck running so that he could warm the cab for Sue Ellen and Sissy. Billy Joe picked Sissy up and put her in the truck. He helped Sue Ellen in then he got in, as he waved at her parents. He drove the truck out of their driveway, heading for home.

Billy Joe stopped the truck two blocks from the house. He gave a red scarf to Sue Ellen. "Honey, I want you to tie this around your eyes." He smiled.

"What? Billy Joe what are you up to?" She grinned.

"You will see. Just put it on, I have a surprise for you. Please." He begged.

"Oh, all right." She laughed as she tied it around her head covering her eyes.

"No peeking." Billy Joe warned.

"This is crazy." She laughed again, "What will people think if they see us like this?" She giggled.

"They will think I'm a kidnapper." He laughed.

"Daddy, you want me to hide my eyes to?" Sissy asked.

"Yes, you too, you can hold your hands over your eyes. No one peeks till I say you can look. OK?" He said.

"OK." They both promised, as he drove to the house. He stopped the truck. "Now just wait till I get out and help you out." He said as he opened his door. He went around to help Sue Ellen and Sissy out of the truck. He took Sue Ellen by her shoulders and turned her to face the house.

"OK, you can look now." He said smiling.

Sue Ellen removed the scarf. "OH, Billy Joe, you painted the house. It is beautiful, and you put shutters up."

"Sissy, look over there." He pointed to the playhouse.

"Wowwee. Look, mommy. Oh, daddy thank you." She beamed. "Can I go see it?" She asked.

"A little later. First I want you to see what I have for you in the house." Billy Joe said as he steered them towards the house. Billy Joe opened the door. Sue Ellen and Sissy stepped inside, Billy Joe followed behind.

"Surprise!" Carl, Margie, and Marcy and Willie, shouted.

"Oh My, is this my old kitchen?" She gasped.

"Look, Sue Ellen, a brand new stove and fridge." Margie pointed to the new appliances.

"Oh, Billy Joe, it's beautiful." Sue Ellen said as she gave him a hug.

"Mommy, my room is gone." Sissy said sadly, looking as if she was about to cry.

"What?" Sue Ellen said as she looked into the room. "I don't understand, Billy Joe, where are Sissy's things?"

"You'll see. Margie take my girls on a tour of their new home."

"You bet. Come on, kids, you come with Sue Ellen and Sissy while I lead the way." She said happily.

"Oh, I can't believe this living room is exactly as I always dreamed it could be." Sue Ellen said as she ran her hands over the new sofa. "How did Billy Joe know I wanted mint green walls, and the dark green carpet and drapes. How on earth did he know?" Sue Ellen said with wonder.

"I knew." Margie spoke up. "Remember when you and I went through the Sears catalogue and you pointed at the stuff you wanted?"

"But how did you get Billy Joe to do all this?" Sue Ellen asked.

"I didn't. He came and asked Carl and I to help him. I picked out the colors and draperies and the furniture. Carl helped Billy Joe with the remodeling. Come on, wait till you see the upstairs." Margie said with excitement in her voice.

"Up stairs, I have never been up there." Sue Ellen said surprised.

They went upstairs. "Now Sissy you go in that door right there, and you will find your room." Margie told her.

"Come on Sissy. Wait till you see it. It's beautiful." Marcy said as she took Sissy's hand in hers.

"Yeah, wait till you see it." William repeated.

Sissy's eyes lit up as she walked in. So did Sue Ellen's eyes, as she saw the white canopy bed with matching furniture. Everything was perfectly matched. Pink wallpaper with white clouds and angels on it. The woodwork and ceiling were done in white, soft pink ruffled curtains and matching pillows and spread.

"I can't believe my eyes." Sue Ellen said.

"But mommy, where is my bed aunt Margie gave me?" Sissy asked.

"Come on, I will show you." Margie said as she led the way to the next room.

They walked into the next room. The bedroom suite that was Sissy's was set up. The walls were papered with cowboys and Indians on horseback. Everything was set up for a little boy's room. "Billy Joe said this room was for the baby." Margie said.

"But what if it's a girl?" Sue Ellen said.

"That's what I said to him, but he is positive you're going to have a boy." Margie laughed.

"Well I hope he is right." Sue Ellen hopefully sighed.

They went to the room across from Sissy's new room, it was very small, but it was all set up as a nursery for the baby. Sue Ellen was very pleased at every thing Billy Joe had done.

"Margie, what did Billy Joe do with all the old stuff?"

"He threw it all away. He and Carl and myself went to town and he bought everything new, except for the stuff I gave you."

"I wonder where he got all the money to do all this?" Sue Ellen asked Margie.

"Honey, Billy Joe has been working seven days a week, and he has been putting in a lot of overtime in, and fixing this place up when he had the spare time. He did this for you and Sissy. Sue Ellen, he has really changed, I have to admit that. I thought I would never be saying such a thing. But he has truly changed for you." Margie said.

"Six months ago would you see Marcy and William in your house with Billy Joe?"

"No. I guess you're right. That's a shock in itself." Sue Ellen commented.

"I haven't seen him take a drink since you left him." Margie said.

"I just hope he stays this way." Sue Ellen said seriously.

"I think he's really going to make things work out this time, because he doesn't what to lose you. He really does love you, Sue Ellen." Margie said firmly.

"Well how bout I fix us some lunch in my new kitchen?" Sue Ellen smiled. "That sounds great." Margie laughed.

"Mommy, can we go out and see my playhouse now?" Sissy said tugging on Sue Ellen's coat tail.

"Sure you can, but don't stay out to long, it's cold out there." Sue Ellen told her as they started down the stairs to the kitchen. Billy Joe and Carl were sitting at the table, drinking coffee. The children ran out to play. Sue Ellen went to the fridge. She opened the door to look inside.

"Billy Joe, there isn't any food in here. What am I going to make for lunch?" Sue Ellen asked.

"Damn, I forgot to buy food. Hey, Carl, let's you and me go to Piggly Wiggly." Billy Joe said as he leaped to his feet.

"I'm ready anytime you are." Carl laughed.

"Billy Joe, wait a minute." Sue Ellen said as she went up to him as he started out the door. She ran up to him, throwing her arms around him, she gave him a long hard kiss. "I love you, Billy Joe Martin. I'm so proud of you at this moment I could just burst with pride. Thank you, baby. I love everything you have done for me and Sissy. I love you." She said as she hugged and kissed him once more.

"I love you, too, darlin' but if I don't go get some groceries, we will all starve." He laughed as he left out the door, joining Carl who was leaning against the porch post grinning big as he saw how happy they seemed to be.

"Well, at least there's coffee." Sue Ellen joked. She poured Margie and herself a cup. They sat at the new kitchen table catching up on lost time. Suddenly Sue Ellen jumped, spilling her coffee as she heard the ringing of the telephone.

"Goodness, I forgot to tell you about the phone." Margie laughed.

"Telephone?" Sue Ellen said with great surprise.

"Yes, aren't you going to answer it?" Margie said with a smile.

"Yeah, I guess I should, but where is it?" Sue Ellen said as she stood up.

"On the little table by the stairs."

Sue Ellen hurried into the living room to answer the phone. She picked up the receiver. "Hello." She spoke into the phone.

"Sue Ellen, I was about to hang up." The woman's voice said over the phone.

"Mom." Sue Ellen stammered. "You knew?"

"Yes, Billy Joe gave me the number this morning when he came to the house to pick you up. He wanted the phone to be a surprise." Her mother giggled a little.

"I'll say it was that all right." Sue Ellen said with a slight laugh in her voice.

"Well, now you can call me once in a while. You don't have the excuse of not having a phone." Her mother said happily.

"Yes, now we can keep in touch more." Sue Ellen answered.

"Well, I got to get going. Your father and I are going over to the center to play bridge. So I will give you a call in a day or two. Give everyone our love."

"Goodbye. I will Mom, same here, I will talk to you later. Bye now." Sue Ellen replied, then hung up. "I can't believe I finally have a phone." She said to Margie.

Carl and Billy Joe returned with the groceries. After they put everything away, Sue Ellen fixed salads and grilled steaks on her new stove. After that day life for Billy Joe, Sue Ellen, and Sissy could not have been better. Sissy enjoyed her childhood with her two little friends, Marcy and William, without the fear her father was going to beat her. Sue Ellen was thrilled with her new home, and her new Billy Joe. She was happier than she had ever been in her marriage. She passed the days now waiting for the arrival of their new baby. Billy Joe kept a balance, for his two wives. He spent Monday through Thursday with Sue Ellen and Sissy. He would leave Sue Ellen at eight thirty on Thursday night, telling her he was promoted to inspector of other plants. That meant he had to travel to plants in other towns Thursday through Sunday. He was home at midnight every Sunday. He gave Sonia eleven thirty Thursday night till eight thirty Sunday night. Everyone was happy with the time he gave them. The only problem he was having is with Red Avery trying to pressure him to come to meetings of the Klan. On Fridays Billy Joe didn't have to be at work till ten A.M. he hid his truck behind the mill so it wouldn't be seen by anyone. He spent Christmas day with Sue Ellen, and Christmas night with Sonia. New Years Eve he have Sonia. New Years Day he gave Sue Ellen. The months passed quickly for him. As March arrived, so did the birth of his son on March second 1958. Sue Ellen gave birth to an eight pound baby boy. Sue Ellen's mother came to stay for a while to help Sue Ellen with the new baby. Billy Joe started feeling like a father. He was actually proud of the fact he had a son.

CHAPTER THIRTY TWO

Elvin ran his dirty hands across the bright red log splitter. He admired it wantonly with his eyes like a child wanting a new bike.

"She's a little beauty, ain't she?" Sam Decker said slapping Elvin on the back. Elvin looked at him, his right eye squinting, twisting his face as he spit out a wad of chew, at his feet.

"How much?" Elvin asked.

"Two hundred fifty." Sam answered firmly.

"Start her up, let's see what she can do." Elvin said.

Sam pulled the pulley rope on the motor. It started on the first pull. He picked up a medium sized log. He laid it long ways in the splitter. He pulled the lever on the side. A loud swooshing sound, and in ten seconds the log split in to four equal pieces.

"Hot DAMN." Elvin said as he danced around. "YAHOOO. That one bad sum bitch. I want it." Elvin said excitedly.

"You give me the two fifty, and it yourn." Sam said.

"Will ya trade fer somethin?"

"Depends on what you got to trade." Sam answered sounding a little interested.

"Take a look at these." Elvin held up a gold wedding set sporting very large diamonds.

"Wow, are they real?" Sam asked as he took them from Elvin holding them up to the sunlight.

"Hell yes theys real. I had them priced."

"You know old Harvey, at the pawn shop? He told me theys worth maybe a few thousand." Elvin informed.

"They sure do sparkle. If they is worth that much how come you want to trade for my log splitter?" Sam asked curiously.

"I don't just wants to trade for that, I wants that flat bed truck, too" Elvin said suddenly.

"I tell you what I will do. Let me find out just how much they are really worth and if they are worth what you say. Well then we got us a deal." Sam said still admiring the rings.

"How do I knows you won't try to cheat me?" Elvin asked suspiciously.

"Cheat you? You know when I give my word I keep it. If you don't trust me, then just forget about trading." Sam said a little annoyed at Elvin. He handed the rings back and started to walk away.

"Wait. Here, I trust you. How long you want me to wait?" Elvin asked.

"Tomorrow, three o'clock. I will have them appraised by a real jeweler. If he says they are worth what my stuff is. Well then you can pick up the splitter and the truck." Sam smiled.

"OK, three o'clock. Don't do me wrong, Sam." Elvin said as he started to leave.

"Hey Elvin, how did you come by them?" Sam yelled out as Elvin was in his pickup ready to leave.

"I traded some stuff for them." He answered, then drove off. Sam took the rings inside his store. He slipped the rings on his pinky finger. He really liked the way they shined. "You sure are pretty, how did you ever end up with a dummy like Gumm?" He said out loud. Suddenly he heard the bells jingle as his door opened. Sam peeked around one of his display shelves, he thought maybe Elvin changed his mind and came back for the rings.

"Oh, howdy, sheriff." Sam said as he realized it wasn't Elvin.

"Sam." Sheriff Jack Maxwell said with a friendly nod.

"What can I do for you sheriff?" Sam asked.

"I need some chain oil for my chain saw."

"Step over here, sheriff. I have three kinds and four sizes." Sam said leading the way. "Here we are, take you pick." Sam smiled. Maxwell took a small can off the shelf.

"I don't know Sam, is this one OK?" He asked Sam.

"What kind of saw you got?" Sam asked.

"A McCullough." Maxwell answered.

"then you will want to get this one." Sam said as he took a can from the shelf holding out for him to see.

"Wow, those are some rings, but aren't they for a woman?" Maxwell asked grinning.

"Oh, they're not mine yet, I'm considering a trade for them, when I find out how much they're worth." Sam boasted.

"Can I take a closer look at them?" he asked Sam.

"Sure can." He said taking the rings off his finger.

"They sure are some beauties. Who did you say gave them to you?" Maxwell asked Sam.

"Well, sheriff, I didn't, but if you're askin."

"I'm askin, Sam." He answered Sam.

"I got them from Elvin Gumm." Sam answered.

"GUMM? How did he come by something this fine?" Maxwell wondered.

"You know them Gumm boys they are always trading for something or another." Sam explained.

"When you supposed to make the trade with him?" He asked Sam.

"Three o'clock tomorrow. You think the rings are stolen?" Sam asked disappointed.

"Maybe." He said. "I need to borrow the rings for a little while, I'll get them back to you as soon as I check them out." Maxwell said slipping the rings into his shirt pocket. He paid Sam for the oil, then he got in his car and left. Sheriff Maxwell went back to his office. He went over to his desk and sat down in his chair. He took a card from one of his desk drawers. He dialed the number that was on the card. "Yes, could I speak to an Agent Fred Wells, please." He said to the operator on the other end.

"Hello. This is Agent Wells."

"Agent Wells, this is Sheriff Jack Maxwell, remember me? I'm sheriff of Tupelo."

"Why yes, how are you?" Wells asked.

"I'm fine. Say, I might have a break in the Green case." Maxwell said sounding very sure of himself.

"I can be there in an hour and a half." Wells said excited.

"You still got them photos of Mrs. Green's rings?" Maxwell asked.

"Yes, I will bring them with me." Wells told him then said goodbye and hung up the phone.

"John get your coat, we got a break in the Green's case." Fred called to John as he hung up the phone.

John grabbed his suit coat off the back of his desk chair. "What you got Fred?" He asked as he followed Fred out the office door.

"I will fill you in on the way to the car." Fred told him as they went down a flight of stairs to the car. Wells and Wallis drove up to the Sheriff's office. They found him waiting outside by his car.

"You must have broke all my speed limits to get here." Maxwell kidded. He pulled the rings out of his shirt pocket. He handed them to Wells through his car window.

"Are they a match?" He asked the agents. Wells took out a magnifying glass from his briefcase. He looked at the inscription on the inside of the rings. "You bet your ass they are." Wells grinned wide. "Were did you get them?" Wells asked.

"Just follow me, and you will soon see." Maxwell said.

"Lead the way. We will be right behind you." Wells assured him. Maxwell went to his car and the agents followed him in their car. They drove over to Sam's Store. Once they were there, Maxwell filled them in on Sam's deal with Elvin. They agreed to stake out Sam's Farm Store the next day to wait for Elvin's return at three o'clock.

Three o'clock the next afternoon, Elvin was right on time. He walked into the store, he wasn't alone. He had brought his twin brother Melvin. They went up to the counter were Sam stood nervously waiting. Elvin was so excited about his deal, he couldn't stop talking to Melvin telling him all about it. They didn't notice Sheriff Maxwell and the two F.B.I. Agents Wells and Wallis who were pretending to be customers browsing the store shelves.

"I'm here. I brought my brother, he can drive the truck home for me. We do haves us a deal right?" Elvin asked eagerly.

Sam stood there stammering for a moment. "Well ah...you see it's like this Elvin." Before he could say anything else, Agent Wells approached the counter. Sam's flushed face with beads of sweat gave a sigh of relief.

"What's your problem? We gots us a deal, don't we? Why ain't you sayin nothin?"

"I'm sorry, Elvin, you don't have a deal." Agent Wells broke in to say.

"WHO AN THE HELL IS YOU?" Elvin said his face snarled up.

"I'm Agent Fred Wells. I work for the Federal Bureau of Investigations, better known as the F.B.I."

"SO WHAT?" Elvin spat.

"Well I and Agent Wallis here are putting you under arrest."

"Arrest for what?" Elvin asked, looking very surprised.

"For starters, how about murder?" Wells said coldly.

"I never killed nobody. You guys are crazy. Melvin tell them." He called to his brother.

"Then tell me why you are trying to sell the wedding rings from a woman who was brutally murdered along with her husband and new born baby?" Wells pushed for an answer.

"I didn't kill that lady. I saved that little baby."

"Elvin you best shut your mouth." Melvin interrupted.

"No, I think it's in his best interest to tell us what he knows." Wells said.

"I ain't got nothing to say." Elvin clammed up, listening to his brother.

"Melvin, what you know about all this?" Sheriff Maxwell said from behind Melvin. "Come on, boys, I think both of you need to go down to my jail so we all can have us a little talk." Sheriff Maxwell said as he put cuffs on Melvin.

"AUH, come on, Sheriff, please don't do this to us. If we go down to your jail, we is dead." Melvin protested.

"Now why would you say somethin like that?" Maxwell asked.

"Why you shakin so bad, Melvin?" Maxwell asked, as Melvin shook uncontrollably.

"Sheriff, please don't take us to your jail, PLEASE."

"Come on boy, settle down." Maxwell said trying to calm Melvin.

"Sheriff, why don't we just take them to the car for now and talk to them there."

"Yeah, yeah, take us to the car, take us anywhere but your jail." Elvin spoke up. They took them in handcuffs out to their car. They put the two brothers in the back seat with Sheriff Maxwell who had rode to Sam's in their car. Wells and Wallis sat in the front seat.

"OK, boys," Maxwell said. "Let's start with the rings. Where or who did you get them from?" Wells asked making the brothers feel uncomfortable from his intense stare.

"I got them in a trade." Elvin answered.

"From who?" Wells asked still staring.

"I...I don't remember." Elvin stammered.

"I think you do, Elvin." Wells said knowing he was lying.

"Lets just take them to my jail. Maybe after they sit there for a while they just might change their minds." Maxwell said getting impatient with their answers.

"No, please. We go there we will be dead by morning. He will kill us." Melvin said getting hysterical.

"Who will kill you Melvin?" Maxwell asked.

"Yes, who? You said that inside. Come on tell us so we can help you." Wells said.

"Otis Macky, that's who." Elvin spoke up.

"Now you done it. We is dead for sure." Melvin groaned.

"Look guys. You tell us what you know, if you weren't involved in the actual murders we can protect you. You help us, and we will help you." Wells said.

"You promise we don't go to jail, and I will tell you whatever you wants to know." Elvin said.

"I can't promise till I hear what you have to say. But if you were involved in the actual killing of one or more of the Greens, then you will have to go to jail. But if you only saw or heard about it, and you didn't take part in any of the killings. As I told you before, you would become witnesses for the state and it would be our job to protect you." Wells told them.

"How is my deputy involved in all this?" Maxwell asked.

"He put up the road block, he told the Greens they had to take the detour cause there was a car wreck up the road." Elvin said.

"Then what happened?" Wells asked.

"Well, he knew they was going to get stuck. Cause earlier him and Red Avery took a tanker truck with water and muddied up the road halfway down that night. They put up the roadblock. Then my brother and .me, we followed Red .Avery and Billy Joe Martin in his truck. Otis was behind us in his cop car. It was just like old Otis figured. They got stuck. Red got out along with Billy Joe. Red walked up to the man. Billy Joe went over to the woman's side of the car. He opened her door and drug her out by the hair. Red shot the Man in the stomach. Didn't kill him right away. Red and Otis drug the man off to the side of the road. That's when Red took out his knife and cut off the guy's balls and dick. Then Billy Joe drug the woman over next to the man and shot her in the head. My brother and me had our guns with us, but we didn't fire a shot. The three of them was standin over their bodies laughin. I saw the lady's belly movin, the baby was trying to get out. So I knelt down beside her, took out my huntin knife, and I cut the baby out. I pulled him out, and he started cryin. He was the cutest thing I ever saw. I was going to keep him and take him home with me. But that Fucking Billy Joe snatched it away by its arm and he shot it in the head. I was so mad at him I took my gun and was going to shoot him. But my brother talked me out of it. I still think I should have shot him in his head like he did my baby." Elvin pouted.

"Well I think you just got a get out of jail pass." Wells said.

"What about you, Melvin? You got anything else to add?" Maxwell asked.

"Like what?" Melvin asked.

"Do you know of any other murders Red and this Billy Joe might be involved in?" Maxwell asked.

"Yes, he does. Go on Melvin, tell them about that nigger woman in Oak Wood, and don't forget all them niggers they killed at the Sugar Shack." Elvin prodded.

"It was Billy Joe who shot that old Mrs. Brock in the head. We was only supposed to scare them a little. But that Billy Joe, well he is mean clean through. I was at the Sugar Shack, but I was outside the whole time. Me and Perry Weeks, we was lookouts. But when we heard all the shooting and screams we left. Billy Joe, Red, Jimmy, Ray and Ricky Parks done all the killin in the bar. Ray Ray Smith told me that Billy Joe killed a nigger boy and his daddy at a lake, then Billy Joe killed another nigger kid and took his sister. They took her to some shack in the woods where him and Red raped her. Ray Ray didn't have anything to do with it. He said he tried to help the girl, but I guess it was to late. He heared she died. He don't want nothin to do with that crazy sunbitch any more either. We ain't been to any of the meetins since all this happened." Melvin said as he dropped his head.

"Sheriff, have you told anyone at your office about these boys?" Wells asked.

"No, I kept this to myself. I didn't want anyone tippin Elvin we were coming here." Maxwell assured him.

"What about old Sam in there?" Wells asked concerned.

"I think if we tell him to keep his mouth shut, he will." Maxwell assured him.

"OK, boys here is how we are going to do this." Wells said as he went on to say. "We got everything you just told us on tape. I'm going to have a typist put it on paper, and you two are going to sign it. Then we are going to get search and arrest warrants for these men. You will stay at our office until we have them all in jail. Then we will take you home and when they go to trial. You will tell the court everything you just told us here today. Oh, and one more thing, where does this Billy Joe keep his gun?" Wells asked them.

"Behind the seat of his pickup. He gots him a special made holster that attaches to the springs on the back of the seat."

"Thank you, Elvin, and thank you, Melvin. You both have been very helpful. But there is still the rings, how did you get them?" Wells asked.

"Billy Joe. He gave them to me on account of he killed the baby. He said it was a fair trade. It really weren't no fair trade. I wanted to keep the little critter, but I took the rings cause I didn't want him to have them." Elvin said.

"Sheriff, can you get a ride back to your car? I don't think these guys should be seen with us." Wells said.

"You're right. I will call my wife to come for me. I need to clue Sam in about keeping all this to himself anyway. What should I do about that damn deputy of mine." Maxwell asked.

"Keep him in the dark." Wells said.

"Don't say or do anything that might tip him off." Wallis finally spoke.

"That's right. We are coming back with fifty agents and warrants. We are going to get them all at one time." Wells added.

"OK, just call me when you're ready. What are you going to do about Ray Ray?" he lives in Cottonwood, that is Bill Combs district. Maxwell said as he got out of the car.

"We will pick him up later, we could use him as a. witness for the little Polke girl." I will call Combs to let him know we got the brake we bin hoping for in this case, Wells replied.

Maxwell left them and went into Sam's store as Agent Wells and Wallis drove the two brothers to Jackson where they got their federal warrants for the arrest of Red Avery, Billy Joe Martin, Jimmy, Ray, and Ricky Parks. Wells made a call to Sheriff Combs as soon as they got back to their office. He knew he was going to make Combs' day.

"Hello, Sheriff Combs. This is Agent Wells. We got them." Wells said with excitement.

"You found the gun?" Combs asked.

"Not yet, we got two maybe three witnesses who saw everything." Wells said.

"That's just great." Combs yelled happily over the phone.

"You want in on the arrest?" Wells asked.

"You bet your ass I do." Combs said.

"We should be there around nine, can you spare a few of your men?"

"How many you want?" Combs answered. "As many as you can spare. These guys might not give up with out a fight." Wells contemplated.

"Well, we will be ready for them if they do." Combs said secretly thinking he wished they would.

"I will have all the warrants with me, hopefully we will find the guns that did all the killings. But if we don't, the witnesses will be enough for a conviction." Wells said sounding confident.

"I hope you're right." Combs said, sounding a little skeptical.

"We are going to get them and bring them to justice. They are going to pay for all the lives they took. I promise." Wells told him.

"I'm hoping." Combs said.

"Well, I better get going if I'm going to get there by nine." Wells said, then hung up.

Red Avery sat kicked back in his shabby brown overstuffed chair, his feet propped on a raggedy footstool. He was clad only in his striped boxer shorts and dingy white undershirt with stretched out dirty gray work socks. He sat there sipping on a bottle of beer as he watched a boxing match on the T.V., unaware that Agent Wells and Wallis were surrounding his house with a team of twenty F.B.I. agents and Sheriff Combs and ten of his best and most trusted deputies. Sheriff Maxwell was riding with Sheriff Combs in his car. Everyone there had a stake in wanting to see these men brought to justice. All the cars rolled up to Avery's run down house with their lights off. They split up into four teams. They completely had his house surrounded.

"Peg, bring me another beer." Red called out to his wife.

"In a minute." She called down to him from the stairs.

"NOW." He yelled demandingly.

"I'm changing the baby, get it your damn self." She yelled back.

"You better hurry your ass up. I'll whoop your ass if you sass me again."

"I don't know why you're so damn cranky. You know I had to get the kids put to bed." Peg said as she slowly came down the stairs. A knock came from the front door.

"Answer the damn door." Red yelled out.

"Get me a beer, answer the damn door." Peg grumbled under her breath. She opened the door, as she did Wells, Wallis, Combs and Maxwell rushed by her. Another agent grabbed hold of her pulling her out to the porch before she could say or do anything.

"Well, woman, who's out there?" Red yelled out, never taking his eyes from the television.

"YEAH, HIT THAT NIGGER, YEAH, GIT HIM" Red shouted at the boxer on the TV.

"Is that what you told your boys when you murdered the Greens?" Wells asked as he stood behind Red.

"WHAT? WHO? AUH." He stammered as he was stunned by the agents and sheriffs who now surrounded his chair.

"Richard Franklin Avery, we have a federal warrant for your arrest and to search these premises." Wells said as he handed him the warrant.

"For what?" Red sneered.

"For murder." Wells answered with a solemn look on his face.

Red stood up, he threw the warrant back at Wells as he said grinning, "Shit. You ain't got nothin. Now get your ass out of my house." Red sneered..

"That's right. We ain't got shit, cause we got you, boy." Combs said as he put his face just inches from Red's face, looking him coldly in the eye. "After we search your house and property, we are going to haul your stinky ASS to jail," Combs added.

"KISS MY ASS, COMBS, you ain't got nothin, just like you and all these F.B.I. boys. You ain't NOTHIN. YOU HEAR? YOU'RE NOTHIN. You all don't know who your messin with." Red said then spit in Combs' face.

Combs grabbed Red by the throat. "AND YOU DON'T KNOW WHO YOUR MESSIN WITH, YOU WORTHLESS PIECE OF SCUM."

"Sheriff, let him go, you're choking him. Come on, sheriff, he is not worth it. Let's do this by the book." Wells said as he pulled at Combs' arm, trying to force him to let go of his grip on Red.

"You're right." Combs said as he released his grip on Red's throat, pushing him down into the chair wheezing and gasping for air.

"Dennis, go outside and ask his wife to get him some clothes to put on." Wells said to one of the young agents.

"Yes sir." He answered as he left to get Red's wife.

After they had Red Avery dressed, they cuffed him and put him in a car with three other agents and one of Combs' deputies taking him to Combs' jail to lock him up till they arrested the others. A team of agents were left to search Red's house. Wells, Wallis, and Combs along with Maxwell left Red's house to go out to the Parks brothers' residence. They used the same method as they used with Red Avery. Jimmy Parks lived in a run down old Airstream trailer out off old highway six. His trailer sat in a wooded clearing. The trailer was dark, the only lights were the head lights of the agents and sheriff cars as they drove into the clearing surrounding Jimmy's trailer.

"He's home. His pickup is here. Everybody stand clear of the door. This old boy's a little crazy, he might come out shooting." Combs warned the others.

Combs stood at the side away from the door as he banged his flashlight on the tin door. "Jimmy Parks, come to the door, it's Sheriff Combs. I need to talk to you." Combs called out, as he banged harder on the door. "Come on, Jimmy, open the door."

"WHAT THE HELL YOU WANT?" Jimmy called out as he got out of his bed from a sound sleep. "Well just hold on a DAMN minute. I got to put on my pants." Jimmy called back to them. A few moments later he came to the door, as they heard him tussling around inside. He opened the door. "What's so all fire important you got to get a man out of his bed for?" Jimmy said angrily.

Wells and Combs grabbed his arm and pulled him to the ground. After they put cuffs on him, they helped him to his feet.

"April Fools Day Jimmy." Combs said. "You are under arrest." Combs smiled.

"FER WHAT?" Jimmy demanded.

"For murder for starters." Wells said.

"I AIN'T MURDERED ANYBODY. You know me, sheriff. Tell them theys wrong."

"No, Jimmy, we aren't wrong. I do know you. I know you helped massacre all those people in the Sugar Shack Bar."

"You blamin me for killin all them niggers?" He said nervously.

"You didn't do it all by yourself, I know you had help and we are going after the rest of your friends. We already have your leader Red Avery. Now we are going to go get your brother's." Combs told him in a menacing tone.

"Why you doin this Sheriff? I can't believe you'd do this over a. bunch of NIGGERS gettin killed." Jimmy said trying to understand his situation.

"That bunch of niggers, as you called them, are human beings, you stupid Klucker. Human beings that you and your other Klucker friends massacred them. You, my friend, are getting better treatment than you deserve. If it were up to me I would just take you out and hang you . I'd be saving the state money." Combs leered at him, anger in his voice.

"So that's how it is. You're another one of those NIGGER LOVERS." Jimmy sneered.

Combs turned to him, then he punched Jimmy hard in his stomach with his flashlight, doubling Jimmy over.

"Sheriff, NO." Wells said as he stepped between Combs and Jimmy before Combs struck another blow.

Jimmy caught his breath. Two deputies helped straighten him up. "You better watch yourself sheriff, it might be you swingin from the end of a rope. And it just might be the people of the great state of Mississippi holding the other end." Jimmy spat.

"Deputies, take this man and put him in the car." Wells said as he held on to Combs.

"Bill, get hold of yourself. He ain't worth it. Let's finish the job. We still have to get the others." Wells said, trying to calm Combs down from his raging anger. "Come on, buddy, let's go trap us some more rat's. What a you say?" Wells soothed.

"You're right. Let's get the rest of those bastards." Combs smiled. The two men walked together back to their awaiting car with Agent Wallis at the wheel.

When they arrived at Rickey Parks' little three-room shack at the edge of town. Ricky was sitting on his front porch in an old rocking chair. His brother Ray sitting next to him on an old wooden crate. they were totally surprised as they saw all the cars roll up stopping in and around Ricky's yard. He stood up wondering what was going on. He relaxed a little when he saw Sheriff Combs.

"Hey, Sheriff." He said smiling.

"Ricky." Combs said giving him a polite nod.

"What you all doin out here this time a night?" Ricky asked innocently.

313

"We are here for you, Ricky and your brother Ray" Combs smiled up at him, as he came up on the porch with the others.

"Fer US? Shucks what you all want us fer?" He asked still smiling.

"Well, Ricky, these other fellows are from the F.B.I. and we have a warrant here for your arrest." And one for your brother Ray' Combs explained.

"Auh, shucks, Sheriff. What did we do?" He asked innocently as they put handcuffs on him and his brother Ray, who was not talking it was thoe he was in shock.

"Don't play that dumb hillbilly act with me, boy. You know what you did." Combs said as he closed and locked the cuffs on his wrist.

"WE didn't do nothin. Why you sayin we did?" Ricky asked with a dumfounded look on his face.

"Come on, Ricky, let's go join your brother." Combs said as he handed him and Ray over to the awaiting deputies.

Ricky didn't resist them, all he kept saying as he walked to the car, as he cried like a little child. "WE didn't do nothin."

Another team of agents began searching Ricky's little house. Maxwell and Wallis joined Combs and Wells on Ricky's front porch. "I just got a call from Agent Stiels. He said to tell you the Martins aren't home, said he checked with the neighbors and they said he took his wife and kids out of town somewhere. It's his oldest kid's birthday, said they won't be home till tomorrow night." Wallis informed.

"Well that's just great. So much for our surprise." Wells groaned.

"Wait a minute, Fred. I think we can still make this thing work." Combs said thoughtfully.

"How? These guys have already probably screamed lawyer." Wells said thoughtfully.

"Not if I tell my deputies not to let them make their phone call." Combs grinned sheepishly.

"Then we would be in violation of their civil rights." Wells remind him.

"No, not really. We can legally keep them for seventy two hours for questioning. It's too late for them to call tonight."

"Yes, but what about tomorrow?" Wells asked.

"I got that covered. Look, all we have to do is question them all day tomorrow for the crimes that took place here, and then we can transport them down to Jack's jailhouse where, by that time, it's too late for them to call. By that time we will have arrested Mr. Martin. After we have him, well then we let them make all the calls they want and there is no chance of our Mr. Billy Joe Martin being tipped off." Combs said proud of his plan.

"That's one hell of a plan, Bill. I like it." Maxwell grinned.

"Remind me never to get on your bad side, Bill." Wells laughed.

"Man you scare me." He added.

"Let's go, we have prisoners to interrogate." Combs said as they walked off the porch.

"Jack, what about your deputy?" Wells asked.

"No problem. I got that covered. He doesn't come on duty till one A.M. That's when I'm going to nail that little son of a bitch. He will be sittin in a cell waitin on his buddies when they join him." Maxwell laughed.

"Well, I guess my guys are going to get overtime tonight." Wells said as he got on his radio to call his two men he had staking out Billy Joe's house. He told Agent Stiels and his partner Agent Thatcher to stay at his post till midnight and they will be relieved by two more agents at that time. They returned back to Sheriff Combs' office to question their prisoners. Wells, Wallis, and Combs were sitting in Combs' office drinking coffee taking a break from there interrogation of their prisoners. The deputies and agents that were left at the Avery house and Parker's trailer had returned with the findings of their search. A deputy Randel and Agent Miller came in to Combs' office.

"Well what did you find?" Combs asked, as Wells and Wallis eagerly listened for their answer.

"No guns, sir." Randel answered.

"Not one?" Combs asked.

"No sir, we turned those places upside down. There was not even a toy gun.

"They must have smelled a rat. There is no such thing as one of these good ol boys not keeping a gun at their house." Combs said as he snapped a pencil he was holding in half.

"Maybe they hid their guns somewhere after the last killings. You know, just in case we came around like we did tonight." Wells said thoughtfully.

"You might be right. These old boys can be pretty smart sometimes." Combs said.

"Not smart enough to figure that one of there own would turn against them." Wells commented.

"I sure hope that will be enough to get them convicted." Combs added.

"Why don't you give Sheriff Maxwell a call to see if he is back to his office yet?" Wells asked.

"I'm sure he is there by now. But I'll give him a call anyway." Combs said as he dialed the number on the phone. "Sheriff's Department. Deputy Barns speaking, how may I help?" The young Deputy asked over the phone.

"This is Sheriff Bill Combs over in Cottonwood. Has Sheriff Maxwell returned yet?" Combs asked.

"No sir. He should be here anytime though. You want him to call you when he gets in?" The deputy asked.

"Yes, I need to know if he has arrested Otis Mackey."

"Yes sir, I will tell him when he gets in." The deputy said as he wrote the message down with a confused look on his face. Then he hung up the phone.

"Well, gentlemen, I guess all we can do now is wait." Combs said as he hung up the phone.

"Maybe he decided to stop at the truck stop and get coffee or something." Wells said.

"Maybe, but he wanted to be at the station before Mackey." Combs said thoughtfully.

"He knows if he misses him he can always radio him and get him back to the station." Wallis spoke as he was dusting off his shoe with his hanky.

"Yeah, I guess your right. I just want to get all of these vermin behind bars where they belong." Combs said slapping his fist into the palm of his right hand, gesturing.

"Easy Bill, we got them now and they are going to get what's coming to them. All of them." Wells said sounding very sure of himself.

"Well, I'm glad you are so sure. Maybe you have forgotten that there has never been a white man ever in the state of Mississippi for killing a colored man. Never." Combs said.

"Well, maybe it's time. When a jury hears the facts on the numbers at the bar massacred together in one place. I'm sure they will do the right thing. They will deliver the verdict of guilty and give them the death penalty." Wells said still feeling very confident that's how it was going to end.

"I'm going to call Maxwell again, he is bound to be there by now." Combs said reaching for his phone. Combs dialed the number, the deputy answered on the first ring.

"Deputy Barns, it's Sheriff Combs again. Is he back yet?" Comb's asked sounding a little worried.

317

"No sir, not yet. I was just getting ready to try and raise him on his car radio again. I tried before when you called the last time. I figured he was out of range." Barns said.

"You go ahead and try to radio him again, then call me back. Let me know one way or another. Oh, has Deputy Macky showed up for duty yet?" Combs asked before he hung up.

"No sir. He hasn't shown up yet, and he is a half hour late." Barns said then hung up.

"I don't like this. I know Maxwell, and it's not like him to be late." Combs said grimly.

"What did the deputy say?" Wells asked.

"He said Jack hasn't made it in yet and neither has Macky." Combs said.

"Well that might just be a coincidence." Wells said.

"Maybe he had car trouble." Wallis spoke up.

"I hope so." Combs said with a heavy sigh.

"How about if we don't hear from him, say, in another twenty minutes why don't one of us just drive the highway to Tupelo and see if maybe he did have car trouble." Wells suggested.

"Not a bad idea. We will give him another twenty minutes, then maybe we should all take that ride." Combs said as he lit up his pipe.

CHAPTER THIRTY THREE

He could see the lights of the truck stop in a distance. Three more miles to go he thought to himself. Then suddenly, he felt his front tire start to thump. "DAMN. Just what I need, a flat tire." Maxwell said out loud as he pulled his car off to the side of the road to come to a stop. He hustled his bulky body reluctantly out of his car. He stretched his arms, and yawned He walked to the front of his car to take a look at his tire.

"Well, Jack, I guess you get to change a tire tonight." He said out loud, as he walked to open his trunk. Jack put his key in the trunk lock, opened the trunk lid, he reached in and took out the spare tire. "DAMN, I don't believe this. IT'S FLAT! That's what I get for giving my brother-in-law this job." Jack said out loud. "All that little son of a bitch has to do is keep the cars running and check out the tires. You wait till I see him tomorrow." He said grumbling to himself. He put the tire back in to the trunk slamming the trunk lid. "Well, Jack, my boy. I guess your going to have to walk." He thought to himself, as he started to walk away from his car.

"Sheriff Maxwell, this is Deputy Barns. If you can hear me, come in please." Barns' voice said coming over Maxwell's car radio. Maxwell reached in his car window for his mike.

"Maxwell here." He said.

"Sheriff, is that you?" Barns asked excitedly.

"Who the hell do you think it is, Mickey Mouse?" Maxwell said sarcastically.

"Sorry Sheriff. It's just that I have been trying to raise you for a while."

"OK. You got me. Now what do you want?" Maxwell asked.

"Sheriff Combs has been calling for you. He asked if you arrested Deputy Macky yet. What's going on, Sheriff?" Barns asked.

"Has Macky come in yet?" Maxwell asked avoiding his question.

"No sir, but why you going to arrest him?" Barns asked.

"Because if you must know, he broke the law. He has tainted the badge he wears. NOW stay off the radio about Macky and listen to me. I have a flat tire and no spare. I'm about a mile from the truck stop. I'm going to walk down there. I want you to send a car out to pick me up. I'm going to get myself a cup of coffee. Call Combs and tell him what's happened. Tell him I will call him as soon as I get to the station."

"Yes sir, I will get Jameson to come pick you up right away." Barns said.

"I will radio you back. I may not need a ride, someone just pulled up behind me. Maybe they will give me a ride to the station. I will call you back in a minute." Maxwell said as he squinted to see who was behind his car with their bright lights on. He could barely make out the tall dark figure walking towards him. He called out to the figure. "Boy am I glad you stopped. You think you could give me a ride?" Maxwell asked with a smile on his face.

"Why not?" The man answered.

"Great, just let me call my deputy to let him know I won't be needing a ride." Maxwell said as he reached back into his car for his mike that lay on the front seat.

The man quickly ran up to Maxwell and shot him in the head. Maxwell's body slowly slid to the ground next to his car. The Man fired again. Maxwell's body made a slight twitch as the second bullet struck his head. He looked down at Maxwell checking to make sure he was dead. The man turned and walked back to his pickup truck he was driving. He was wearing his uniform. His name tag read Deputy Otis Macky. Macky made a u-turn in the road and headed for his house where he packed up what little he owned, loaded it in his truck. He left Tupelo and drove to Kentucky where he had some cousins that were Klan members. He knew they would let him hide out where no one would ever come looking for him.

Barns sat by the radio for about fifteen minutes waiting for Maxwell to call him back. Finally he decided to call him. "Sheriff Maxwell, come in, please." There was no response. He tried for five minutes. He decided to send Deputy Jameson out to look for him. It was another twenty minutes when Jameson arrived at the truck stop. When he didn't find the Sheriff he drove down the road to see if he could locate his car. He spotted the car on the other side of the road, he made a u-turn pulling behind Maxwell's car. His headlights shined on Maxwell's body crumpled in a heap beside his car.

Wells and Wallis rode in Combs' cruiser towards Tupelo. They decided to go look for Maxwell when they didn't hear back from Deputy Barns. As they rounded the bend about two miles from the truck stop. They saw flashing red lights, an ambulance, and three or four sheriff cruisers. They could see as they came closer, several deputies directing traffic around all the lit flares on the road. Combs pulled his cruiser off to the side of the road parking behind one of the deputies' cruisers with it's flashing red lights. "Must have been a bad accident." Wells said as they came to a stop. A young thin deputy approached them as they got out of the car.

"What's going on deputy?" Combs asked as he got out of his car.

"Something very bad, sir." The deputy said, his eyes filled with tears, as he went on to say. "Someone killed Sheriff Maxwell. They just shot him in the head." He said, tearfully trying hard to keep composure.

Combs looked towards the ambulance to see them loading Sheriff Maxwell's body. "Son, who is your under sheriff?" Combs asked.

"That would be Joe Weederman, sir." The Deputy answered.

"Has he been notified?" Combs asked.

"No sir, he is probably in bed." The Deputy answered.

"Well don't you think you need to wake him up?" Combs said sternly.

"Yes sir, I'll do that right now, sir." The Deputy said a little nervous.

"Tell him we will meet him at the Sheriff's office."

"Yes sir." The deputy said as he turned and went over to his cruiser to radio for the Under Sheriff.

Combs and the two agents with him got back into his cruiser and drove off for the Tupelo Sheriff's station.

Under Sheriff Joe Weederman was waiting in Sheriff Maxwell's office when Combs, Agents Wells and Wallis came in. The four men shook hands as they introduced themselves to one another. Combs filled Weederman in on the investigation. Maxwell, himself, and the two agents Wells and Wallis were conducting.

"So what your telling me is that Jack was going to arrest our Deputy Otis Macky?" Weederman asked looking skeptical.

"Correct, but as you know, Jack never made it. And neither did your Deputy Macky." Combs said getting a little agitated with Weederman.

"Jack never told me of any of this. I'm his under Sheriff, why did he not fill me in?" Weederman said feeling betrayed by his boss.

"Jack didn't want anyone tipping Macky off." Combs told him.

"Well someone must have." Macky hasn't reported to work." Weederman said.

"I think it might have been me, sir." The tall blond Deputy Barns said standing in the doorway, his eyes red from crying. Everyone looked up at him.

"You, how? You telling us that Sheriff Maxwell confided in you, and not me?" He said feeling a little agitated.

"No sir, the sheriff didn't say anything about Otis. I found out when you called, Sheriff Comb's. Then when you told me to keep trying to radio, I'm afraid I repeated what Sheriff Combs said over the radio. It's possible that if Otis was on his way in he might have heard my transmission over his radio in his truck." Barns said regretfully.

"How many times did you broadcast it?" Combs asked, adding that he repeated what he had said exactly.

"Well on the first call I said Sheriff Maxwell if you can hear me, Sheriff Combs called and was wondering if you had served the arrest warrant on Otis Macky yet. I didn't say it again till I finally got the sheriff on the radio. That's when he got after me for saying it over the airways. So I guess it's my fault the sheriff got killed." Barns said breaking down into tears.

"Take it easy deputy, we can't be sure that Sheriff Maxwell was killed because you left it slip about Macky." Combs said, putting his arm on his shoulder.

"Then why isn't Otis here right now?" Barns asked.

"I think we need to find that out. Has anyone been to Macky's residence?" Combs asked.

"Not as far as I know." Weederman said.

"I guess we can. Where does he live?" Combs asked.

"Wait a minute. I can't let you go over there. This ain't your jurisdiction." Weederman protested.

"Well, Wallis and I can." Wells spoke up.

"You can?" Weederman said.

"That's right. I can go anywhere in the United States of America to investigate a suspect in a federal crime. Killing a Law officer is a federal crime." Wells said reminding him of his status of being an F.B.I. Agent.

"That's right. Deputy Barns, get the address for us. Lets go fellas." Combs said with a chuckle.

CHAPTER THIRTY FOUR

"I think our moms and dads really had a great time, don't you?" Sue Ellen said as she gave the baby a bottle.

"Yeah, I think they did. Hell your dad even said more than ten words to me." Billy Joe commented.

"Oh, honey, he's warming up. I think this trip to the Opry is really showing him that you have changed for the better." Sue Ellen assured him as he drove down the highway.

"I know my Dad had a good time. He loves that Roy Acuff." Billy Joe said smiling.

"Well, I know my mom and dad were really impressed with this station wagon. I only wish we could keep it. It's so much nicer than your pickup." Sue Ellen sighed.

"Well, we can't keep this one because it's a rental. But maybe we can buy one like it next month." Billy Joe grinned.

"Oh, honey, could we, really? Do you think we can afford it?" Sue Ellen said with excitement.

"Sure we can. Remember I got that promotion. I know it keeps me on the road a lot, but it is giving us a better life." Billy Joe said earnestly.

"Yes, we have had a wonderful four days. I know it will be something Sissy will never forget. She just loved the zoo and the amusement park was a child's dream come true. And I think you had just as good a time as the rest of us." Sue Ellen kidded as she tickled his ribs.

"You're right. I did. I have always wanted to go to the Grand Old Opry House. I would like to go to see Elvis one of these days too. He's the Man." He said smiling big.

"Yaha, I would like that too." Sue Ellen answered thoughtfully.

"Well here we are. There's Ole Bessy." Billy Joe said as he turned into the car rental lot. "I will unlock the truck for you. You and the baby go ahead and get in. I will wake Sissy up and get her in the truck." Billy Joe said as he parked next to his truck.

Sue Ellen and the baby got into the truck. Billy Joe woke Sissy, he led her to his side and had her slide in the middle. After he unloaded everything from the wagon, he locked it and tossed the keys in the night slot.

Billy Joe got into his truck after he dropped the keys in the night slot in the front door of the car rental. "So you really like that wagon, do ya?" Billy Joe said as he shut his truck door.

"Yes, I think it's a beautiful car." Sue Ellen answered.

"Well, I think if I'm going to get a car like that I think you should learn how to drive."

"ME drive? My daddy went crazy trying teach me in our old Buick." She laughed.

"Well, I'm not your daddy, and you won't be driving in an old Buick. You will learn in a new car, and it will be an automatic, you won't have to worry about learning how to shift." Billy Joe said seriously.

"Well, I guess it can't hurt to try." Sue Ellen said thinking how scary it sounded to her.

"Margie drives and so do lots of other women." Billy Joe pointed out to her.

"I said I would try, but don't be disappointed if I mess up." Sue Ellen warned.

"Don't worry honey, you will do fine. I promise." He smiled as he leaned over and gave her a kiss on her cheek.

"Thank you. I'm glad you got all this faith in me." Sue Ellen smiled.

"Is he all right? He sure does sleep a lot." Billy Joe said, looking over at his baby son in Sue Ellen's arms.

"Of course he is. He's just a good baby, that's all."

"I guess I just don't remember Sissy being that quiet." He replied.

"Sissy honey, wake up. We are home." Sue Ellen said shaking Sissy's leg gently.

"Sure is a lot a cars parked on the street." Billy Joe observed as he turned into his driveway.

"Maybe someone is having a party." Sue Ellen remarked.

"Could be, but all the houses are dark." He said wondering.

"Maybe they are stay overs." Sue Ellen said trying to explain it.

"Oh well, it's none of our business." He said as he opened the door for Sue Ellen.

"Come on, Sissy go in the house with your mommy." He told her as he unloaded the truck. Arms loaded, Billy Joe followed Sissy and Sue Ellen into the house. Sue Ellen took the children upstairs and put them to bed. Billy Joe sat the suitcases on the floor next to the toys and souvenirs. He fixed himself a cup of coffee, took it into the living room turning on the TV, made himself comfortable on the couch. Sue Ellen came down and joined him a few moments later. She curled up with him on the couch. They watched a little TV together. Then they made love on the couch.

"I wish you didn't have to go." Sue Ellen said as they were still locked in each other's arms. Billy Joe still on top of her, as he kissed her neck.

"I know I wish I could stay too. But if we are going to get that new car, I have to go to work." Billy Joe teased. Then raised himself off her. "Honey, I will only be gone for five days. Then I will be home and give you some more of this." He said with a smile as he leaned down and kissed her breast. "I got to take a shower and get ready to leave. You going to join me?" He held out his hand to her. His lean naked body glowed in the reflection of the TV. They went into the bathroom and took a quick shower together. Sue Ellen threw on a robe as Billy Joe got dressed.

"Do you have everything you need in your suitcase?" Sue Ellen asked.

"Yes, I'm pretty sure, honey." Billy Joe replied as he zipped up his pants. He put his arms around her. "I'll be home before you know it. You won't even have time to miss me." He smiled then he kissed her long and hard. "I love you." He whispered.

"I love you too." She answered softly.

"OK, honey, I got to go. Don't forget I will call you day after tomorrow." He said as he let her go, picked up his suitcase and went out the door to get in his truck. Sue Ellen stood in the doorway looking out at him as he gave her a wave. She started to wave back when suddenly she saw several men surround Billy Joe slamming him against the front of the truck.

"F.B.I. Billy Joe Martin, you are under arrest in the murders of Jane Green and her infant son." Wells said as he read the charges on the warrant.

Sue Ellen came running out of the house down the porch barefoot in her bathrobe screaming hysterically. "What are you doing to my husband?"

"Sue Ellen, go back in the house. It's just a mistake. I'll be OK." Billy Joe told her as they handcuffed him.

"Mam, listen to your husband. You need to go back into the house and stay with your children." Wells said as he pulled her away from the truck.

"You're wrong, my husband wouldn't kill anyone." She cried.

"Mam, that's for a court to decide now. The Best thing you can do for your husband now is wait till morning and get him a good lawyer." Wells said, feeling sorry for her.

Carl and Margie were awakened by the shouting. They could see what was happening from their front window. They came out of their house when they saw Sue Ellen being held by the shoulders to calm her down by two F.B.I. agents. As they crossed the street they saw Billy Joe being put in to the back seat of the sheriff's car in cuffs. "What on earth is going on?" Carl asked.

"They are taking Billy Joe to jail. They think he killed somebody." Sue Ellen cried. She jerked away from the agents' hold on her. She ran to Margie throwing her arms around her crying.

"Where are you taking him?" Carl asked.

"He will be at the Cotton Wood Jail for tonight. He will be transported to Tupelo or Jackson by tomorrow afternoon. You will have to call the Sheriff's department in the morning. They can tell you more about it." Wells said coolly. He looked at Sue Ellen. "I'm sorry for you, Mam, but you don't know all the facts about your husband." Wells said as he tipped his hat and went to his car with his two agents to leave.

"Sue Ellen, let's go into the house." Carl said.

"Yes, honey, you're going to catch a death of a cold out here with no shoes on." Margie remind her. The three of them went into the house. Margie made a fresh pot of coffee as Carl sat down at the table with Sue Ellen.

"All of this must be over that stupid ring Billy Joe bought for me last year." Sue Ellen said as she sobbed.

"Look, Sue Ellen, Billy Joe may not be an angel, but I don't think Billy Joe had anything to do with those murders. I got a friend of mine who is a criminal lawyer. I will give him a call in the morning."

"Oh yes, that's right, dear. Carl is talking about Ben Stien. He is an excellent attorney. We will all go down to the jail as soon as Carl calls him. I'm sure he will take Billy Joe's case." Margie said trying to sound reassuring for Sue Ellen's sake.

"That's right, Sue Ellen. Don't you worry about a thing. We are friends and friends help each other out." Carl smiled.

"You get some rest now. We will talk to you in the morning." Margie said.

She slowly opened her eyes to focus on the soft warm glow of the fireplace. The leather sofa she was lying on squeaked under the movement of her body as she stretched her arms. She yawned, as she got up from the sofa. She bumped into the suitcase sitting in the doorway to the kitchen as she went in. The cabin was dark except for the glow of the fireplace.

"Ouch." Sonia said as she stubbed her toe on the suitcase. She turned on the light over the sink. She looked up at the clock hanging on the wall over the kitchen stove. "Ten after four" she said out loud. "Oh, Joe, we missed our train," she thought to herself. She decided to fix herself a cup of coffee. She sat down at the table, waiting for the coffee to brew. The quietness of the house gave her an eerie feeling.

"Get hold of yourself, Sonia." She said out loud as she shifted her shoulders. "Oh, Joe baby where are you?" She said out loud again. She poured herself a cup of coffee. She sat back down, trying to figure out why her husband hadn't showed up yet. He had never been late before without calling her. And to not show up for a little Vegas getaway they had planned together a month ago just wasn't like him she thought. He just wouldn't buy tickets and not call without a good reason.

"Oh, God," she thought out loud, "What if he had an accident out on the highway somewhere? Maybe he is hurt, and lying in a hospital somewhere, or worse. Surely someone would call me." She started to cry. "I need to call someone, but who?" she thought. "I know, I will call the highway patrol first." She thought to herself, as she jumped up and ran to the phone. Sonia picked up the phone an dialed the operator.

"Hello operator? Could you please give me the number for the Mississippi State Highway Patrol?" She asked as she pulled out a pen and paper from the phone stand drawer. Sonia wrote down the number as the operator gave it to her. She pushed the receiver button down, and the quickly let it up to get a new dial tone. Then she dialed the number the operator gave her.

"State Highway Patrol, Officer Jay Thomas speaking, how may I help you?"

"My name is Sonia Martin. My husband Joe Martin was supposed to be home by one A.M. We were supposed to catch a train at two thirty for Kansas City. It's after five now." Sonia said trying to hold her composure.

"Well, Mam, maybe he had car trouble or something." The officer said.

"Or something. Maybe he had an accident. Have you had any car accidents last night or this morning?" Sonia said trying to control herself.

"No Mam, everything has been quiet. Not even a fender bender tonight." He told her.

"Well, then I want to file a missing person's report." Sonia said.

"Mam, the highway patrol doesn't do missing persons. That would be your local police department and they won't take a report, till he is missing at least seventy-two hours. Mam, he is probably just late. I'm sorry I can't be of any help to you. Just give him a little more time. I'm sure he will come home and have a very good explanation." The officer tried to sooth her concerns.

"Thank you." Sonia said then hung up the phone. She called the Jackson police department. They told her the same thing the highway patrolman told her. She couldn't file a report for seventy-two hours. She decided to call as many hospitals as she could find in Arkansas, Alabama, and Mississippi. She didn't have any luck. So she just decided to wait, hope and pray that her Joe would be coming through the door soon with some good reason as to why he was late. She sat down in the big leather chair next to the phone stand. She cried herself to sleep.

CHAPTER THIRTY FIVE

Billy Joe was led in handcuffs by the two F.B.I. agents to a large cell where Red Avery and the Parks brothers lay stretched out on the bunks. They sat up when they heard the cell door being opened.

"OK Martin. Once you're inside, put your hands through the hole in the door. Then I will remove the cuffs." One of the agents told him. Billy Joe walked into the cell. He saw Red sitting on the edge of one of the bunks grinning wide. He turned and slid his hands through the hole as the agent removed the cuffs Billy Joe could hear Jimmy and Ricky mumbling something in the background to each other.

"I was beginning to wonder if you were going to join us." Red said snidely.

"Well, it sure is not by choice." Billy Joe snapped back.

"I thought maybe you turned rat when you weren't here last night." Red said.

"Rat? Why would I do something like that?" Billy Joe said angrily.

"Well, you weren't here and all the charges they read to us and the fact you have been acting like you're better than us. Well, you know." Red said shifting his red hairy shoulders.

"I don't know where they got all that stuff from. I was out of town with my family. We just got back a couple hours ago. The next thing I knew, I was being throwed over my truck hood by a bunch of guys in dark suits." Billy Joe said, anger building by the moment.

"Well, maybe it's that Jew bastard that lives across the street from you." Red said.

"You talking about Carl and Margie Holt? No way. They don't know anything about what I do. Besides I heard the suits say they had witnesses. That means that somebody had to have been there and seen everything." Billy Joe said as he lit a Lucky.

"I think you just might be right. I think I know who it is." Red said thoughtfully.

"Yeah, who? A minute ago you thought it was me." Billy Joe said angrily.

"I'm sorry, I thought that because you weren't in here with us last night. But you said you were out of town, so now I'm pretty damn sure who it is." Red said shaking his head with that get even tone of voice.

"Well, who?" Ricky asked.

"Look around you. Who isn't here?" Red said.

"The Gumm twins. Na, it might be that maybe they's somewheres too." Ricky said.

"Have you ever known them to go anywhere for more than a few hours at a time?" Red said more convinced as he thought about it.

"What about Ray Ray?" Billy Joe asked.

"What about him? He wasn't there when them niggers got it." Red defended him.

"What about the girl?" Billy Joe asked.

"What about her? He didn't have anything to do with it. Besides he was passed out from bein dead drunk. Na, it wasn't him. He wouldn't say nothin, he's too henpecked." Red laughed.

"Yeah, maybe your right. That Elvin doesn't like me. So maybe he did it to get even with me." Billy Joe said as he jumped up on a top bunk.

"Well, if we don't see them in a day or two, well then, we will know." Red said as he lay back on his bunk.

"Well ain't nothin we can do right now. We shouldn't be sayin nothin in here anyway. You don't know who might hear us. Besides we don't know if it's the Gumms or not. I'm tired, the only thing we can do is get us some shut eye for now." Jimmy Parks said as he gave in to a big yawn. "Goodnight guys." He said turning over on his side.

Billy Joe laid on his back staring up at the ceiling. His thoughts were on his situation and the look on Sue Ellen's face as the agents took him away. Then he thought of Sonia, waiting on him to come home so they could go on their trip to Vegas. "I have got to call her he thought to himself. But how? They won't let me make any calls. I got to get a message to her somehow, he thought.

"Billy Joe, you still awake?" Red whispered to him.

"Yeah, I'm awake." Billy Joe answered.

"I just wanted to tell you, they ain't got no evidence. You know the guns are not around. If all they got is some blabber mouth, well let's just say, suppose that blabber mouth just disappears? Anyway this is Mississippi, and there ain't no court around these parts going to convict a white man for killin some niggers. Well, we ain't got nothing to worry about. We will just play those F.B.I. boys' little game and I will guarantee you that we all are going to walk away from all this heroes. Mark my word, heroes." Red promised.

"Rise and shine boys." A deputy said as rapped the bars with his night stick.

"Go away. What we got to get up fer?" Red said sounding grumpy.

"If you want your continental breakfast, you'll come get it now. Cause you all are bein moved today and you might not get nothin for quite a spell." The deputy said as he rapped on the bars one more time.

Red got out of his bunk. "Movin us. Movin us where?" Red asked.

"I guess they ain't told you yet. You boys are going to Jackson." The deputy said handing Red a cup of coffee and a donut.

"Why Jackson?" Red asked.

"I don't know. I do know that you boys are famous now. You made the papers. Even got your pictures in it. Here, I brung one for you to look at while you have your breakfast." He said smiling as he gave Red the newspaper and handed the others their coffee and donuts.

"Well, see ya, TEE HEE." The deputy laughed as he pushed his breakfast cart down the hall. Red sat on the edge of his bunk, reading the paper out loud for the others. The F.B.I. arrest five Klu Klux Klan members in the brutal murders of Doctor Markus Green and his wife Jane Green and their infant son. Charges are also being sought in the Sugar Shack massacre and four separate murders. The four Klan members are Richard Avery, better known as Red. Billy Joe Martin, and three brothers, James L. Parks Raymond A Parks and Ricky Lee Parks. All residents of Cotton Wood, Mississippi. there are mug shots they took of us, sure don't do us justice." Red laughed.

"I need to make a phone call." Billy Joe interrupted Red as he jumped off the bunk.

"Guard, guard, I need to make a phone call. Guard." Billy Joe yelled.

"Relax, man, they will let us have our phone calls when they are good and ready." Red said looking up from the paper. "Sit down over here and take a look at your picture." Red grinned.

"You think this is some kind of fucking joke? You think getting our fucking names and pictures in the newspaper is something to brag about?" Billy Joe turned away from Red to yell for the guard again.

"Boy, you better stop all that yellin. Now you best settle down or me and these deputies here will settle you." The jail guard told him as three other deputies stood behind him.

"I want my phone call. I have that right. NOW OPEN UP THIS FUCKING DOOR and LET ME MAKE MY CALL." Billy Joe screamed at him angrily.

"I'm warnin you boy, SHUT THE HELL UP." The guard yelled back at Billy Joe.

Red and Jimmy got up from the bunk, and walked over to stand beside Billy Joe. Red took hold of Billy Joe's arm. "Billy Joe, come on man, let's go back over here and sit down. These guys are just waitin for an excuse to crack your head open."

"You better listen to your friend buddy." The guard said as he glared at Billy Joe.

"Come on Billy Joe," Jimmy said soothingly.

"I just want to make a phone call." Billy Joe said in a low murmur as he was being led over to the bunk by Red and Jimmy. "You don't understand. She's waiting on me. I need to call her. We are going to Vegas." Billy Joe rambled.

Red and Jimmy thought he was talking about his wife. "It will be all right. We will have a lawyer real soon when they read the paper and the lawyer will get us out. We just have to be patient." Red said trying to calm him down. Billy Joe crawled back up on his bunk. He closed his eyes as tears streamed down his face from the corners of his eyes as he saw the image of Sonia waiting and wondering where he was. It was four o'clock when they were moved to the Jackson jail. Once they were there, they were put in separate cells.

It was six P.M. when a jailer came for Billy Joe. "Martin, I'm here to take you down to make your phone call. I won't put the cuffs on you if you promise to behave yourself. You promise?" The jailer asked with a friendly smile.

"I promise. All I want to do is make my call." Billy Joe said sincerely. The jailer unlocked the door and led Billy Joe to a little room that had a wooden telephone booth with folding doors with glass windows.

"You got fifteen minutes." The jailer told him.

"Thanks, man." Billy Joe said with relief in his voice. He dialed the number for Sonia. The second the phone rang, Sonia picked it up.

"Hello Joe, is that you?" She cried.

"Yes. I'm sorry, honey, I worried you, but I was tied up on a job where there was no phone. Look, honey, we are going to have to postpone our trip for just a little while. Now, I'm not going to be able to come home till this thing with my work is finished." Billy Joe tried to reassure her that everything was all right.

"Do you know just what you have put me through? I was frantic! I didn't know if you were in an accident, or what." Sonia cried.

"I'm sorry honey! I just couldn't get to phone. The job site I'm working on has no phone. I was in a situation to where I couldn't leave the job." Billy Joe lied.

"I love you Joe and I miss you so much. Please don't ever put me through something like this again." Sonia said still upset and crying.

"I promise. I'm so sorry, I love you so much, honey, and I miss you terribly. I promise I will be home real soon. I will call you every chance I get OK?" Billy Joe said trying to smooth things over with her.

"OK, but do you know when? And are we still going to Vegas?" Sonia asked.

"Yes, honey, we are still going to Vegas! You just keep everything packed and I will call you in a couple of days, OK?" He said soothingly.

"All right. But I will still miss you." Sonia pouted child like.

"I miss you too, honey. And when I do get home, first I'm going to make mad passionate love to you, and hold you all night long. Then we will get up and go on our trip and when we get there I'm going to make love to you again, and maybe we might find some time to go gamble. This time we are going to stay for three weeks." He told her with a slight 7laugh.

"Three weeks? Can you get that much time off?" She said sounding much happier now.

"You bet. After this they owe me, big time." Billy Joe said.

"I can hardly wait." She said delighted with the news.

"Listen honey, I got to go, I don't want to, but the sooner I take care of this the sooner I can get back home to you. I love you, baby, and I will be thinking of you every minute" Billy Joe told her as he was getting a signal from the guard to hang up.

"I love you too, darling. I will be here waiting for you. I miss having your arms around me." Sonia said her goodbye to Billy Joe.

"Bye sweetie, I love you." Billy Joe said then hung up the phone.

"Was that your lawyer?" The jailer asked.

"No. It was my wife." Billy Joe answered.

"Most guys in your situation call their lawyers first then their old lady's." The jailer said surprised that he would call his wife first. He took Billy Joe back to his cell where Billy Joe spent the rest of the day.

After Sonia hung up the phone she decided to take a shower. She was feeling happy inside as well as very relieved to know that her Joe was OK and would be coming home.

Sue Ellen wasn't feeling so elated. She had went to the Cotton Wood jail with Carl and Margie Holt only to find out that she couldn't see Billy Joe because he was no longer there. He had been transferred to Jackson. Sue Ellen was very upset over this news. As they were on their way out of the jail, they ran into the lawyer Carl had called. "Ben." Carl called out to the short thin well-dressed gray haired man as he got out of his car. He walked towards Carl, who was walking towards him as Margie and Sue Ellen followed close behind Carl.

"Ben I'm so glad you came." Carl said as they shook hands. "Ben this is Billy Joe's wife! Sue Ellen Martin. Sue Ellen, this is Ben Stien." Carl said introducing them.

"Glad to meet you, Mrs. Martin." He said as he shook hands with Sue Ellen. "I was just on my way in to see your husband!" Ben smiled.

"He's not there," Carl broke in. "They took him to Jackson."

"I see. Well, I will have to go there tomorrow, it's too late to go there now. But I will go to see him first thing in the morning." Stien said.

"Thank you, Mr. Stien. I know they are wrong about the charges they have against my husband. I know my husband could not have killed all those people." Sue Ellen said tearfully.

"Now, now, don't you worry, dear. You need to stay strong for your husband. I'm going to see what they think they have against him. Then we will work everything out from there. Carl, you and your lovely wife need to see that she gets home. I will call you tomorrow when I know for sure what evidence they have." They said their goodbyes. Carl and Margie took Sue Ellen home where her mother waited with Sissy and little Joe.

Sue Ellen was sitting at the kitchen table holding little Joe in her arms feeding him a bottle, her mother was doing the dishes from lunch. Carl and Margie were sitting at the table with Sue Ellen.

"What time do you have to take the baby to the doctor?" Her mother asked as she rinsed a plate putting it in the strainer.

"Ten-thirty." Sue Ellen answered.

"Would you like me to take you?" Margie asked.

"I don't know! Margie you and Carl have done so much for me already." Sue Ellen smiled.

"Don't be silly! If you need to take our little angel to see the doctor, it's no trouble."

"OK, if you're sure?" Sue Ellen said.

"Is this just a regular check up?" Margie asked.

"No, the doctor is going to run some test." Sue Ellen answered.

"Test? What's wrong?" Margie said very concerned.

"I called the doctor last week about his check up. I was concerned about the way Joey acts." Sue Ellen said with concern and worry.

"Acts! How do you mean?" Margie asked with a puzzled look.

"Think about it! Have you ever heard him cry?" Sue Ellen asked Margie.

Margie thought for a moment, a perplexed look on her face. She looked at the baby. "Come to think of it I don't think I have ever heard him cry." Margie said.

"That's right he has never cried." Sue Ellen said sadly.

"Oh, Sue Ellen! Do you think he might be deaf?" Margie asked.

"I don't know, that's why I'm taking him to the doctor. I really need to find out." Sue Ellen said.

"I will come over in the morning and take you and the baby to the doctor. After that if you want to go see Billy Joe, we can go there." Margie said smiling.

"I think I should come right back home. Remember Mr. Stien said he was going to go see Billy Joe and that he would call me after." Sue Ellen remind.

"That's right. I forgot about that." Margie said.

"I have to find out when Billy Joe can have visitors anyway. I was planning on calling as soon as I hear back from Mr. Stien. I want to thank you and Carl for getting Mr. Stien for Billy Joe." Sue Ellen said.

"Sue Ellen, maybe you're just worrying too much." Sue Ellen's mother said.

"Mom, how can you say that? You had Sissy and Joe most of the day today and did Joe cry once today?" Sue Ellen asked.

"Well, no, he slept most of the day. I think he is just one of those babies that are just real good." Her mother said giving her opinion.

"Mom, Sissy was one of those good babies. But she cried, not a lot. But she did cry and she moved her arms and legs and even tried to hold her head up. None of which little Joe does at all-he just lays there and stares or just sleeps. And to me mother, well it's just not normal." Sue Ellen said frustrated.

"Now, now, Sue Ellen. Please try not to fret. You're taking him to the doctor tomorrow. So let's wait and see what he has to say about little Joe. I'll almost bet anything he's going to say he's just a late bloomer." Her mother said putting her arm around Sue Ellen's shoulder.

"I hope your right mom. Well, I guess I need to put him in his cradle. As you can see, he has went back to sleep again." Sue Ellen stared down at her sleeping baby with a deep sigh.

"Well, Carl and I should be going. We will see you in the morning, Sue Ellen." Margie said as she got up from the table with Carl. They said goodbye and went home. Sue Ellen put the baby in his cradle. She and her mother sat down to watch a little TV. Sissy was over to Marcy and William's house playing.

CHAPTER THIRTY SIX

Sonia was feeling elated, since she finally heard from Joe. She decided to go down to the Pink Lady were she used to work. She wanted to visit some of the girls she used to work with. She moved the packed suitcases from the hallway to the bedroom. She changed her clothes and freshened her make up, combed her hair, and happily left for the club.

She arrived at the Pink Lady around eight that evening. "Hi Marty." She said to the young, good-looking bartender.

"Hi Doll. Long time no see." He said cheerfully from behind the bar.

"Oh, I have been pretty busy since I got married you know." She said as she flashed her diamond ring at him smiling.

"Wow. I knew you had quit, but I didn't know you got married." He smiled as he held her hand admiring her ring.

"Is Peggy here?" Sonia asked.

"Yeah, she in the back." Marty said as he went back to wiping shot glasses.

"It's OK if I go back isn't it?" Sonia asked.

"Oh sure." Marty smiled.

Sonia walked to the back of the club where the dressing rooms were located behind the stage. She stopped at the first door and knocked. "Who is it?" Peggy called out as she sat in front of a large lighted mirror combing her hair.

"It's Sonia." She called back to Peggy.

"OH MY." Peggy squealed out with delight as she jump't to her feet to run to open the door for Sonia. She flung open the door, immediately throwing her arms around Sonia. They hugged each other, laughing and giggling with happiness to see each other.

"Girl we got so much to catch up on. Come on in. I want to hear all about what you been doin and why you haven't come by before now." Peggy said excitedly as she closed the door behind Sonia. I was going to come down and see you a long time ago, but I have been so tied up.

"To tied up that you can't come by and say Hi to your friends?" Peggy kidded.

"I was in Vegas. I got married there." Sonia said as she flashed her ring in Peggy's face.

"WOW, that's some hunk of glass." Peggy's eyes lit up. "Who's the lucky guy?" Peggy asked.

"His name is Joe Martin. I met him here. We fell in love, and the rest you know." Sonia smiled.

"Was he that tall dark haired handsome one that look a lot like Elvis?" Peggy asked.

"That's the one." Sonia beamed.

"Are you guys living up North?" Peggy asked.

"No. We live just a few miles out of town from here." Sonia answered.

"Oh, you haven't had any trouble out of other people?" Peggy asked curiously.

"I know what your trying not to say, Peggy."

"I...I just was worried. You know how some of these white men think around here. How some of them feel about mixed marriages." Peggy explained.

"We both understand that. We stay to ourselves a lot. We are very careful when we do go somewhere together. We are free to do as we please when we go to Vegas. Joe and I have talked about maybe moving to California someday." Sonia said.

"Well you just be careful. You should know better than anybody about how evil some of these people can be." Peggy warned.

"I know. We are being careful. Thanks for worrying about us." Sonia said with a smile.

"Well I hope so. I sure don't want to lose one of my best friends." Peggy said seriously.

They stayed and talked together till it was time for Peggy to go on stage. "Well I better get going. Joe might call and I wouldn't want to miss his call." Sonia said as she got ready to leave.

"Hey Sonia, could you do me a favor be for you go?" Peggy asked as she slipped on her G-string.

"Sure, what do you need?" Sonia asked.

"There's a quarter on my dressing table, could you go out to the paper box outside and get me a paper?" Peggy asked.

"Sure, I can." Sonia said.

"Thanks. You don't have to bring it back here. Just leave it with Marty. I will get it later." Peggy smiled. They hugged each other and then Sonia went out to get Peggy the paper.

Once outside Sonia went over to the paper box out front by the curb. She started to put Peggy's quarter in the machine, when the headline caught her eye. The color drained from her face as she read the headlines and saw the pictures on the front page. Her hand shook as she dropped the quarter in the slot to take out the paper. Her eyes began to well with tears as she stared at Billy Joe's picture alongside Red Avery and the Parks brothers. She felt faint as she read the newspaper quickly. She took the paper in and gave it to Marty.

"This is for Peggy. I will see you later. I got to go." Sonia said as she ran out before Marty could say goodbye. She dug in her purse and took out a quarter to buy another paper. She went to her car. She sat there crying as she read the whole story about Billy Joe and the others who were being held for the murders of the Greens and forty other murders. She cried uncontrollably as she read the part that said Billy Joe had a wife and two children. Once she got hold of herself she drove home to try to come to grips of the situation. She knew she had to find out if her Joe was really Billy Joe who was now sitting in the Jackson Jail.

Sonia had went home to think things out. She knew that Joe had kept some papers in the safe. She went over to where the floor safe was and threw back the throw rug that covered the little trap door over the safe. She knew the combination from watching Joe open it on many different occasions. She pulled back the trap door, and turned the dial on the safe. In the bottom of the safe was an envelope on top of the thirty thousand dollars Billy Joe had won in Vegas. She took the envelope out and opened it. Inside was the deed to the cabin. She burst out into tears as she read the name on the deed, Billy Joe Martin. Also in the envelope was a plant I.D. for the textile mill in Tupelo. It had his photo, name and old address on it. She sat cross-legged on the floor crying as she stared at his photo. She started to put every thing back in the envelope when she noticed that another photo had fallen out onto the floor in front of her. She picked it up and stared for a long moment of the blond girl holding a little girl about a year old. She turned it over to read the writing on the back, Sue Ellen and Sissy age two. She put everything back except the photo of Sue Ellen and Sissy. She started to close the safe, then she stopped, she reached in and took out the three bundles of money. She held them in her hand. She fanned her chin with the money thinking. Suddenly she tossed one of the stacks in the safe and slammed the lid and spun the dial to lock it. She put the throw rug back over the trap door after she closed it. She put the photo of Sue Ellen and Sissy on the fireplace mantel. Then she took the money into the bedroom with her where she pulled out a large suitcase. She tossed the money into it and took the rest of her clothes from the closet and dresser drawers and packed them into the suitcase with the money. She went back in to the living room. She sat down at the desk that sat in front of the bay window. She took a pen and writing tablet out of the desk drawer. She began writing a letter to Billy Joe, a very long letter. After she finished the letter, she put a stamp on the envelope. Then she called the jail and asked for their address and if Billy Joe would get the letter if she mailed it. The jail operator gave her the instructions on how to address it. She thanked the operator and hung up the phone. She took her suitcases and loaded them into her car. She closed up the cabin and mailed the letter on her way out of town.

CHAPTER THIRTY SEVEN

Sue Ellen waited in the hospital waiting room with Margie and Carl by her side. The Doctor had sent her over to the hospital from his office for blood test and X-rays of her baby little Joe. They waited for what seemed like twenty-four hours instead of just three hours.

"Sue Ellen, I'm sure everything is going to be OK." Margie said trying to cheer her up.

"I hope you're right. But I feel it in my heart that something is very wrong with him." Sue Ellen said, her face very haggard. Her doctor finally came in and pulled up a chair facing her. He took her hands in his.

"Mrs. Martin, did you have a fall or injure yourself while you were in at least your second trimester?" He asked as he looked into her eyes.

"Yes, I fell and broke my arm and some of my ribs, as well as my hip." Sue Ellen told him nervously.

Margie and Carl both sat there silently as they listened. Knowing that Sue Ellen just didn't fall, but they felt it wasn't their place to speak up.

"What does that have to do with my baby?" Sue Ellen asked.

"I'm getting to that." He said as he went on to say. "It seems that your baby has suffered some kind of brain damage. That had to have occurred from the fall you took or from the birth canal during delivery. It seems that the brain cells that signal his speech and his motor skills are the ones that are damaged now. As time goes by some of those cells may repair themselves. But you must know now that he may remain in a vegetated state. That means he may never walk or talk, or be able to express his feelings. In laymen's terms I'm afraid your son is severely retarded. We will just have to wait and see how he progresses in the next six months. He may gain some motor skills. We just have to wait and see. I'm sorry" he said as he squeezed Sue Ellen's hand. He stood up to leave.

"You can pick him up in a few minutes to take him home."

Sue Ellen sat there stunned by the news.

Margie put her arms around her. "Oh, honey, I'm so sorry, but maybe he might get better like the doctor said. Only time will tell."

"Maybe you're right." Sue Ellen answered, her eyes welling up with tears as she fought hard not to cry. "I need to go get my baby. Then we need to go home, I need to know what Mr. Stien found out." Sue Ellen said as she got up from the chair.

"Do you want Carl and I to come with you?" Margie asked.

"No, I will be fine. You and Carl go on ahead. I will meet you at the car."

"OK, we will pull around to the front so you won't have so far to walk."

"Fine I'll see you there." Sue Ellen answered.

Sue Ellen walked down the hall towards the nursery as Carl and Margie went to their car. A Nurse met her in the hall and lead Sue Ellen into the nursery where her baby lay in a crib. She put the baby's clothes back on him and wrapped him in his blanket. She picked him up and held him close to her. Sue Ellen closed her eyes and fought back the tears as she whispered to him. "Mommy loves you, baby, no matter what the doctors say. You will get better. I know you will." She told him then she carried the baby to the awaiting car where Carl and Margie drove them home. Sue Ellen's mother was in the kitchen sitting at the table when Sue Ellen came in.

"What did the doctor tell you?" She asked, anxiously waiting for Sue Ellen to tell her.

"Mom, would you mind putting Joe in his crib? I have to make a phone call, then I will tell you everything the doctor told me." Sue Ellen said as she handed her the baby.

Her Mother took the baby from her arms, "Sure, honey, you go make your call, I will make us some coffee after I put Joey to bed. Oh, Sissy is over playing at her little friends' house." She said as she started for the stairs to put the baby in his room.

Sue Ellen went to the phone and dialed Ben Stien's number. "Hello, my name is Sue Ellen Martin. I would like to talk to Ben Stien if he's there." Sue Ellen told the secretary that answered the phone. A moment later she heard Ben Stien's voice answer.

"Yes Mrs. Martin, I was about to call you myself. I saw your husband today and I read the police report on his case and I think we have a chance of beating this. Now he is going to be arraigned in the morning. I'm going to ask for bail. I think he might get it. This judge we are going before, well let's just say he's an old time Southerner." Stien said with assurance that he could get Billy Joe out.

"I hope so. When do you think I will be able to see him if he doesn't get bail?" Sue Ellen asked.

"I will call you tomorrow after the arraignment." Stien said sounding hopeful.

"Thank you, Mr. Stien, I will be waiting for your call." Sue Ellen said then hung up the phone. She went into the kitchen to join her mother who was now seated at the table patiently waiting for her to fill her in on what the doctor had to say about Little Joe's condition. Sue Ellen explained to her what the doctor had told her about the baby's condition. She had just finished telling her mother when Sissy came in. Sissy couldn't understand why her mother and grandmother were sitting at the table crying and looking so unhappy.

"Hear yee, Hear yee, this court is now in session. The honorable Judge Buffard J. Calhoun presiding for the state of Mississippi. The balding bailiff said as the Judge came into the courtroom taking his seat on the bench.

"You may all be seated." The Judge said as he looked through a stack of papers he brought with him. Billy Joe sat at a long table with his attorney Mr. Stien.

Red Avery and the Parks brothers were seated next to Billy Joe's attorney, and their attorney, Harvey Nivels, a lawyer for the Klan.

"Is the prosecution ready to state their case for arraignment and bail?" Cahoon asked.

"Yes, your honor." Attorney Albert Rollins said.

"State your charges." Cahoon said as he took a sip of water from a glass.

"The state charges are capital murder in the first degree, forty-two counts, your honor, and five counts of kidnapping in the first degree, and thirteen counts of rape and sodomy in the first degree. The State asks that there be no bail at this time, your honor." Rollins said as he straightened his tie.

"I will take note of that, Defense rise. How do you plead?" Cahoon asked.

All four men stood up with their Attorneys. Judge Cahoon asked them one by one how they pled.

"Mr. Billy Joe Martin, how do you plead?" Cahoon asked.

"Not guilty, your honor." Billy Joe said swallowing hard.

"Mr. Richard Avery, how do you plead?"

"Not guilty, your honor." Red answered with a grin.

"Mr. James Parks, how do you plead?"

"Not guilty, sir, I mean your honor." James said nervously.

"Mr. Richard Parks, how do you plead?"

"Not guilty, your honor." Mr. Raymond Parks how do you plead?" "Not guilty, your honor." Raymond said, clearing his throat. "Are you Parks Boy's related?" Brothers, Your Honor" Raymond answered.

So "Noted." Calhoun answered. "Does the Attorneys for these defendants have anything to add?"

"Yes, your honor, if it's all right with Mr. Martin's Attorney, Mr. Stien, I would like the court to take in consideration that all of these men before you are family men and all have steady employment. I would like to ask for the lowest bail the court will allow, your honor."

"Mr. Nivels and Mr. Rollins, I'm going to take all of this in consideration. Are all the defendants property owners?" Cahoon asked.

"Yes, your honor." Nivels answered.

"Good. Then I'm setting bail at five hundred dollars cash or bond."

"Your honor, that's unheard of. This is a capital murder case. You can't do that." Rollins said outraged at the judge's decision. Judge Calhoun a look of contempt on his face at Rollins, as he said.

"Outraged or not Mr. Rollins. This is my court and I can set the bail any way I please. Now court adjourned till ten-thirty at which time I will hear the next case." Calhoun tapped his gavel as he stood up to leave.

"All rise." The bailiff commanded as the judge left the bench.

"He can't be serious." Wells said to Combs as they stood up in the gallery to walk over to the prosecutor Rollins. "He can and he did. I have always thought him to be a Klansman." Combs said angrily.

"Well, I think maybe we need to have the trial moved to another Judge. Mr. Rollins can't you ask for another judge?" Wells asked.

"I can but I have to show cause as to why." Rollins answered.

"Cause, hell look at what he just did." Wells said angrily.

"Well, I'm afraid it's up to the judge on the amount of bail that is set by him." Rollins said.

"Yeah, what if HE is a member of the Klan?' Combs asked.

"Hell Bill, over half of the judges and business men in the whole state of Mississippi, not to mention Georgia, Arkansas, Alabama, Tennessee."

"You made your point, counselor." Combs interrupted him before he could name all the states in the south.

"All right. So what do we do?" Wells asked.

"Wait till he sets a trial date. Then we pick a jury and go to trial. With any luck we get a conviction. You just make sure our witnesses get to court on time." Rollins said closing his briefcase. "Now if you gentlemen will excuse me, I would like to get a cup of coffee before I have to come back in here. I will have the date for you this afternoon." Rollins said as the three men walked together out of the courtroom.

Billy Joe had his Attorney pay his bail, Billy Joe told him he would bring the money to his office the next day. Red, Jimmy, and Ricky, had to stay in jail till Red's wife came down with the bail money to bail them all out. Billy Joe got his wallet, watch and ring back when he made his bail. He had a hundred dollars in his wallet so he called a cab to take him to his cabin.

As he started to leave from the payphone were he had just called for the cab. A deputy called to him. "Billy Joe Martin."

Billy Joe turned towards him. "Yeah." Billy Joe answered wondering what he wanted.

"The clerk forgot to give you this. It came in the mail this morning." The deputy said, handing him the letter.

"Thanks." Billy Joe said, taking the letter from the deputy's hand.

Billy Joe went outside to wait for the cab. He sat down on a stone bench under a shade tree. He opened the letter and began reading it. His heart fell as he read through the letter.

"Dear Joe or should I say Billy Joe, I don't know where to start. I guess I really want to ask why? Our whole life together is a lie. I don't want to believe that you had anything to do with the killing of all those people. But in my heart I think you did and there is no way I can live with the thought that you belonged to the Klan. It was Klan that killed my mother and father. My mother was white, and she fell in love with my father who was a black man. When my mother became pregnant with me, my mother's father, who was a

Klan member, he got some of his Klan buddies together and they took my father out to a woods where they first castrated him, then they hung him from a tree, then shot him repeatedly. Riddling his body with a hail of bullets. They let my mother have me, then they took me and left me on my father's mother's doorstep. I guess he couldn't bring himself to kill me when I was born. My mother was so distraught that she slit her wrist and died in her bathtub. So I think that maybe it is all right for a white man to have a colored woman, but not for a white woman to have a colored man. And one other thing, you can't be married to two women at the same time. One, it's against the law, and two, that means our marriage isn't legal and I refuse to live as the other woman. So I decided to leave all of the rednecks in this so called deep Southland and go someplace where all of this hate and violence doesn't exist. By the time you get this letter I will be gone and someplace where I'm free. I will always love you. But I hate you for hurting me this way. I have taken twenty thousand of your money. It's for me to start a new life. I feel you owe me that much. Love Always, Sonia.

    Tears streamed down his cheeks as he folded the letter and put it in his pocket. The cab pulled up and he got in. He gave the cabbie the address and he leaned his head back against the seat, as he tried to think. He knew he had to go to the cabin one more time before he went home to Sue Ellen. He kept thinking that when everything was all over, maybe Sonia would come back to him. The cab left Billy Joe out in front of his cabin. After he paid the cabdriver he went inside. He felt the stillness inside. He went over to the fireplace. He saw the photo of Sue Ellen and Sissy sitting on the mantel. Along with their wedding photo in Vegas, and her wedding rings. He flopped down on the couch. He gave out a big sigh as he took out Sonia's letter and began reading it over and over. After about an hour he decided to walk down to the little market two miles down the road where he bought six bottles of Johnny Walker whisky. He took the quart bottles back to the cabin, where he sat drinking one bottle after another. This took him a little less than two hours. After he had started on the third bottle, he decided to go over to the trap door where his safe was located in the floor. He took the remaining ten thousand from the safe. He divided the money into two separate folds. He shoved a fold into each of his front pockets of his jeans. He went to the phone and called for another cab. He was a little drunk, but in complete control of himself.

The cab showed up about twenty minutes later. He had the cab drive him to the Chevy dealers in downtown Jackson. Where he bought a brand new cream colored station wagon.

Billy Joe arrived home at his house in Cotton Wood at nine thirty that night. When he came into the house he found Sue Ellen sitting in the living room watching the Jack Benny Show. He stood leaning in the doorway. "Well, I guess you really didn't miss me much." Billy Joe said in a hurt tone of voice. The sound of his voice startled Sue Ellen at first. She jerked her head up with a surprised look on her face.

"Where have you been? I was told you would be home this afternoon." She said elated with excitement as she ran over to him throwing her arms around his neck.

"Miss you. I have been going crazy for three days just trying to get someone to let me see you." She cried as she kissed his neck hugging him tightly.

"I missed you too. Come outside with me. I want to show you why I'm so late getting home." Billy Joe said pulling towards the kitchen. Sue Ellen followed alongside him with a puzzled expression on her face.

"Billy Joe, what are you up to?" She giggled.

"Just come with me. You will see." Billy Joe grinned. "Close your eyes." Billy Joe told her as he turned the porch light on. He took her out on the porch. "OK, now you can look."

Sue Ellen opened her eyes. "Oh, Billy Joe, it's so beautiful." She gasped excitedly as she ran down the porch steps to the car. She ran her hands over the car's fenders.

"It's yours, you just have to learn how to drive it now." Billy Joe smiled.

"Who's going to teach me?" She asked.

"Well I guess it will have to be me." Billy Joe said winking his eye at her.

"Only if you promise not to get to mad at me when I do something stupid." She said sounding serious.

"I promise. But we can't start tonight. Let's do it after breakfast tomorrow." He grinned, as he went on to say. "How bout you fix this old man something to eat? I'm hungry."

"Old man? You ain't that old yet." She laughed as she went back on the porch, giving him a kiss.

"Sure I am. I bought a station wagon didn't I?" He laughed, then kissed her passionately. After they kissed they went inside where Sue Ellen made him something to eat. Afterwards they went upstairs and made love. Billy Joe sat his back propped against the headboard of the bed smoking a Lucky Strike cigarette. Sue Ellen had her arm across his chest.

"Billy Joe, I need to talk to you about Joe." She said as she ran her fingers through his chest hairs.

"What about him?" Billy Joe asked giving her his full attention.

"Took him to the doctor. They ran some tests. The tests show that Joe has some damage to his brain, he is never going to be right in short, our baby is retarded." Billy Joe stubbed out his cigarette.

"How and the hell did he get brain damage?" He said angrily.

"Before you start losing your temper, it's partly your fault. He got the brain injury while he was still inside me. He got it when you beat the hell out of me." She said trying not to be sounding like she was blaming him.

Billy Joe sat there silent, his face drained and haggard. "I need some coffee." He said as he got out of bed.

"I will get us both some." Sue Ellen said as she got up too. They both went down stairs to the kitchen. They sat at the table drinking coffee and working things out on how they were both going to cope with the condition of their son. They decided that they weren't going to dwell on how he got that way, but how they were going to handle his care. Afterwards they went to bed so they could get up and Billy Joe could give her her first driving lesson.

Billy Joe survived the three days of giving Sue Ellen driving lessons. He was back into his work routine. He pulled his truck into the parking lot of the mill. Red Avery was just getting out of his truck when Billy Joe parked his truck next to him.

"Well how does it feel to have to come back to work after your little vacation?" He said with a big grin on his face.

"Well I don't really know just yet." Billy Joe said coldly.

"Hey boy, don't you think it's time you knock off this 'I'm better than you act'?" Red sneered at him.

"Look, you need to understand something. We may go to jail for the rest of our lives or maybe worse. I probably wouldn't have done the things I did if I hadn't been brain washed by you and your organization." Billy Joe said looking Red straight in the eyes.

"Why you little son of a bitch, let me tell you somethin. In case you forgot, it was your brilliant idea to do the niggers at the bar." Red remind.

"Yeah, it was. But if I hadn't been so brain washed by every thing you said to me, I'm just saying things might have been different, that's all." Billy Joe said a little anger in his voice.

"Is that why you got you a Jew lawyer?" Red said smugly.

"My wife got him for me." Billy Joe said curtly.

"Oh she did, did she? Well, you could have used our lawyer. It looks to us like you are trying to act like it was all our doing, and that you're some kind of goody two shoe's." Red said hatefully.

"Well I really don't want to be a part of you in anyway. I know I'm going to have to pay for what I did and so will all of you. The cops got themselves a couple of witnesses." Billy Joe said being realistic.

"Well let me tell you a little secret. By the time we go to court, the cops won't have no witnesses and the judge is one of us. You know, the ones you don't want any part of any more." Red said coldly.

Billy Joe looked at Red blankly for a moment. "I need to get inside before I'm late." Billy Joe shrugged past Red, as he went to his work station.

"You best think about what I said, boy." Red yelled after him as Billy Joe went inside the mill. Billy Joe's boss, Mr. Jeb Turner was waiting at the time clock when Billy Joe went to clock in. He reached for his time card but it wasn't there. "Billy Joe I need to talk to you." Turner said.

"I'm not late, Mr. Turner. My time card isn't here." Billy Joe said.

"No, your time card isn't there because I told the timekeeper not to put one there for you. For that matter Red Avery either. Oh, there he is now. Red, would you mind this concerns you too." Turner said.

"What concerns me? What's going on, Mr. Turner?" Red asked curiously.

"Look, fellas, I'm going to have to let you go." Turner said.

"What the hell for?" Red said, a little anger in his voice.

"I'm sorry, guys. But this has come from the big bosses. You guys have made news nationwide. We have buyers in Chicago and New York and with this kind of publicity you guys are getting right now, well, our buyers will stop their orders and that means we will have to close our doors and besides that, if I let you stay on, that would be a slap in the face to all the colored workers we have. I'm sorry, guys. I have to let you go. I have your final checks here." Turner said, handing Red and Billy Joe the brown envelopes containing their checks.

"I can't believe your doin this. Hell, we haven't been convicted of anything yet." Red snapped. "Hell, what about all the years we gave to this plant?" Red remind.

"I'm sorry fellows. You have fifteen minutes to clear out your lockers and leave the premises." Turner said, then went back into his office. Billy Joe stood there stunned.

"Well if that don't beat all." Red said.

"What's that you said? You and your group are untouchable?" Billy Joe spoke up. Then he turned to leave.

"You ain't seen nothin yet. You will see what my group can do, and it will be more than just killin a bunch of niggers in a bar." Red said angrily.

"Yeah, whatever you say. That ain't getting us our job back." Billy Joe said in a pissed off tone.

"You will see, my friend. At least I won't be standin alone." Red said angrily to Billy Joe as he went out the door. Billy Joe jumped into his truck and sped out of the parking lot. He just started driving down the highway trying to think. He was thinking about Sonia, his baby, and now his job he just lost and all the things Red had said and the trial he was soon to be facing. It wasn't long before he found himself sitting in his truck in front of the cabin that he and Sonia had shared. He went inside and started drinking the bottles he hadn't finished from the last time he was there. He went into the bedroom and lay across the bed staring at a photo of him and Sonia.

Billy Joe spent the whole day , drinking and trying to sort things out in his mind. He was on his last bottle sitting in front of the fireplace, watching the flames flicker. Suddenly he threw the bottle into the fireplace smashing it. The contents splashed on and into the fire causing the flames to leap out onto the wooden floor, quickly spreading to the bear skin rug, catching the end table and leather couch on fire. Billy Joe stood up and calmly went to the front door. He took one last look at the inside of the cabin. He closed the door behind him. Got into his truck and drove off, as the entire cabin was now engulfed in flames. By the time the fire department arrived on the scene, the cabin was completely destroyed. There were nothing left except ashes. Billy Joe never went back. He closed the book on that part of his life. He was now deciding how he was going to handle his son's problem.

He knew he was going to have to deal with Red Avery and the court very soon. He wasn't sure how just yet. He knew he still had enough money to see him through till he could get another job. But he was worried how much of the money he would have to pay the lawyer.

He decided he was going to have one last fling before he had to go to court. He thought if he had to go to jail for the rest of his life, he might as well enjoy what freedom he still had. He went home to tell Sue Ellen that he no longer had a job. He didn't want her finding out from anyone else. As he pulled his truck into his driveway he saw Carl mowing his lawn. He waved to him as he got out of his truck. He went into the house.

Sue Ellen was fixing dinner. "Hi, honey." Sue Ellen said smiling as Billy Joe came in the door.

"Honey, come over here and sit down with me. I need to talk to you." Billy Joe said sounding serious. Sue Ellen washed her hands and went over to the table and sat down across from Billy Joe. She could see something was really bothering him.

"What's wrong, honey?" she asked concerned.

"I lost my job today." He said calmly.

"Oh honey, why?" She asked.

"Because of this court thing." He answered.

"What are we going to do?" She asked concerned.

"I will get another job. I got enough money saved. I'm not going to look for another job until I can put this court thing behind us. Mr. Stien is pretty sure I'm not going to jail.

I know I haven't really talked to you about it. But honey, I want you to know, I didn't do those things they said I did." He said convincingly.

"I know you didn't, honey. I know in my heart you couldn't do those terrible things." Sue Ellen said convinced of his innocence.

"You think your mother would take the kids for two weeks?" Billy Joe asked.

Sue Ellen looked puzzled. "I'm sure she will, but why?" she asked.

"Because I want to take my best girl some place special." He answered.

"OK, how about I call her after dinner? But I need to tell her where we are going." She said.

"You finish fixing dinner, and I will tell you when I come back from Carl's. I need to see him. It won't take long, I promise." He said as he kissed her forehead.

He went out the door, going over to Carl's house. Carl was finished mowing, and was bent down on one knee cleaning the bottom of his mower.

"Hey, buddy, when can you take a vacation?" Billy Joe asked with a boyish smile on his face.

"Vacation?" Carl said startled.

"Yeah, vacation." Billy Joe said again.

"I guess anytime I want one. Why do you ask?" Carl grinned.

"Can you take off for two weeks?" Billy Joe asked still sounding mysterious.

"I can take three if I want. Why all the questions about my vacation time?" Carl said, thinking Billy Joe was going to pull a joke on him.

"I'm taking Sue Ellen to Vegas, and I want to take you and Margie with us. I will pay for the plane tickets and the hotel, and I will even give you a thousand dollars for you and Margie to gamble with." Billy Joe beamed.

Carl looked at him stunned for a moment. "Are you serious?" Carl asked.

"Hell yes, I am. I wouldn't joke about something like this." Billy Joe said with a big smile.

"Can you afford to do something like that?" Carl asked.

"Well, if I couldn't I would not have asked." He told Carl.

"Hell, yes I would like to go. But man you don't have to give us a thousand dollars." Carl said.

"I want to, you are my friend. You and Margie have always helped us out, so this is my way of saying thanks. So say yes you will go." Billy Joe smiled.

"Yes. When do you want to go?" Carl asked.

"Is Friday too soon?" Billy Joe asked.

"Friday will be fine. That gives me time to clear it at work. Can you leave town like that before the trial date?" Carl asked concerned.

"Sure I can. Nobody has told me I can't go out of state. Besides, I will be back long before the trial. Carl I want you to know, I didn't do what they say I did." Billy Joe said.

"I know you didn't buddy. I never thought you did. That's why I got you the lawyer." Carl smiled.

"Thanks for believing in me. You and Margie come over after supper. I haven't told Sue Ellen yet. Don't tell Margie. Let's tell them together. Let's surprise them." Billy Joe grinned.

"You got it, pal." Carl answered.

"See you after supper then?" Billy Joe asked.

"You bet. About seven OK?" Carl asked.

"Seven is fine." Billy Joe answered, then went back across the street to his house.

Billy Joe came in the door just as Sue Ellen was setting the table. "Dinner will be ready in a few minutes." She smiled.

"Do I have time to shower?" He asked her.

"If you can do it in fifteen minutes." She kidded.

"I can do that." He said as he started for the hall to the stairs.

"Hey, you going to tell me why I'm asking my mother to keep the kids?" She asked before he left the kitchen.

"After dinner. Oh yeah, I forgot, Carl and Margie are coming over at seven."

"You're up to something, aren't you?" She grinned at him.

"WHO ME? I don't know what you're talking about. I have to go take my shower now. See ya." He laughed as he hurried through the doorway.

"Oh, you. You can't fool me. I know you are up to something for sure now." She called out to him.

Billy Joe took his shower, after he dressed in a tee shirt and clean pair of jeans he went downstairs to the kitchen where Sue Ellen was putting food on Sissy's plate. The baby was in his basinet next to the table where Sue Ellen sat. Billy Joe took his seat at the table. Sue Ellen served him his food. "Thank you, darlin." Billy Joe said as Sue Ellen filled his plate. He sat there eating and smiling between chews. He knew it was really getting to Sue Ellen. But Sue Ellen just sat there eating, playing along with his game.

"Mommy, I'm finished. Can I go see Superman on TV?" Sissy asked.

"Sure baby." Sue Ellen answered softly.

"Go watch the TV in your playroom." Billy Joe ordered.

"OK, daddy." Sissy said as she slid off her chair, and ran to her playroom.

"Don't turn it up to loud Sissy. We got company coming." Billy Joe called to Sissy.

"I won't daddy." Sissy called back as she peeked her head around the doorway.

"Are you going to tell me now?" Sue Ellen asked.

"Tell you what?" Billy Joe toyed with her.

"Why I need to ask my mother to watch the kids." Sue Ellen said getting frustrated.

"Later." He said grinning at her frustration.

"OH, You'ooooooh You are making me crazy." Sue Ellen groaned. She got up from the table and began clearing the dishes. Billy Joe sat there blowing smoke rings teasing her.

Sue Ellen was drying the last plate when Carl and Margie knocked on the door. "You all don't have to knock, just come on in." Billy Joe said through the screen door.

"Well, we thought it to be appropriate to knock, bein guests and all." Carl laughed.

"Hi guys. Want some coffee?" Sue Ellen said cheerfully.

"You bet. You make the best coffee in town." Carl said with a big grin on his face. Sue Ellen served up the coffee to everyone as they sat down at the table. She poured herself a cup of coffee, and sat down next to Billy Joe.

"Well, has Billy Joe been acting mysterious?" Margie asked as she took a sip of her coffee.

"I'll say he has. He's been driving me crazy." Sue Ellen said looking at the devilish look Billy Joe had on his face.

"Well, shall we tell them?" Billy Joe said with a sheepish grin.

"I think we better before the suspense kills them." Carl laughed.

"Well, come on. Tell us." Sue Ellen said excitedly.

"OK, OK, I guess we better tell them. Carl and I have decided to take you gals to Vegas for two weeks." Billy Joe said coolly.

"VEGAS? LAS VEGAS?" Sue Ellen and Margie squealed excitedly together.

"Yep. We are going to leave on Friday." Billy Joe said as Sue Ellen was hugging him around his neck. Margie was doing the same to Carl.

"Oh, Margie come upstairs with me. I need help finding the right thing to wear." Sue Ellen said excitedly.

"Then after, we can go to my house and you can help me." Margie said as she and Sue Ellen chatted excitedly heading for the stairway.

"Hey, what about us?" Billy Joe called out.

"Oh, we will pack you something too. But I think Sue Ellen and I are going shopping tomorrow." Margie giggled.

"Well, there goes any money I thought I might have extra." Carl sighed.

"Don't worry, man. I'm going to talk them into waiting till we get to Vegas to shop." Billy Joe said.

"I don't think you know my wife, she will buy the stores out here first. Then she will do the same when we get to Vegas. The plane will be lucky if it can get off the ground." Carl joked.

"Well I guess I can give Sue Ellen and Margie a couple of hundred they can shop here with." Billy Joe said.

"Hey buddy, did you rob a bank or something?" Carl asked kiddingly.

"No I just saved all my money when I was working all the extra jobs I was doing and along with the raise I got and the bonuses, well let's just say I didn't get rich, but I'm well set. I can afford to spend at least three thousand for a fun vacation with two of my best friends." Billy Joe said as he slapped Carl gently on the back.

"We feel the same way about you and Sue Ellen, and the kids too." Carl smiled. Billy Joe got up to get them some more coffee.

As he was holding the coffee pot to pour into the cups, "Hey, what was that? Did you get a cat?" Carl asked as his attention was on the funny sound he was hearing. Billy Joe sat the coffee pot down craning his neck trying to figure out where the sound was coming from. Suddenly his eyes became fixed on the bassinet. Carl got up from the table and looked in the bassinet. "Wow. He's crying, Billy Joe, do you hear him? He's really crying." Carl said, a shocked look on his face.

"Sue Ellen," Billy Joe shouted. "Sue Ellen get the hell down here, now." He shouted once more. His eyes still fixed on the bassinet. Sue Ellen heard Billy Joe yelling for her. She knew something was wrong by the urgent sound in his voice.

"I'm coming." She yelled as she and Margie hurried down the stairs. Out of breath and a scared look on her face, "What's wrong?" she asked as she was catching her breath.

"It's the baby." Billy Joe said.

"Is something wrong with him?" she asked concerned as she ran over to the bassinet.

"Listen." Carl said, then smiled.

"What? Oh, my God. He's crying, he's crying. Margie, look, he's crying." Sue Ellen said as tears of joy ran down her face.

"And that's not all, he's kicking his feet." Carl pointed at his tiny feet. Sue Ellen bent down and lifted the baby from the bassinet.

"I think he's trying to tell us he's hungry." Sue Ellen smiled at the baby.

"Oh, Sue Ellen, this is so wonderful. The doctor told you to give him six months. Heck, he isn't waiting that long. I think he is going to be all right." Margie said joyfully, as her eyes were filled with tears too.

"Does this mean that doctor is wrong about him being retarded?" Billy Joe asked.

"I don't know. He did say there was a possibility he would regain some mobility, but he might be slow in his learning. I need to take him back to the doctor in the morning." Sue Ellen said as she gave the baby his bottle.

"Well, this proves one thing. His vocal cords are working." Margie said happily.

"I think I will go with you to the doctor I want to hear what he has to say about this." Billy Joe said.

"I think that is a great idea. You should be there." Sue Ellen said, thrilled that he wanted to go with her.

"How about we all go, then after the girls can go shopping." Billy Joe suggested.

"That's a good idea. But I can't go. But Margie can. I have to work tomorrow." Carl said.

"Margie would you mind getting Sissy, I need to put the baby to bed. Sissy needs to get her bath and get ready for bed too." Sue Ellen asked.

"No problem." Margie said.

Sue Ellen took the baby up to his room, and Margie went into the playroom where Sissy was fast asleep on the floor in front of the TV. She turned the TV off and picked up Sissy from the floor into her arms and carried her upstairs to her room.

After the children were put in their beds, the four of them played cards and chatted about the baby and their trip to Vegas. They quit a little after eleven. Carl and Margie went home to their bed and Billy Joe and Sue Ellen retired to their bed.

They got up early the next morning to take the baby to the doctor and do their shopping. Sue Ellen had called her mother before they left to tell her the good news about the baby and ask her if she would care for the children while they went to Vegas. Her Mother agreed to take care of the children. But suggested she and Sue Ellen's father stay at their house where Sissy could be able to play with her friends and toys.

"Doctor does this mean that he is getting better?" Sue Ellen asked, as she stood by the baby lying on the table.

"I do believe he is. This is a good sign that his brain cells are regenerating. I don't want you to think this means he will be normal. This just means there is still hope of him being able to learn. He will more than likely be slow. But at least he won't be a vegetable like we first thought. We will just have to monitor his progress one step at a time. We will know more as time goes by.

"But are you telling me that he may be retarded?" Sue Ellen asked.

"Not in the way you are thinking. He may have problems on learning to walk and talk and then, on the other hand, he may learn to do everything a normal child does. Just at a slower pace. It's just to hard to say at this time. Like I said we just have to wait and see. I don't want you to hold to high of hopes for him, only to be letdown if he doesn't develop like we hope he will." He told Sue Ellen. Billy Joe stood there leaning against the wall. He didn't say anything, he just listened to the doctor.

"Just keep talking to him, and encouraging him as you would your other child." The doctor told them.

"We will, doctor. I'm not giving up on him." Sue Ellen smiled as she picked the baby from the table.

"I'm glad to hear you say that. Well, then I will see you and the baby in six weeks." The doctor said smiling back at her.

"Thank you doctor." Sue Ellen said as she carried the baby out the door.

"Thanks, Doc." Billy Joe said to the doctor as he shook his hand. They walked out to the waiting room where Margie sat with Sissy on her lap, thumbing through a magazine.

"Hi, mommy. Is little Joe all right?" Sissy asked as she slid down off Margie's lap running over to Sue Ellen holding the baby.

"You girls ready to go shopping now?" Billy Joe grinned.

"You got your wallet unlocked?" Sue Ellen kidded.

They left the doctor's office and spent the next four hours shopping, talking and having a great time doing it. Billy Joe was having a better time than he thought he was going to have with two women and two kids. When they returned home the wagon was loaded with packages. Billy Joe was shaking his head and kidding them about buying out the stores.

CHAPTER THIRTY EIGHT

Sissy stood on the porch with her grandmother waving goodbye to Billy Joe, Sue Ellen, Carl and Margie as they drove away on their way to the airport. Sissy stood there waving till the station wagon was out of sight.

"Come on, honey, let's go back into the house with your brother." Her grandmother said as she held Sissy's hand as they started to go inside.

Sissy stopped as she heard her name being called. "Granma, it's Marcy and William. Can I go and play?" Sissy said looking up at her with those big blue eyes.

"Sure honey. Maybe your little friends would like to stay and have lunch with us." She said as she smiled down at her.

"OK, I will go ask them." Sissy said as she hurried off down the steps.

"Hi, Marcy. My granma says you and William can have lunch with us. Please say yes." Sissy said as she clung to her old doll.

"I wants to, but we gots to ask momma first."

"All right. I have to wait here. Granma says I have to stay in the yard." Sissy said a little sad.

"OK, we will run home real fast and ask." Marcy said with a big grin on her face.

"I'm tired. I wants to stay here." William pouted.

"All right. You stay with Sissy you big baby." Marcy scolded.

"I will watch out for him." Sissy said trying to sound grown up.

"I will run real fast." Marcy called back to Sissy as she started running for home. Sissy and William went over to play on the swings till Marcy came back. Marcy returned a short time later; they played together in the playhouse till they were called in for lunch. The three children were sitting at the table eating their ham and cheese sandwiches.

"Granma, can we go pick flowers?" Sissy asked.

"Well honey, I don't know. I told your mother I would make sure you stayed in the yard." Her grandmother said.

"Mommy lets me pick flowers all the time." Sissy answered.

"How far do you have to go for these flowers?" She asked Sissy.

"Just past the back gate." Sissy said with pleading eyes.

"If I let you go, will you be able to hear me if I call for you to come home?" her grandmother asked. "Ahua." Sissy said nodding yes.

"OK, but you better come when I call because if I have to come for you there will be no TV. Understand?" She said to Sissy.

"Yes granma. Does this mean I can go?" Sissy asked.

"Yes you may go." She said with a smile.

"YIPEEE." Sissy said excitedly. "I will bring you back the prettiest flowers I can find." Sissy said as she and the other two children scampered out of the house.

They ran to their favorite place and sat down and began picking the wild flowers. "I bet you miss your mommy and daddy." Marcy commented as she picked a flower.

"I miss my mommy, but I don't miss my daddy. I wish he would never come back." Sissy said with a pouting look.

"Why? Your daddy isn't mean anymore is he?" Marcy asked.

"Yes he is. He is the meanest daddy in the whole wide world." Sissy said, a little anger in her little voice.

"Does he still hit you?" Marcy asked.

"No." Sissy said in a low voice.

"My mama says he found Jesus, he had the devil in him before."

"So if he ain't hurting you no more, why you still hate him?" Marcy asked, a confused look on her little round face.

"I said he don't hit me no more, but he still hurts me." Sissy said looking like she was about to cry.

"How does he hurt you?" Marcy asked.

"Well sometimes when mommy ain't around he makes me touch his peepee then he sticks his finger in my peepee and it hurts." Sissy started to cry. "And he makes me bend over the bed and he puts his peepee in the crack of my butt, his peepee gets real hard and real big, then white icky stuff comes out all over my back." Sissy said with a look of shame on her little face.

"Why don't you tell your mommy?" Marcy asked.

"Cause my daddy said if I ever told anyone, specially my mommy, he would kill me and even kill my baby brother and mommy too." Sissy said as she started to cry hard.

"Don't cry, Sissy. I hate him too." Marcy said in a hateful tone. "I know who you can tell." Marcy said soothingly.

"Who?" Sissy asked wiping her eyes with the back of her hand.

"Tonight when you go to bed you tell God and then ask your guardian Angel to look after you and to make your daddy stop doing those bad things to you." Marcy said, sure that was the answer.

"All right. I will ask them tonight." Sissy said sadly.

"I think I should tell my momma." Marcy said.

"NO, you got to promise. You can't tell nobody. Promise me. PLEASE." Sissy begged.

"OK, I promise." Marcy promised crossing her heart.

"If you are really and truly my friend you won't tell no one." Sissy said making sure Marcy would keep her promise. "You better not tell anyone or I won't be your friend any more."

Sissy made her swear again. "I told you I won't tell nobody." Marcy pouted.

"OK, let's pick our flowers." Sissy smiled, pushing her sadness aside.

The children spent the rest of the day picking flowers and playing make believe. They played till Sissy's grandmother called her home.

The plane landed at the Las Vegas airport right on time. When the four of them got off the plane, Carl, Margie and Sue Ellen were impressed by the limo driver standing by the arrival gate holding a sign with their last names on it. The driver loaded their luggage in the trunk. After he held the limo door for them to get in, he drove them straight to the Sands Hotel and Casino. Sue Ellen, Margie and Carl's eyes lit up like children excited seeing Christmas tree lights for the first time. None of them had ever been inside a casino before or ever seeing a place like Vegas. After they were settled in their rooms they all went down for dinner, then Billy Joe and Carl turned the girls loose in the Casino to play the slot machines. Carl played a few table games with Billy Joe but he found that he liked the slots better. Billy Joe wandered off on his own. He decided to walk down the street to visit one of the other casinos. He had had a lot to drink, but held it well like he always did. As he started to go inside the casino a young attractive girl called out to him. He turned to see who was calling him. His heart skipped a beat, the voice sounded just like Sonia's, but when he came face to face with her he could clearly see it wasn't her. For his Sonia would never dress like her. But she did remind him of Sonia. She was a lot darker skinned, she looked more like a Negro girl. Sonia never did.

"Hey baby, how you doin? You want some company?" She said. Her large white teeth glistened between her ruby red thick lips as she smiled a big friendly smile at Billy Joe.

"I don't know. Maybe." He hesitated, as he looked her up and down. She was wearing five-inch heels; they were a bright sequined red. She had on skintight short shorts, that just barely covered her hips, they rode above her pubic hair line. Her midriff was bare, the only thing covering her breast was a scanty criss cross halter top. Her hair was tightly pulled back into one long braid that hung down her back touching her round firm buttocks.

"Honey' you can have me for the night for five hundred."

"Oh, yeah, and just what do I get for the five hundred?" Billy Joe asked with a big grin on his face.

"Anything you want, sugar." She teased.

"You got a place?" Billy Joe asked.

"You ain't got no room?" She asked, surprised.

"Yeah, I got a room, but it's got my wife in it." He grinned.

"Oh, well in that case, sugar, I know a little out of the way motel a block from here on a side street. But the room is fifty extra."

"Lead the way." Billy Joe gestured, smiling big.

"You got to pay up front, honey." She held out her hand, giving him a business before pleasure look.

"How do I know if you won't just take my money and disappear on me?" Billy Joe said cautiously.

"How do I know you won't just take me, then not pay me?" She said firmly.

"OK, I tell you what. How bout I give you the money for the room and half now for you and the other half once we get into the room. Look at me do I not look like an honest John?" He said grinning his boyish grin.

"OK, but you best not fuck with me or you will wish you never thought of it." She warned, as she took the money from him. He followed her to a seedy looking motel on a dark side street. Billy Joe waited outside while she went in to pay for the room. He stood off in the shadows so the desk clerk couldn't see him. The girl got the key and led him to the room. The room wasn't to bad he thought, except it had a mildew smell. He handed her the rest of the money. He opened the quart bottle of whisky he bought on his way there. She put the money in the little purse she carried, went in to the bathroom returning naked with two glasses in her hand. She sat down in Billy Joes lap, as he sat in a straight back chair next to a round wooden table. He filled the glasses with the whisky. Billy Joe downed his in one gulp. She just sipped on hers. Billy Joe poured himself another, and did the same.

"Wow, you sure can down the booze. You better slow down, honey, if you want to be able to get it up." She laughed.

"Don't you worry baby. If there's one thing I can do, it's get it up no matter how much I drink." He said downing another glass, then he put his glass on the table and swooped her up like she was as light as a feather and threw her on the bed. He took a pack of rubbers from his pants pocket. Then he stripped.

"Ooowweee, sugar, you are well endowed. Shoot I might just do you for free." She smirked as she stared at his large penis. He climbed on the bed with her. He spread her legs apart, he leaned over her as he thrust himself inside of her. At first he just started making love to her. Then Visions of Viola saying almost the same words to him the night he took her at Sugars. He began losing control as he started biting her shoulder, then her breast. She yelled out in pain, then she scratched his face. He reared back and punched her in the face. She tried to fight him off, but he was much too strong for her. He pulled himself out of her then he flipped her on her stomach, and began sodomizing her. The more she struggled the more he became excited, and violent in his sexual rage. He bit her neck, back and thighs. He flipped her back over on her back and he bit her nipple off her breast, just like he did to Viola be for he killed her. She tried to scream but all she could do was a low moaning sound as he smashed her face repeatedly with his fist knocking her unconscious. He raped and sodomized her for hours before he left.

Billy Joe walked the few blocks to the strip. He went into the Flamingo casino. He pulled out a roll of hundred dollar bills that he had taken off the prostitute he had just murdered by slitting her throat. He went over to a dice table he bought five hundred in chips. He placed a two hundred dollar bet, then rolled the dice. He ended up winning twenty five hundred dollars. He stopped and went to the slots. He won another four hundred. He returned back to the casino were he found Carl still playing a slot machine. Sue Ellen and Margie were playing in the next row.

"Hey buddy, where you been?" Carl said with out really looking away from the machine he was playing.

"I went down the street to one of the other joints." Billy Joe replied.

"Did you have any luck?" Carl said as he turned to face Billy Joe. Then he saw the scratches on Billy Joe's face. "Damn, what happened to your face?"

"Oh, I broke up a fight between two women in front of the Flamingo. One of them must have scratched me. Is it bad?" Billy Joe asked innocently.

"Is it bad? It looks like you had a fight with a wild cat." Carl laughed.

"I'm going up to the room to change, if you see Sue Ellen tell her I will be back down in thirty minutes. Tell her to stay here." Billy Joe said as he started for the room.

"I will keep her here, but hurry back before this damn machine takes all my money." Carl laughed as he dropped in two more coins.

Billy Joe took off his clothes and took a shower. He looked in the mirror after he got out of the shower. He examined his scratches on his face and chest. "DAMN bitch." He said out loud to himself. He went into the bedroom picked up his clothing he had been wearing earlier. He stuffed them into a brown paper bag. After he dressed he took the bag with him and threw them in a waste bin in the hall by the elevators. He got on the elevator pushing the down button to the casino floor where he joined the others. Sue Ellen had won two hundred dollars in quarters. She was grinning from ear to ear. Margie won a hundred fifty dollars and Carl had finally won a jackpot of sixteen hundred on the machine he was playing.

The four of them went to dinner and just had fun dancing in one of the dance clubs where a live band played through the night. It was four A.M. before they went up to their rooms and settled in for the night.

CHAPTER THIRTY NINE

The shadowy figure made its way in the darkness past the rear of the big warehouse. The shadowy figure was a man called Boomer Malone. He was the enforcer for the Klan. As he made his way into the back door passed the night janitor Rosco Cliffton. He had been with the mill for twenty years. It was his job to keep all the cotton halls swept up from the floor around the separator. He was wearing his bib overalls he always wore, with an old faded red handkerchief hanging out his back pocket. His black balding head shined under the dim light as he swept. He was in his late fifties, he hummed an old blues tune as his chubby hands pushed the broom, keeping time with his tune. He didn't notice Boomer slipping in the darkness behind the big cotton separator bin. Boomer made his way to the boiler room, where he planted his home made bomb behind the big boiler furnace that supplied the steam to wash and clean the cotton, as it made it ready for processing.

Very carefully he put the bomb in place, then set the timer. He made his way back to where Rosco was still sweeping the floor. He waited for his chance to slip by him unseen. Once he made it back out of the building he ran as fast as he could in the darkness to his pickup truck he had parked in the field in back of the plant. He started his truck and sped off towards the dirt road. As he turned on to the dirt road the bomb went off rocking the entire neighborhood in a one-mile radius. The Mill went up in a large ball of fire sending smoke and flames that could be seen as far away as Tupelo. Rosco staggered out of the back door his clothes were ablaze as he fell to the ground. Two truck drivers who were on the out side when the blast hit saw Rosco as he came out the door in flames. They ran over to him, throwing their jackets over his body to put out the flames. Rosco was burned over ninety percent of his body. Several people came running and screaming out of all the exit doors of the warehouse. They were all badly burned. By the time the Fire Department arrived the entire building was ablaze. A hundred and twenty workers perished in the fire as the building collapsed. Rosco and four other colored women died on their way to the hospital. Fourteen others suffered severe burns. The Cotton Mill was completely destroyed.

Red Avery and Boomer Malone along with Ricky and his brother Jimmy Parks stood in the huge crowd of people across the street watching the mill burn.

"Well Boomer, it looks like you out did ol Billy Joe. You took out more niggers at one time than he did with a little help from us at that old nigger bar." He said with a big grin on his face. "Now all you got to do is take out those fucking stool pigeons, and that will make you the King of the Hill." Red said giving Boomer a friendly slap on the back, grinning.

"Don't you worry none. Those pigeons are as good as cooked right now." Boomer laughed.

"That's what I like to hear. Now let's go get us a cold beer. Come on boys." Red said as they left the fire scene and headed for their meeting place.

Once they were at the meeting place they sat around drinking beer, and planning the murders of Melvin and Elvin Gumm.

"I want those fuckers dead. But it's got to look like an accident." Red said as he took a swig from his beer bottle.

"Don't worry, I will make it so good the cops will have to say it was an unfortunate accident." Boomer bragged.

"You better be as good as you claim. This different than a cotton mill. I don't want anything tracing back to us. I mean there can't be any survivors. You got to make sure they are good and dead." Red said seriously.

"I told you, don't worry, I got it all worked out. There won't be any survivors. I guarantee it." Boomer smirked.

"I want you to wait until next week. I will tell you when. I want to make sure we all have an iron tight alibi when you do it." Red said.

"That's right, cause them F.B.I. guys are watching the Gumm's place. So it ain't going to be easy to get to them." Jimmy said making his point.

"Don't you worry none about those F.B.I. boys. I am just going to have to figure out a diversion to get them away from those Gumm boys, that's all." Boomer said as he puffed on his cigar.

"Well, it better be a good one, cause those ol boys are like watchdogs, they don't fool so easy." Red said as he lit Boomer's cigar.

"You just call me when you're ready, and I will take care of the problem." Boomer smiled.

A week later after their meeting at the Klan headquarters Red Avery and Boomer came up with a plan. He and the Parks brothers met in town at a local bar called The Happy Clown.

Boomer sat in the woods behind the Gumm's rundown house. He knew they would be going into town for supplies as they always did on Thursdays. He also knew that the F.B.I. would follow them to make sure they stayed safe. He knew that they left at noon, just as they always did for the past fifteen years. Red Avery and the Parks brothers walked into the Happy Clown Bar at one P.M. they started playing a game of pool and drinking beer. They played for about an hour.

"You cheated." Ricky yelled at Red.

"I CHEATED? WHY YOU LITTLE FUCK, I'm going to kick your ASS." Red yelled back. The bar had several people sitting at the bar. Their attention was on Red, and the Parks brothers.

"HEY, YOU BOYS TAKE IT OUTSIDE." The bartender yelled at them from behind the bar.

"Mind your own business, barkeep." Red shouted at him.

"This is my business. Take it outside or I'm callin the cops." The bartender said as he picked up a phone from under the bar, he started dialing the phone as he sat it down on top of the bar.

"Call the damn cops, I don't give a fuck. I'm still going to kick this little bastard's ass for calling me a cheat." Red said as he gave Ricky a shove backwards pushing him against the pool table."

"Don't you push my brother." Jimmy said as he gave Red a little shove, putting himself between Red and Ricky.

Red threw his bottle of beer against the wall, smashing it, splattering beer down the wall onto the floor. Jimmy swung his pool cue he was holding at Red. He missed Red as he ducked. The cue broke in half as it struck the wall. Red picked up a chair and hurled it towards Jimmy. Jimmy side stepped and the chair hit the corner of the pool table. Ricky grabbed the chair to throw it back at Red when two big city police officers came in the bar.

"Put the chair down boy." He ordered. Ricky dropped the chair. "OK, now what's going on here?" The officer asked.

"Officer, I want them out of here. I want to press charges against them for damages to my place. The bartender demanded.

"OK, Berry. How bout I get them to leave and pay you for whatever they broke?" The officer said trying not to arrest them.

"Fine, have them give me fifty bucks and get them out of here." The bartender agreed.

"OK, boys, you heard the man. Just pay up and we can all go home." The officer said trying to sound friendly.

"Hell, no. I ain't givin that fat bastard no fifty dollars for a two dollar pool stick and a broken beer that I already paid for." Red sneered.

"Boy, you tellin me you would rather go to jail than pay him and go home?" The officer asked.

"That's right. We ain't given him no fifty dollars. We was just havin a little disagreement." Red said.

"Well, you know if you go before the judge, it's going to cost you boys three times that much for each one of you." The officer said trying to reason with them."

"Look, officer, forget the fifty, just get them the hell out of here." The bartender said.

"There now. You hear that boys?" He is going to be a good guy and drop the complaint. Now come on, let's go on out peaceably." The officer coaxed as he took Red by the arm to lead him out. Red yanked his arm away from him.

"I can lead myself out. I don't need you to put your hands on me." Red sneered.

"Look here, son. Don't make this hard." The officer said just as two more police officers came in. The officer took hold of Red again. Red took a swing at him, Jimmy and Ricky started fighting with the other policemen. then their brother Ray jumped in. They didn't struggle too hard, they let the policemen cuff them and take them to jail.

All four of them, were booked for drunk and disorderly and resisting arrest. But they had planned it that way so they would have a good alibi.

Boomer crawled under the Gumm's house after they left for the day. He planted twenty sticks of dynamite under the floor of the house placing each stick in key places. He then rapped four more sticks together and planted them in a shrub were he knew the Agents always parked their car. He then set the timer for midnight. He knew they would be sound asleep by then. When he was finished he left to go meet up with two more men from out of town. They were going to take care of Ray Ray Smith. He was the last witness against Red, Billy Joe and the Parks brothers. Red, Jimmy, Ray and Ricky had the perfect alibi. They were in jail. Billy Joe was still in Vegas.

Boomer slinked back in to the woods being very careful I not to be seen by anyone. He walked about three miles through the woods before he came to the clearing were he had his pickup hidden. Once he was safely back in his truck he drove out to meet the others and to seal Ray Rays fate.

Boomer drove twenty miles out of town to a place called Harpers Pond. He found Monty Becker and Dicky Bird leaning against an old forty nine Buick with rusted out fenders and running boards.

"It's about time you showed up." Dicky said as he spit his plug of tobacco on to the stone road next to his car.

"I ain't late, you're early." Boomer grinned wide exposing his missing front teeth and the discolored remaining ones. He rubbed his stubbly unshaven chin.

"When we goin after this yellow belly stool pigeon?" Dicky asked as he stood by his car relieving himself on his tire.

"Red told me he goes out to his workshop every night around nine o'clock. He stays out there till eleven or so." Boomer said.

"What's he do that fer?" Dicky asked.

"He's makin him a boat." Boomer answered.

"I guess he ain't goin fishin in it after tonight, is he?" Dicky chuckled.

"Maybe he is makin his coffin." Monty said as they all started laughing.

"Come on, boys, let's go get us a few beers at my house, till it's time to go. My old woman is at her sister's helping out with her new youngin." Boomer said as he climbed back in his truck. Monty got into Dicky's car and they followed Boomer home where they sat around drinking beer and talking about how they were going to kill Ray Ray.

Ray Ray helped his wife MaryAnn put their children to bed, she went downstairs to watch her program on TV. "I'm goin out to the shop for awhile." Ray Ray called to his wife as he started out the side door of his house.

"OK, honey, but please don't stay out there too late." His wife called back to him as she turned on the TV.

"Now don't you worry none. I will be back in to watch the news with you." He told her as he went out, gently closing the door so he wouldn't wake the children. He went out to his shop that he set up in an old barn "next to his house. He opened the barn door to go in, reaching for the light switch as he entered. He flipped the switch, but the light didn't come on.

"Damn it. I hope I didn't blow a fuse." He mumbled to himself as he took out a book of matches to light one. Just as he struck the match Boomer turned a flashlight on him.

"Hello Ray Ray, you need a light?" He chuckled.

"Shit man, you scared the fuck out of me. What the hell you doin out here in my barn?" Ray Ray asked shaken from the surprise visit.

"Oh, we come to give you a message from Red."

"From Red? Why didn't he just come?" Ray Ray asked nervously.

"Oh, he wanted to be here, but he is a little tied up at the moment. So he sent us. You see, it seems that you been doin some talking to them F.B.I. boys and Red, well, let's just say he ain't to happy about it." Boomer sneered.

"Yeah, I talked to them, but I didn't tell them nothing, cause I don't know nothin." Ray Ray said as he started backing up towards the barn door only to find that he was suddenly grabbed by his arms by Dicky Bird and Monty Becker. He tried to struggle free, but he couldn't. They drug him to the center of the barn where Boomer slipped a rope over his head. Ray Ray felt the knot on the noose tighten suddenly he was hoisted in the air, hanging by his neck. His body convulsed as he struggled for his last breath. His body relieved itself, Ray Ray was dead. Boomer and Dicky laughed as they watched Ray Ray die. "Come on Dicky He won't be ratting anybody out now. "Monty make sure that stool is kicked over, it has to look like he killed himself. "Already did that! Monty said as he headed for the door to leave the barn. "Great! now let's get the Hell out of hear! I want to get across the state line be for the Gum boy's fry. The three men very quietly left out the back door of the old barn. Boomer pushed the lever on the power box that set next to the back door as he went out. A light came on at the inside front of the barn were Ray Ray's body hung from the rafters, slowly swaying back and forth as it cast an outline of his shadow in front of his unfinished boat. Boomer and his men slipped away unseen in the darkness into the woods. A slight fog was starting to drift in. The two F.B.I. agents who was assigned to watch Ray Ray and his family were setting in their car drinking coffee from a thermos. Across the road in front of Ray Ray's house. Agent John Carter took a sip of his coffee then said to Agent Tom Malone sitting next him on the passenger side of their car. "Ray Ray is running a little late tonight going out to his barn. He said as he saw the light come on thru a side window in the barn. "Hell" I didn't see him come out of his house! Did You? Carter said. "Nope, must be the fog and because it is dark as shit out here. Malone then took another sip of his coffee. "What time is it? Carter ask. "ten after eleven" Malone answered. "SHIT" we have three hours and fifty minutes to go be for our shift ends. Carter groaned. "How bout we stop at the truck stop on the highway for breakfast be for we go back to the motel? Malone ask. "sounds good! Carter answered, as he went on to say, "What do you think he does in that barn every night? "I was told he is restoring an old boat" Malone answered. "Wish I had a boat! I would love to do some deep sea fishing. Carter said wistfully as he leaned his head back on the car seat. The two agents sat across the road watching Ray Ray's house and barn. Meanwhile inside the house MaryAnn sat on the sofa watching the TV the news was over and the Steve Allen show was on. She sat there yawning as she looked over at the clock on the wall. Eleven Forty five" she said out loud to herself. That man and his Dam Boat! I guess I better go out and tell him what time it is. she said as she raised her self up off the sofa. She pulled her robe closed as far as it would go to cover her large stomach, she was eight months pregnant. She went into the kitchen to a side door that led out to small porch facing the side door of the barn about forty feet away. She flipped on the porch light as she stepped out on to the porch, calling out Ray Ray's name. The light got agent Malone and agent carter's attention right away. "Heads up! Malone said as he saw the porch light come on. Carter sat up strait as watched MaryAnn step out on to the porch. "Man she look's like she is due any time, Carter said. "He is in trouble now! She is on her way to the barn, and she don't sound very happy about him not answering her calling to him. Malone said. "I would not want to be him right now if she is anything like my wife, Carter said jokingly. MaryAnn walked across the yard as she said to herself, "Dang man" I bet he done fell asleep out here. She reached for the door handle to the barn door, she opened the door an went in side, as she called out his name. Ray Ray" she called out as she approached the side of his boat. She heard a creaking sound coming from above her at the bow of the boat, as she approached the bow she saw the shadow moving ever so slowly, as she looked up she saw her husband's body hanging from the rafters. She gave out a blood curling scream as she reached out and grabbed hold of his boots. Malone and Carter jumped out of the car gun's drawn as they ran to the barn to were MaryAnn's wailing scream's came from. As they burst in thru the barn door, they saw MaryAnn clinging to Ray Rays Boots crying hysterically. The Agent's put their gun's away as soon as they saw Ray Ray's body hanging and his sobbing wife. Carter took hold of MaryAnn by her shoulders, He spoke very soothingly getting her to let go of her husband. "Get her in to the house! I will call it in, and get a Doctor out here for her. Malone said as he went back to the car to call it in on the car radio. "Dispatch this is agent Malone, patch me thru to Cottonwood Sheriffs station. "right away Agent Malone" Dispatch replied. "Sheriffs Department" Deputy Morgan speaking! How may I help you? "This is F.B.I. Agent Malone, I need you to get hold of Sheriff Combs. Tell him to contact Agent Well's and meet me out here to the Smith stake out, it seems to look like Ray Ray Smith hung himself. I also need a Doctor for his wife, the Coroner ,and as many Deputy's as you can find. HELL JUST SEND OUT EVERY ONE! "Yes Sir I will get right on it" Deputy Morgan said. Malone walked back to the barn, to secure the scene. Sheriff Combs arrived at twelve fifteen A.M. followed by the coroner and a dozen deputy's. Agent Malone walked over to Sheriff Combs car as Combs stepped out. "You must be Sheriff Combs" Malone said holding out his hand to Combs with a big smile on his face. Combs Shook Malone's hand as he said with a solemn face, "What the Hell happened? "It looks like Ray Ray hung himself" Malone answered. "show me" Combs said. "Follow me, he is in the barn. Malone said. They both headed for the barn. As they started to go inside the barn, the coroner walked up and went inside with them. As they approached Ray Ray's body hanging from the barn rafters. Combs scanned the seen with his eyes. "I guess we need to cut him down the coroner said. "NO" NOT YET" Combs said. "NOT YET" WHY NOT? The Coroner said a little agitation in his voice. I cant examine his body up there. The coroner said sounding more agitation in his voice. "That is right Doc, just give me a few more moments, then we will cut him down. The coroner shook his head yes, as Combs turned to Malone and said to him. "That over turned stool over there, is that what he supposedly stood on? Combs said pointing to the over turned stool. "Yes" Malone answered. "How far would you say it is from the bottom of his boots to the floor? Combs ask." I don't know maybe three or four feet! Malone said. "grab that stool and set it under his boots" Combs said. Malone picked up the stool and set it up under Ray Rays boots. Malone's jaw dropped, as he said. Sonofabitch! "Do you still think he hung himself? That stool is at least a foot and a half short under him, He could not have stood on it, even on tippy toes. Someone else strung him up to make it look like he killed himself. Combs pointed out. "But WHO and HOW? We never took are eyes off this place. Malone said. "The Klan! They are sneaky little Bastard's! Combs replied. "you can cut him down now Doc! Combs said with a sigh in his voice. "I will let you know what I find when I get him on my table Sheriff" the Corner said as two deputy's lowered Ray Ray's body down to two other Deputy's who held on to his body and laid him on the floor. "Well there is nothing more we can do out here till morning, all we can do is seal everything off and try to get prints and find out where and how they got in here without being seen. Let's go in to the house and talk to the wife. Combs said as he turned and stated for the door. "I don't think she is going to be of much help" She is a hysterical mess, She found him hanging. Malone said as he followed Combs to Ray Rays house. Just as they approached the steps to the porch to go knock on the side door. A voice called out from the darkness. "BILL wait up" it was Agent Fred Wells. "Fred" is that you? Combs called out. "yes it is me he said as he came into the glow of the porch light. "We lost Ray Ray" Combs said as Fred came up by him at the bottom of the step's. "Not just him" We lost the Gum brothers as well as two of my agents! Fred said with anger in his voice. "HOW"? Bill ask. "There was an explosion at the Gum boys place, it was suppose to look like a propane gas leak. But it was Dynamite. My men and the Gum Boy's never knew what hit them. Fred in a angry shaking voice. "You know what this means Fred"? "Yes" those Sonofabitches are going to walk! Fred said angrily.

"We need to find those gun's Bill said. "We need to stop trial" Fred said, with a deep sigh in his voice. "STOP THE TRIAL! We still have the Grand Jury testimonials from the Gum Brothers and Ray Ray! Bill pointed out. "Bill you know that is not enough for a conviction. if they get a not guilty verdict, We can never try them again for those crime's because double jeopardy is attach. Fred reminded Bill. "Your right, so How do you plan to get the trial stopped? Bill ask. "I will call the D.A. in charge of the case, and get him to drop the charges. Once he knows that all the whiteness are Dead. I am sure he will do it. Fred said. "If we find some more whiteness to come forward we need to put them and their Family's in protective custody, and I know there are some more out there. And we need to find those Dam guns. Bill said to Fred in a serious tone in his voice. "You Bet Your Ass! We will get them all, and for all the murders they did tonight as well. So lets go in and talk to the wife. Fred said trying to give a little smile on his face. Combs Morgan, and Wells went up the step's Combs knocked on the door as he opened it and the three of them went inside. They found Ray Ray's wife sitting in a over stuff chair crying as her Sister sat on the arm trying to console her in her grief. "Mrs. Smith We need to talk with you. Combs said with sympathy in his voice for her. She looked up at the three men standing be for her. Her voice became in raged with anger, as she blurted out, "YOU" You were suppose to protect my RAY RAY! He did not kill himself, THAT ROTTEN GOOD FOR NOTHING RED AVERY AND HIS KLAN BUDDIES KILLED MY RAY!! She screamed at them. Mrs. Smith Red Avery did not kill your husband. He and the three Parks brother's have bin locked in my jail sense three this after noon. Combs said in a soft tone of voice. Then Mrs. Smith spat back. Let Me tell you something Sherriff Red Avery may have not done it himself! But He planed it and gave the order to kill my Ray Ray to another one of his Klan members. You know he calls himself the Grand Wizard of the KLU KLUX KLAN! She said anger in her voice. "You may be Right Mrs. Smith, But we need to get proof of his involvement, and who did the killing of your husband and the others. we need evidence and eye witness to these crimes. It will take us some time, but we will get them! All of them!! Combs told her. "I will testify" My Ray Ray told me every thing they did to that little girl. Mrs. Smith said. "Im sorry Mrs. Smith, it has to be some one who was there and at the seen of the crime and witness the crime first hand. Combs said. "I Know some one" She said. "WHO? Fred Wells spoke up with a little excitement in his voice. "Mike Parks, He quit the Klan around the same time my Ray Ray did! She answered. "Do you know were he lives? Wells ask taking a note book from his breast pocket of his suit coat. "I am not sure, but I think he lives some were on the north side of town. My Ray Ray and him worked together at the mill. She told him. I will get his address from the motor vehicles. Combs spoke up. "What time did your husband go out to the barn? Wells ask. "He went out at ten o'clock, the Honey Mooner's were coming on the T V. she answered. He was suppose to come back in to watch the news at eleven. When he did not come in when the news was over and the Steve Allen show came on, I went out to get him. She added. "They must have bin waiting on him to come out to the barn, and turned off the power some how, and killed him in the dark. That is why we never saw Ray Ray come out of the house. We thought he went out to the barn when we saw the lights come. they must have turned the lights back on when they left. Malone said. "There is a switch box by the back door of the barn. Mrs. Smith said. " I will make sure the print boys check it for prints Combs said. "Mrs. Smith You get some rest now, we will talks some more later if you think of any one else that might be of some help in getting these Guy's Malone told her as they were getting ready to leave. "Oh one more thing" Why didn't your husband turn on the porch light be for he went out to the barn? Malone ask. "Some times he did and some times he didn't. That was just Ray Ray being Ray Ray. She answered. "I wish he had turned that porch light on we would have seen him go out to the barn, and bin able to tell if something was not right. Malone said to her as he turned to leave with Combs and Wells.

CHAPTER FOURTY

Billy Joe and Sue Ellen sat across the table from Carl and Margie, in Caesars Palace having dinner. Carl tapped on his wine glass with a spoon, as he cleared his throat. "I would like to make a toast, but first I would like to say! Thank You Billy Joe. Thank you for giving my wife Marge and I one of the greatest exciting fun two weeks we have ever had in our life. Besides that if you had not took us here, we would have never had the chance to see and meet Elvis, let alone have our photo taken with him. You and Sue Ellen will always be one of closes Dear and Best Friends we have ever had, may all of us be friends for life. WE LOVE YOU! BILLY JOE AND SUE ELLEN!! They all raised their glasses and took a drink of wine. Then Sue Ellen said to them as she sat her glass down. "We Love You to!! " Now that we got all that out of the way" How are our wife's getting home? Carl chuckled. "What do you mean How are we getting home? Margie said with a puzzled look on her face. "Well Billy Joe and Sue Ellen came with three suitcases and you and I had three, Now we all have twelve suitcases. "That's Right! I guess the girl's will have to stay behind and get the next plane out day after tomorrow! Billy Joe laugh jokingly. "You cant be serious! Sue Ellen gasp, Margie cut in to say, "we only have souvenirs and a few things we needed. Billy Joe and Carl burst out laughing. "The look on you girls face" Carl said still laughing. "We are just kidding with the two of you! Billy Joe added. "OH YOU GUY'S Margie said as she playfully punched Carl's arm. "Come on Carl! Lets take our Girls Dancing, let's live it up for our last night here. They all left the dinning area and headed for the Ball Room to dance, be for retiring for night to their rooms, to get some rest be for the air port limo picked them up to drive them to catch their flite for home.

They arrived at the airport at seven A.M. checked in and boarded the plane by eight thirty A.M. Sue Ellen and Margie sat together on the plane chattering away about all the gifts they were taking home for friends and family members. Billy Joe and Carl sat together talking on a more serious matters. It was Billy Joe who spoke first as the plane leveled off in flite. "Carl if I have to go to jail, can I count on you to look after Sue Ellen and the kids? " You know you can. But you are not going to jail, Ben is a great Lawyer, he knows that you did not kill all those people. We all believe in you Billy Joe. Carl smiled. "I hope you are right Pal, as you know the trial is just a week away. " Have you thought about what you are going to do when all this is over? Carl ask. "You mean if I don't go to jail? Billy Joe said a little despair in his voice. "You got to have faith my friend. God won't let you down, I know he won't I feel that in every bone in my body. God is on your side .Carl said trying to reassure him. They talked for a little while then leaned their heads back on the seat closed their eyes and fell asleep. Carl woke up when he heard the captain say over the intercom. Please fasten you seat belts we are about to land. thank you for flying with us at United air lines. "Billy Joe! Wake up! We are about to land, put your belt on. Carl said as he shook him awake. They departed the plane after it landed, waited for their luggage. Billy Joe went for the car and brought it to the loading zone. After the car was loaded they started on the long drive home. Billy Joe was a little somber and quiet, as he drove the car. Everyone else chatted excitedly about all the fun things they did and seen. And all the fun they had shopping for gifts.

It was ten till six P.M. as they arrived in Cottonwood. As they drove down the main street just three miles outside of the city of Cottonwood, Sue Ellen Gasp," OH MY GOD! Billy Joe! Look The Mill!! Billy Joe pulled the car over and stopped. They all stared out the car windows at the twisted melted metal that was once the mill. burned out cars lined in front and under the twisted metal that was the parking lot for the workers cars. Two men wearing yellow hard has stood on the side walk talking. Billy Joe and Carl got out of the car and walked up to the men. "What The Hell Happened? Billy Joe ask one of the men. "Not sure yet! The F.B.I. and Special Fire inspectors are inside now trying to find out. The man said. " Was any one hurt? Carl ask. "Yes" The entire second shift! Only nine people are still barely alive. A hundred and forty are dead. The man said sadly. "What could have caused a fire that big? Carl ask." I cant really say for sure, but the rumors going around by some folks are saying it was a bomb! The man said. "That's horrible" who would want to Bomb a Cotton Mill? Carl said. "When did this happen? Billy Joe ask. " five days ago the man answered. " Thanks Man for telling us. We got to get home now its bin a long day for us. Billy Joe said as he held "out his hand to shake hands with both men. Billy Joe and Carl went back to the car and left for home.

Sissy was sitting on the porch steps as she saw Billy Joe drive into the drive way. She jumped up and ran to the screen door as she shouted out. " GRANMA GRANPA!! MOMMYS IS HOME! Then she rand down the steps out to the car, as Sue Ellen got out and thru her arms around Sissy lifting her up and hugging and kissing her cheek. "Oh Mommy I Missed you SO MUCH! " I missed you to Baby! Sue Ellen said as she hugged her tight then gently putting her down. " Were is my hug and kisses? Margie said Holding out stretched arms to Sissy. With a big smile on her little face, Sissy ran over to Margie jumping into her arms, as Sissy gave her a big hug and a kiss. " I missed you to Aunt Margie. " About Me? Carl ask with a big grin as stood next to Margie. Sissy reached over putting both her little arms around his neck and giving him a kiss on the cheek. "Love you kiddo! Carl said as he took Sissy from Margie. " I Love you to Uncle Carl. Sissy said as he put her down. Billy Joe walked to the front of the car. " Hey! Were is my Hug? He said with a big grin as He looked down at Sissy. Sissy walked slowly to him, as He picked her up, her little body stiffened as Billy Joe hugged her and kissed her cheek. then he whispered in her ear. "Daddy Loves You, and I am sorry for all the times I have hurt you. I will never ever hurt you again. Then He Kissed her cheek, and put her down. " Let's all go into the house, rest up and we can unload Vegas later! Billy Joe said as every one laugh with him. As he turned to walk to the house, he saw his Father and Mother standing on the porch with Sue Ellen's Mother and Father. "WOW! What a surprise! Billy Joe said as he Hugged his mother then his father, as he went on to say. " What brings you Guys here. He ask with a smile. " We came to go to court with you and show are support for our Son. His Father said. " Thank You Daddy" But You and Mom don't have to make all those long trip's just to show your support for me! Hell I already know how you feel about me, and I love you both for that. Billy Joe said getting a little teary eyed. " Oh Yes We do" We are going to be there every day, and so are your Sisters. His Father said. " Lets all go inside, we can talk about this later. Sue Ellen's Mother and I made dinner for all of us. So lets go eat be for it gets cold Billy Joes Mother Jane smiled. Everyone went inside and sat down at the dinner table. They sat around at the table chatting about Vegas and the children and all the gifts they had for everyone. After dinner and the dishes were cleared washed and put away, all the men went out to Billy Joes car and brought in His and Sue Ellen's suitcases. Then they took Carl and Margie's suitcases over to their house. After the children were put in bed, an hour later Carl and Margie went home to go to bed. Sue Ellen and Billy Joes parents retired to their rooms for the night. Billy Joe told Sue Ellen to go on up to bed, He told her He would be up later, said He was going out on the porch to smoke a cigarette. She gave him a kiss and went upstairs to their room. Billy Joe walked out to the porch, he sat down on the porch swing and lit up a cigarette, he took a drag and blew out the smoke as he looked out at the night sky. Thought's of Sonia ran thru his mind, He knew it was because of her that he stopped drinking and he could now see how evil the Klan was. He also knew that Sue Ellen had tried to tell him the same thing. But he just would not listen to her. It took falling in love with a Negro girl to show him Negro's were people with feeling's just like him. He knew that he would have to pay for all the people's lives he had taken.

" Can I have one of them smokes? Billy Joes Father said as he came out on the porch to join his son on the swing. " sure Billy Joe said handing his father the pack of Lucky's. He took the pack pulled out a cigarette as he sat down on the swing next to his son, he handed the pack back as Billy Joe held out his lighter to lite the end of the cigarette. "Thank you son. His Father said as he took a puff on the cigarette. "Cant sleep? Billy Joe ask his Father. "I just thought I would spend a little time alone with my Son. His Father said. "I guess we haven't spent a lot of alone time this past year! Billy Joe said with a sigh as he took another puff on his cigarette. "Not sense you joined the Klan! His Father said in a resentful sounding voice. "I know "Daddy! I should have listened to you, I started Drinking the hard stuff. Almost lost Sue Ellen, She left me, because I beat her and Sissy in my drunken rages. But she forgave me and took me back, only if I stopped my drinking and made a better life for us. And I have bin really trying to do that. But now I may go to jail, because I let Red Avery brain wash me in to joining up with the Klan. But Daddy, I swear those things they are charging me with was not me! Billy Joe said confessing to his Father of his mistakes. "Do you remember John Tucker and his son Cory? "Yes! You and Mr. Tucker use to cut wood for winter together. "That's right! And you and his son Cory were best friends, you and Cory were always playing Daniel Boon in the woods. His Father said reminding him of his childhood. " Yes we were eight years old then they moved away and I never saw them again. Billy Joe said. "They didn't move away, I told you that because I thought you were to young to understand what happened to them. "What happened to them? Billy Joe ask a concerned look on his face. " it was Valentines Day, little Cory made a Valentine card made like a heart. He gave it to a little white girl he liked. Her Daddy was a Klansman. So he took three other Klan members with him over to Johns place, they grabbed Cory from his back yard, striped off his shirt two of the men held him as the girls father took a whip to Cory's back, John ran out when he heard Cory scream. John grabbed the whip out of the fathers hand and knocked him on his ass. The other men thru Cory to the ground, and jumped on John. It took all four men to take John down, They Hung John and Cory on a large branch from the big old oak tree in Johns back yard. His wife and his two other children whiteness the whole thing. After the funeral she sold the farm and moved back east were her sister lived. John was a Negro man, But he was a good man. And He was a Dear Friend to ME! And that is why I hate the Klan and everything they stand for. If I would have told you back then, just maybe, you would not have joined the Klan. But I was trying to protect you. " You know Daddy! I was so mad at Cory for years because I thought He moved away, and never said Good By to me. Billy Joe said sadly as images of his child hood friend Cory flashed thru his mind. "Son Do like I do, just remember all the good times you had together, and hold those memory's close to your heart. His Father told him as he stood up and stubbed out his cigarette in a ash tray sitting On a little stand next to the swing. "Thanks Daddy, Now I know Cory was still my friend. Billy Joe said feeling sad but relieve in his voice. "Well I guess I need to turn in, Billy Joe! Look down the street there, I noticed it while we were talking. There is someone inside that car smokeing,who ever it is just flicked a cigarette out the window. Billy Joe got up from the swing and stood next to his father as he looked down the street to were the car was parked. "It is probably just the Fed's Daddy making sure I will show up in court Wednesday. Billy Joe said to his father not to worried about the car. "Well I guess I will say Goodnight. His father said. "I guess I better turn in to! Good night Daddy. Billy Joe said as he followed his father in to the house.

The car parked down the street was a black 54 Chevy the driver was Red Avery, on the passenger side was Boomer Malone, in the back seat was Dicky Bird jugging on a flask of shine. "Why don't I just put a few sticks of dynamite under his house and get rid of all of them at one shot? Boomer said. "HELL KNOW! Not with all the Fucking FEDS in town. Avery snapped. "I forgot! I guess you is right. Boomer said. " But what if he makes a deal with the feds? Dicky Bird said. "He ain't gonna do that because I got his gun he shot all them niggers with! Red said with a big grin on his face. "But what if you all go to jail? Dicky Bird ask. "WE AINT GOING TO JAIL! The FEDS AINT GOT NO CASE! They Don't got any so called witnesses no guns THEY GOT NOTHING! Red pointed out. Then he started the car as he said, lets get the Hell out of here and go do some more drinkin, at the meeten hall as he drove off. " Hey RED! What you got's in mind for old Billy Joe? Dicky Bird ask as they drove down the street. "Oh I got's something real good in mind for him, his Jew Friends and his whole Fucking Niger Loven family! Red said slyly. "When? And how you gonna do it to them? Dicky Bird said excitedly. "IM just going to wait till the feds leave town, and things die down. Then we will strike when everyone least expect it. I will let everyone in the Klan know when the time is right. Red said in a sneaky sly voice and a sneering grin on his face. " Dicky Bird giggled, I can hardly wait! Boomer and Red Laughed, as red added You will wait till I tell you the plan. They arrived at the meeting hall, went in and drank the booze red had on ice till they all passed out.

Next Morning Sue Ellen and Billy Joes Mothers were in the kitchen making breakfast. Sue Ellen came down stairs with the Baby in her arm's as she went in to the kitchen. "You Guy's are up early, Sue Ellen said as she came in to the kitchen. "Good Morning Honey! We both woke up early, so we decided to get breakfast started for everyone. Sue Ellen's mother said as she scrambled some eggs in a bowl. "There's our little man "Billy Joes Mother Jane said as she held out her hands to take the baby in to her arms smiling. Sue Ellen handed Jane the Baby. " I came down to feed little Joe, I thought we were the only one's up. Sue Ellen said as she opened the cabinet taking out a jar of baby food for Little Joe. "We got up an hour ago, we put the coffee on had a little chat and decided to fix breakfast for everyone. Her Mother said. Then went on to say. Sit down Honey and have some coffee, then she poured coffee from the pot into a cup sitting on the table in front of Sue Ellen. "Thanks Mom" I really need a cup to wake me up, I got to get all three suit cases unpacked and hand out all the gifts we got for everyone. Sue Ellen said then took a sip of coffee. "Oh My" I was wondering why you had so many cases. Her Mother said with a little giggle. "Oh Honey" I forgot to tell you last night, I put all your mail on the table by the phone. "Thanks Mom, I will get to it be for I get to the suit cases. She looked over at Jane as she gave the last spoon full of food to the baby. "He finished the whole jar, that is so great! Mom has he bin eating that good all the time? Sue Ellen said smiling at Little Joe as he smiled back at her. "He sure has, and that's not all he has bin doing, He has bin rolling himself over. Her Mother told her. "OH MOM"THAT IS SO WONDERFULL! I think He is going to be just fine. Sue Ellen said in a happy tone of voice. "Mother Jane would you mind holding Little Joe for a few more moments while I check the mail? Sue Ellen ask as she got up from the table. "NOT AT ALL,I want to spend as much time as I can with him. Jane said with a big smile. Sue Ellen walked in to the living room, she picked up the mail and started to sort it when she came to a letter that read it was from the federal court in Jackson, she put the rest of the mail down and opened the one from the court, Her heart skipped a beat as she read the letter it had a check attached to it for five hundred dollars. Her hands were shaking as she picked up the phone and dialed Ben Stine's number. "Stine Law Office a woman's voice said over the phone. " Yes my name is Sue Ellen Martin, I would like to speak to MR. Stine Please. Sue Ellen said. "Are You a Client? The woman ask. "Yes. Sue Ellen said. "ONE MOMENT"I WILL PUT YOU THRUE" The woman said. "SUE ELLEN! I WAS ABOUT TO CALL YOU! Stine said as he answered the phone. "YOU WER! IM calling you because I just got a letter with a check from the court. Sue Ellen said. Stine spoke up be for she could go on. "The Court Dropped the charges, the check is the return of the bail money. "That means it is over? Sue Ellen said with a sigh of relief in her voice. "Maybe not" they can refile if they get any real hard evidence against Billy Joe! I do not think they will, because I feel Billy Joe is innocent. But He Needs to stay away from the rest of the Klan members. Stine told her. "He already has, Billy Joe quit the Klan months ago. Sue Ellen told Stine. "That is good, But if they do refile You call me right away. NOW GO GIVE YOUR HUSBAND THE GOOD NEW'S And Stay in touch! You Have a Great Day. " Oh Yes we will" Thank You MR. Stine" Thank You" Sue Ellen said as they both said good by and hung up the phone. Sue Ellen let out with an excited Yell as she ran up the stairs to the bedroom were Billy Joe was still asleep. She jumped on him as he woke up in a shock look on his face. "HAVE YOU GONE CRAZY WOMAN? Billy Joe said trying to set up as Sue Ellen sat on him, saying "It is over" THANK GOD IT"S OVER! "WHAT IN THE HELL ARE YOU TALKING ABOUT? Billy Joe Shouted at her. "LOOK "LOOK" you do not have to go to court. She said as she held up the letter for him to read. Then she told him about the phone call to Stine and everything he told her. "OH HONEY! THIS IS GREAT! Billy Joe said as He gave Sue Ellen a big kiss. "Come on get up and get dress, our Mothers are making us breakfast. I want us to go down and give every one the great news. Sue Ellen said with a big smile on her face. "Hell I think everyone knows. The way you were yelling you woke the whole house up! Billy Joe kidded her, as he got out of bed. "Get dressed and I will see you down stairs. Sue Ellen said as she went out the door of the bed room, as she stepped out in to the hallway she ran in to her father and father in law. She gave them both a hug as she told them what all the ruckus was about. All of them went down the stairs chattering happily with each other. Sue Ellen and Billy Joes Mothers were standing at the bottom of the stairs as the three came down, Sue Ellen gave them the news about Billy Joe, everyone was hugging and rejoicing as they went into the kitchen. Billy Joe joined them a few moments later with Sissy perched on his shoulders. "LOOK" MOMY! DADDY GAVE ME A HORSEY RIDE! SISSY said with a happy smile. Billy Joe lifted her off his shoulders and sat her on a chair at the table. As Billy Joe sat down next to Sue Ellen, Sissy spoke up. "Daddy can I have a real pony? "Maybe Santa will bring you one for Christmas, Only if you are a good girl! Billy Joe answered. "Well it isn't Christmas, But after we finish with breakfast, we all need to go in to the living room so I can give everyone their gifts we got in Vegas. That is why the three suit cases are sitting there. Sue Ellen said smiling. "Yeha Sue Ellen and Margie brought half of Vegas back with them, That is why Carl and I had to buy all those extra suit cases. Billy Joe laugh. Everyone at the table broke out laughing. "OH You" We only brought back little gift's for all the people we love! Sue Ellen said with a little giggle in her voice.

The Family went into the living room were Sue Ellen handed out the gifts to everyone. Carl and Margie came over with the gifts Margie bought for Sissy and Little Joe. After lunch Sue Ellen called Ida May and told her she was bringing her Family to meet her Family. And Carl and Margie was coming also, to bring gifts from Vegas for her Family. Ida May was thrilled with the ice tea serving set Sue Ellen and Margie brought her that had the Las Vegas logo on it.as well as the matching salt and pepper shakers. Marcy, William, and Ben as well as their father Emit got matching jackets that had the Vegas logo on the back. The three children also got two sets of clothing. Billy Joe gave Ben a transistor radio. He gave Emit an autograph photo of Sammy Davis JR. "THANK YOU MR.MARTIN! How did you know I like Him? and how was you able to get him to write his name on it, and how did he know my name? "Emit said a little teary eyed. "Well Your Wife told my Wife, and my Wife told me, and I got tickets to see his show. after the show I went up to him and ask him for a photo just for you. I told Him what a great Fan you were to him. And well here it is. Billy Joe told him with a smile. Thank You Again MR. Martin, Emit said as he shook Billy Joes hand. " Call me Billy Joe! MR. Martin is to formal. "You can call me Emit! Billy Joe. He said feeling more relaxed around all the white people. Carl came up to Billy Joe and Emit, he was all excited. "MR. Johnson! Were did you ever get such a great grill! It is fantastic. "You can call me Emit Son, what do you want me to call you? "You can call me Carl Sir! Please tell were you got that Grillers Dream? Carl begged. "I built it. Emit said. "You Built IT! OH MY GOD! EMIT HOW MUCH WOULD YOU

CHARGE TO BUILD ONE FOR ME? Carl ask all excited. "I guess I could if you buy the materials, do it for say a hundred dollars. Emit said giving it a deep thought, But I cant do it till after I get all my planten done. "That is great! Just give me a list of what you need when you are ready, and I will get it. Carl said with a big grin as he ran his hands over the big grill. Then he looked up at Emit saying. "Emit" I got a great idea! Why don't we have ourselves a big cook out" I will do all the cooking and supply the food. What do you say Emit! Carl ask with pleading eyes. "Sounds ok to me! But it's kind of early to have a cook out. Emit said. "We won't do it right now, first I will have to go home and get the stakes and potatoes, foil and go to the store for ice and drinks, and the Ladies can whip up the side dishes. " Well I guess it's ok! But the kids won't eat steaks, we best make hamburgers and hot dogs for them. Emit said smiling. "Great" Billy Joe you want to come with me? "IM going to have to, you will need my truck to haul everything. Let's go tell the ladies. Billy Joe said. "Can Rodger and I be of some help? Billy Joes Father Joe spoke up. Emit turned to them and said, Yes you can. You can help me get the tables and chairs from my garage, and set them up. Carl and Billy Joe Left to go shopping and Sue Ellen went back to her house to get bottles and diapers for the baby. She returned a short time later and began helping the other Ladies with the sides. Emit, Rodger and Joe set up the tables and chairs. Carl and Billy Joe arrived back at Emits house two hours later. Billy Joe drove his truck in to a drive way that came off from the street that crossed His street were he and Carl lived on. The drive way was heavily treed and tall shrubs made it impossible to see Emits house and back yard. The drive way also lead down to a large barn. Billy Joe parked next to the edge of Emits back yard, as he and Carl got out of his truck, He and carl were amazed at how great every thing was so perfectly set up, "WOW" Carl said as he started to unload the food. They really bin working. It looks like a real fancy banquet set up. "Yes it does He really takes good care of his place. Billy Joe said as he pulled the boxes filled with bags of ice. Emit Rodger and Joe came over to the truck. "Your Back" Rodger said. "Looks like you bought the store out! Joe said. "You Boys got enough there to feed an army, Should we invite the whole Community? Emit chuckled. Carl set the meat down on the counter at the end of the grill. Suddenly, Carl smacked his forehead with the palm of his hand as he yelled out. " OH MAN! I FOR GOT THE CHARCOAL!! Every one burst out laughing. "Boy" You don't need no charcoal, That stuff will poison your food. This grill don't use no charcoal. Emit said grinning. "Well How am I going to cook the food? Carl ask with a perplexed look on his face. "You take some sweet grass and cherry tree limbs and peach limbs spread a bunch of walnut shells and acorns, pour some melted pork fat on it and lite the fire. If you look behind you, will see the grill is ready for the meat. Emit said with a chuckle. Carl was very impressed, He rushed around and began preparing the meat and putting it on the grill to cook. Every one sat around the table as Emit Led every one holding hands as they said the Lord's prayer, be for eating and having a great time as they bounded together with a life time friendship. Making new memories for ever. Billy Joe said a silent prayer of his own. Asking God to forgive him for all the horrible things he had done. He promised He would do everything in his power to do good things and treat people right, and take care of his family. Emit and Ida May invited Billy Joe and his family as well as Margie and Carl to come to their church on Thursday evening at seven P.M. for a special service to hear the Reverend Martin Luther King. Billy Joe and his family agreed to be there, as did Carl and Margie. Billy Joe had ask Emit if his church would be ok with him inviting white people to attend the services. "We aren't like some white people, we believe that we are all Gods children, no matter what color the skin may be. In our hearts we are all the same in Gods eyes. Our Church is not for coloreds only, like it is in some churches in the south that is for whites only. We consider our church as Gods House and in his house everyone is welcome. Emit told Him. Billy Joe smiled at him as he said. "We will be there, it is only three days away, my parents and my wives parents aren't going home till Sunday. So you can count on all of us coming. "I think you will like the services. Now I guess we got that settled, we best go help with the clean up and get things put away, be for we end up in the Dog house with the Ladies. Emit chuckled. Every one helped put things away and cleaned up. Afterwards every one hugged and said good night. Billy Joe and Carl put Sissy and the baby in the truck, Carl held the Baby, Sissy sat in the middle. Sue Ellen Her parents and Billy Joes Parents along with Margie all walked back home together as they talked about the good time they had with the Johnsons. After they were home the children was put to bed, Carl and Margie went home. Two hours later every one turned in for the night. Except Billy Joe, he went out on to the porch to smoke and collect his thoughts of the new feelings he was having about Negros and about GOD. And what really happened to his best child hood friend Cory. He was seeing for the first time in years what the Klan was really about. He was beginning to feel nothing But HATE FOR THE KLAN!

9A.M. Thursday

Sheriff Combs was sitting at his desk drinking a cup of coffee as he read the night shift reports. He looked up as he heard a knock at his door. "Come in" He said as he gave a wide grin at the well dressed man entering his office. What brings you to this neck of the woods? Combs said still smiling? "I missed your great coffee, and I was lonely. Agent Fred Wells chuckled as he sat down. "The coffee is over there in the corner, grab yourself a cup and tell me what up. Combs said nodding at the coffee pot in the corner of the office. Wells went over to the coffee pot and pored himself a cup then he sat back down taking a sip of the coffee. I am here to let you know, your getting an out of town visitor. "Reverend King "Combs said be for wells could finish. "How did you know? Wells ask a little surprised. "I got a memo over the teletype last night. Combs said. "I came here to ask you for back up support for me and my men, I did not know if you would get notified or not, this being such a small town. Wells said. "Well this isn't Mayberry" we do have up to date equipment, Combs laughed. "IM sorry" Bill I wasn't making fun of your Department, I wasn't sure how you might feel about King coming here. Wells said. "I have the highest respect for Reverend King. He is trying to bring change to the South and all of America. And he is doing it peacefully. Bill said. "Yes He is all about peace and change for all men women and children. But the Klan is all about hate murder and just plain evil. And if the Klan gets their way, they will stop at nothing to find a way to Kill Him! Fred Wells said in serious tone in his voice. "Yes they will! And it is up to men like us to protect him and keep him safe, and try to prevent and destroy the Klan to bring about that change. Bill said. "Speaking of the Klan" How are your Klan Boys behaving? Fed ask. "WELL" Red Avery is still having his regular meetings at that old run down church on the south side. I think he has lost a lot of his members, because the head count is down. And that Billy Joe Martin has not bin there in months. Bill said. "You know he was in Vegas for two weeks with his wife and two friends, I had Agents from the Vegas office keep an eye on him. Just in case he was planning to jump his bail. Fred said. "But He didn't he came back a week be for his trial date. Now that has bin canceled. He has just bin spending his time with his family. Bill said. "You still think he is guilty? Fred ask. My Gut says yes! But his actions these past months say no! Bill replied. "Well getting back to what's at hand right now, I have got twenty Agents coming here by one o' clock, and the state police is escorting Kings car to the church, they should be there by four P.M. How many of your Deputy's do you have? Fred said. "I have ten plus myself. Bill replied. "Great" We should have everyone in place by three P.M. Fred said. "Have You located Otis Mackey yet? Bill ask Fred. "NO Not yet! But we will get him! Fred said remembering how he Killed Sheriff Jack Maxwell. Mean while Red Avery was holding a special meeting at his Klan headquarters of his own. There was more than a hundred fifty Klan members getting ready for a march in front of the Baptist Church on the North side of town.

 All of Agent Fred Wells agents arrived on time. Bill Combs and his Deputy's all joined forces and took their places at the First Baptist Church on the North side of town. Reverend King arrived at the church he was surrounded by his body guards and members of his movement as he met with Reverend Earl Thomas who was the pasture of the church. People had already filled the church waiting for Reverend Kings arrival. they all went inside and the service began. First with the church quire as their voices filled the air with heavenly music. Reverend King gave a sermon, then He talked about up coming peace marches asking people to join him and fellow marchers and volunteers for the right to vote and equal rights movement. After the services were over and people starting to leave the church, The calm happy feelings of God was interrupted as Shouts of obscenities towards The negro's as well as the white people who were supporters of Reverend King. All of a sudden Breaking glass and screams filled the air as car windows were smashed and cars being set on fire. There was fighting in the street sidewalks and lawns between the Klan,

Deputy's and State troopers and F.B.I. agents along with civilian's. Rocks and beer bottles were hurled thru the stain glass windows of the church. Reverend King was rushed out the back door of the church by his body guards to an awaiting car and drove off thru a back ally way. A Klansmen ran up to the church with a bottle filled with gas an a rag stuffed in the neck, as he was about to lite the rag on fire. Sheriff Combs stepped in front of him ordering him to drop the bottle. He ignored Combs and lit the rag. Combs Shot him in the leg, He dropped the bottle on the ground. Combs quickly put out the fire by stomping it out. The Klansman lay rolling and screaming in pain as he yelled curse words at Combs. He drug the Klansman to the steps of the church and cuffed one of his hands to the iron railing. "Didn't your Momma ever teach you not to play with fire? Combs ask as he snatched off the Klansman's hood off. "FUCK YOU! He spat at Combs. "YEHA YEHA" Don't go no were. Combs chuckled to himself as he walked away to get into the trunk of his car. Agent Wells came over to Combs as he was pulling out a tear gas rifle. "I called in for more back up and for the Guard to help! Fred said. "Here take one! Combs said handing Fred one of the Guns. "Think this will hold them off till the others get here? Fred ask. "I sure as Hell hope so! Each gun as fifty rounds we need to shoot in the middle of the street, Hopefully that will make most of them scatter and go back to the rock they crawled out from. Combs said as he added. We need to stop this shit be for to many innocent people get hurt. I hope my jail can hold all of them ASSHOLES! Use the smoke grenades first, that will give our guys a chance to put on their mask. Combs instructed Wells. "The blue shells are the smoke, the red ones are the tear gas, Now lets Rock and Roll! Combs said as they walked to the center of the street and started firing. All the Klansmen started running in retreat towards the City Park were they left all their cars. Combs and Wells walking behind firing smoke grenades. The Feds and Deputies had about sixty Klansmen sitting cuffed on the curb, as the fire truck came and put out the burning cars. The street looked like a war zone with many injured people laying in yards and sidewalks as well as in the street. The injured were taken to the hospital by ambulance and by cars. Combs and Wells were walking back to Combs cruiser as the Klansman was being loaded in to an ambulance. "COMBS" YOU SONOFABITCH! YOU SHOT ME! YOU ARE GONA GET YOURS!

YOU THINK YOU SAVED THAT NIGGER PREACHER! WELL YOU DIDN'T! He yelled at Combs as he was put in to the ambulance. "YOU ARE GOING TO JAIL AFTER THEY PATCH YOU UP! Combs yelled back at him. Wells tugged at Combs arm as he said. "Come on Bill that piece of trash is not worth your time! The Reverend Thomas was standing by Combs cruiser as Bill and Fred approached Bill opened the trunk and put the guns away. "I just wanted to thank you two for saving my church, and Reverend King so he could go see the other folks at their church. Reverend Thomas smiled. Bill snapped his head around to look at the Reverend slamming the trunk lid closed. "What OTHER CHURCH? Bill said with a worried look on his face. "Well HE told me he had a prayer meeting at the little church in the woods were his Father went when he was a boy. Reverend Thomas said. "Fred! Get in and call your men and have them fallow us. Reverend where is this church? Bill said urgency. "It is two miles down on Willow road South. The Reverend told him. "What's going on Bill? Fred ask with a puzzled look. "This was a set up to keep us here so they could get to King! Bill said. They jumped in to the car, Fred radioed to the other Agents and Deputy's to follow Bills car with lights and sirens, as the sped down the street heading for the Church.

Thursday 7 P.M.

Billy Joe and his family were seated in a pew by the door with Carl and Margie and The Johnson Family next to them. Billy Joe sat next to the isle that lead down to the pulpit, were Reverend King was about to speak. All the pews were filled with several other white Families who came to hear Reverend King speak, and to show their support for him and their Nabors. Two state troopers sat outside on their motorcycles in front of the church. Suddenly a black convertible came racing past the troopers as two men in the back seat thru bottles of beer at the troopers smashing against the rear of their motorcycles. The troopers started their cycles and gave chase with sirens and lights on. A pickup truck pulled up were the troopers were parked moments be for. Three men jumped out of the back of the truck wearing Klan hoods and robes. Two of the men pulled out a wooden cross from the truck bed, carried it to the front lawn of the church and planted it, as they set the gas soaked cross on fire, the third man burst in to the front door of the church with a shot gun. All heads turned to look at the man holding the gun aim at the Reverend King, people gasp in horror as they froze in fear in their pews. Reverend King stopped in mid sentence then he stared strait in to the mans eyes, as he shrugged off his body guards trying to pull him away. "THIS IS A HOUSE OF GOD! PUT THAT GUN DOWN! AND COME WORSHIP WITH US! Reverend King said with no fear in his voice. "SHUT THE FUCK UP YOU BLACK DEVIL! IM GOING TO SEND YOU BACK TO HELL WERE YOU CAME FROM!! The Klansman Yelled out, just as he started to pull the trigger of the gun. At that split second Billy Joe jumped up from the pew He pushed the gun upward as it fired in to the ceiling. Then Billy Joe yanked the gun away from the man as he used the butt of the gun to hit him and knock him backwards out the church door down the steps and on to the stone walk way. The other two Klansman ran towards Billy Joe to attack reaching for their pistols. Billy Joe pumped the twenty cage and fired at their feet, they stopped and turned run back to the pickup. The man on the ground jumped up an ran for the truck, then He stopped and turned to fire a pistol that one of the other men handed him. Billy Joe saw the gun and he fired the shot gun again at the man striking his arm, He yelped as he dropped the gun and jumped in to the back of the truck. The truck sped off as they heard the sirens and saw all the flashing lights coming down the road. The burning cross lit up the night sky as well as the whole front lawn of the church. A state trooper car and a Deputy Sheriffs car gave chase to the pickup. Billy Joe stood on the stone walk in the glowing light of the burning cross still holding the shot gun, when all of the other Sheriffs cars and F.B.I. cars rolled up to a stop in front of the church. Combs and Wells Followed By other Deputy's and agents jumped out of their cars with guns drawn. All guns were pointed on Billy Joe. "PUT THE GUN DOWN! Combs yelled out at him. Billy Joe stood there a little frozen for a moment. Then he slowly and gently laid the gun on the ground. "NOW STEP AWAY FROM THE GUN AND GET DOWN ON YOUR KNEES! Combs demanded. Billy Joe complied, he got down on his knees as Combs came up to him and put hand cuffs on Billy

Joe. "This time I got You! Combs whispered in Billy Joes ear. "You got it wrong, Sheriff! I was only trying to help. Billy Joe said. Fred Wells had went inside to check on the people and Reverend King. People started coming out of the church as Combs got Billy Joe to his feet. Reverend King came out with Billy Joes Family, Carl and Margie and the Johnson Family close behind him. Reverend King walked up to Sheriff Combs as he put his hand on his shoulder, he said. Sheriff Please take the cuffs off this young man! He saved my life as well as all these people tonight! Bill looked at him with disbelief on his face. "But he was holding a gun when we rolled up. Bill said. "Because He took that gun away from the Klansman that was about to shoot me. Referend King said. "That's Right Bill! Everyone here tells the same story. Fred told him. Combs took the cuffs off Billy Joe. Billy Joe turned to face Combs as He said. "Sheriff" I know you think I did all those things I was accused of because I was a Klan member. That wasn't Me! I quit the day I was arrested and heard all those horrible charges against me. And because I also lost my job at the mill because of it. If I was like the Klan! Do you think I would be here in church with these people? Billy Joe ask giving him that innocent look. "I guess not! IM Sorry MR.MARTIN. Bill said apologizing. "I want to shake your hand and thank you for saving my life and the lives of all the people in the church! Reverend King said holding his hand out to Billy Joe. He shook hands with Billy Joe, and ask him if he would like to help with his movement. "I will help in any way I can Reverend! But Sheriff Combs here will more than likely arrest me for shooting that Klan Guy. Billy Joe told him. "SHOOTING" YOU SHOT THE GUY? Combs said. "Well Yes! He pointed a pistol at me, and I fired be for he did, I think I hit him in the shoulder cause he dropped the gun over there by the road. Billy Joe said pointing to were he saw the gun dropped. "ARREST"YOU! HELL BOY THIS IS GOING TO HELP US CATCH THAT POINTED HEAD FOOL! Combs said. "How? Billy Joe ask. "Well we can get his prints from those guns, and if he has a record then we will know his name. and if he took a lot of buck shot, he will need medical attention. And we will get him for sure. Combs said with a big grin on his face. "I will call it in Fred Wells said as he headed to the car. A small framed black man with gray hair approached Billy Joe ask as he shook hands with him. "Thank you for being here tonight, I am Pastor Rubin Brown Will you and your family be joining us on Sunday? That is if you don't mind the hole in the ceiling. I don't know when I can get it fixed. "I would like to come with my wife and kids if you don't mind. Billy Joe said with a smile. Then he went on to say, How bout I come here on Saturday, and I get my Pal Carl to help me fix that hole. after all I put it there! Billy Joe smiled. "You are a good man" maybe you and your family would like to join our little church? Pastor Brown said. "Why not! I think I am going to like it here. Billy Joe told him. Be for Billy Joe and his family could go home, every one that had bin in the church came up to him thanking him and shaking his hand and giving him hugs. Billy Joe was feeling like a real HERO.

The State troopers on their motorcycles that was chasing the black convertible, lost site of the car as they turned off their head lights and turned into a wooded area. The troopers cruised around several roads searching for the car. They called it in and headed back to Sheriff Combs office. Same thing happened with the pickup with the Klansman being chased by Sheriffs State Troopers and Feds, The Klansman gave them the slip by driving into a barn on another Klansman Farm. They knew the area better than the men chasing them. The driver of the pickup with the wounded man, called a Doctor across the state line who was a Klan member. The Doctor told them how to care for the mans wound and as soon as the coast was clear bring the man to his office, He told them he would go there and wait for them.

Thursday 11P.M.

Sheriff Bill Combs and F.B.I. Agent Fred Wells were sitting together in Bills office, talking about the Day's events, a young Deputy came in to the office a shot gun in one hand and a brown evidence bag in the other as he said. "Sheriff" Here are the guns they were dusted for prints, the shot gun had two sets of prints, and the colt had one set of prints that was the same as the one set on the shot gun. Bills eyes lit up with excitement as he ask grabbing the brown bag tearing it open. "COLT! IS IT A COLT 45? "Yes it is Sheriff! The Deputy answered. "Bill You Thinking What IM THINKING? Fred said with excitement now in his voice. "OH Yes" Bill said as he pulled the gun out of the bag holing it up as he admired it. "I think this little Beauty is going to give us the evidence we need to put the Greens Killer and the Sugar Shak murders away forever. "Bill let me take the colt to our lab in Jackson to test it and see if the bullets match the ones we have from the murder victims. Fred said with hope in his voice. "It is kind of late, I guess it will have to wait till morning. Bill said. "Give me the Colt and I will take it to our lab and pull the expert out of bed myself. Just give me a few hours and I will have the answer if that is the gun or not. Fred told him. "OK" Let's make sure the chain of custody isn't broken. And by then maybe we will know whose prints are on the guns. Bill said as he handed the brown evidence bag back containing the gun. Fred took the evidence bag signed the voucher left the Sheriff's office and drove his car to Jackson F.B.I. Headquarters to run the ballistic test on the colt 45. Sheriff Combs waited in his office for the prints to come in with a match.

Friday 2:30 A.M.

A dark green 55 ford wagon drove down the highway heading for the state line, a man by the name of Delbert More laid down in the back seat covered with a blanket. Leroy Davis sat in the last seat in the back of the wagon. Elliot Barker was driving his wife Jennifer sat next to him on the passenger side of the car. They crossed the state line in to Alabama and drove to a small town by the name of Ludlow. As they came to the street were the Doctors office was they turned in to an Ally way behind the office. Doctor James Lee came out the back door with a wheel chair. He went to the car Him and the other two men helped Delbert out of the car and in to the chair, and wheeled him inside were two nurses stood in scrubs in the operating room. They got Delbert on to the table, he was incoherent Doctor Lee unwrapped his shoulder, the packing and bandages were soaked in blood. "God" This is bad! He is Shockey! We got to get fluids in him, I can't operate till he is more stable. Hellen hang two units of plasma and Sheila put a I V with ringers in him. He told the nurses as they hurried to get Delbert more stable. "You folks need to come with me to the waiting room. I have some hot coffee out there, you look like you all could use a cup! Doctor Lee said as he led them to the waiting room. Doctor Lee went over to a phone in his office to call in another Doctor he knew for help with the surgery. "Hennery! James here! I need your help, I got a gun shot wound that is pretty bad! "Are you at the hospital? Hennery ask. "No" My office! This is a special case, No paper trail. James told him. "I understand, give me twenty minutes I will be there. Hennery said as he hung up. Just then a tall thin dark haired man walked in to the waiting room waring scrubs. His name was Doctor Donald Potter Anastacia's. "I see the patient isn't stable yet. Potter said filling a cup with coffee. "He should be in about thirty minutes Doctor Lee told him. "You going to be able to do the surgery by your self? Potter ask. "I got Hennery Blake coming to help. Lee answered. Blake came like he said he would, and when Delbert was stable he was put to sleep and the surgery began. It took six hours. they had to amputate Delbert's arm. The damage was just to great to save it. He was taken to the local hospital and admitted as a farm accident. Doctor Lee was His Doctor. No one ever knew it was a gun shot wound. Barker and his wife along with Davis drove back to Mississippi on Saturday morning. The other two men that was in the truck with Delbert and Davis, had painted the truck black and put their Georgia plates back on the truck when Davis returned and told them about Delbert, they left the Barker farm and went back to Georgia were they all had family. Delbert had no family he lived by himself in an old camper by the lake.

Friday 6: A.M.

Combs was stretched out on his couch in his office sleeping. When the phone rang, he jumped up to answer it. "Sheriff Combs here! He said rubbing his face. "Bill" Its Fred! WE GOT A MATCH!! Fred said with excitement on the other end of the phone. "ARE YOU SURE? Bill ask. "Yes! It is a perfect match. That gun was used in all the murders.

Fred said. "Now all we got to do is find the guy who used it. Bill said. "The prints haven't came in yet? Fred ask "No not yet! Bill answered. "Well all we can do now, is hope this guy has a record. Fred said. "If he don't have a record, than we are back to square one. Bill sighed. "Well IM going home to get some sleep. You should do the same. Just give me a call when you have something. Fred said sounding a little weary. "I won't argue with that! I need to let my wife and kids know I still live there. Bill laughed. Bill said good by to Fred then hung up the phone, and headed home to his family.

6:15 P.M. Friday.

Billy Joe and Carl arrived at the little church in the woods to fix the damage to the ceiling and roof made by the shot gun. Pastor Rubin Brown was standing on the front steps of the church. "You Young Men really keep your word! Pastor Brown said with a big smile on his face. "We told you we would be here today, and here we are. Billy Joe and I will have that hole fixed like new in no time at all. Carl said as he pulled a latter off Billy Joe's truck. Billy Joe and Carl started on the roof first, repaired the hole and put new shingles on and went inside the church and repaired the hole in the ceiling with new plaster and paint. They finished up by nine P.M. that night. No one could tell there was ever a hole in that ceiling. Pastor Brown Thanked them, said good by as Billy Joe and Carl drove off heading for home.

9: P.M. Friday

The Cottonwood jail cells were full with all the Klansmen that were arrested for the riot they caused. Some of the Klansmen were transported to the Tupelo jail. Red Avery was back from the hospital were he had twelve stiches to his head. He was sharing a cell with Dicky Bird, Boomer Malone, and Ricky Parks. "Has any one heard if King is dead or not? Red ask. "Not a word Red". Ricky replied. "DAM! IT SHOULD HAVE MADE THE PAPPERS BY NOW! Red sneered. "Maybe we can ask one of the Guards. Dicky Bird said. "ARE YOU NUTS! We can't say anything! They have no Idea we are involved. And I want to keep it that way. Red told him. "All we can do for now is just wait till we hear something about it. If everything went according to the plan, King and all the rest of those Niggers in that church are dead, and the gun that killed King has bin planted in Billy Joes truck. And he will be charged with all the bodies that are on that gun. And he will be in a cell till they take him out and hang him. Red laughed. "How did you get Billy Joes gun Red? Dicky Bird ask. "Red said with a big grin on his face, He gave it to me. I told him we had to hide our guns be for the feds came around. So he gave me his gun, and helped me take all our guns to my hiding place. I would not have done this to him if he hadn't turned traitor to us. So now he is going to get the Death penalty for turning against us. Red told all the men in the cell with him.

The one thing Red Avery did not know was that Billy Joe went to the cemetery a few months be for and picked the lock on the door, he took out his gun and bought another gun made the same year make and caliber as his. He switched the barrel firing pin and cylinder on the guns. He left the new gun and took his gun home and locked it in his floor safe.

9: A.M. Saturday

Sheriff Combs was sitting at his desk, when one of his Deputy's came in. "Sheriff! We got a hit on the prints! He said smiling. Sheriff Combs looked up with a excited look, as he said. "What's His name? "Delbert More He is from Fillmore Georgia, He did two years in Macon for assault with a deadly weapon charge. And he is a Klan member. "This is great news! I will call Agent Wells to let him know. The Feds can find him now. "Thanks Wilson" Combs said as he picked up the phone to call Fred Wells.

Three weeks later Delbert More was picked up from the hospital in Alabama by two Klan members to take him back to his home in Georgia. He was happy to be leaving the hospital, but still upset about losing his arm. All he would talk about was going back to Cottonwood and killing every one in the little church and burning it down. What he didn't know was that the Grand Dragon of the Klan, was upset with for not following orders. He was not to go in to the church alone. he was to wait till the cross was set afire and the other three men was to go in with him and shoot everyone in the church and make sure Reverend King was killed first.

He was driven to a rock quarry and shot in the head and his body was dropped in a hole and covered with a ton of dirt.

Red Avery and all fifty members of the Klan, were sent to fourteen months in the county jail for inciting a riot, assault and battery arson, destruction of property, and trespassing. Each member was to pay a thousand dollars each for damages. Red found out that Reverend King was still alive, and that The gun recovered was linked to another Klan member. He made a vow that when he got out of jail, he and his pals were going to get Billy Joe and His Family as well as Carl and Margie Holt.

Billy Joe Became a Born again Christen He was Happy with his life and his Family now. He and Carl along with Sue Ellen and Margie were helping the cause for voting rights for Negros. Little did he know that his life was about to change again. He went out on the porch to get the mail out of the box. He saw a letter address to him, he opened it with his pocket knife ,as he started to read the letter His legs felt shaky, he sat down on the swing just as Carl came on the porch. "Hey Buddy You look a little pail! Are You OK? Carl ask with concern. Billy Joe looked up at him. "I "I Bin Drafted. Billy Joe stammered. "Drafted! Carl said. Just then Sue Ellen came out on the porch. "Drafted" Who has bin drafted? She ask. "Me Billy Joe said then went on to say. I have to report for a physical in Jackson ten days from now. "I guess I will be getting my notice pretty soon two. Carl said. "Oh Billy Joe! Do you have to go, can you get out of going? Sue Ellen said in a worried voice. "Not unless You want me to go to prison for twenty years! Billy joe answered. "OH MY" Can they do that? Sue Ellen ask. "You know" This might be a good thing for you, You have bin talking about starting your own bull dozer and back hoe business. "How is that? Billy Joe ask. " Well you can choose the branch you want to serve under. So you tell them you want to join the Army CORRS of engineers. Carl told Him. "YOU KNOW YOU JUST MIGHT BE RIGHT! THAT SOUNDS LIKE A GOOD IDEA! Billy Joe said feeling very confident about going. "LETS Go in and have some coffee and talk about it. Bill Joe said as he put his arm around Sue Ellen and went inside with Carl.

TO BE CONTIUED IN PART 2 OF

THE COLOR OF ANGLES